BLIGHTY

BLIGHTY

BRITISH SOCIETY IN THE ERA OF THE GREAT WAR

GERARD J. DEGROOT

LONGMAN
London and New York

Addison Wesley Longman Limited,
Edinburgh Gate,
Harlow, Essex CM20 2JE, United Kingdom
and Associated Companies throughout the world.

*Published in the United States of America
by Addison Wesley Longman, New York*

First published 1996
Second impression 1998

ISBN 0 582 06138 5 CSD
ISBN 0 582 06137 7 PPR

British Library Cataloguing-in-Publication Data

A catalogue record for this book is
available from the British Library

Library of Congress Cataloging-in-Publication Data

De Groot, Gerard J., 1995–
    Blighty : British society in the era of the Great War / Gerard J.
De Groot.
        p.   cm.
    Includes bibliographical references and index.
    ISBN 0–582–06138–5 (casebound). — ISBN 0–582–06137–7 (pbk.)
    1. Great Britain—History—George V, 1910–1936. 2. Great Britain–
–Social life and customs—20th century. 3. World War, 1914–1918–
–Great Britain. I. Title.
DA577.D37   1996
940.3′41—dc20   95–45475
                                                                         CIP

Set by 20 in 10/12pt Sabon
Printed in Malaysia, PP

CONTENTS

PREFACE

This book began about five years ago over a delightful lunch with Andrew MacLennan of Longman UK, who sought my suggestions for books for my courses. I said that, in my teaching, I had become aware of the need for an up-to-date and affordable text on British society during the Great War. I was not plugging myself as a possible writer, but Andrew seemed to think I was just the person. I am grateful for his confidence in me, and for the kindness and support he has shown over the years.

I have a number of others to thank. My good friend and colleague Dr Barry Doyle helped a great deal more than he ever realised by allowing me access to his phenomenal knowledge of obscure sources. It was also reassuring to test my ideas on him and to receive his perceptive comments. Dr Niall Barr, Elizabeth Quigley and Corinna Peniston-Bird helped with the work on newspapers. I am especially grateful to Corinna, whose eye for a good story is acute. My former students Luke Yates and Ian Kirby allowed me to borrow some of their specialist knowledge.

But, most of all, I have to thank my dear wife Sharon Roe for showing so much confidence in me, and my precious daughter Natalie for always keeping me in touch with the important things in life. Natalie, born during the preparation of Chapter 10, is blissfully unaware of the insights relevant to that chapter which she provided.

Dr Gerard J. DeGroot
St Andrews, 1995

ACKNOWLEDGEMENTS

We are grateful to the following for permission to reproduce copyright material:

Paul Berry, Literary Executor of Vera Brittain for her poem 'To My Brother' and four lines from 'Perhaps . . .' by Vera Brittain from *Verses of a V.A.D.* Erskine Macdonald, 1918 and the Imperial War Museum, 1995; Burns & Oates Ltd for part poem 'A Recruit from the Slums' by Emily Orr from *A Harvester of Dreams* (1922); New Statesman & Society for poem 'High Wood' by Philip Johnstone from *Nation* 16.2.18; Routledge for part rhyme 'Sing a Song of Wartime' by Nina Macdonald from *War-Time Nursery Rhymes* (1918); George T. Sassoon as Literary Executor of the Estate of the late Siegfried Sassoon, for part poems 'Suicide in the Trenches' & 'The Rank Stench' by Siegfried Sassoon; authors' agents on behalf of the Estate of the late Dame Edith Sitwell for poem 'The Dancers' by Edith Sitwell from *Clowns Houses* (Blackwell, Oxford 1918); Macmillan Press Ltd for tabular material from J. Winter, *The Great War and the British People.*

We have been unable to trace the copyright holders of the poems 'Preaematuri' by Margaret Postgate Cole, 'Wind on the Downs' by Marian Allen, 'Invitation au Festin' by Aelfrida Tillyard, and would appreciate any information which would enable us to do so.

INTRODUCTION

Once upon a time in the 1960s – the decade of hope and progress – Britain seemed a dynamic and fluid society. Historians, perhaps unconsciously affected by the temper of those times, gazed upon the previous half-century of British history and saw a great ferment of change fired by the catalyst of war. War encouraged women toward emancipation, governments toward social responsibility, and workers toward consciousness and assertiveness. Class and gender barriers began to crumble.

Thirty years later, with the millennium approaching, change does not seem as profound, nor progress so direct. Politics is still dominated by the party of conservatism and tradition. Even Mrs. Thatcher's brief period of radicalism seems to have been absorbed and contained by her party. There is a striking similarity between the individuals who dominate politics today and those who dominated during the Great War. (Even some of the names are the same.) Despite a century of 'progress' in education and social welfare, the vast majority of working class children leave school early and the vast majority of middle class children go on to university. The arguments which were used to constrain women within the sphere of the home remain popular to this day. Those women who manage to pursue a career still receive lower pay for equal work and find advancement severely restricted.

I cannot claim that we are wiser now than historians who wrote in the 1960s. But every historian is affected by the generation in which he or she lives. My experiences of over fifteen years living in Britain tell me to look again at the Great War and to be aware not just of change, but also of the countervailing forces at work in society which constrained or absorbed change. Progress was profound, but so was the power of convention, tradition, authority and repression. One can never ignore the deep worship of the past which exists within the British psyche. Britain is a very old country and, seemingly, a country which wants to remain old.

Socialists and feminists have seen behind the lack of social progress a conservative conspiracy. Yet the groups who would presumably have benefited most from progress have often been those most prescriptive. Many ordinary women feel no desire nor need to be emancipated. One has to accept that after the war most women positively yearned to leave their wartime jobs and return home to husbands and family. As for the workers, I have to thank Arthur Scargill for teaching me a lesson in working class conservatism. During the 1984 miners' strike, he said the dispute was not about pay, but about the future of the industry – the chance for sons of miners to be miners. For an American raised on rags to riches myths that statement seemed bizarre: surely a miner would want for his son something better than a life down the pits? Close study of workers during the Great War has rendered Scargill's position much more understandable. Class consciousness renders class barriers more impregnable.

It is a measure of the quality of Arthur Marwick's *The Deluge* that for nearly 30 years it has been the unrivalled source on British society during the Great War. It is a beautifully written book, packed with information and insights which remain useful. But some of the assumptions which seemed perfectly logical a generation ago now seem as incongruous as the clothes we wore back then. It is therefore time for a reassessment of the war. I do not claim to be the first historian to embark on such a venture. Trevor Wilson's *The Myriad Faces of War* is exactly the sort of revisionism which the subject deserves. I have to admire his enthusiasm and energy in collecting the material for such a massive work, one which I found immensely helpful in the preparation of this book. Unfortunately, all but the most enthusiastic students are put off by its bulk. J. M. Bourne's *Britain and the Great War, 1914–1918* errs to the opposite extreme. It is useful, but by its brevity it demonstrates the folly of trying to cover politics, society and the military in one short volume.

I have relied heavily on the work of specialist historians who have studied all aspects of this subject. This book is designed to point the student interested in additional detail in their direction. But, beyond that, it is an attempt to distil the accumulated knowledge about the war into a form which students will find useful, readable and interesting. My great regret about the progressive specialisation of history which has occurred during my lifetime is that historians appear to have lost the ability to communicate. They have created for themselves myriad magic circles into which only those who speak the secret language are admitted. This book is therefore an attempt to demystify the history of Britain in the Great War.

This is a history of Blighty during the war. Blighty was a place, an idea and a set of warm-heated, cozy emotions. This book is therefore by definition a social history. It is not intended to be a study of politics during the war. I have not neglected politics, but have intentionally included only enough political detail to make social developments more understandable. Were I to deal adequately with the formation of the coalitions, the Asquith–Lloyd George split, etc., *and* cover the effect of the war upon society, I would end up with a very large book, which would be self-defeating. Students interested in wartime politics should therefore seek out John Turner's excellent *British Politics and the Great War* or other sources mentioned in my bibliography. If the balance of coverage in this book does not seem logical to some critics, I can only plead that all books are a reflection of the tastes of the author. Freed from restraints upon length, I could have created a vast and truly comprehensive book, but in doing so would have rendered it unmanageable and unsuccessful.

Nevertheless, every author experiences profound depression at what he is forced to delete. I would have loved to have told readers about the surge in the popularity of dog wool, the woman accused of bigamy whose husband was serving time for bigamy, the biggest selling toy for children at Christmas 1918 (a miniature tank) and the strangely familiar tale of a woman who failed to realise that the husband who returned from the Dardanelles was an impostor. But, alas, I could find no room.

Perhaps this book will inspire readers to dig deeper.

1 'CLAD IN GLITTERING WHITE'

After 1918, British intellectuals commonly attributed the outbreak of the Great War to a malaise which had descended upon Britain like a fog. A wide variety of phenomena were cited which together convinced the British people that war was not only tolerable, but positively good. Even that ever popular culprit, the British weather, figured prominently in the factors inspiring belligerency. (An unusually warm summer caused either restless tension, or carefree complacency, or primal aggression – depending on one's point of view.) Although analysts offered widely different explanations for this malaise, they shared a certitude which is only possible in hindsight. The lesson is clear, but often missed despite its clarity: fears, hopes, anxieties and illusions buffeted Edwardian Britain in many different directions; it is only in retrospect that a straight line to war seems apparent.

A typical postwar opinion was that of Caroline Playne, who maintained in *The Pre-War Mind in Britain*:

> the thoughtful, no less than the others, were under the spell of an immense crowd infection even before it finally took hold of them in the hot dog-days of 1914. The desire went out from the more primitive-minded, those to whom force made a supreme appeal – militarists, chauvinists, imperialists. The mental contagion – it was a contagion, something more immediate than a suggestion – swept down the mindless, expectant, half-frightened, wondering crowds, and . . . swept down progressives, earnest people, intelligent people as well. But these last had to sublimate motives, to idealize, to call evil good, to invent specious pretexts for following on with the multitude. None the less they were victims of the infection.[1]

Winston Churchill, like Playne more inclined to purple prose than logical reasoning, reflected: 'The old world in its sunset was fair to see. But there was a strange temper in the air. Unsatisfied by material prosperity, nations turned restlessly towards strife, internal or exter-

---

1 C. Playne, *The Pre-War Mind in Britain*, pp. 329–30.

nal.'[2] It is fascinating how the inexplicable (like a war) often arrives on the ether – as cloud, contagion or storm. Thus, Mary Agnes Hamilton recalled how her friends

> seemed always to be waiting for something from outside which was going to decide what they thought. It was appalling, but it was there. They sat and watched it coming as they might have sat and watched a thunderstorm approach.[3]

The factors contributing to this mood can be recited like a catechism by any student of pre-war Britain. According to the accepted scenario, the public schools encouraged an ethos of anti-intellectualism and false sentimentality, turning the spirit of the playing field into a dangerous martial obsession. Militaristic youth movements produced boys eager not just to drill but to fight. The popular press and 'invasion novels' encouraged a paranoiac fear of rampant Germany imposing her sadistic will upon enfeebled Britain. Meanwhile, anguish over suffragettes, militant trade unionism and Irish republicanism encouraged a tendency amongst the people to look outward for diversions and fresh challenges. For the government, war seemed a welcome escape from internal troubles, a chance to unite a fractured country.[4]

Some episodes in this grand *mise en scène* have a factual basis, others are mere whimsy. But since we know that war did break out, the factors which contributed to it naturally seem obvious and important and those which worked against it seem insignificant. We ignore, for instance, the tremendous impact and popularity of Norman Angell's pacifistic book *The Great Illusion;*[5] the enormous progress made in international cooperation, especially in banking, transportation and communication; the worldwide interest in the Olympic movement since 1896; the civility which the Hague Conferences of 1901 and 1907 contributed to international relations; the popularity of pacifist groups, especially those socialist-inspired; the reverence for Germany among British intellectuals and businessmen;[6] and the fact that the Anglo-German naval rivalry had eased by 1912,

2 Ibid., p. 19.

3 M. A. Hamilton, *Dead Yesterday*, p. 43.

4 An idea effectively demolished by M. Gordon in 'Domestic Conflict and the Origins of the First World War: The British and the German Cases', *Journal of Modern History* (1974). See also Z. Steiner, *Britain and the Origins of the First World War*, p. 153.

5 See H. Weinroth, 'Norman Angell and *The Great Illusion*: An Episode in Pre-1914 Pacifism', *Historical Journal* 18 (1974).

6 See Gordon, p. 207, and S. Wallace, *War and the Image of Germany*, passim.

as had many other international tensions. Had war not occurred, historians would today point to these phenomena as clear harbingers of a dawning era of peace.

Furthermore, there is a fundamental misconception in the arguments of Playne, Hamilton and those of similar ilk, namely that the popular will can carry a nation into war. 'In terms of foreign policy', writes Zara Steiner, 'it should be remembered that we are dealing with a very small group of individuals rather proud of their isolation from the masses.'[7] The Foreign Office preferred that the public remain ignorant of international affairs; it thus avoided 'the embarrassing and no doubt thankless task of revealing what British foreign policy was, what it was based on, and what consequences it might entail'.[8] Governments go to war not because of mysterious forces swirling in the air but for pragmatic reasons. Popular opinion is important; politicians will usually hesitate before committing a nation to a decidedly unpopular war. But no amount of 'war fever' will drive a government to wage a war not in the national interest. It is therefore essential that any study of why Britain intervened should begin with high diplomacy and only then examine popular sentiment.

By 1914, 99 years had passed since Britain had fought a war on the European continent. During this time she was the world's leading industrial power and she had amassed the largest empire in history. That she was able to avoid war against any or all of her European rivals is a testimony to skilful diplomacy and to the strength of her navy, not to mention to her pacific nature. At least as far as European power politics was concerned, Britain was a peaceable kingdom. True, she was an aggressive imperial power, but her aggression was carefully directed. Her numerous imperial 'wars' were essentially police actions. Two points deserve emphasis: firstly, in August 1914 it would not have been the natural British reaction to intervene and, secondly, because Britain was inclined to be peaceful, she was militarily weak.

This weakness was recognised by the War Office official Sir Henry Brackenbury in 1899: 'We are attempting to maintain the largest Empire the world has ever seen with armaments and reserves that would be insufficient for a third-class power.'[9] In the same year,

7 Steiner, p. 167. See also pp. 142, 151, 169, 248–9.

8 K. Wilson, 'The New Foreign Office and the "Education" of Public Opinion Before the First World War, 1906–1914', in K. Wilson, ed., *Empire and Continent*, p. 41.

9 J. McDermott, 'The Revolution in British Military Thinking from the Boer War to the Moroccan Crisis', in P. Kennedy, ed., *The War Plans of the Great Powers*, p. 101.

Lord Rosebery described Britain as 'so lonely in these northern seas, viewed with so much jealousy, with such hostility, with such jarred ambition by the great empires of the world, so friendless among nations which count their armies by embattled millions'.[10] As will be demonstrated in the next chapter, it was beyond Britain's capacity to respond to weakness by becoming strong. There were too many other demands on the public purse to finance a meaningful expansion of Britain's military forces. Nor was there much popular desire to do so.

'So long as you are isolated', Joseph Chamberlain asked in 1898, 'can you say that it is not possible, can you even say that it is not probable, that some time or another you may have a combination of at least three Powers against you?'[11] The only conceivable response to this predicament was diplomacy. Britain took the crucial step of entering into entangling agreements, the avoidance of which had been central to the ideal of Pax Britannica since 1815. The first significant departure from diplomatic custom came with overtures to Japan, culminating in the alliance of 1902. Under its terms, Britain agreed to remain neutral in a war between Russia and Japan alone, but promised to provide support to Japan if Russia were joined by another European power. The agreement provided Japan with the confidence to pursue her expansionist ambitions at Russia's expense, even, as it happened, to the point of war. Britain was not overly concerned by the prospect of Japanese killing Russians, or vice versa, as long as Japan steered clear of British interests in East Asia. Japan's ambitions were thus safely contained, as were, more importantly, those of Russia. Britain hoped that Russia's consequent preoccupation with the Japanese threat would curb her aspirations on the Indian subcontinent and in the Persian Gulf. With Russia effectively neutralised, Britain could safely reduce naval commitments in East and South Asia, allowing their redeployment in more critical areas around Europe.

Next came France. If after two world wars the Entente Cordiale of 1904 seems natural, it is well to remember that at the time it constituted an abrupt change of heart. Less than a decade earlier the British and French had nearly come to blows during the Fashoda crisis. The Anglo-French Entente was again a pragmatic attempt by Britain to protect Imperial interests through compromise with a rival. It was not motivated by warm feelings toward France; there was

10 R. R. James, *Rosebery*, p. 412.
11 J. L. Garvin, *The Life of Joseph Chamberlain*, p. 302.

very little that was 'cordiale' about it. It dealt with specific areas of competition, in particular Morocco and Egypt, and was not, as far as Britain was concerned, supposed to affect European relations. In other words, it was not directed against Germany. Unfortunately, France had a hidden agenda; she saw the Entente as a way to isolate Germany. This reveals both the naivety of British diplomacy and also the dangers of agreements born of desperation. At the price of peace in Africa, Britain was drawn into the European vortex.

Desperation breeds cynicism, and there were few more cynical agreements than that forged with autocratic Russia, especially considering Britain's earlier pact with Japan. By 1898, the biggest threat to the British Empire was not France, nor Germany, but Russia – or so it was thought. Russian interests in Persia threatened the Imperial jewel, India. 'A quarrel with Russia anywhere, about anything, means the invasion of India', Balfour warned in 1901. The Committee of Imperial Defence warned that the army would not be able to defend India in the event of a determined Russian invasion. 'As long as we rule India we are the greatest power in the world', Lord Curzon argued. 'If we lose it we shall drop straight away to a third-rate power'.[12] The massive size of Russia's army (potentially 3,600,000 men) was a problem, but even more daunting was the fact that she was the one power in Europe virtually invulnerable to Britain's naval might. The Anglo-Russian convention of 1907 resolved this predicament satisfactorily for the British, but, again, at the cost of drawing Britain deeper into European affairs.

The safety of the Empire was insured, but with the result that Britain was more at risk of entanglement in a European war. These agreements are far more important to Britain's decision to intervene in August 1914 than are any of the manifold instances of Anglo-German antagonism which occurred after 1890. One should not discount entirely the significance of the naval rivalry, the bumbling intervention of the Kaiser in the politics of Southern Africa, the Agadir Crisis, or the building of the Berlin–Baghdad railway. But those problems pale in comparison to the much more pressing dilemma of protecting an empire which could no longer be protected by the usual means, namely military power. It might reasonably be asked why, during this period, Britain did not strike a bargain with Germany. There were those, including Lloyd George, who wanted to, but the essential motivating factor was missing: Britain only struck deals with her rivals, and Germany was not a rival. Britain's

12 M. Howard, *The Continental Commitment*, p. 14.

interests were mainly imperial, Germany's mainly continental. There was little the two could offer each other as the basis for a deal. Germany was the one European power with whom Britain could co-exist in relative harmony.

Most Britons saw the Empire as the source of British strength. In fact it was the root of her weakness. Its grand façade hid a decidedly ramshackle structure. Supposedly secure Imperial markets had encouraged complacency in Britain, such that Britain's industrial lead was constantly eroded by more dynamic entrepreneurs and innovators in Germany, Japan and the US. Germany surpassed Britain in steel production during the 1880s; the United States did the same during the following decade. The cost of defending and administering the Empire increased at a much faster rate than profits accruing from it. But, more worrying, the Empire was no longer performing its single most important function: that of a safe import/export conglomerate. As time passed, Europe superseded the Empire as the main focus for British trade. Between 1880 and 1900, exports to Europe increased by 23 per cent, imports from Europe by 27 per cent. Perhaps more worrying was the fact that imports exceeded exports by approximately five to three.[13] Over the course of the Victorian period, Britain became a highly specialised economy, rendering her dangerously dependent upon foreign producers for the goods she chose not to produce.

The significance of this shift was clear to a perceptive few: Britain could no longer remain aloof from Europe. Thus, even without the agreements with Russia and France, Britain would have been drawn inexorably into European affairs. One need only consider the fact that at the beginning of Pax Britannica, Britain was self-sufficient in food, and by its end, she could feed herself for less than 125 days out of a year from domestic production. By 1900, she produced only 50 per cent of the meat she consumed, 20 per cent of the wheat and about 35 per cent of dairy products. Even though not all food imports came from Europe, Britain's geographic position rendered her vulnerable to the weapon of hunger (i.e. blockade) even with a strong navy. The Royal Navy offered little protection against Britain's greatest threat: that of one hostile power gaining hegemony over Europe. If that were to happen, she could face being shut out of Europe's lucrative markets, whilst simultaneously being threatened militarily on an overwhelming number of fronts.[14] 'We could not be

13 B. Porter, *The Lion's Share*, pp. 120–1.
14 See K. Bourne, *The Foreign Policy of Victorian England*, pp. 7–8.

indifferent to . . . a destruction of the balance of Europe, which rests upon the assumption that no Power is in the position to dictate absolutely to the rest', the *Daily News* recognised in 1911.[15]

Britain was tied to Europe, but could do little to influence its affairs, as events following the assassination of Archduke Franz Ferdinand revealed. Like it or not, a European war was her war. This was cogently recognised on 23 July 1914 by the Foreign Office official Sir Eyre Crowe:

> Should this war come and England stand aside, one of two things must happen: (a) Either Germany and Austria win, crush France and humiliate Russia . . . What will be the position of friendless England? (b) Or France and Russia win. What would then be their attitude towards England? What about India and the Mediterranean?[16]

Staying out of the war would jeopardise the carefully constructed web of agreements designed to protect the Empire; neither Russia nor France would see any reason to behave themselves in India or Africa if Britain let them down in Europe. But, at least as important, Britain could not stand aside while the war produced a dominant European power – such as Germany – determined to exploit British vulnerability.

Thus, Britain declared war on 4 August 1914, after the ultimatum to Germany expired. For the British, this was a conflict about empires, capitalism, trade and food, not about democracy, honour, civilisation or the defence of trusted friends. But when Germany attacked poor little Belgium, a war of markets became a war of morality. Graf von Schlieffen's strategic solution to the problem of Germany's encirclement by two enemies – France and Russia – was to arouse the righteous indignation of a third enemy – Britain. Because of the reasons stated, Britain would have gone to war even without the violation of Belgium. But she would have done so with a Liberal government in disarray (if not destroyed) and a country uneasy about intervention. While British participation in the war may seem inevitable now, it did not seem so at the time – neither to the majority of the people, nor to a significant section of the government. Sir Arthur Nicolson, Ambassador to Russia, complained:

> So many people regard the maintenance of the equilibrium of Europe as merely an abstract principle, for the support of which it is not worth firing a shot, and they do not understand that were the Triple Entente

---

15 *Daily News*, 24 July 1911.
16 K. Wilson, *The Policy of the Entente*, pp. 79–80.

broken up we should be isolated and compelled to do the bidding of the Power which assumed the hegemony of Europe.[17]

That was the irony of Empire: it obscured British weaknesses and permitted a comfortable but dangerous indifference to European affairs.

But once defenceless Belgium was invaded, Britain had a purpose. The war became just, righteous, even holy. On 6 August the Prime Minister Herbert Asquith confidently told the Commons:

> I do not believe any nation ever entered into a great controversy . . . with a clearer conscience and a stronger conviction that it is fighting, not for aggression, not for the maintenance even of its own selfish interest, but . . . in defence of principles the maintenance of which is vital to the civilization of the world.[18]

Asquith claimed that Britain had

> a solemn international obligation, an obligation which, if it had been entered into between private persons in the ordinary concerns of life, would have been regarded as an obligation not only of law but of honour, which no self-respecting man could possibly have repudiated.[19]

In truth, Britain had no obligations, moral or otherwise, to Russia and France, as Asquith confirmed in March 1913 when he denied that Britain 'was under any obligation . . . which compels us to take part in any war'.[20] A formal alliance might in fact have acted as a deterrent to German belligerence, and ensured greater harmony with French foreign policy. But most British abhorred the idea of a binding commitment. Britain's only obligation was to herself; 'when Germany declared war on France in 1914', writes Trevor Wilson, 'Britain was morally obliged to act, because implicit in France's survival was the highest of all moral causes: the survival of Britain'.[21]

Nor were ties to Belgium based on love and sympathy, however much they may have seemed so to most British. The long-established commitment to Belgium arose from a pragmatic acceptance of that country's strategic importance.[22] Britain's trade with the continent

---

17 Wilson, 'The New Foreign Office', pp. 38–9.

18 *Hansard*, 6 August 1914.

19 Ibid.

20 *Daily News*, 25 March 1913.

21 T. Wilson, 'Britain's "Moral Commitment" to France in August 1914', *History* 64 (1979), p. 385.

22 See B. Gilbert, 'Pacifist to Interventionist: David Lloyd George in 1911 and 1914. Was Belgium an Issue?', *Historical Journal* 28 (1985), and T. Wilson, 'Britain's "Moral Commitment" '.

required that a friendly (or at least neutral) power should control the ports of Ostend and Zeebrugge. Their importance is clearly demonstrated by the enormous damage caused to British shipping by German submarines operating out of them during the Great War and by Britain's costly (but futile) attempts to capture them.

The invasion of Belgium gave this war a purpose it otherwise lacked. The British suddenly saw that underneath Germany's civilised exterior beat a mad militaristic heart which had to be torn out. An idealistic age needed a war of ideals, as Lloyd George recognised when, on 19 September 1914, he told a Queen's Hall audience:

> We have been living in a sheltered valley for generations. We have been too comfortable and too indulgent ... and the stern hand of Fate has scourged us to an elevation where we can see the great everlasting things that matter for a nation – the great peaks we had forgotten, of Honour, Duty, Patriotism, and, clad in glittering white, the great pinnacle of Sacrifice pointing like a rugged finger to Heaven.[23]

This was, of course, a lot of tripe, but the British are fond of tripe. Precisely because the British had lived in sheltered valleys (or rather empires), they still naively believed that everlasting values like honour, duty and patriotism mattered in a struggle between industrial nations.

The war became a crusade and the British inspired crusaders. Their war was fundamentally conservative and traditional. Britain fought not for change but to protect the values at the heart of her greatness. Germany, it was argued, promoted mad, irresponsible modernism which would upset the peaceful world order. She needed to be taught a lesson in British moderation. The British self-image and the way they perceived their enemy had a certain accuracy. British culture *was* proudly repressive, Germany's *was* erratically progressive. 'If Germany was the principal activist, and hence modernist, nation of the *fin-de-siècle* world', writes Modris Eksteins, 'then Great Britain was the major conservative power. ... Britain showed on the whole comparatively little interest in the manifestations of modern culture.'[24] Britain felt a comfortable fondness for things old; she was not ravaged by antimodernist angst of a sort which could have been exploited by right wing extremists.[25] Her cultural traditionalism harmonised perfectly with foreign policy. Her 'position as "Number One" was ... the essential British prob-

23 *The Times*, 20 September 1914.
24 M. Eksteins, *Rites of Spring*, p. 117.
25 See Gordon, especially pp. 200–1.

lem', Paul Kennedy argues. 'Having achieved the pinnacle of worldly success, [she] had nothing to gain and much to lose from changes in that global order. Britain was now a *mature* state, with a built-in interest in preserving existing arrangements.'[26] This maturity produced a peculiar blend of repressiveness and liberalism. Liberty meant 'not the right to do as you pleased, [but] the opportunity to do as you should'.[27]

But did this conservatism extend down to the great mass of common people who would, presumably, have been the chief beneficiaries of progressive change? Strange as it seems, the answer is yes. The workers were very conservative. Their pride in Empire, the monarchy and British tradition was high; most believed, despite their poverty, that they were superior to any workers elsewhere in the world. Gradual enfranchisement had given them the impression that they were being empowered politically, without encouraging in them false hopes of a New Jerusalem. It might nevertheless be argued that the *avant garde* was a concept unknown to ordinary people, therefore the claim that the British were reacting to the threat of rampant German modernism is spurious. But some evidence suggests that ordinary people did see the war in precisely these terms. A soldier told his parents in October 1914 that

> we should remind ourselves that it is our great privilege to save the traditions of all centuries behind us. It's a grand opportunity, and we must spare no effort to use it, for if we fail we shall curse ourselves in bitterness every year that we live and our children will despise our memory.[28]

Faith in traditional values was also expressed in the war poetry – throughout the war. The accepted view holds that the war caused poets to abandon romanticism, rigid both in ideals and structure. Whilst this may be true of Sassoon, Owen and their ilk, theirs was not the poetry which the people actually read. Approximately 2,225 poets were published during the Great War; those we associate with the war today were a neglected minority back then.[29] A great deal of 'bad' patriotic poetry continued to be published in newspapers throughout the war, seemingly unaffected by the collapse of illusions which occurred at the front. Lloyd George's Queen's Hall speech was specifically calculated to appeal to this same populist sentiment,

---

26 P. Kennedy, *The Realities Behind Diplomacy*, p. 69.
27 Eksteins, p. 118.
28 Ibid., p. 119.
29 C. Reilly, ed., *Scars Upon My Heart*, p. xxxiii.

as was the wartime propaganda which played heavily on the motif of the English rural idyll, a sturdy symbol of tradition. To the urban industrial worker that idyll may have been as familiar as the surface of the moon, but the ideals it evoked were widely cherished.

One essential characteristic of a noble and just war was that it should be fought in a civilised manner, according to an accepted set of rules, like a serious game of rugby. Since British society equated games with war,[30] it naturally approached war as if it was a game. Evidence that this incredible fantasy survived into the war can be found in a letter to *The Scotsman* in January 1915 in which a British soldier described a dogfight involving one German aircraft against sixteen French and British. What made the experience so wonderful was that the German escaped unscathed. 'And we gave him a great cheer', the correspondent wrote, 'for the odds were against him, and he must have been a great chap.'[31] Keen young officers, direct from the public schools, would sometimes lead their men over the top by kicking a football in the direction of the German trenches, the most famous eccentric of this sort being Captain W. P. Nevill, who kicked off at the Battle of the Somme on 1 July 1916. (Nevill was immediately shot dead, but by all accounts the kick was impressive.[32]) Such incidents probably occurred much less often than legend would have us believe, but it is the myth which is important in shaping the British self-perception. The British believed they were fighting a good game and papered their lives with colourful stories to reinforce this belief. The *Daily Mail* offered an allegorical tale of fraternisation between British and German soldiers which began with the trading of pleasantries across No Man's Land, moved to the throwing of tobacco and chocolates to the other side and ended with a jolly snowball fight. But the amiable exchange ended when a German, true to form, put a rock in a snowball which subsequently struck a Tommy in the eye. Some people just did not know how to play the game.[33]

This approach to war did not allow for a great deal of anti-German hatred. It is difficult to generalise about popular attitudes toward Germany, but it appears that in the pre-war period anti-German feeling was not as rampant as might be expected. The naval

---

30 A point discussed at length in Chapter 3.

31 Eksteins, p. 124.

32 C. Veitch, ' "Play up! Play up! and Win the War!" Football, the Nation and the First World War 1914–15', *Journal of Contemporary History* 20 (1985), pp. 363–4.

33 *Daily Mail*, 31 December 1914.

race was not like the Cold War after 1945 but more like a healthy rivalry between two closely matched schools. Rates of ship construction were presented in the newspapers like football league tables. Sir Charles Hardinge, Permanent Under Secretary at the Foreign Office, complained as late as 1909 that 'Public opinion in England has not as yet grasped the danger to Europe of Germany's ambitious designs.'[34] Anti-German bigotry was not completely absent, but in most cases it was safely hidden beneath a veneer of British tolerance. As will be seen, once the war began, the veneer quickly cracked and hatred seeped through, especially on the home front, where it was encouraged by propaganda. But, before August 1914, there was considerable admiration for Germany and certainly a greater sense of harmony than was felt toward the 'ally' France, a much more dependable object of hatred.

It is therefore erroneous to assume that invasion literature – books like *The Riddle of the Sands*, *The Invasion of 1910* and *The Battle of Dorking*, and plays like *An Englishman's Home* – was responsible for stirring anti-German feeling in the decades before the Great War. Granted, the books and plays were popular and the enemy was usually German. The literature was intended as a warning of an impending threat, but that does not really explain its appeal. This generation, like any other, had a healthy fascination for intrigue and espionage. Thrillers are always more credible if the bad guy is believable; linking the fictional enemy to a contemporary adversary provided the requisite verisimilitude.

The British in 1914 perceived for themselves a righteous mission, which, regardless of their lack of preparation, made them formidable. The national mood allowed the Liberal government the confidence that the war would be supported by a people united in their belief in a just cause. The unifying effect of war can be seen in the reaction of the *Daily News*. Staunchly anti-interventionist during the July crisis, it quickly brought itself into line with popular temper: 'We have said our last word of controversy . . . Being in, we must win.'[35] Victory in the war would not only protect the world from what Germany represented, it would also restore a sense of rectitude to Britain, after a period in which righteousness had been in decline. 'I'm anxious that England may act rightly', Rupert Brooke confessed to his friend Edward Marsh in July 1914.[36] Even those who perceived

34 Wilson, 'The New Foreign Office', p. 38.
35 *Daily News*, 5 August 1914.
36 Eksteins, p. 131.

an opportunity for change wanted change of magnitude not funda-mentals. Lord Milner hoped that the war would force into being stronger government, leading in turn to a strengthened empire, a more formidable military and a disciplined society. 'War would "ring out the feud of the rich and poor". The imperial ideal would replace the class struggle and "ancient forms of party strife".'[37] The war seemed to present a lucky escape from the pre-war turmoil caused by the Irish problem, the trade unions and the suffragettes, turmoil which had seemed to presage a doomed Britain in which old values no longer counted. Thus, the war would be a purgation, a return and a renewal. 'A sour, soiled, crooked old world [was] to be rid of bullies and crooks and reclaimed for straightness, decency, good nature', recalled C. E. Montague.[38] For Brooke, soldiers marching to war were like

> swimmers into cleanness leaping,
> Glad from a world grown old and cold and weary.[39]

Britain would win because her noble values would rise to the surface.

Thus, a war about economics and European hegemony was transformed into one 'about values, about civilization, about sports-manship, and especially about the relationship of the future to the past'.[40] The popular mood placed severe limits upon the change which war would effect. The British feared change, resisted it for as long as possible and, when it became inevitable, did their best to incorporate it within a restrictive cocoon of tradition. This war was fought not to change the world, but to bring it back to the certainties of the Victorian age, certainties undermined during Edward's reign. The war would be worthwhile if it led not to something new, but to something gloriously old.

---

37 J. M. Bourne, *Britain and the Great War, 1914–1918*, p. 230.
38 C. E. Montague, *Disenchantment*, p. 10.
39 R. Brooke, '1914', in T. Cross, ed., *Lost Voices of World War I*, p. 55.
40 Eksteins, p. 132.

2   VIRTUOUS INFERIORITY

When war erupted in 1914, Britain found herself in need of an army. Germany's standing army was ten times larger than Britain's and she had access to a vast reservoir of trained reserves. The British prided themselves on the fact that their volunteer force, though small, was professional. But there was cold comfort in this reasoning. 'Professional' in this case described the relationship between the soldier and the army; the British were career soldiers, not conscripts. 'Professional' did not necessarily mean high quality; these soldiers were well-drilled, but generally ignorant of modern war. The army was like an antique fire engine: spotless, shiny and in perfect working order, but not very good at putting out big fires.

In some ways, the army mirrored Edwardian society. It had rigid class distinctions and its officers were educated in the same public schools which produced civilian society's leaders. Thus, a common belief system existed among officers and their peers in the civil service, politics, the judiciary and the church. But, as the sociologist Morris Janowitz has observed, armies are better at magnifying than mirroring prevalent social values. Officers generally consider themselves superior to their civilian counterparts – the self-appointed guardians of tradition in an ever-changing world.[1]

The separation between army and society extended further. The 'workers' – enlisted men – were not a microcosm of the civilian working class. Rather, ordinary soldiers tended to be vagabonds who could find no better occupation: recruits from the bars and brothels of urban slums or the human detritus thrown up by the shrinkage of agricultural Britain. This separation between army and society was more pronounced in Britain than in other European industrialised countries because the British Army was a volunteer force. In France and Germany, conscription produced a more socially homogeneous army, with recruits from all sectors of society. But, since Cromwell's time, the British were suspicious of a large standing army. This in

---

1 M. Janowitz, *The Professional Soldier*, p. 80.

part explains their abhorrence of conscription, but also reveals why the army became a closed caste – ignored and often abhorred by wider society. Soldiers complained as late as 1891 that they were often denied admission to bars and theatres.[2] When his Winchester headmaster learned of Archibald Wavell's intention to join the army, he protested to Wavell's father: 'I do not think that you need take this extreme step, since I believe that your son has sufficient brains to make his way in other walks of life.'[3] The mother of the future Field Marshal Lord Robertson, upon hearing of his enlistment, wrote: 'I would rather bury you than see you in a redcoat.'[4]

Thus, the pre-war army was a 'vestigial appendage'[5] – an institution, rather like the police today, which everyone believed essential, but few really loved. Imperial wars produced many a romantic fantasy about brave, noble warriors, but *real* soldiers were pariahs.[6] The army nevertheless performed an immensely valuable function. By keeping the Empire quiet, it allowed a false sense of security – commonly known as Pax Britannica. It allowed the British to ignore world affairs and concentrate on their day-to-day lives. Few yearned for a vast army like that of Germany, which might become too powerful and too politically ambitious. It is therefore no wonder that Britain found herself, in 1914, with an army ridiculously ill-suited to the task which confronted it.

Complacency toward the army was affordable because of the sense of security which the Royal Navy provided. That Britain ruled the waves may have been a cliché but it was not a myth. Since Britain was an island nation, and since an airborne attack was still some way off, the security the navy provided *was* real. True, the idea of Pax Britannica, which held that Britain could remain aloof from European affairs, was a fallacy, given her growing dependency upon continental markets. Nevertheless, the strategic fact remains: Britain did not feel *physically* threatened by the German or French armies.

The role of the Royal Navy was therefore to protect Britain and the Empire from foreign invasion, a task it performed rather well.

2 A. Summers, 'Militarism in Britain Before the Great War', *History Workshop Journal* 2 (1976), p. 108.

3 A. Wavell, *Soldiers and Soldiering*, p. 138.

4 J. Keegan, *The Face of Battle*, p. 220.

5 Janowitz, p. 4.

6 A point misunderstood by G. Wilkinson in ' "Soldiers by Instinct, Slayers by Training": The *Daily Mail* and the Image of the Warrior, 1899–1914', *Journal of Newspaper and Periodical History* 8 (1992).

The army's role was that of an Imperial police force designed to deal with riots, rebellions and mutinies in Britain's myriad overseas possessions. During Queen Victoria's reign, the army performed this function in 72 separate campaigns, usually successfully, but not always conspicuously so. Out of these campaigns there grew a small war mentality which impeded the serious study of developing military science. Fought in exotic places against unpredictable enemies, small wars did not seem to conform to classical principles. Their lessons could therefore be safely ignored – or so it was felt by those who fought them. The army instead held to sacred Napoleonic principles unadapted to developments which had occurred since Waterloo. This shortcoming was exacerbated by the country's reluctance to plan for war. The prejudice against a large standing army went hand in hand with an aversion to strategic plans formed in advance of a crisis. Both, it was felt, smacked of militarism. Historians who contend that Britain was a militaristic society before 1914 have failed to explain this abhorrence of military planning.[7] Britain preferred instead a pragmatic army, capable of reacting to crises when they occurred.[8] Stated differently, the British saw virtue in muddling through.

Pragmatism was the enemy of professionalism; without theory, there could be no proper study of war. The British held that victories in small colonial wars came about when disciplined soldiers acted like the automatons they were trained to be. Failures occurred when discipline broke down. Senior officers therefore perceived little need to develop new tactics to suit new weapons. Lessons about modern firepower arising from the Franco-Prussian or American Civil Wars were largely ignored. Launcelot Kiggell, Commandant of the Staff College and later Chief of Staff of the British Expeditionary Force (BEF), expressed a typical attitude:

> History proves . . . that in all ages the moral has been to the physical as three is to one. Courage, energy, determination, perseverance, endurance, the unselfishness and discipline that make combination possible – these are the primary causes of all great successes, and in turning our thoughts to new guns or rifles or bayonets, we too often forget the fact.[9]

In truth, the 'moral' only wins battles if the physical will allow. In

---

7 See Summers, 'Militarism in Britain'; G. Best, 'Militarism and the Victorian Public School', in M. J. Bradley and B. Simon, eds, *The Victorian Public School*.

8 G. Harries-Jenkins, *The Army in Victorian Society*, pp. 171–9.

9 Quoted in ibid., p. 197.

her small Victorian wars, Britain had the better guns, rifles and bayonets. Her soldiers were often of superior physical stock and were better trained. It was therefore easy to be brave. What the British seemed loath to accept was that their superb morale resulted not from superior character, but from greater wealth and development in comparison to colonial adversaries. The emphasis upon moral qualities exacerbated a dangerous traditionalism. 'When change *was* discussed it often tended to focus on the line of least resistance – the individual', argues Travers. 'It was easier to think of changing individuals, in terms of training, discipline, morale, offensive spirit, etc. than it was to consider basic changes in technology or tactics.'[10]

Small wars encouraged other dangerous assumptions. The conflicts were usually dominated by a single commander who imposed his will upon the campaign, or failed to do so. This encouraged the belief that good generalship was solely a question of character, not a skill to be learned. Small wars thus provided large heroes who mistakenly assumed that they could go it alone without the help of trained technical advisers. The campaigns also created the impression amongst the public that war was a distant adventure with little bearing upon everyday life.[11] Casualties were always small (especially compared to the enemy), victory usually inevitable. All of this reinforced the tendency to ignore the army, except to the extent that it provided excellent raw material for boys' adventure stories.[12] It also encouraged a habit of judging campaigns only by their success or failure, not by their price. Neither the army nor the government nor the people asked whether lives were squandered. Because the army was victorious, it was a success.

For its officers, the army preferred gentlemen to professionals. Professionalism, like planning, smacked of militarism and was therefore abhorrent. Courage and honour were valued far more than knowledge or ability. Leadership was an attribute of birth; not something to be learned. Because he was a gentleman, the officer was beyond reproach; he underwent no periodic reviews of his performance which professionalism would have implied. He operated according to a code of practice universally accepted but never tested. 'While eccentricity was acceptable, deviancy was not', writes one historian

---

10 T. Travers, 'The Offensive and the Problem of Innovation in British Military Thought 1870–1915', *Journal of Contemporary History* 13 (1978), p. 546.

11 Harries-Jenkins, pp. 199, 215.

12 For instance: G. A. Henty, *With Kitchener in the Soudan.*

of the pre-war army. High on the scale of deviancy was the cad who studied the science of war in an ambitious, but misguided, attempt to secure promotion.[13] Advancement instead occurred on the basis of an ad hoc, highly personalised system, itself an outgrowth of the amateur, traditional ideal of war.[14]

Britain had an officer class, but it was in no way similar to the Prussian Junkers, a closed caste for whom the science of war resembled a religion. Members of the British military elite saw themselves as gentlemen first and officers second. Until 1871, a system of purchase governed entry into the army and subsequent promotion. In 1860, a lieutenant-colonelcy in the cavalry cost around 14,000.[15] Promotion might occasionally come without payment, but exceptions were made not on the grounds of merit but rather at the whim of the Commander in Chief. Purchase was abolished in 1871, but the army did not immediately become a meritocracy. The new criteria for entry and advancement were in truth as restrictive as the old. Henceforth, a potential officer was judged on the basis of his education and his financial standing. In the case of the former, the prestige of his old school was more important than what the candidate actually learned. In 1891, all 373 Sandhurst entrants came from just 55 prestigious public schools and universities.[16] Since 'good' public schools placed heaviest emphasis upon a classical education and athletic prowess, it could be said that Britain built her army from men who could conjugate Latin verbs and kick a ball into touch.

As for the influence of money, it was more subtle than under the old purchase system, but hardly less significant. In the late Victorian period, a middle class male required an income of at least £700 per year to support himself in a style which suited his position in society. (If he aspired to an army career he needed more.) Since only around 280,000 of the 7,000,000 households in Britain could have afforded such a sum, the pool of potential officers was very small, especially since that pool had also to provide politicians, diplomats, clergy and other elevated authorities.[17] Membership in a regiment required that the officer be able to afford mess expenses and other

13 Harries-Jenkins, p. 44.

14 See T. Travers, 'The Hidden Army: Structural Problems in the British Officer Corps, 1900–1918', *Journal of Contemporary History* 17 (1982), p. 537.

15 P. E. Razzell, 'Social Origins of Officers in the Indian and British Home Army: 1758–1962', *British Journal of Sociology* 14 (1963), p. 258.

16 Ibid., p. 259.

17 P. Laslett, *The World We Have Lost*, pp. 227–8.

incidentals; the more prestigious the regiment, the higher these costs. Even recreation was expensive, though essential to advancement. Careers were often made on the connections forged at lavish parties. Prowess in field sports – particularly polo and shooting – was a prerequisite of the gentleman-officer. All these costs increased with promotion. These expenses undoubtedly deterred many who might otherwise have considered a military career and discouraged able but less affluent officers from seeking promotion.

The army was therefore a reflection of wider society, but a distorted one. Class stratification was, if anything, more rigid. Granted, within the officer corps there was some opportunity for upward mobility. An officer could advance up the social scale through promotion, as long as he had the money to absorb the consequent costs of his rise. In 1912, 59 per cent of officers were middle class, 32 per cent landed gentry and 9 per cent aristocracy. Middle class officers came predominantly from rural smallholdings (under 3,000 acres) and saw the army as an opportunity to attain status not otherwise available through their landed interests alone.[18] But while this might seem evidence of a mild democratisation, in fact appearances are deceptive. The middle class officer may have been in the majority, but he was not consequently powerful. In the period up to the First World War the proportion of aristocrats in the rank of major-general and above was two and a half times that of their distribution within the rest of the officer corps.[19] In fact, as the army became more middle class, the upper classes became more dominant within it. Field Marshal Lord Robertson, who entered the army as a private, was the most significant intruder into this highly closed caste. But, as he readily admitted, his was an exceptional case; before 1914 only about four or five officers per year were promoted from the ranks.[20]

The army did not accept any young gentleman. Unsuitable candidates were weeded out by a competitive examination designed to test appropriate soldierly qualities. But the problem with examinations is that they are biased toward the intelligent, and the army was more interested in character than intellect. During the Victorian period, it was discovered that the exam was too difficult for some otherwise promising candidates from the better public schools. It was consequently made easier in order not to exclude those with the desired

---

18 Razzell, 'Social Origins of Officers', p. 253.
19 Ibid., p. 254.
20 W. Robertson, *From Private to Field Marshal*, pp. 29–31.

social characteristics.[21] The exam was structured with those characteristics in mind. Two compulsory subjects, mathematics and English, had to be taken along with three options. Among the latter, the Classics paper was weighted three times more heavily than the other options, which meant that in order to pass, the candidate was virtually forced to choose Classics as an 'option'.[22] A solid grounding in the Classics was still the mark of a gentleman, and gentlemen made the best officers. Since the exam was little more than a test of memory, wealthy candidates employed crammers (at great expense) in order to increase their chances of passing.

Army education was designed more to test an individual's gentlemanly qualities than to train him as a soldier. In the army's scale of priorities, breeding and birth were more important than experience and training. This is revealed by the quotas restricting admission to the Staff College. Each year 30 officers were admitted after taking a competitive entrance examination. But only six officers from the artillery and engineers were allowed. Because those branches were more scientific than either the infantry or cavalry, they attracted bright middle class technicians – not a type thought to make good senior commanders. A quota had to be enforced because if the competition had been fair, artillerymen and engineers would have swept the board. As it was, they usually occupied the top dozen places after the examination. But rather than admit more than six, the army often accepted cavalry and infantry candidates who had failed the exam in order to make up the numbers. Douglas Haig was among those who benefited from this rather heavy-handed example of class prejudice.[23] As Geoffrey Best has remarked, 'There seems to have been no limit to what you didn't have to know to get into the infantry or the cavalry.'[24]

The elitist character of the army can also be seen in the dominance of the cavalry within it, even after that arm began a sharp decline into obsolescence. During the Great War, both Commanders in Chief of the BEF (Haig and Sir John French), all of the Chiefs of Staff and five of nine Army Commanders were cavalrymen. Yet the cavalry made up less than one-tenth of the army's total personnel. The cavalry was like 'old money', a socially pure elite group untainted by the technological advance of warfare and the conse-

21 Harries-Jenkins, pp. 124–5.
22 G. DeGroot, *Douglas Haig, 1861–1928*, pp. 27–8.
23 Ibid., pp. 38–9.
24 Best, 'Militarism and the Victorian Public School', p. 131.

quent rise of the middle class. Because cavalry engagements occurred at close quarters – man to man – the cavalryman was thought to embody the gentlemanly qualities and moral fortitude which the army prized. Thus the cavalry's dominance of the army's higher echelons confirmed the importance of character over intellect and at the same time hindered moves toward modernisation. Modernity threatened the obsolescence of those personal qualities upon which the army's elites based their status.

In the late Victorian period it became increasingly important for the ambitious officer to be a Staff College graduate. But this did not mean that intellect was superseding character or that professionalism had suddenly become important. Breeding still remained the essential prerequisite of a good commander, but it was gradually accepted that those of good character could improve themselves through professional training. Nevertheless, probably the majority of officers doubted the value of education right up to the eve of war.[25]

Although the increasing emphasis placed upon a Staff College education was a sign of progress, the instruction which potential commanders received remained antediluvian, even as late as 1914.[26] One problem resulted from the army's uncertainty over the staff's proper role. The idea of staff officers – professionals trained to advise the commanders and plan campaigns – contradicted the army's sacred belief in inspired leaders who succeeded through individual genius. The College also encouraged a dangerous delusion that war could be 'normal', in other words, 'decisive, offensive, mobile but structured, won by morale and determined personal leadership'. Students were taught that warfare was 'structured, short, reasonably simple and predictable'.[27] The College's faults – an emphasis on rote learning, class bias, confusion over the role of the staff and over the nature of war – were deficiencies which characterised the army as a whole, and the rest of society.

If the officers in the Victorian army were society's elite, the enlisted men were its dregs. A Royal Commission, reporting in 1867, concluded that men enlisted 'for want of work, pecuniary embarrassment, family quarrels, etc.'. The Superintendent of Recruiting admitted that the richest source for 'volunteers' were the public houses, adding, 'you must go where you can find the material'. The situation did not markedly improve over subsequent decades; the army

25 B. Bond, *The Victorian Army and the Staff College*, pp. 29–30.
26 Ibid., pp. 305–6.
27 T. H. E. Travers, *The Killing Ground*, pp. 87–8.

remained the last resort of the destitute. The pay in 1892 was 1s 2d per day, minus 4½d for rations. At the same time the British agricultural worker made 13s to 15s per week and privates in the US Army, the only other large volunteer army, earned the equivalent of 1s 9d per day with free meals, twice as much in real terms. The poverty of soldiers affected their standard of health. For most of the period the death rate for enlisted men, excluding wars, was double the national average.[28]

The senior officers who would command in the Great War grew up in the Victorian army, in which conformity was prized, change occurred gradually and reform was by definition suspect. The Duke of Cambridge, Commander in Chief of the Army from 1856 to 1895, stubbornly argued that 'There is a time for all things. There is even a time for change; and that is when it can be no longer resisted.'[29] Nevertheless, between the end of the nineteenth century and the advent of war in 1914, two events did breach the ramparts of tradition. The first was the Boer War of 1899–1902, a massive embarrassment for the army and a huge shock for the country as a whole. The second event, the Haldane reforms, arose out of the collective fright that events in South Africa caused.

Taken unaware by the ferocity and determination of the Boers, British troops found themselves quickly encircled at Mafeking, Kimberley and Ladysmith during the first few weeks of the war. Then came Black Week (10–15 December 1899) with humiliations at Colenso, Magersfontein and Stormberg. The nation began to question whether the army was adequate even for its limited task of policing the Empire. Sir Redvers Buller, the Commander in Chief in South Africa, was hastily replaced by Britain's favourite General, Lord Roberts, who brought with him as Chief of Staff another hero, Herbert Kitchener. A series of methodical set-piece engagements followed, eventually resulting in the surrender of Pretoria on 5 June 1900. But conventional war then gave way to guerilla warfare, and again the British were taken by surprise. Over 450,000 British and Imperial troops, more than 22,000 deaths, £200 million and nearly three years of fighting were required to defeat the Boer forces, which never numbered more than 50,000.[30]

The war's lessons were widely misunderstood. Once Buller had

---

28 B. Bond, 'The Late Victorian Army', *History Today* 11(1961), p. 623.

29 R. Blake, 'The Crimean War to the First World War', in M. Howard, ed., *Soldiers and Governments*, p. 29.

30 T. Pakenham, *The Boer War*, pp. 572–3.

been sacked, Roberts's conventional war had been reassuringly short, effective, and most of all mobile, thus seeming to confirm the ortho-doxy handed down from generation to generation and enshrined in Staff College teaching. The cavalry interpreted one short, insignificant but nonetheless dramatic charge prior to the relief of Kimberley (in which Haig took part) as proof of its continued importance.[31] But since the war seemed, for the most part, weird, its hard lessons were discounted. British officers failed to notice how effective machine-guns had proved, and how entrenched Boers employing concentrated fire were able to hold up forces many times the size of their own. The Boer fondness for trenches was in fact seen as evidence of their lack of breeding – real gentlemen would stand and fight. The small but significant tactical errors which occurred in South Africa did not generally inspire a subsequent reconsideration of tactics by senior British commanders. The Boer War should also have taught the Brit-ish that a determined population, mobilised for war, could carry on for a very long time, thus demonstrating the importance of long term logistical planning. But, as with the war's other lessons, this one was ignored because it seemed a strange war.

The British government was more frightened than the army by the South African fiasco. Nearly all the troops available to the Crown had been sent to the war, leaving Britain and the rest of the Empire virtually undefended. When the government called upon its citizens to supply reserves for the army, they were found wanting, not in spirit but in health. 'The want of physique', argued the Director-General of the Army Medical Service in 1903, 'is not only serious from its military aspect, it is serious also from its civil standpoint, for if these men are unfit for military service, what are they good for?'[32] If Britain could not easily defeat a small force of untrained farmers, how could she possibly cope with a huge continental army? Finally forced to confront her vulnerability, Britain began a frantic attempt to prepare for a European war.

Along with the new diplomatic directions discussed in the last chapter came a modernisation of Britain's military – a long and painful process. Since the army, due to its poor performance in South Africa, seemed in need of the most urgent reform, attention focused in that direction. A committee headed by Lord Esher proposed sig-nificant structural reforms, including the formation of a General Staff

---

31 See G. DeGroot, 'Educated Soldier or Cavalry Officer?: Contradictions in the pre-1914 Career of Douglas Haig', *War and Society* 4 (1986), pp. 54–8.

32 Summers, 'Militarism in Britain', p. 111.

on the German model. Esher's ideas were accepted by the Conservative government in February 1904, but progress then ground to a halt. It fell to the traditionally pacific Liberals to complete the job after their victory in 1906. Although relations with Germany had worsened over the preceding decade, it was not the German threat which motivated the new War Minister, Richard Burdon Haldane. Rather, his two most important priorities were to create the largest and most efficient army within the confines of a strict budget of £28 million and to create a reserve force in a country habitually averse to a standing army and conscription. These restrictions, rather than the requirements of a continental strategy, shaped the reforms.[33] In his postwar autobiography, Haldane attempted to defend himself against charges, levelled by the right wing press during the war, that he had failed to prepare Britain for war on the continent. He claimed that, from the beginning, he had worked on the assumption of an inevitable clash with Germany and had organised the army to meet that threat. His memoirs exaggerate both his perspicacity and the scope of his achievement, perhaps understandably given the circumstances. Had Haldane genuinely intended to prepare the country for a continental war, he would have pushed for larger army estimates and a compulsory service law. He would also have failed. Neither the government nor the country was prepared to accept the massive militarisation of society which a continental strategy implied. Thus, Haldane achieved the maximum possible. His reforms were a political solution to a military problem and, as such. inadequate to the challenges ahead.

Haldane's reforms can be grouped into three areas. The first, the formation of a General Staff, fell far short of Esher's proposals, which had called for professionals skilled in the science of war to provide tactical and strategic advice continually updated in line with improvements in weapons technology – in other words, a 'brain of the army'. Instead Britain ended up with a General Staff of an essentially administrative, logistical character. Esher's more ambitious reforms were opposed both by the army and by influential civilians, on the grounds that they would result in a dangerously powerful military elite, as in Germany. The second area of reform involved creating an Imperial General Staff, which would allow the various colonial and dominion forces to fight harmoniously with those from

---

33 See R. B. Haldane, *Before the War*, pp. 30–1. For an effective counter-argument see E. Spiers, *Haldane, An Army Reformer*.

Britain. This meant standardising weapons and training, and planning for the mobilisation of Imperial forces in time of war.

The final area of reform consisted of those changes most difficult to achieve, namely the organisation of Army Commands, the creation of a reserve and the formation of the British Expeditionary Force (BEF). The government wanted an army that could be easily mobilised and quickly expanded on the outbreak of war. The reserve was created by converting the old auxiliary units – Militia, Yeomanry and Volunteers – into a single force of part-time soldiers, renamed the Territorials. It was an important proviso of the Territorial and Reserve Forces Act, passed on 19 June 1907, that the Territorials and Special Reserve (the old Militia) would not be sent overseas without their prior permission. They were intended for home defence while the BEF fought on foreign soil.

In comparison to the problem of a reserve, the formation of Army Commands and the BEF went relatively smoothly. Before 1907, a proper expeditionary force did not exist. The army was merely a collection of diverse regiments with only one suitably organised corps at Aldershot. The Army Order of 1 January 1907 coordinated this disorganised mass into one cavalry and six infantry divisions, a force of 120,000 men intended for rapid mobilisation on the outbreak of war. Consolidation reduced waste and inefficiency; the army reached its maximum possible size within the confines of its limited budget. But this meant an actual *decrease* in numerical strength, a point which again demonstrates that Edwardian Britain was hardly gripped by militarist mania. Some field batteries and infantry battalions were retired, but, significantly, the cavalry came through this rationalisation unscathed. The BEF, designed to be mobilised within 14 days, was essentially the force which went to war in 1914. It was, within its strictly defined limits, a well-organised force which mobilised smoothly. But it was unsuitable to the task it encountered in France and Belgium: it was too small, it could not be rapidly expanded, and most of its commanders were too set in their ways, incapable of the strategic and tactical improvisation which the war would demand.

There were those who recognised that the army was woefully ill-suited to the war ahead. Critics came in two general types: those who doubted its quality and those who ridiculed its size. Among the former was a small but vocal group who argued that failures in South Africa arose from an obsessive British faith in the amateur ethic. One such critic, George Brodick, argued in *The Nineteenth Century* that 'The young Englishman of this great leisure class is no dandy and no coward, but he is an amateur born and bred, with an amateur's lack of training, an amateur's contempt for method, and an amateur's ideal of life.' Amateurs, Brodick argued, dominated politics, the civil and foreign service, and, most dangerously, the army. The young officer 'seldom takes his profession seriously, and is hardly encouraged to do so. There is little enough "shop" talked in mess rooms, and little real enthusiasm except for sporting and social amusements; military duties are not evaded, but they are recognized by most as a "bore".'[34]

The solution, Brodick argued, was not better organisation and education, as advocated by Esher, Haldane and Haig. No amount of training or experience could possibly be effective if soldiers were tainted with the 'amateur spirit'. After all, the remarkably successful Boer generals,

> while they were not professionals in training . . . were not amateurs in spirit. Having for their single object the defeat of the enemy, they were hampered by no rules of military etiquette and few scruples of military honour, exercising the utmost ingenuity and sparing no pains to inflict the greatest possible injury upon our troops with the least possible injury to themselves.[35]

The argument showed extraordinary insight and, bearing in mind the British experience during the Great War, considerable perspicacity. But, in a culture where amateurism was a positive virtue, Brodick's advice was never likely to receive serious consideration. A typical response was that of Sir Herbert Maxwell in the same journal:

> Every institution is known by its fruits; if these are sound there is not much to complain of in the trunk. . . . My contention is that there are no signs of decay – no abatement of zeal – no withering of fidelity – in the public services . . .[36]

The reformers of the post-Boer War period thought that they were addressing the problems which the war exposed. Haldane and his acolytes proved proficient at creating new bureaucratic structures, but they did not understand the need to change minds. Amateurism was deeply rooted in the British ethos and would not be eradicated by mere restructuring of the army. Officers had to be encouraged to think differently about war and British society had to learn to value

34 G. Brodick, 'A Nation of Amateurs', *The Nineteenth Century* 48 (1900), pp. 526–7.

35 Ibid.

36 H. Maxwell, 'Are We Really a Nation of Amateurs?', *The Nineteenth Century* 48 (1900), p. 1063.

professionalism and planning – in other words, it had to exorcise its fears of an efficient army.

The problem of amateurism was far too subtle for the average British citizen. A more popular solution to the army's deficiencies was to increase its size through the cure-all of conscription. The National Service League, founded in 1902, addressed this simplistic sentiment. The League called for compulsory military training for all able-bodied male citizens. The idea had appeal beyond the fact that it seemed an effective response to the German threat. National service, it was argued, would allow Britain to avoid the fiasco of the Boer War when 60 per cent of volunteers were rejected as unfit for service. Soldiers would be brought to fitness *before* a conflict arose, though how military training alone, without adequate social welfare and income redistribution, would achieve this was not adequately explained. Conscription also harmonised with popular conceptions of citizenship which held that the individual owed a debt of service to the state. National service seemed an effective antidote to the juvenile delinquency and social disorder which plagued the inner cities. Finally, the idea seemed to provide a solution to the problem of relative industrial decline. After military service, the worker would return to the factory with the 'alertness, the docility and the disciplined promptness' of the German working man.[37]

Under the patronage of Britain's favourite soldier, Lord Roberts, the League received considerable publicity during the period up to 1914, with a peak membership of just under 100,000. Among its supporters were Leo Maxse, Lord Milner, Leo Amery and Robert Baden-Powell. *The Times, Daily Mail, The Observer, Daily Telegraph* and other prominent papers threw their weight behind the cause. But while the League claimed support from 177 MPs of all parties, in truth few politicians backed it enthusiastically. Despite all its efforts, including an average of 240 local meetings per month in 1912, the League never succeeded in becoming a truly mass movement and therefore never came close to achieving its goal.[38] It was opposed not only by liberals and the left, but also by conservatives and traditionalists who saw compulsion as thoroughly un-British. Senior army officers, among them Haig and Kitchener, argued that volunteers were by nature more committed and dependable soldiers.

37 S. Low, 'The Future of the Great Armies', *The Nineteenth Century* 47 (1899), pp. 390–2.
38 The data on support for the League is from Summers, 'Militarism in Britain', p. 113, who draws entirely different conclusions.

The League's failure provides yet more evidence of the decidedly non-militaristic nature of pre-war British society.

Deficiencies in the army could be tolerated because the British remained confident that the Royal Navy would be their salvation. But this sense of security did not give rise to complacency; from the end of the Boer War to August 1914, a great deal of energy was directed toward naval reform, in particular by Sir John Fisher, First Sea Lord, from 1904 to 1910. He was responsible for improvements in officer training, the redirection of fleets to home waters, the scrapping of obsolete vessels and the creation of an active reserve on the basis of the nucleus-crew system. But Fisher's most important effect lay in the decision to build the 'Dreadnought' class of battleship. These reforms were not at first directed toward the growing threat of Germany, being instead part of a periodic modernisation programme. In fact, until 1904, calculation of the navy's size did not even take Germany into account; the two-power standard (whereby Britain calculated the size of her navy according to the combined size of the next two largest forces) was measured in relation to France and Russia.

But it gradually dawned on the British that the German naval bills of 1898 and 1900 were designed to give Kaiser Wilhelm a navy to rival the British. In February 1904 Lord Selborne, First Lord of the Admiralty, told the Cabinet that henceforth Germany would replace Russia in the calculation of the two-power standard. The energetic self-publicist Fisher delighted in the confrontation with Germany which this implied. In December 1904, he decided to re-orientate the British fleet so as to concentrate battleships in home waters. A new base at Scapa Flow in the North Sea was established. Fisher spoke openly and belligerently of his desire to 'Copenhagen' the German fleet. Thus began the Anglo-German naval race – technically a misnomer, since Britain's continued adherence to the two-power standard meant that she had to stay ahead of Germany and France combined. Few stopped to consider whether this calculation remained logical, especially in view of Germany's rampant ambitions and France's friendliness. But if doubts were raised, they were not likely to be heard above the din created by the right wing popular press, which delighted in an issue so perfectly suited to inflame jingoistic passions. The average British citizen had no trouble understanding an issue which could be so simply expressed as 'lots of big ships'.

The Anglo-German naval race, which began in earnest after the launching of HMS *Dreadnought* on 10 February 1906, was based on the uncritical assumption (derived from the writings of Captain Alfred Thayer Mahan) that political and economic hegemony was determined by sea power. What is astonishing is the way in which Mahan's already suspect thesis was rendered even more absurd by a concentration on sheer numbers of big ships, without much attention to their effectiveness nor to the quality of the sailors who manned them. 'Dreadnoughts' were built because it was assumed that future naval encounters would follow the classical pattern of massed forces meeting in a set-piece battle like two grand masters sitting down to a game of chess. The humiliation of the Russian navy by the Japanese at the battles of Tsushima and Port Arthur had unfortunately reinforced this flawed notion. Behind it lay the same short war mentality that gripped European armies, also wedded to classical patterns of war.

In fact, since the state of military technology militated against a short land war, a set-piece battle at sea became in consequence unlikely. No naval power (especially not an island nation) would risk the destruction of its entire fleet in one massive battle if the war was likely to be long. Since big battles were unlikely, big ships were less important. In a long war, the navy's role is to maintain a blockade, keep shipping lanes open, transport troops and protect merchant shipping, all of which are best performed by considerably smaller ships than those in the 'Dreadnought' class. But this argument was beyond the ken of the British people, their government and indeed the Admiralty. They saw Germans eager for a race and sprinted off without bothering to check which direction to run. There was little the government could have done differently (even if it had understood the issues) given a rabid public fired by lurid invasion stories and newspapers shouting 'We want eight and we won't wait'. Britain, mesmerised by German production in the 'Dreadnought' class, failed to notice the steady expansion of Germany's submarine fleet, ships immensely more useful in a long war.

The debate concerning Britain's military capabilities which followed the Boer War was much more energetic than any which occurred during the Victorian period. But, despite the crisis of confidence, the army and navy which went to war in 1914 were remarkably similar to those which had existed in 1899. The Royal Navy had been superficially modernised, but it retained a faith in the patterns of ancient naval battles and, most of all, remained confident of its own invincibility. The army had, thanks to Haldane, been administratively restructured and was made capable of speedy mobilisation. But the costs of naval modernisation (the construction of

'Dreadnoughts') and a burgeoning social welfare budget had limited its size to a mere 120,000 men. And it was still essentially a Victorian army; senior commanders who would control its fate were the product of that era and were wedded to traditions which pre-dated Edwardian reforms.

After extended argument, Britain had decided to stick with the status quo, rejecting the advice of those who wanted a larger or more professional military. She remained satisfied that the practices which had served her well in the past would enable her to meet any crisis which lay ahead. It is in this way that Britain's military was most accurately a reflection of her society. The faults in the army and navy were not ones exclusive to those institutions; they were instead manifestations of the wider social ethos. The military was shaped by both the insecurities and the egotism of Edwardian and Victorian Britain. The public's faith in the amateur ideal, its suspicion of large armies, its adherence to liberal conceptions of freedom, and its belief in its capacity to muddle through gave Britain the army and the navy she deserved.

In early 1914, war loomed on the western, not eastern, horizon. The possibility that the army might be called upon to enforce Irish Home Rule frightened everyone, since no other issue seemed so severely to test the loyalty of the officer corps. It was therefore something of a relief that war broke out in Europe, not Ulster. Popular opinion held that it would be a short and glorious war, an opportunity not to be missed. Staff officers who should have stayed at home to study the strategic and tactical problems of this war, not to mention the logistics of expanding the army, instead rushed off to join the fray. And who could blame them? But the war they encountered was not the war they expected. After a brief period of mobility, stalemate descended like a thick, impenetrable fog. War, contrary to all expectations, was static, costly, horrible and long. It was also unexpectedly deadly: by the spring of 1915 the army of Victoria by way of Haldane was all but obliterated. A new army had therefore to be created. Britain's ability to muddle through would be severely tested.

3 'TO DIE YOUNG'

On 1 May 1914, the regular army was nearly 11,000 men short of the size prescribed by the Army Order of 1907, proof of the population's lack of enthusiasm for military service.[1] Four months later, after the outbreak of war, the army was swamped by a flood of recruits too large to be processed. When Britain was forced to improvise an army, her population responded with alacrity. The men who came forward proved, superficially at least, the perfect raw material for an army. From the public schools came potential officers of limitless zeal, unquestioning patriotism and unwavering confidence in their ability to lead. From the working class came the perfect foot soldiers: deferent, fatalistic men who expected little from life and for whom the army often meant an improvement in living standards. This flood of recruits seemed to justify the British faith in muddling through.

MUSCULAR CHRISTIANS

R. C. Sheriff, author of *Journey's End*, tried to secure a commission in autumn 1914:

> 'School?', inquired the adjutant. I told him and his face fell. He took up a printed list . . . 'I'm sorry,' he said, 'but I'm afraid it isn't a public school.' I was mystified. I told him that my school, though small, was a very old and good one – founded, I said, by Queen Elizabeth in 1567. The adjutant was not impressed. He had lost all interest in me. 'I'm sorry,' he repeated. 'But our instructions are that all applicants for commissions must be selected from the recognized public schools and yours is not among them.'[2]

Since the public schools had produced the gentlemen officers of the Victorian and Edwardian army, the army naturally looked to them

1 E. M. Spiers, 'The Regular Army in 1914', in I. Beckett and K. Simpson, eds, *A Nation in Arms*, p. 44.
2 R. C. Sheriff, 'The English Public Schools in the War', in G. A. Panichas, ed., *Promise of Greatness*, p. 137.

for new recruits. But beyond mere custom, this was also a pragmatic response predicated by war's emergency. 'It was a rough method of selection', Sheriff concluded, 'a demarcation line hewn out with an ax; but it was the only way in the face of emergency, and as things turned out, it worked.'[3] By selecting public schoolboys, the army ensured that its officer recruits had a consistent standard of basic training and a belief system relevant to military service. On the eve of war, 150 schools and 20 universities had established Officer Training Corps – a Haldane reform. Thus, the public schoolboy had rudimentary military training; he knew how to handle a rifle and was familiar with basic drill. Furthermore, the school environment – the hierarchy of the prefectorial system and teamwork rewarded by decoration, not to mention its monasticism, discipline and austerity – was roughly similar to army life.[4]

But, bearing in mind the prevalent amateur ideal, it is unlikely that practical benefits alone explained the public schoolboy's worth. What appealed most was the boy's character, supposedly suited to leadership in battle. In the latter half of the nineteenth century the schools had shifted their emphasis from 'godliness and good learning' to a more vigorous and manly training suited to an expanding and dynamic Empire. Often referred to as Muscular Christianity, this ideal was epitomised by Rugby School and its headmaster, Thomas Arnold. Athletic prowess took precedence over intellectual development. In Arnold's vision, 'sport . . . would give a young man the body of a Greek and the soul of a Christian knight'.[5] Boys were supposed to be muscular *and* Christian, but the Christianity was adapted to suit Imperial aspirations. Sermons taught that Jesus, a virile carpenter, was a paragon of manliness.

Manliness should not be confused with what today is called machismo, since it encompassed a raft of attributes including honour, duty, sacrifice, honesty, and of course physical strength and endurance. Good character was supposed to arise from a strong will, which was in turn a sign of a healthy mind. Since the health of the mind and that of the body were inextricably linked, Victorians assumed that by looking after the body the will could be strengthened. Studies of the Victorian public school have tended to judge these ideas ill-founded, obsessive and bizarre, yet the schools were merely acknowledging the link between a healthy body and a healthy

3 Ibid., p. 139.
4 See R. Wilkinson, *The Prefects*, pp. 17ff.
5 M. Eksteins, *Rites of Spring*, p. 120.

mind, which few question today. Furthermore, team sports undoubtedly *do* encourage discipline, self-sacrifice, teamwork, etc. – attributes which have practical applications in later life. One wonders in fact whether the preoccupation with exercise was any more pronounced than is the case today. The big difference was that before 1914 the obsession was confined to the upper classes (and to males) and was seen as a way for the young to become adults rather than for adults to stay young. 'Unfortunately the more adult aspects of this concept of manliness... were less easily assimilated by posterity', writes Norman Vance.[6] In other words, the boys sometimes failed to understand that games were not just games. As time passed, 'manliness declined from the moral strenuousness of Arnold's conception and approximated to the cult of the physical'.[7]

If there was an obsession, it was in the way building character was linked to physical exercise, to the exclusion of other stimuli. Between the 1850s and the outbreak of war in 1914, educators held that it was not necessary to exercise the mind with challenging intellectual problems if mind and character were being more effectively developed on the playing field. The army agreed. One senior officer who served on the Royal Commission on the Militia and Volunteers argued in 1904 that 'Situations may arise in a good cricket or football team requiring as quick a decision, perhaps a shade quicker, than a company commander with his line of skirmishers in the field.'[8] The army's *Field Service Regulations*, the officer's bible, stipulated that 'Success in war depends more on moral than on physical qualities. Skill cannot compensate for want of courage, energy and determination.'[9] Those qualities could best be developed on the playing field, not in the classroom. In 1902, the Assistant Commandant of Woolwich Academy argued that teaching cadets science narrowed their minds. 'Our great point is character, we care more about that than [science] subjects.'[10]

H. H. Almond, headmaster at Loretto, felt that a school did not need a rifle corps if it possessed a rugby field.[11] War was merely a

6 N. Vance, 'The Ideal of Manliness', in M. J. Bradley and B. Simon, eds, *The Victorian Public School*, p. 122.

7 Ibid., p. 124.

8 G. Best, 'Militarism and the Victorian Public School', in Bradley and Simon, eds, p. 142.

9 *Field Service Regulations, Part I (Operations)*, p. 11.

10 T. Travers, 'Technology, Tactics and Morale: Jean de Bloch, the Boer War, and British Military Theory, 1900–1914', *Journal of Modern History* (1979), p. 286.

11 Best, 'Militarism and the Victorian Public School', p. 142.

higher form of athletic contest, therefore the best way to prepare for war was to play games. Boys' adventure stories began with the hero cutting a swathe through the rival school's defence and ended with him doing the same to a horde of raving Dervish. The theme is best illustrated in 'Vitai Lampada', by the Poet Laureate Sir Henry New-bolt, oracle of Empire and manliness:

> The sand of the desert is sodden and red,
> Red with the wreck of the square that broke –
> The Gatling's jammed and the Colonel dead,
> And the regiment blind with dust and smoke.
> The river of death has brimmed his banks
> And England's far, and Honour a name,
> But the voice of a schoolboy rallies the ranks;
> Play up! play up! and play the game![12]

A Marlborough College song had a similar message:

> Be strong, Elevens, to bowl and shoot,
> Be strong, O Regiment of the foot,
> With ball of skin or lead or leather,
> Stand for the Commonwealth together.[13]

Equating war with games encouraged the assumption that both were played to a single set of rules. Warfare was civilised, fought by gentlemen, and won by the morally pure. One could not, of course, expect uncivilised races to play the game properly, which explains in part why the British occasionally had difficulty defeating them. Haig, for instance, was dismayed to find that the Dervish at Omdurman would pretend to surrender, then rise and fire at his men from the back.[14] In contrast, war between civilised Europeans was generally expected to be the purest form of combat. When Fisher suggested that poison gas and aerial bombardments might be employed in future wars he was treated with polite condescension, like a once-reputable gentleman who had sadly slipped off his rocker. The British failure to prepare adequately for submarine warfare can in part be explained by a belief that civilised powers would never be so cowardly as to wage war in such a fashion.

The component qualities which made up the manly character

12 H. Newbolt, 'Vitai Lampada', in *Poems New and Old*, pp. 78–9.

13 J. A. Mangan, 'Athleticism: A Case Study of the Evolution of an Educational Ideology', in Bradley and Simon, eds, p. 157.

14 G. DeGroot, *Douglas Haig, 1861–1928*, p. 66.

help to explain the behaviour of the young men who volunteered in 1914, and indeed that of the existing officer corps. One important quality was loyalty. By playing for a team, the boy learned to place the interests of the group before his own. Once developed, loyalty for the school or house was easily redirected to the regiment. It was instinctive; the individual did not question whether the institution was worthy of his devotion. *The Times* praised school spirit as a force which encouraged boys to 'distrust individual intellects and do an unselfish job'.[15] Thus, not only was the public school anti-intellectual in its emphasis upon character over intellect, its stress upon loyalty militated against the exercise of reason. But this suited an army which did not want its junior officers to think.

Another quality encouraged at the public schools was 'good form'. The concept encompassed both physical and moral qualities, with little distinction between the two. Beautiful manners and impeccable dress symbolised moral virtue and a 'clean' soul, or, in the case of a soldier, an impressively appointed uniform suggested courage, honour, self-sacrifice and, again, loyalty. The aesthetic and the moral – form and content – were inextricably fused. Loyalty and good form stifled insight and imagination, but that was the idea. The loyal individual tended toward moderation, compromise and restraint. New ideas, by nature disruptive, were treated with suspicion. This bias against progress was manifested in the public school curriculum; budding officers could recite Plato in the original Greek, but had little knowledge of physics or chemistry.

In *The Loom of Youth*, Alec Waugh described the public schoolboy as 'easy-going, pleasure-loving and absolutely without a conscience . . . he has learnt to do what he is told, he takes life as he sees it and is content'.[16] No wonder these boys went eagerly off to war. Jane Harrison, then a Cambridge lecturer, was astonished at the reaction of students and dons to the call to arms: 'it came to me as something of a shock to find that many of them . . . went, not reluctantly, but with positive alacrity'. In her opinion, the obsession with teamwork and self-sacrifice produced a herd instinct which stifled creative thought and critical enquiry. The warriors of 1914 were 'driven by a thirst for primary sensations'; they sought to 'drown their individual consciousness in collective militancy'.[17]

For this generation, the war was an opportunity not just to crush

15 Wilkinson, p. 83.
16 A. Waugh, *The Loom of Youth*, p. 90.
17 J. Harrison, *Alpha and Omega*, p. 227.

the Germans or to save Britain, but also to satisfy primal yearnings and to experience a spiritual purgation. In *Desmond's Daughter*, Colonel Wyndham described war as

> the great paradox, the greatest in human history. It spells horror, but it spells also heroism, which is possibly what commends it to most healthy minded men. . . . Call it what you like, a terrible medicine or an intermittent eruption of evil; it is still . . . the Great Flail that threshes the wheat from the chaff. So, in the long run, it makes for the ethical advance of the race.[18]

According to David Newsome, the public schools, by trying to teach manly virtues through games playing, 'fell into the opposite error of failing to make the boys into men at all'. He feels, rightly, that the 'code of living became so robust and patriotic in its demands that it could be represented as reaching in its perfection a code of dying'.[19] H. A. Vachell's *The Hill*, standard reading at school after its publication in 1905, described the perfect death:

> To die young, clean, ardent; to die swiftly, in perfect health; to die saving others from death, or worse – disgrace – to die scaling heights; to die and to carry with you into the fuller ampler life beyond, untainted hopes and aspirations, unembittered memories, all the freshness and gladness of May – is not that cause for joy rather than sorrow?[20]

Death in fetid mud did not figure in Vachell's vision, nor did the slow agony of gas poisoning or the horrors of an endless artillery bombardment. The loyalty, courage, self-sacrifice and patriotism a boy learned at school were without question attributes relevant to soldiering. They enabled him to withstand hardships otherwise unendurable. But somewhere along the line the schools lost sight of the fact that the object of war is not to die heroically, but to win.

SPREADING THE GOSPEL

Confidence in the beneficial effects of Muscular Christianity inspired attempts to spread the ethic lower down the social order. Enthusiasts were not so sanguine or democratic as to believe that by teaching an urban wastrel the discipline of the scrum he could be transformed into a future Field Marshal. But they did feel that a good dose of

18 W. J. Reader, *At Duty's Call*, p. 23.
19 D. Newsome, *Godliness and Good Learning*, p. 258.
20 H. A. Vachell, *The Hill*, p. 236.

manliness might transform a feckless, unhealthy, undisciplined slum boy into a worthy servant of the Empire.

Among those so inspired was William Alexander Smith, Glasgow businessman, YMCA member and Lieutenant in the Lanarkshire Volunteers, who formed the first company of the Boys' Brigade in Hillhead in October 1883. Beyond mere Muscular Christianity, the Brigade was a pragmatic attempt to keep boys suitably occupied during their early teens, when idleness might otherwise tempt them toward delinquency. Religion alone, Smith believed, could not achieve this purpose since, being too sedentary and effeminate, it had no appeal for spirited boys. Smith regretted that Sunday School teachers were invariably women who encouraged 'among boys an impression that to be a Christian means to be a "molly coddle" '. The Brigade sought to redirect the boy's manly instincts:

> All a boy's aspirations are towards *manliness*, however mistaken his ideas may sometimes be as to what that manliness means. Our boys are full of earnest desire to be brave true *men*; and if we want to make them brave, true *Christian* men, we must direct this desire into the right channel. . . . We must show them the *manliness* of Christianity.[21]

Christianity became manly when its lessons were worldly and heroic and when it was combined with the discipline and order of military-style drill and athleticism encouraged by team games. The Brigade was among the first voluntary movements to introduce working-class boys to organised sports, hitherto the preserve of the public schools. In Smith's perfect world, boys would talk 'to each other in the most perfectly natural way about the Company Bible-Class before all their comrades on the football field'![22]

Smith's example was widely copied. A wide array of youth organisations were established, all combining religion, athleticism and military discipline. The Anglican-inspired Church Lads' Brigade, the Jewish Lads' Brigade, the Duty and Discipline Movement and the National Council of Public Morals carved out inner-city constituencies. But the most famous youth movement was undoubtedly the Boy Scouts. Begun in 1908 by General Sir Robert Baden-Powell, it was yet another manifestation of the quest for national efficiency which followed the South African embarrassment. Baden-Powell, hero of Mafeking, went beyond the traditional games ethic, stressing instead the beneficial properties of life on the Imperial frontier. 'Football is a good game', he argued, 'but

---

21 J. Springhall, 'Building Character in the British Boy', in J. A. Mangan and J. Walvin, eds, *Manliness and Morality*, p. 55.
22 Ibid., p. 57.

much better than it, better than any other game, is . . . man-hunting.'
Thus, scouting was a spiritualistic response to the problem of an
unhealthy population (during the Boer War, approximately 70 per cent
of volunteers were judged unfit for military service), and as such was
typical of the conservative element in society who blamed society's
problems on character deficiencies. Boys from the slum would be turned
into worthy servants of Empire simply by being taken into the countryside, where they would learn the moral purity and discipline of patriotic
scouts. This aim is clearly stated in *Scouting for Boys*; scouts would
learn to emulate the 'pioneers, explorers and missionaries' who had
built the Empire:

> real *men* in every sense of the word, and thoroughly up on scout craft,
> i.e. they understand living out in the jungles, and they can find their
> way anywhere, are able to read meaning from the smallest signs and
> foot-tracks; they know how to look after their health when far away
> from any doctors, are strong and plucky, and ready to face any danger,
> and always keen to help each other. They are accustomed to take lives
> in their own hands, and to fling them down without hesitation if they
> can help their country by doing so.[23]

In South Africa, it was unfortunately the Boer soldier who proved
himself the more accomplished scout. Baden-Powell was determined
that the next war would find Britain better prepared. 'Every boy
ought to learn how to shoot and obey orders, else he is no more
good when war breaks out than an old woman', he argued.[24] 'Be
Prepared' was not simply a vague command to young scouts, but a
very specific injunction: 'BE PREPARED to die for your country . . .
so that when the time comes you may charge home with confidence,
not caring whether you are to be killed or not.'[25]

The message of manliness and preparedness was driven home in
the boys' literature of the time, prodigious propaganda for Muscular
Christianity. Whilst the works of Jules Verne and Rudyard Kipling
have some literary merit, the great majority of the manly tales are
now of interest only to the social historian. Yet these stories and
poems were hugely popular. G. A. Henty produced two or three
books between the early 1880s and his death in 1902, with each
edition selling around 150,000 copies. Each novel kept to a strict

23 J. M. Mackenzie, 'The Imperial Pioneer and Hunter and the British Masculine
Stereotype in Late Victorian and Edwardian Times', in Mangan and Walvin, eds,
p. 177.

24 Ibid., p. 176.

25 From *Scouting for Boys*, in Travers, 'Technology, Tactics and Morale, p. 280.

formula: a magnificent manly hero, lashings of adventure, a sprinkling of suspense, an element of verisimilitude (books were often linked to real events) and an agreeable climax: right always triumphed. Like Smith, Henty recognised that boys were not likely to be attracted to the piousness which characterised juvenile literature of the mid-Victorian period. It should come as no surprise that Henty served as an Honorary Vice President of the Boys' Brigade.

The *Boy's Own Paper* took the Henty formula and published it in an affordable weekly magazine (price: 1d) which, according to one survey, was read by two-thirds of Britain's schoolboys.[26] The magazine was started by the Religious Tract Society as a response to the 'penny dreadful', which, it was feared, tempted boys down unChristian paths. At its peak, it sold over 50,000 copies per week, with each copy probably passed among at least three boys. Contributors included Verne, Rider Haggard, Talbot Baines Reed, R. M. Ballantyne and the ubiquitous Henty.

It would be tempting to judge the popularity of the *Boy's Own Paper* and of Henty, the Boys' Brigade, the Boy Scouts and similar organisations as evidence of rampant militarism. The evidence is certainly compelling. Within two years of its establishment, the Boy Scouts claimed 100,000 members.[27] Over 40 per cent of all male adolescents belonged to some kind of youth organisation by 1914.[28] Haldane, defending plans for setting up officer corps in schools and universities, confessed to the Commons that 'you are not in danger of increasing the spirit of militarism there, because the spirit of militarism already runs fairly high'.[29] But if this was militarism, it was an impotent strain, especially in comparison to the militarist mania which gripped German society. A definition is perhaps helpful. True militarism requires the domination of government and society by military elites, a tendency to overvalue military power and the dissemination of military values into wider society. Britain failed to satisfy the first part of this definition and only partially satisfied the second (witness the lukewarm response to military preparedness and compulsory service). As for the third part, it is true that military

---

26 Springhall, 'Building Character', p. 64. The survey was published in the *Fortnightly Review*. It was probably taken among public schoolboys, as those from the poorer classes would not have been able to afford the *Boy's Own Paper* even had they wanted to read it. The figure of two-thirds of the total readership is therefore somewhat misleading.

27 Z. Steiner, *Britain and the Origins of the First World War*, p. 159.

28 I. Beckett, 'The Nation in Arms, 1914–1918', in Beckett and Simpson, eds, p. 5.

29 M. Howard, *Studies in War and Peace*, p. 92.

values did spread into wider society. But one should ask why they spread. The 'militarism' of the public schools, Boys' Brigade and *Boy's Own Paper* was not designed to prepare Britain for war nor even to turn all boys into soldiers. Its primary aim was instead social control, not unlike the knee-jerk response of certain groups who advocate the reintroduction of national service whenever English football hooligans run riot in Amsterdam or Dublin. One aim of the Boy Scouts was to counter the lure of football grounds, where there gathered 'thousands of boys and young men, pale, narrow-chested, hunched-up miserable specimens, smoking endless cigarettes, numbers of them betting, all of them learning to be hysterical as they groan or cheer in panic unison'.[30]

One also needs to question how effectively military values were disseminated. Over 40 per cent of boys in youth organisations is an impressive constituency. But while those organisations might have had a militaristic intent, one should not assume they were successful at spreading the martial gospel. Wily, opportunistic young boys probably took what they wanted from these groups and ignored the boring or disagreeable. When the Boys' Brigade extended its recruitment beyond established church congregations, it found that new recruits were less likely to attend church regularly – they swallowed the muscular morsel but discarded the Christian wrapping. The salient point about the Brigade, the Scouts and the Henty novels was that they were fun. A bit of Christian indoctrination and some innocent drill was probably a small price to pay for the opportunity to play a good game of football on a real pitch with a real ball or to read a cracking good story.

And what of the six out of ten boys who did not join youth movements? These were the very ones Smith and Baden-Powell were most eager to indoctrinate, in other words the 'hooligan' element in the inner cities. This was especially true of the Boy Scouts, which, try as it might, could not shed its elitist tag. The problem was partially one of means; scout uniforms, outings and paraphernalia, no matter how well subsidised, cost money which the very poor did not have. Even the Boys' Brigade, though not as expensive, mainly attracted boys who had already made a good start in life, from skilled working class homes (or better), who went to church and were already apprenticed to a respectable trade. The 12th Earl of Meath, honorary President of the Dublin Battalion of the Brigade, admitted in June 1902 that the Brigade was attractive only to the

30 Travers, 'Technology, Tactics and Morale', p. 280.

'better-behaved lads, those who have already a desire for something better, [and] a tendency towards religious organisations'. It could 'never hope to obtain the rough lads from the great mass of the population'.[31]

Beyond these financial constraints, there existed a distinct abhorrence of youth groups among lower working class boys. They possibly saw uniformed youth movements for exactly what they were, namely methods of social control. Thus, a refusal to join was an assertive expression of lower working class independence. This rejection even stretched occasionally to violence against boys who were members. 'Many a company in those ancient days was conscious of a highly organised underground movement whose purpose was to conduct a continuous guerilla campaign against the Boys' Brigade', recalled one former member. 'Often was a drill parade conducted under a fusillade of stones and bricks.'[32] Similar, if less hyperbolic, stories of violence against Brigade members abound. Members of the Catholic Boys' Brigade of South London chose to change into their uniforms at the meeting hall, so as to avoid the possibility of being attacked en route.

The lower class boy also read a different type of magazine, if he read at all. The Henty books, at a shilling each, were beyond his means, and the *Boy's Own Paper*, at 1d per issue, could be afforded only by the 'boy with a future' who joined the Brigade and the Scouts. The less fortunate read those priced at ½d per issue, such as *The Union Jack* and *The Halfpenny Marvel*, exactly the coarser magazines which the *Boy's Own Paper* had been specifically set up to counter. Frederick Willis recalled that 'a very distinct barrier' divided 'that section of society which had a penny to burn and that which had only a halfpence'.[33] But the cheaper magazines were not totally devoid of the Muscular Christian message. The Harmsworth weeklies *The Gem* and *The Magnet* published stories by Frank Richards about a fictional public school called Greyfriars, where manly heroes abounded. But Frank O'Connor recalled that though boys from his humble origins enjoyed the stories, they did not always absorb the underlying moral lessons:

> I kept in training by shadow boxing before the mirror in the kitchen, and practised the deadly straight left with which the hero knocked out the bully of the school. I even adopted the public school code for my

31 Springhall, 'Building Character', p. 58.
32 Ibid., p. 59.
33 Ibid., p. 67.

own, and did not tell lies, or inform on other boys, or yell when I was beaten. It wasn't easy, because the other fellows did tell lies, and told on one another in the most shameless way, and, when they were beaten, yelled that their wrists were broken, and even boasted of their own cleverness and when I behaved in the simple, manly way recommended in the school stories, they said I was mad or that I was 'shaping' (swanking), and even the teacher seemed to regard it as an impertinence.[34]

The phantasmagoric world of the public school was for most boys simply too far removed from reality to inspire imitation. For the street corner youth, to be manly meant to smoke, drink, swagger, lie, cheat and fight – and preferably fight dirty. Christian manliness was supposed to be an antidote to hooliganism, yet for the dispossessed to be manly meant to be a hooligan.

THE RUSH TO THE COLOURS

Pre-war strategic plans were based on the assumption that a European war, should it occur, would be short. Manly myths of war relied on the same assumption; in order for war to be romantic, it had to be brief, decisive and glorious. But within a week of the first shots being fired, British preconceptions collided head-on with the realities of modern war. It became obvious that the war would be long and would use up men at a prodigious rate. Lord Kitchener, the newly appointed Secretary of State for War, concluded that Britain should immediately begin to raise an army in excess of one million men. By nature a loose cannon, Kitchener in one precipitous step cast aside the Army Order and the Territorial and Reserve Forces Act, which stipulated that both the regular army and the Territorials would employ their respective recruiting machinery to expand as required in time of war. Possessing little faith in the Territorials, Kitchener decided instead to start from scratch by building a new army, drawn entirely from volunteers.

The Territorials were not simply consigned to the scrap heap. Originally intended as a home defence force, some were re-employed at Imperial outposts, in order to free regular army battalions for despatch to France and Belgium. Necessity eventually dictated their transfer to the Western Front; the Loos offensive of September 1915 would not have been launched without their assistance. But each decision which brought the Territorials closer to active service abroad

34 Ibid., p. 69.

was taken reluctantly by Kitchener. There are a number of reasons for his misgivings, many of them justified. Firstly, they were intended for home defence, and the threat of invasion, in Kitchener's mind at least, remained real. Secondly, their terms of engagement were not particularly appropriate to this war. For them to serve overseas necessitated rewriting their conditions of service. Given the voluntarist ethic, this required the permission of the troops concerned. Territorial soldiers enlisted for just four years, extended to five in time of war. The force would therefore shrink as time passed, not a pleasant prospect in a long war. It was also feared that new volunteers might opt for the Territorials, seeing home service as a soft option. Thirdly, the cherished integrity of Territorial units, a legacy of their proud past as Volunteers, Yeomanry and Militia, militated against breaking them up to reinforce existing regular army units. Fourthly, Territorial units varied greatly in quality. At the time of mobilisation, upwards of 20 per cent of the troops in some units were unfit for service. The 42nd Territorial Division was nearly at full establishment when it left Britain, but when it arrived in Egypt in September 1914, the GOC, Sir John Maxwell, found 100 men technically blind, 1,500 riddled with vermin, one dying of Bright's disease and 'hundreds . . . so badly vaccinated they could hardly move'. One officer concluded that the division had 'picked up any loafer or corner boy they could find to make up the numbers'.[35]

But the most important reason for Kitchener's reluctance to allow the Territorials to form the nucleus of an expanded army was his lack of respect for part-time amateur soldiers – what he called a 'Town Clerks' army'.[36] He felt that when it came to creating soldiers a little knowledge (such as the Territorials possessed) was much more dangerous than none at all. Kitchener preferred to start from scratch with a new army unencumbered by tradition, trained according to the demands of this war, enlisted for the duration, and able to be sent wherever necessity dictated. This desire inspired Alfred Leete's famous poster which had the imposing figure of Kitchener proclaiming 'Your Country Needs You'.

The response was enormous. Between August 1914 and December 1915, 2,466,719 men enlisted, the largest volunteer army in any country in history. This great rush to the colours might seem an enormously unselfish response by citizens of all classes to their country's call. But it is important to realise that these men did not

---

35 I. Beckett, 'The Territorial Force', in Beckett and Simpson, eds, p. 134.
36 Ibid., p. 130.

share a common will to serve. Only by studying the various motivations for volunteering can we understand the type of army which eventually evolved and the effect which war had upon those who served.

The mass of volunteers can be divided into two groups: those from the public schools, most of whom became officers, and those from the rest of society who made up the ranks. Of the former group, it has been argued that their willingness to volunteer is easily explained since they had most to lose if Britain were defeated.[37] But an explanation which relies so heavily upon self-interest seems ill-fitting a generation of boys so naive and devoid of cynicism, so conditioned to believe in honour, glory and self-sacrifice. It has become a cliché to quote Rupert Brooke in this context, but it is in the nature of clichés that they are often singularly apropos. Granted, Brooke was extraordinary, but only in the eloquent way he described the emotions which young men from his peer group felt:

> If I should die, think only this of me:
>   That there's some corner of a foreign field
> That is forever England. There shall be
>   In that rich earth a richer dust concealed;
> A dust whom England bore, shaped, made aware,
>   Gave, one her flowers to love, her ways to roam,
> A body of England's, breathing English air,
>   Washed by rivers, blest by suns of home.[38]

This generation was raised to believe in manly, chivalric values, yet had little opportunity to test their relevance in the real world. The unreality of its vision of war is revealed in a National Service League pamphlet by Canon J. H. Skrine of Merton College, Oxford:

> War is not murder ... war is sacrifice. The fighting and killing are not of the essence of it, but are the accidents, though the inseparable accidents; and even these, in the wide modern fields where a soldier rarely in his own sight sheds any blood but his own, where he lies on the battle sward not to inflict death but to endure it – even these are mainly purged of savagery and transfigured into devotion. War is not murder but sacrifice, which is the soul of Christianity.[39]

---

37 J. Winter, 'The Army and Society: The Demographic Context', in Beckett and Simpson, eds, p. 197.

38 R. Brooke, '1914', in T. Cross, ed., *The Lost Voices of World War I*, p. 55.

39 A. Summers, 'Militarism in Britain Before the Great War', *History Workshop Journal* 2 (1976), p. 120.

Like another martial race, the samurai, public schoolboys worshipped war but seldom actually fought; thus their ethos was exaggerated into farce. Images of war came from Henty, Newbolt and Kipling, not from shattered veterans of Balaclava and Omdurman. Even when old boys told war stories on school speech days, they did not tell of chaos and slaughter, but instead perpetuated the myths of heroic war – a type of war long obsolete, if indeed it had ever existed. It was generally expected that war against a civilised European enemy would be war at its most sublime, the ultimate embodiment of the public school education: not a calamity, but a sacred rite of passage which only the most fortunate would experience. Graham Greene recalled: 'My brothers and I were delighted at the speed with which [Namur] had fallen because the prolonged defence of Liège had threatened a speedy determination of the war. As long as the war continued, we might one day be involved and the world of Henty seemed to come a little closer.'[40]

'I adore war', wrote Julian Grenfell after just one month of fighting; 'it's like a big picnic without the objectlessness of a picnic. I've never been so well or happy. No one grumbles at one for being dirty.' Muscular Christian values had been so well disseminated that Grenfell could freely write of war in this way without being judged mentally unbalanced. Nicholas Mosley later explained that Grenfell's reference to dirtiness was 'meant physically, but psychologically it was relevant too. For the first time a generation brought up to be clean and bright and brilliant could, without guilt, be fierce and babyish and vile.'[41] Perhaps, but for this generation there was nothing fierce, nor babyish, nor vile about war. It may have been dirty, but spiritually it was pristinely clean. Vachell, it will be recalled, described death in war as like the 'freshness and gladness of May'. War's dirt had the purifying effect of baptismal water.

Granted, there were some iconoclasts who refused to conform to the standards of the typical public school patriot. J. B. Priestley was one such, yet he too answered Kitchener's call with alacrity. As he later explained, he was unaffected by peer pressure, by patriotism, by Kitchener's call, by visions of a great heroic crusade, or by anything

> that was rational and conscious ... I went at a signal from the unknown ... there came out of the unclouded blue of that summer, a challenge that was almost like a conscription of the spirit, little to do

40 P. Vansittart, *Voices from the Great War*, p. 35.
41 Ibid., p. 44.

really with King and Country and flag-waving and hip-hip-hurrah, a
challenge to what we felt was our untested manhood. Other men, who
had not lived as easily as we had, had drilled and marched and borne
arms – couldn't we?[42]

Priestley perhaps described a universal male condition; war brings
out the hidden soldier which lies within many men. But one suspects
that this conscription of the male spirit was stronger in this innocent
and manly age than in almost any other. As much as he might have
denied it, Priestley was influenced by the temper of his generation,
however subliminally.

As for the workers, they were slightly freer than those of higher
status to make up their own minds since they were less brainwashed
by prevailing conceptions of duty. They volunteered for a wide
variety of reasons. The rush to the colours was not one monolithic
mass, but rather some two million separate individuals, each with a
different set of reasons for volunteering. In varying degrees, these
recruits were deferent, desperate, drunk, bored, destitute or deluded;
many sought glory, others were drawn by a patriotic duty, and many
simply did what they were told.

The concept of a 'rush to the colours' is in fact misleading, at
least as it is commonly presented. Nearly 300,000 men enlisted in
August 1914, a good many before Kitchener made his urgent call.
The most productive recruiting period lasted from the final week of
August to the second week of September. If there was a rush, it was
over by the 9th. Fewer men enlisted in all of October than during
the first four days of September. This is illustrated by the matter of
height requirements. When the war began, the army set a minimum
standard of 5 feet 3 inches (1.6 metres). On 11 September the
decision was taken to raise the standard to 5 feet 6 inches (1.68
metres) in order to control the flow of recruits. But, as was subsequently apparent, by that stage the flow was beginning to diminish.
On 14 November the army returned to the original requirement and
began in fact to organise bantam units consisting of men below 5
feet 3 inches. As one correspondent to *The Times* recognised, short
men had certain advantages: 'besides lessening the size of the target
for the enemy to hit, he requires shallower trenches to hide or protect
him'.[43]

Much has been written of men who volunteered on the assumption that the war would be short and that the chance for glory must

42 Ibid., pp. 261–2.
43 *The Times*, 26 August 1914.

not be missed. These sort existed, but there were also those who waited to see whether the country's need was genuinely urgent. Recruitment varied according to occupation and social standing. Men employed in the commercial and distributive sectors volunteered more readily than those in agriculture, manufacturing or transport,[44] and the young went more quickly than the old, perhaps understandably given that the latter usually had more binding commitments.[45] Those who had no firm ties to family or employer went first, especially if economic circumstances made volunteering an attractive option. Nevertheless, for all but the lowest paid, enlistment meant financial hardship.[46] It is no coincidence that the high rate of enlistment in August and September corresponded to a temporary but dramatic rise in unemployment. Industries, frightened by economic uncertainty, reacted by cutting jobs; nearly 500,000 men were made redundant by the end of August, and many more were forced onto part-time status. These men would not have had any idea how temporary their jobless state would be. Thus, the very first rush of recruits was dominated by the sort who had always volunteered for the army, namely the young, unskilled, unemployed and desperate.[47] The Local Government Board in Bristol instructed charities in August 1914 not to grant relief to able-bodied men of military age. Some 90 per cent of relief recipients promptly enlisted, causing the local unemployment rate to drop by 1½ per cent. By November Bristol's factories were inundated with new orders and the enlistment rate fell sharply.[48]

Some historians have suggested that the worker's willingness to volunteer can be explained by the fact that his life of drudgery, dirt, low expectations, hard labour, subsistence wages and low life expectancy was not altogether different from life in the army. But, as the worker well knew, civvy street carried little risk of being shot. Familiarity with drudgery might explain why the worker made such a resilient soldier after enlistment, but it cannot explain why he joined. Nevertheless, as with the recruits from the public schools, the worker's willingness to volunteer was based upon an assumption that the war would be neither long nor very deadly. It is difficult to

44 Beckett, 'The Nation in Arms', p. 9.

45 I. Beckett, 'The British Army, 1914–1918: The Illusion of Change', in J. Turner, ed., *Britain and the First World War*, p. 104.

46 P. Dewey, 'Military Recruiting and the British Labour Force During the First World War', *Historical Journal* 27 (1984), p. 206.

47 C. Hughes, 'The New Armies', in Beckett and Simpson, eds, p. 103.

48 Beckett, 'The Nation in Arms', p. 10.

imagine volunteers coming forward so enthusiastically had they been fully aware of the horrors of this interminable war.

The Bristol example mentioned above shows that destitution was an important motivator only during the first two months of recruiting. After that time, orders for munitions and supplies made employment plentiful and there would have been no economic reason for a man to resort to the low pay and dangerous conditions of being a soldier. There is no consistent pattern between rates of pay and willingness to volunteer.[49] Thus, one needs to look for other reasons why, for instance, by January 1915, approximately 10,000 skilled engineers and 160,000 coal miners had enlisted.[50] Jay Winter provides a possible explanation:

> Unemployment did not fill the ranks of Kitchener's Army, popular sentiment did. The protection of 'little Belgium', the defence of the empire, the need to be seen to be doing one's military duty alongside the men of one's district or village: these may sound like outworn clichés today, but in 1914 they had force and substance in the minds of ordinary people.[51]

The statement requires some qualification, but is basically sound. As we have seen, unemployment was important during the early months of war. But after that time, popular sentiment seems to have been the prime inspiration, and age the prime determinant,[52] for joining. Words like duty and honour occur nearly as often in working class diaries and letters as in those from the middle class.[53] This is interesting because, strictly speaking, the workers would have been defending a social system which had not treated them well. Their willingness to serve certainly perplexed the pacifist poet Emily Orr:

> What has your country done for you,
>   Child of a city slum,
> That you should answer her ringing call
> To man the gap and keep the wall
> And hold the field though a thousand fall
>   And help be slow to come?
> . . .
> 'What can your country ask of you,
>   Dregs of the British race?'

49 Dewey, 'Military Recruiting', p. 207.
50 Hughes, 'The New Armies', p. 102
51 Winter, 'The Army and Society', p. 197.
52 See Dewey, 'Military Recruting', pp. 211, 218–19.
53 D. Winter, *Death's Men*, p. 33.

'She gave us little, she taught us less,
And why we were born we could hardly guess
Till we felt the surge of battle press
And looked the foe in the face.'[54]

Given the high level of industrial unrest before the war, one might expect there to have been a widespread reluctance to come to Britain's aid. In fact, the British working class was, and remains, an intensely patriotic group. One profound, but often discounted, element of British working class consciousness is a love for Britain and a willingness to defend her.

The patriotism of the workers was very easily manipulated. Generally speaking, they were a deferent group naive about politics and inclined to accept that Britain was in danger, that her cause was good and that Belgium needed defending. The psychological impact of Kitchener's pointing finger was enormous: the poster beckoned, commanded, threatened, cajoled and shamed all at the same time. The message – YOUR COUNTRY NEEDS YOU – was one which the lowly worker would not have heard often. He was needed.

Along with national pride, a vast reservoir of local solidarity could be tapped. The War Minister Lord Derby is commonly credited with the idea of 'Pals' battalions, units formed in a locality or among workers from a single industry or business. In fact, Derby's function was mainly one of lending prestige; the proposal was first discussed in the War Office twelve days before Derby's formal announcement of the scheme on 24 August, and the very first Pals battalion, the 'Stockbrokers' of the Royal Fusiliers, began recruiting on the 21st.[55] Whatever its origin, the idea was brilliant. It played on the herd instinct, one of the prime reasons for volunteering, and also solved many of the problems of establishing group solidarity which basic training addresses. In other words, men joined because their 'pals' were joining and automatically felt a sense of identity with the battalion. The various units illustrate the variety of sources from which they were recruited: 'Accrington Pals', 'Grimsby Chums', 'Glasgow Corporation Tramways', 'University and Public School Brigade', 'Tyneside Scottish', 'Tyneside Irish', 'Cotton Association', etc. Boys' Brigade or OTC units often formed the nucleus of a Pals battalion, as would athletes or supporters from local football, rugby or cricket sides.

54 Emily Orr, 'Recruit from the Slums', in C. Reilly, ed., *Scars Upon My Heart*, p. 87.

55 P. Simkins, *Kitchener's Army*, p. 83.

Before 1914, those opposed to professionalisation and prepared-ness took refuge in the argument that, in the event of a war, the British capacity for improvisation would carry the country through the crisis. Immediate reactions to the crisis seemed to justify this confidence. The Parliamentary Recruiting Committee redirected political party constituency organisations into recruiting, thus making use of their local knowledge, access to halls, canvassing techniques, talents for public speaking and access to voter lists. The PRC pro-duced an estimated 54 million posters, leaflets and other publications, in addition to organising 12,000 meetings and 20,000 speeches.[56] In July 1915, the PRC joined with the Women's Emergency Corps in distributing among West End shoppers leaflets urging them to carry home their own parcels, thus freeing deliverymen for service at the front.[57] In other ways, individuals did their bit. The Post Office had postmen switch to mufti and donated over 100,000 blue uniforms to the army.[58] The retired principal of a ladies' college offered her services as a nanny free of charge to any widower prevented from volunteering because of the need to look after his motherless children.[59] Recruiting messages were emblazoned on taxis and printed on the back of London tram tickets.

Those who would not willingly jump into the army were pushed, with increasing force as the war progressed. Government, press and Church were not above shaming men into volunteering. One famous recruiting poster showed a humiliated father being asked by his children: 'Daddy, what did you do in the Great War?' Millions of men were forced to consider how they would answer their children. One tends to forget that in this poetic age the most popular poems were not those of Sassoon, Owen or even Brooke, but heavy-handed verses published in the daily newspapers and written to mobilise an ever greater war effort. Harold Begbie, for instance, lent his rather modest rhyming skills to the recruiting effort:

> What will you lack, sonny, what will you lack,
> When the girls line up in the street,
> Shouting their love to the lads come back
> From the foe they crushed to beat?
> Will you send a strangled cheer to the sky
> And grin till your cheeks are red?

56 Reader, pp. 112–13.
57 *The Times*, 7 July 1915.
58 Ibid., 11 February 1915.
59 Ibid., 3 September 1914.

But what will you lack when your mate goes by
With a girl who cuts you dead?[60]

Perhaps the most popular practitioner of this genre was the irrepress-
ible Jessie Pope, whose excruciatingly condescending poem 'The Call'
firmly established her as the high priestess of humiliation:

Who's for the trench –
    Are you, my laddie?
Who'll follow French –
    Will you, my laddie?
Who's fretting to begin,
Who's going out to win?
And who wants to save his skin –
    Do you, my laddie?

Who's for the khaki suit –
    Are you, my laddie?
Who longs to charge and shoot –
    Do you, my laddie?
Who's keen on getting fit,
Who means to show his grit,
And who'd rather wait a bit –
    Would you, my laddie?[61]

The most famous example of coercion through humiliation began in
September 1914, on the encouragement of Penrose Fitzgerald, a
retired admiral, who advised women to distribute white feathers to
men not in uniform. Evidence suggests that the 'white feather ladies'
were more often derided than admired, but as one contemporary
remarked, 'The bellicosity of these females was almost as terrible to
the young man who had no stomach for fighting as an enemy with
banners and guns.'[62] 'Would not the feather-brained Ladies . . . be
better advised to learn to nurse the wounded, and thus become
useful, instead of offending nuisances to the community?', an angry
correspondent to *The Times* wrote.[63]

    While it was theoretically possible for the thick-skinned to carry
on in a world of white feathers and Jessie Popes, other forms of
coercion were impossible to ignore. Lord Derby announced publicly
that 'When the war is over I intend, as far as I possibly can, to

---

60 Reader, p. 116.
61 Jessie Pope, 'The Call', in Reilly, ed., p. 88.
62 Simkins, p. 124.
63 *The Times*, 20 January 1915.

employ nobody except men who have taken their duty at the front.'[64] One soldier recalls journeying to his depot in 1914 with eight servants of a peer who had announced that younger members of his staff 'ought' to volunteer.[65] The Nestlé company publicly announced that it expected all single male employees between 18 and 30 to volunteer. It hoped that the public 'will excuse any unavoidable delay in despatch of goods ordered'.[66] A firm of stockbrokers in London, ironically owned by Quakers, told its staff that 'The firm expects that all unmarried staff under 35 years of age will join Earl Kitchener's army at once, and also urges those who are married and eligible to take the same course.'[67] Volunteering was not, in other words, always a matter of free choice.

Recruiting had a shady side, and a distinctly sleazy one. Early in the war, recruiters were paid a minimum of 2s 6d for each man enlisted. The less scrupulous turned a blind eye toward those volunteers too old or, more often, too young. (The payment was reduced to 1s in October 1914, which meant that recruiters had to work harder, or be less honest, to earn the same reward.[68]) In autumn 1914 medical officers had to inspect up to 200 men per day, a situation which naturally resulted in errors and iniquities. Men were often judged not according to their fitness at the time of examination, but on a prediction of their health after three or four months of healthy army life.[69] Doctors were paid (until May 1915) 2s 6d for each man passed fit, thus inviting abuse. It was also not unknown for recruiters to prey upon the inebriated in public houses. One Fulham recruiter would habitually roam the streets, aided by two chauffeurs and a boy scout, and round up the 'unemployed and idlers'.[70] Perhaps the most notorious case involved a recruiter who persuaded men to enlist, take their King's shilling, and then desert, whereupon he sold their kit and split the profits.[71] In October 1914, Londoner Ernest Adams was sentenced to two months' imprisonment for volunteering and drawing pay from at least six different recruiters.[72]

64 Reader, p. 120.
65 Hughes, 'The New Armies', p. 102.
66 *The Times*, 7 August 1914.
67 Reader, pp. 120–1.
68 Hughes, 'The New Armies', p. 103.
69 J. Winter, *The Great War and the British People*, pp. 50–3.
70 Reader, p. 119.
71 Hughes, 'The New Armies', p. 110.
72 *The Scotsman*, 16 October 1914.

But the darker side of recruiting should not detract from what was, by any calculation, a massively impressive response to the call for volunteers. Between the outbreak of war and December 1915, nearly 2.5 million men joined the army without any legal compulsion. This constituted almost half of the total enlisted during the war. Some 29 per cent of the volunteers joined in August and September 1914. Granted, a good many of these men, especially those who delayed joining, were bullied. But cynicism seems inappropriate; no amount of qualification can explain away what was an extraordinary willingness to serve. If there was a typical volunteer, it was perhaps George Coppard, who in a single paragraph of his memoirs demonstrated the futility of trying to categorise reasons for joining:

> Glossing over my childhood, I merely state that in 1914 I was just an ordinary boy of elementary education and slender prospects. Rumours of war broke out and I began to be interested in the Territorials tramping the streets in their big strong boots. Although I seldom saw a newspaper, I knew about the assassination of the Archduke Ferdinand at Sarajevo. News placards screamed out at every corner, and military bands blared out their martial music in the main streets of Croydon. This was too much for me to resist, and as if drawn by a magnet, I knew I had to enlist straight away.[73]

If one leaves aside the obvious indicators of Coppard's class and background, his testimony could have been echoed by so many of those who volunteered, be they wealthy, poor, educated or common. This innocent, gullible generation still believed in heroes, duty and the glory of war. War was not a disaster but an opportunity, a chance to prove oneself and do one's bit. Britain needed men and they responded.

---

73 George Coppard, *With a Machine Gun to Cambrai*, p. 1.

4   BUSINESS AS USUAL

On Christmas Day 1914, British and German troops met in No Man's Land, played football and exchanged gifts. The Germans gave the British cigarettes which in all likelihood were British-made. This may seem odd: during war belligerents are supposed to cease trading. That was certainly the British government's intention, but the evidence speaks for itself: tobacco exports to Holland increased from 367,680 pounds in 1913 to 3,601,000 pounds in 1915.[1] Since it is impossible to believe that Dutch nicotine addiction increased tenfold in two years, it is safe to assume that the huge haul of cigarettes was mainly smoked by Germans.

It is perhaps inconsequential that harmless items like tobacco penetrated the blockade, but evidence suggests that more essential commodities also did so. And, strictly speaking, since total war means that every citizen becomes a combatant, it follows that every commodity becomes contraband. Unfortunately, the British government was slow to understand the implications of total war, therefore anomalies like trading with the enemy occurred. The fault did not lie with unscrupulous British businessmen, though some corruption existed, but rather with the government's failure to provide coherent economic direction. If it had a strategy it was 'Business as Usual', but it hardly seems appropriate to grace that misbegotten policy with the status of a strategy.

A STRATEGY OF SORTS

On 4 August, David Lloyd George, speaking to businessmen in Blighty, promised that the government would 'enable the traders of this country to carry on business as *usual*'.[2] This statement has been

---

1 J. McDermott, ' "A Needless Sacrifice': British Businessmen and Business as Usual in the First World War', *Albion* 21 (1989), p. 274.

2 D. French, *British Economic and Strategic Planning, 1905–1915*, p. 92. Italics from the original.

interpreted as an attempt to calm widespread fears of unemployment, inflation and trade collapse. It was undoubtedly that, but, according to David French, it was also part of a wider war strategy, toward which Britain drifted in the decade before 1914:

> The Navy was to bring about Germany's defeat by blockading its ports and causing its economy to collapse. Protected by its *Dreadnoughts* the British economy would be able to function almost as usual and so Britain would be able to supply its continental partners with all the munitions they required to conduct the land war.[3]

Business as Usual was an outgrowth of nineteenth-century economic liberalism, the ideology which had made Britain powerful and, it was presumed, had produced a century of peace. Edwardian Britain took shelter in the illusion that the worldwide system of trade could not tolerate a protracted war, an idea encouraged by Norman Angell's *The Great Illusion*.[4] War would bring economic ruin, massive unemployment and widespread starvation; economic dislocation which would limit its duration. It is out of this thinking that Business as Usual arose. As a strategy, it was in truth the best of a bad job. By the Edwardian period the linkage between prosperity, free trade and small armies had begun to unravel, yet Britain still adhered to its attendant military implications. She planned, in the event of war, to do what she did best: British banks would loan money to allies to buy British goods, which would be carried in British merchant ships, protected by the Royal Navy. As Maurice Hankey (later Cabinet Secretary) described, Britain's task would be to

> continue our trade, and so to keep the economic conditions of life in this country tolerable, whilst they are becoming progressively more intolerable to the inhabitants of the enemy's country. By this means not only shall we enable ourselves to outlast the enemy, but we shall be in a position to render to our allies ... assistance of a material nature ... enabling them to sustain the burden of war while the enemy is rapidly consuming his resources.[5]

But, as Hankey understood, in order for Britain to maintain this role, she had to avoid 'tremendous drains on our labour supply' – in other words, she could not tolerate British workers dying on the battlefield.

---

3 Ibid., p. 1. See also idem, *British Strategy and War Aims, 1914–1916*, and idem, 'The Rise and Fall of Business as Usual', in K. Burk, ed., *War and the State*, pp. 7–31.

4 See H. Weinroth, 'Norman Angell and *The Great Illusion*: An Episode in Pre-1914 Pacifism', *Historical Journal* 18 (1974).

5 French, *British Economic and Strategic Planning*, p. 34.

The strategy depended on a number of conditions. The war's impact upon the British economy would have to be minimised so that business could indeed carry on as usual. The blockade (of goods both leaving and entering Germany) would have to be sufficiently tight to cause the enemy economic and social ruin, but without annoying neutral nations, especially the United States. British manufacturers would have to capture German export markets disrupted by the blockade. But, as Hankey realised, such a scenario was possible only if Britain avoided the drain on her work force which a large army implied. Finally, allies would have to be satisfied with an arrangement whereby they suffered enormous casualties while Britain enhanced her economic position by being the bank, the larder, the factory and the arsenal of the Entente.[6] In fact, none of these conditions could be assured, which meant that Britain's plans for the management of the war economy were totally irrelevant to the conflict in which she was engaged.

The inspiration behind the military 'strategy' of Business as Usual was undoubtedly a desire to preserve and strengthen liberal Britain. This meant that in the management of the war economy liberal principles would remain predominant. Free enterprise would be preserved as far as possible and the government would intervene only on an ad hoc basis when it became apparent that the free market was not delivering the goods. No government minister at this stage argued that far-reaching state intervention was intrinsically good.

The government nevertheless anticipated a number of areas in which intervention might be necessary to facilitate Business as Usual: namely, food supply, transport, maritime insurance and the money market. As regards food, a large proportion of essential items like sugar and fats came to Britain from Germany and vast amounts of wheat came from Russia, a supply which would be cut off if the Dardanelles were closed to shipping. Indeed, supplies of virtually all imported foods would be interrupted at least initially, with prices consequently rising. This was indeed what transpired. The war was not 24 hours old when the *Scotsman* reported widespread increases in food prices and panic buying: 'A well-dressed lady was seen to leave a [Glasgow] provision warehouse wheeling a small barrow on which was a bag of flour.'[7] Since a large proportion of Britain's population lived a hand-to-mouth existence, a sudden rise in food

6 Ibid., p. 98.
7 *The Scotsman*, 5 August 1914.

prices was worrying. It was widely feared that a starving population might force the government to make peace.

As regards transport, it was anticipated that disruption would be confined to the first two weeks of the war, when the rail system would be flooded with mobilised troops. Looking further, some officials predicted that naval action in the Channel might render east coast ports too dangerous for merchant traffic. The possibility of shifting all incoming traffic to west coast ports was investigated, but was quickly discovered impracticable, since the ports were ill-equipped to handle the anticipated volume, and the consequent cross-country transport would swamp the rail system. Trains owned by one company would, for instance, be forced to travel on tracks owned by another. Merchant shipping presented a similarly bleak outlook. For Business as Usual to work, seaborne trade could not be impeded by the war. But maritime insurance companies, motivated by profit rather than patriotism, were reluctant to insure ships sailing in a war zone. And crews were justifiably frightened. On 19 August ten sailors of the cargo ship *Trevaylor* were jailed after refusing to sail in the North Sea unless they received compensation for the risks involved.[8] Rates threatened to reach exorbitant levels, making British exports less affordable and imports (like food) more expensive. Again, the answer seemed to lie in the government taking a more active role by guaranteeing all shipping.

Finally, Britain's position at the centre of the international financial market was frighteningly precarious. In 1914, German liabilities to London banks totalled about £1 million per day. If, in the event of war, repayment were to cease, the effect upon the banking and finance systems would be catastrophic, causing an inevitable run on gold. But an even worse situation would result if Britain declared an embargo on gold exports. Free trade in gold was essential to the international system of trade upon which the Business as Usual edifice was built.

All of these problems were recognised before 1914, but, by the eve of war, no coherent plan for how to manage a war economy had emerged. This lack of preparation should not come as a surprise, given the complacency described in earlier chapters. Because the military was ostracised from wider society, a belief developed that the conduct of war could be left to soldiers and sailors with little effect upon civilians. Government's role would be to ease the disturbance to the domestic economy which war would cause rather than

8 Ibid., 19 August 1914.

to mobilise the economy for war. There was surprisingly little accept-ance of the need for civilian and military sectors to work in harmony.

Once war broke out, the government's initial efforts on the home front were designed to make Business as Usual work. Of profound concern was how the working class would react to war. Both Keir Hardie, the Independent Labour Party (ILP) leader, and Ramsay MacDonald, the Labour Party leader, along with some prominent trade unionists, had boasted that organised labour would stop a war in its tracks by calling a general strike. The government, while not underestimating the power of organised labour, nevertheless felt con-fident that redundant workers would act as strikebreakers. But mass unemployment still posed a serious public order problem. Plans for preserving public order in the event of war were in place as early as January 1913. The Metropolitan Police, in cooperation with the War Office, drew up arrangements for protecting public buildings and utilities, food storage depots, abattoirs, flour mills and bakeries from rioters. These plans were implemented with reasonable efficiency even before war was officially declared. Armed guards were mobil-ised on 2 August, the same day that MacDonald appealed to workers with an anti-war speech in the Commons.[9]

Aware of the adage that the revolt of the hungry ends at the baker's shop, the government took immediate steps to insure a steady supply of food. A Cabinet Committee on Food Supplies was estab-lished, chaired by Reginald McKenna. Parliament on 8 August passed the Unreasonable Withholding of Foodstuffs Act, giving the Board of Trade power to seize the stocks of anyone suspected of hoarding food for the purposes of profiteering. From the 12th, McKenna's committee began purchasing large stocks of foodstuffs previously supplied by Germany, most notably sugar, of which £260,000 worth was bought in New York in one week alone. A Royal Commission on Sugar Supplies was soon established to oversee this trade. In addition, under the authority of the Admiralty, all British ships carry-ing food to enemy countries were directed to unload their cargoes in Britain, even if the commodities originated in a neutral country. This naturally annoyed the Americans who suspected that an ulterior motive was to drive down American wheat prices.

Steps were taken to ensure that the transport of food was not disrupted. Control of the railways was assumed by the Railway Executive Committee, but the government, still expecting a short war and still determined to minimise the disruption of the economy,

9 See *Hansard*, 2 August 1914.

limited its jurisdiction to one week only, 'so that for the next four and a half years the ritual of requisition had to be repeated every seven days'.[10] An Admiralty committee provided daily bulletins on the safety of sea routes and the capacity of ports to handle goods. The Huth-Jackson war risk insurance scheme, introduced to Parliament on 3 August, sought to alleviate the concerns of shipowners. Pre-war objections to intervention of this nature melted away. Echoing the spirit of Business as Usual, McKenna defended his committee by declaring that 'our purpose has been not to interfere with ordinary trade at all, but to leave the traders to conduct their own business'.[11] In fact the government was interfering, but always with the aim of creating an illusion of tranquillity amidst the chaos of war. Business as Usual implied an unusual level of government intervention.

Benign governmental interference came also in the form of encouragement to British traders, specifically in markets hitherto dominated by Germans. The aim was not only to cripple Germany during the war and to help finance the British war effort, but to give Britain an automatic lead in postwar trade. The economist and Liberal MP Leo Chiozza Money optimistically predicted that

> The British trader . . . who desires to take a hand in a most interesting and important game may confidently count upon several years' freedom from German competition in which to prosecute fruitful experiment.[12]

Trade fairs were organised at which were displayed German goods earmarked for supplanting by British manufacturers. Walter Runciman, President of the Board of Trade, relaxed patent laws, thus allowing free copying of German goods, including china, jewellery, clocks, glassware, haberdashery and especially toys. The Commercial Intelligence Branch of the Board of Trade reported in August 1914 that German toy exports to the United Kingdom totalled £1,147,400, with another £2,756,500 worth exported elsewhere. During the same year, the communiqué pointedly announced, British toy exports totalled only £629,200.[13] But opportunities which seemed brilliant on paper were difficult to realise. British manufacturers, in order to move into new areas, required huge amounts of investment capital, in addition to concrete assurances from the government that markets would be protected after the war. Since the government remained

10 T. Wilson, *The Myriad Faces of War*, p. 215.

11 *Hansard*, 8 August 1914.

12 L. Chiozza Money, 'British Trade and the War', *Contemporary Review* 106 (October 1914), p. 482.

13 *The Scotsman*, 31 August 1914.

ideologically opposed to intervention, it was seldom able to satisfy manufacturers.

No other problem was more important in the early days of the war than that of establishing stability in the money markets. Even before war had been declared, a financial crisis had begun which threatened to drain the country's reserves and grind trade to a halt. If left unchecked it would make it impossible to finance the war – and to feed the population. On 29 July panicked sales of securities began at stock exchanges in Europe and New York; two days later the London Stock Exchange was forced to close. Joint-stock bankers called in loans, rendering it impossible for accepting houses to finance international trade. True to form, investors began urgently demanding gold, prompting the Bank of England on the 30th to raise the bank rate from 3 to 4 per cent in an attempt to stem the outward flow of reserves. On the following day the rate doubled to 8 per cent. In three days (29–31 July) the Bank lost £6 million, or 16 per cent of its reserves.

On 31 July a Cabinet Committee, chaired by Lloyd George, met to deal with the crisis. Its objective was to create the conditions necessary for Business as Usual, in other words, to restore trade as near as possible to pre-war levels. This explains Lloyd George's speech of 4 August, the first time the government actually used the words 'business as usual' to describe its policy. The Committee quickly introduced a one-month moratorium on all debts and extended the August bank holiday for three days. The Chancellor resisted the temptation to suspend specie payment, but paper money in denominations of £1 and 10s, designed to relieve the pressure on gold, was issued. The notes carried a promise that they could be redeemed in gold, a promise which the Bank hoped it would not be called upon to keep.

By 7 August some confidence had returned, but banks were still not prepared to lend sufficient money to industry to restore trade. Later in the month, Lloyd George threatened sanctions unless the banks took a more liberal line. But bankers knew that this was mere bluster; the government's power to regulate was minimal. It instead opted to guarantee bankers against losses, through the Bank of England. This policy, along with the extension of the moratorium to 4 November, combined to revive trade to a satisfactory level. In the process the government learned a compelling lesson: war had not changed the basic axiom that finance was amoral and unsentimental; patriotism was irrelevant in the quest for profits. Business would not therefore carry on as usual unless the government made it worthwhile for businessmen. When one compares the government's actions in this area with its preparations to use force to meet the threat of bread riots, one sees the first hint of what became a consistent pattern: business cooperation would be won with a carrot, that of the workers with a stick.

Unbeknownst to the government, a much more serious threat to Business as Usual than that posed by the financial crisis came with the appointment of Lord Kitchener as Secretary of State for War on 5 August. The appointment seemed to make perfect sense. Since the Curragh Crisis in March (when J. E. B. Seely was forced to resign) the government had essentially been without a War Minister, Asquith having assumed that portfolio in addition to his own. It seemed a brilliant coup for a party burdened by pacific tendencies to draft in Britain's most highly respected soldier. The appointment was immensely popular, helping to unite the country behind the war while convincing doubters in and out of Parliament of the Liberal government's determination. 'We need hardly say with what profound satisfaction and relief we hear of Lord Kitchener's appointment', commented *The Times*.[14] But Asquith, perhaps sensing the difficulties ahead, referred to the appointment as a 'hazardous experiment'.[15] Kitchener, it should be noted, was reluctant to take up the post.[16]

If Kitchener had ever read *The Great Illusion*, he was certainly not impressed by its warnings about the economic disaster of modern war. He had waged a successful campaign in the Sudan on a tight budget and was confident that he could do the same in Europe. Surveying the size of the continental armies and the issues at stake, he immediately forecast a war lasting at least three years. But, Kitchener's confidence aside, it was impossible for business to carry on as usual during a war of such duration. (The government's plans for the management of the war economy presumed a war of no more than nine months.) An even more damaging blow came when Kitchener, on his second day in government, told Cabinet colleagues: 'We must be prepared to put armies of millions in the field, and to maintain them for several years.'[17] He called for 500,000 men, a demand he shortly doubled and then doubled again. Conducting normal business would be impossible if two million workers were

14 *The Times*, 6 August 1914.
15 R. Jenkins, *Asquith*, p. 342.
16 T. Royle, *The Kitchener Enigma*, p. 254.
17 P. Magnus, *Kitchener: Portrait of an Imperialist*, p. 339.

withdrawn from the labour supply, nor could the export market withstand the diversion of resources which equipping such an army implied. Thus, Kitchener's appointment rendered Business as Usual dead on arrival, though a long time would pass before the government accepted its demise.

One might question why the government tolerated this immediate and drastic contradiction of its plans. The answer is simple: having created a Messiah, they were forced to follow where he led. He was, Runciman regretted, 'the unattackable K'.[18] As Sir Edward Grey confessed, Kitchener's prediction

> seemed to most of us unlikely, if not incredible. . . . I believed the war would be over before a million new men could be trained and equipped, but that, if this expectation were wrong, the million men should of course be sent abroad to take part in the war. It was, therefore, clear that we should all agree to what Kitchener wanted.[19]

To be fair to Kitchener, he did not intend that his policy should entirely supplant Business as Usual. That policy could exist as part of the allied wearing out process which would occur while Kitchener raised his armies. 'Our Army should reach its full strength at the beginning of the third year of the War, just when France is getting into rather low water and Germany is beginning to feel the pinch.'[20] In other words, Britain would benefit from the exhaustion of both enemy and ally. She would put her force into the field at a time when it could dominate affairs and thus render Britain the prime shaper of the peace. In the meantime, Kitchener reminded Sir John French, the Commander in Chief of the BEF:

> The numerical strength of the British Force, and its contingent reinforcement, is strictly limited, and with this consideration kept steadily in view, it will be obvious that the greatest care must be exercised towards a minimum of losses and wastage.[21]

Unfortunately, events in France and Belgium did not conform to Kitchener's patient plans. On the one hand, France expected and was to an extent dependent upon immediate British military aid. On the other, British generals, instinctive attackers, were certain that bold offensives would bring quick victory.

18 C. Hazlehurst, 'Asquith as Prime Minister, 1908–1916', *English Historical Review* 85 (1970), p. 528.

19 E. Grey, *Twenty-Five Years, 1893–1916*, Vol. 2, pp. 68–9.

20 D. French, 'The Meaning of Attrition', *English Historical Review* 103 (1988), p. 388.

21 Magnus, p. 349.

Just as Business as Usual hardly deserves to be called a strategy, so too Kitchener's policy which undermined it. He shot from the hip, reacting impulsively to a seemingly catastrophic situation, without considering the consequences of his actions. Rejecting the procedures for expansion set out in Haldane's army reforms, he instead 'with a wave of his baton . . . started to conjure new "Kitchener Armies" out of the ground, formed in his image'.[22] 'The result was the confusion which arises from a sudden departure from settled principles', Haldane remarked bitterly.[23] The army had barracks sufficient for only 175,000 men. Munitions factories were equipped to supply a force of 100,000, not one five or ten times that size. Hankey reflected:

> the government had no national plan for an expansion of the Army. . . . None of the problems had been worked out or thought of at all . . . there was no basis for programme making or for estimating future requirements and supplies, no warning was given to the armaments firms of what would be expected of them.[24]

Kitchener's policy was as divorced from economic realities as Business as Usual was from military ones. He failed to consider how such a vast army was to be housed, fed, clothed and armed, especially if those who would ordinarily supply the army were downing tools to become soldiers. Among the volunteers who joined prior to January 1915 were 10,000 skilled engineers, 145,000 building trades workers and 160,000 miners – their skills would be wasted in the trenches.[25] Some men were sent back, but the army could not easily reject willing and able-bodied volunteers; it did not want to give the impression that its needs were not as urgent as Kitchener claimed. The only way to regulate the flow of men and to minimise the damage to essential industries would have been to introduce conscription. Although the country might have accepted compulsion at this stage, the Liberal government would not. In any case, the early flood of recruits seemed proof enough that conscription was not remotely necessary.

Thus, just when export trade was recovering and factories were returning to full production, Kitchener began to undermine economic stability by making huge demands upon the labour force. Under Business as Usual any topping up which the army required would

22 Ibid., p. 348.
23 R. B. Haldane, *Autobiography*, pp. 278–80.
24 French, *British Economic and Strategic Planning*, pp. 127–8.
25 C. Hughes, 'The New Armies', in I. Beckett and K. Simpson eds, *A Nation in Arms*, p. 102.

have come from the derelicts and dossers upon whom it customarily depended. Instead Kitchener's New Army took the cream of the work force. As has been suggested, Kitchener's plans could not co-exist with Business as Usual. Unfortunately, until at least May 1915 these two approaches were forced to work in tandem. The result was anarchy.

THE PEOPLE RESPOND

The pace of activity provided an illusion of security, thus militating against a more ordered response to the war. The same spirit of voluntarism which brought millions of men to recruiting centres was apparent throughout society. A dentist, Austrian by birth, but a naturalised British subject, offered to extract teeth free of charge from any man who volunteered. A man whose poor eyesight prevented his volunteering advertised for someone (preferably, for propriety's sake, a gentleman) to teach him to knit.[26] An injured airman who needed skin grafts advertised in *The Times* for donors. He received over 50 responses the next day.[27] During November 1914, schoolchildren in Grangemouth were encouraged to bring a potato to school every day. Two tons of potatoes were collected for Belgian refugees.[28] During 'Million Egg Week' in August 1915, 1,036,380 eggs were collected from private citizens for soldiers at the front.[29] A charitable group hoping to establish a hospital in France advertised for the loan of a milk cow. Not only were a number of cows donated, but middle class ladies volunteered to be milkmaids, dairy appliance firms donated equipment, and a moneylender offered to loan (at a reduced rate) sufficient funds to purchase a cow, if a donation was not secured.[30]

Among the comfortable middle class, a proliferation of charitable organisations sought to relieve distress, be it among Belgian refugees, or the destitute families of British servicemen. The government itself received, unsolicited, £25 million during the first ten months of the war, an impressive sum given that during the same period income tax doubled and other taxes ate into disposable income.[31] Every

26 *The Times*, 4, 7 September 1914.
27 Ibid., 29 April 1915.
28 *The Scotsman*, 30 November 1914.
29 Ibid., 3 September 1915.
30 *The Times*, 23 June 1915.
31 B. Waites, *A Class Society at War*, p. 158.

day the papers were full of appeals to worthy causes, some rather imaginatively presented:

> Dogs and cats of the Empire! The Kaiser said: 'Germany will fight to the last dog and cat.' Will British dogs and cats give 6d each to provide a YMCA Soldiers Hut in France?[32]

> Flashlight, a New Forest pony, appeals to all four-footed friends for donations towards an ambulance for wounded horses. She will gratefully acknowledge all money sent to her.[33]

So profound was the charitable spirit (or at least the enthusiasm for collecting donations), that in March 1916 established charities demanded a system of licensing. Cases of fraud were not unknown, and so prolific were volunteers collecting donations on the streets that the public began to complain of the nuisance.[34]

Workers who did not volunteer still exhibited an impressive willingness to serve the cause. The war was hardly a few days old when, at a number of factories, the labour force agreed to suspend restrictive practices. Strikes, frighteningly frequent before the war, became a rarity. Even on Clydeside and Tyneside, traditionally militant areas, an ambiguous but still significant industrial truce was declared. Industrial harmony was confirmed with settlements between workers and government, like the Shells and Fuses Agreement and the Treasury Agreement.[35] Granted, these harmonious covenants did not all stand the test of time. But the patriotic desire of workers to help their country is impressive.

Although the unions surrendered a great deal, they did so willingly. Theoretically, at least, the government was not the dominant party in the negotiations. If ever a time existed when the unions had enormous potential power, it was surely in March 1915, when labour was scarce and the BEF was hungering for ammunition. But, significantly, the workers (or at least their representatives) never contemplated extracting profit from the nation's predicament. Responsible patriots that they were, they agreed to help their country, confident that their sacrifices would be rewarded at war's end. As will be seen, some shop floor workers judged the Treasury Agreement a sham. But most shared their leaders' sense of trust and optimism. The agreement was an outward manifestation of an inward truth: namely

---

32 *The Times*, 29 January 1915.
33 Ibid., 6 February 1915.
34 See ibid., 13 February, 25 March 1915.
35 These are discussed in more detail in Chapter 6, pages 111–14.

that patriotism among workers was always stronger than class solidarity or socialist commitment.

An equally impressive reaction to the demands of war came from women in the suffrage movement, who had previously made nuisances of themselves with marches, arson and vandalism. The militant Women's Social and Political Union, led by Mrs Emmeline Pankhurst and her daughter Christabel, made an immediate pledge to the war effort, demanding that the government make proper use of women. Mrs Millicent Fawcett's more moderate National Union of Women's Suffrage Societies was equally eager to contribute. She had opposed the war up to its outbreak, but on 7 August wrote in the suffrage paper *Common Cause* of her satisfaction that 'our large organization, which has been completely built up during past years to promote women's suffrage, can be used now to help our country through this period of strain and sorrow'.[36] A week later she urged followers: 'LET US SHOW OURSELVES TO BE WORTHY OF CITIZENSHIP WHETHER OUR CLAIM TO IT BE RECOGNIZED OR NOT.'[37] As this suggests, the feminist reaction was not merely patriotic; it was also opportunistic – war seemed to offer access to hitherto male preserves, which would in turn hasten emancipation. But not all feminists were keen to serve, nor were all those who came forward motivated by a quest for liberation. Emmeline's other daughter, Sylvia, rejected the position of her mother and sister, maintaining a strident opposition to the war through the socialist Women's Suffrage Federation. Equally significant, half of the NUWSS committee resigned in protest against Fawcett's decision to commit her organisation to the cause.[38] But for the vast majority of women, as for male workers, the overwhelming reaction to war was a patriotic desire to serve.

For some women, the war offered the possibility of being able to imitate men, an understandable desire given the barriers to achievement in patriarchal society. Mairi Chisholm and Elsie Knocker, experienced motorcycle riders and mechanics, somehow manoeuvred their way to the front around obstacles of male prejudice. Flora Sandes actually fought with the Serbian Army. But, while interesting anomalies, these women were not the sort respectable society admired; there was no widespread yearning to redefine standards of femininity. Therefore, despite the demands of the suffrage

36 *Common Cause*, 7 August 1914.
37 Ibid., 14 August 1914.
38 See A. Wiltsher, *Most Dangerous Women*, pp. 63–81.

campaigners, the war did not bring immediate opportunities for women to 'discover' themselves through useful employment. It was not that the government failed to recognise the potential of women to contribute, but rather that it did not anticipate labour shortages. The war was, after all, supposed to make male workers redundant, not provide opportunities for females. Business as Usual was gender-specific: men and women would contribute to the war effort within their established spheres. Even women with undeniably valuable skills were often rejected by a patriarchal establishment. When the pioneering Scottish doctor Elsie Inglis offered her services to the War Office (she wanted to form her own ambulance unit), the authorities reacted: 'My good lady, go home and sit still.'[39]

Women were instead supposed to continue doing womanly things, and thus minimise war's disruption. They were considered valuable to the war effort, but in ways strictly confined to their own sphere. They could knit socks, send parcels to soldiers at the front, and generally keep the home fires burning. The ubiquitous Jessie Pope offered advice to mothers about what to send a boy at the front:

> Some candles and a bar of soap,
>   Cakes, peppermints and matches,
> A pot of jam, some thread (like rope)
>   For sticking khaki patches.
> These gifts, our soldier writes to say,
>   Have brought him untold riches
> To celebrate his natal day
>   In hard-won Flanders' ditches.[40]

The newspapers were full of patriotic advertisements encouraging women to send products to loved ones at the fronts. Horlicks Malted Milk Tablets were 'invaluable to a soldier in the field and most efficient in relieving hunger and thirst and preventing fatigue'.[41] Knitting, advised Pope, was not only productive, it diverted attention from the trials endured by a husband, son, brother or boyfriend:

> Shining pins that dart and click
>   In the fireside's sheltered peace
> Check the thoughts that cluster thick –
>   20 *plain and then decrease.*

39 F. Balfour, *Elsie Inglis*, p. 144.
40 J. Pope, 'The Nut's Birthday', in C. Reilly, ed., *Scars Upon My Heart*, pp. 88–9.
41 *The Times*, 18 November 1914.

> . . .
> Wonder if he's fighting now,
>> What he's done an' where he's been;
> He'll come out on top, somehow –
>> *Slip 1, knit 2, purl 14.*[42]

A 'needlework mania' gripped the country. One correspondent to *The Times* complained that his wife and daughter, whose abilities as seamstresses were limited, had turned his parlour into 'a sort of factory'. 'My heart goes out to poor suffering Tommy Atkins if he is to be condemned to endure these miserably cut, uncomfortable and irritating garments.'[43]

The most useful service women could perform was to encourage men to volunteer. Baroness Orczy, author of *The Scarlet Pimpernel*, encouraged membership in the Women of England's Active Service League, 'whose sole object will be that of influencing men to offer themselves at once to the nearest recruiting officer'.[44] White feather ladies were merely the most blatant of a common type. 'We women . . . recognize that, as women, we have no use for the man who will not fight for his King and his country', wrote one woman to *The Times*.[45] 'He is not fit to be the father of our children.' An advertisement addressed to 'the Women of London' reminded fainthearted females of their patriotic duty:

> Is your 'Best Boy' wearing Khaki? If not don't YOU THINK he should be?
> If he does not think that you and your country are worth fighting for – do you think he is worthy of you?
> Don't pity the girl who is alone – her young man is probably a soldier fighting for her and her country – and for YOU.
> If your young man neglects his duty to his King and Country, the time may come when he will NEGLECT YOU.
> Think it over and then ask him to
> JOIN THE ARMY – TODAY[46]

One mother, whose great misfortune it was to have no sons of military age, offered her two year old son as a mascot to any regiment which would have him.[47] The famous recruiting poster which showed

42 J. Pope, 'Socks', in C. Reilly, ed., pp. 89–90.
43 *The Times*, 28 August 1914.
44 C. Haste, *Keep the Home Fires Burning*, p. 57.
45 *The Times*, 16 January 1915.
46 Haste, pp. 56–7.
47 *The Times*, 16 January 1915.

women at a window watching their men march away under the caption 'Women of Britain Say – GO!' was clearly designed as much to influence women as men. The poster was the perfect symbolic representation of how separate spheres and Business as Usual combined to constrain women.

But many women were uncomfortable with their restricted roles. War, they regretted, brought the most profound separation of the sexes. One woman told a recruiter: 'Take myself, an able-bodied woman, aged 27, sound in health, and fond of a scrap. You have only to say the word.'[48] The poet Nora Bomford rued the accident of her birth which rendered her

> So dreadfully safe! O, damn the shibboleth
> Of sex! God knows we've equal personality.
> Why should men face the dark while women stay
> To live and laugh and meet the sun each day?[49]

A large number of women, Vera Brittain notable among them, salved their frustration by becoming nurses, predominantly in the Volunteer Aid Detachment. Their contribution was undoubtedly significant but it still reinforced the traditional female role of carers. And strict rules determined where women were allowed to do their nursing. Most were not allowed anywhere near the fighting front.

Mere eagerness to serve was not enough to move a government and an industrial sector reluctant to employ women in war-related work. The Board of Trade in March 1915 did institute a Special War Register, designed to take note of women willing to serve, but two months later fewer than 1,816 of the nearly 78,946 registered had been given work.[50] In the first year of the war, total female employment increased by just 400,000, while male employment increased by 1,000,000. Vacancies in civilian employment caused by men volunteering were filled to the largest extent by other men. Cognisant of this fact, Pankhurst and Fawcett organised a massive demonstration on 17 July 1915, with banners like 'We Demand the Right to Work', 'Shells Made by a Wife May Save a Husband's Life' and 'Women's Scissors Will Cut The Red Tape'.[51] But by then they were pushing at an open door, since the scandal over the supply of

---

48 Ibid.
49 N. Bomford, 'Drafts' in Reilly, ed., p. 12.
50 D. Lloyd George, *War Memoirs*, I, p. 174
51 *The Times*, 8 July 1915.

shells had finally exposed the need for labour – and the farce of Business as Usual.

A NATION DIVIDED

The patriotic commitment of the people was not enough on its own to ensure effective prosecution of the war. One hidden problem of Business as Usual was that it militated against emotional mobilisation; it encouraged the attitude that the war would not affect the home front. Thus, as the example of women demonstrates, the enormous surge of popular patriotism in Blighty which followed the outbreak of war could not be fully exploited. But, even more serious, a dangerous gulf developed between home front and fighting front, growing wider and deeper as the war progressed. Amidst a great fluster of activity there survived the traditional British attitude that war should be fought by soldiers who could be left alone while the rest of the population got on with life. R. H. Tawney complained in *The Nation* about the 'dividing chasm' which separated those at home, with their 'reticence as to the obvious physical facts of the war', from those doing the fighting – 'the people with whom I'm really at home, the England that's not an island or an Empire, but a wet populous dyke stretching from Flanders to the Somme'.[52] That chasm was partially unavoidable given that civilians, aside from the occasional bombing raid or shore bombardment, were unaffected by the fighting. But it was widened by the popular pretence that the war was a calamity confined to the continent.

Nowhere was Tawney's dividing chasm wider than between men and women. Bomford blamed this gulf on the shibboleth of sex, but it was undoubtedly encouraged by the active perpetuation of gender stereotypes. Wartime rendered it even easier for men to act strong, virile and heroic and for women to conform to sensitive, caring and motherly images. The novelist Storm Jameson was one of few to recognise the futility of those like Pankhurst and Fawcett who wanted to use the war to bridge the gap between the sexes:

> Why do not women know that in any war, the enemy is not on the other side? Their enemy is war itself – which robs them of their identity: and they cease to be clever, competent, intelligent, beautiful, in their own right and become the nurses, the pretty joys and at last the mourners of their men.[53]

52 *The Nation*, 21 October 1916.
53 M. S. Jameson, *No Time Like the Present*, p. 211.

Cultural stereotypes provided a convenient shelter in which to hide from the realities of war. The truth was at times unpalatable; witness, for instance, Vera Brittain's horror when her beloved Roland Leighton showed her his 'vicious-looking steel dagger' useful (for cutting throats) in trench raids. While she admired Leighton's chivalric qualities, she confessed that 'the sight of the dagger in the hand of one of the most civilized people of these ironically-named civilized times depressed me to morbidness'.[54] The problem with stereotypes is that they hinder understanding of another's predicament, as was evident in the vitriol penned by the war poets:

> You smug-faced crowds with kindling eye
> Who cheer when soldier lads march by,
> Sneak home and pray you'll never know
> The hell where youth and laughter go.[55]

To the government, the gulf was not a problem, but an asset to be encouraged and perpetuated. The nation, it was thought, fought best in ignorance.[56]

There was also a gulf between those for whom war meant loss and those for whom it meant profit. Returns submitted in 1916 showed that in the coal, shipbuilding, iron and engineering industries, average profits rose by 32 per cent over the pre-war level. The shipbuilding firm Cammel Laird saw its profits increase 74 per cent. Farmers, benefiting from the scarcity of imported food, also made vast profits. According to E. M. H. Lloyd, opportunities for lucrative speculation were plentiful:

> Any one who could offer supplies could name his own price; and in order to get a contract, it was not always necessary even to possess the goods. An option was sufficient. The banks were quite willing to advance money on a War Office contract and thus enable the contractor to buy what he had already sold.[57]

A complete novice in the yarn trade made £150,000 in six months, with hardly any capital outlay. As Lloyd George essentially admitted in January 1915, the government turned a blind eye to profiteering as long as supplies remained dependable:

54 V. Brittain, *Chronicle of Youth: War Diary 1913–1917*, p. 244.
55 S. Sassoon, 'Suicide in the Trenches', in *Collected Poems*, p. 78. Sassoon's greatest scorn was reserved for women: see 'Glory of Women', in J. Silkin, ed., *The Penguin Book of First World War Poetry*, p. 132.
56 See Chapter 9.
57 E. M. H. Lloyd, *Experiments in State Control*, pp. 26, 32.

The first interest of the taxpayer is that the supplies should be secured. With this object it may be to the public advantage to conclude contracts in the negotiations of which the prime necessity of securing expeditious and satisfactory delivery has been regarded as of more urgent importance than the actual terms of the bargain.[58]

Profiteering was one thing, trading with the enemy another. The freedom accorded the commercial sector and the lure of profits at times encouraged exporters to ignore issues of belligerency. Businessmen do not appear to have been overly bothered by the moral implications of this type of trade. The problem resulted in part from contradictions within Business as Usual. British exports to Germany, massive before the war, could not continue as usual if German ports were blockaded by British ships. In the true spirit of Business as Usual, some exporters argued that they should not be denied access to German markets if the commodities in question were not for military use. *The Economist* even maintained that one-way trade with Germany provided an excellent way to bleed the German economy of foreign exchange.

The government failed to provide a lead. Producers were confronted with mountains of red tape and layer after layer of confusing bureaucracy but no workable guidelines for the new system of restricted trade. 'It is a curious comment on our old Free Trade system', commented *The Times*, 'that when we come to the necessity of restrictions in trade we seem only able to improvise in this blundering manner.'[59] Under the terms of the Trading with the Enemy Act of September 1914, it was, for instance, left to the exporter to determine whether goods shipped to a neutral country were destined for a belligerent one, a task exporters were ill-equipped to handle. Given the very high profits in trade of this kind, it is not surprising that some businessmen occasionally failed to exercise appropriate vigilance. Montagu complained that trade with Germany, which was occurring 'on a very large scale', was 'done not so much by men who know that they are trading with the enemy but by men who take no trouble to make sure that they are not'.[60] In the amoral climate of Business as Usual, British exporters usually blamed the government for providing the opportunities for them to become obscenely rich.

Under the terms of the Treasury Agreement, profits of firms

---

58 French, *British Economic and Strategic Planning*, p. 134.
59 *The Times*, 12 August 1915.
60 McDermott, ' "A Needless Sacrifice" ', p. 277.

engaged in war work were limited. But it did not take a particularly clever accountant to find ways to sidestep the duties. Generous allowances were made for depreciation, increased output and capital expenditure. Industrialists sank profits into buying up defunct businesses or plant rather than surrender it to the government. Thus, the attempt to limit profits of war industries had no significant effect before mid-1917, when a government commission admitted that

> We have committed a serious mistake in making excess profits duty the cornerstone of our war taxation. This tax does not take the money out of the rich man's pocket in the same way that direct tax on his income would have done, and it has consequently failed in its moral effect on the working classes as a symbol of sacrifice.[61]

And, since legislation applied only to war industries, there was no attempt to limit profits on basic commodities like food or coal which workers had to buy. This exacerbated the workers' sense of outrage. The General Federation of Trade Unions found in February 1915 that the price of grains had increased by between 34 and 72 per cent. The poorer classes were forced to buy lower grades of meat. The expense and scarcity of fish meant that virtually rotten samples were still sold on stalls and the Bishop of London publicly announced a policy of leniency regarding the Friday fast.[62] Household coal prices rose on average by 20 per cent.

Little was done about the problems of excess profits and trading with the enemy because they did not seem adversely to affect the conduct of war. But the government failed to appreciate how these issues affected a population which had developed a keen sense of moral rectitude. The word 'profiteer' attained common usage among workers as early as the spring of 1915. They could not fail to notice that their patriotic sacrifices were not being matched by industrial and commercial magnates who put profits first. They naturally wondered why a moratorium on profits, to match that upon strikes, could not be effected.

STRATEGY IN DISARRAY

Kitchener's desire for a mass citizen army depleted strategically important industries of valuable manpower. Skilled workers in essential industries were often shamed into volunteering by a public ignor-

---

61 Waites, p. 69.
62 *The Times*, 6 February 1915.

ant of the contribution they were already making. Kitchener recognised this problem and offered a partial solution by granting war service badges to essential workers, thus allowing them to demonstrate their importance to the war effort. He would have liked to have banned all skilled men from volunteering, but this idea was vetoed because it contradicted the spirit of voluntarism and interfered with labour agreements.[63]

Shortages of essential commodities and raw materials were evident in Blighty virtually from the first month of the war. By December 1914, employment in mining was down by a net 11 per cent, but since those who had entered the industry since August 1914 were less productive than those who had left it to join the army, the problem was worse than the figures suggested.[64] The Treasury Agreement was supposed to alleviate the labour shortage by making it easier to introduce unskilled and semi-skilled workers into industry. But by early 1915, voluntary labour agreements were proving insufficient; a more dynamic programme of government direction was essential.

Harbingers of the labour shortage were apparent early in the war. But since this government was not noted for its perspicacity, only a fully fledged emergency would motivate it to act. That emergency came when troops at the front began to run low on ammunition. The fault lay not with British industry but with government. The Boer War had revealed how Britain's armament industry was incapable of responding to the demands of a protracted war. Yet the government had responded not by expanding the industry but by cutting back in the interests of economy. In 1907, the Murray Committee decided to scale down the national ordnance factories. It was left to private armouries to respond to fluctuations in demand, a burden they could not possibly handle. When war came, armaments firms were suddenly expected to produce 176 million rounds by the end of August 1914, when their capacity was just three million rounds. From 25 August to 1 October the War Office ordered as many artillery pieces as it had in the previous ten years.[65]

The problems were exacerbated by the unexpected nature of this war. Most military experts had anticipated a war of movement using small calibre mobile guns firing shrapnel shells. Heavy artillery was

63 Royle, p. 284.
64 Wilson, p. 151.
65 C. Trebilcock, 'War and the Failure of Industrial Mobilisation: 1899 and 1914', in J. M. Winter, ed., *War and Economic Development*, pp. 152–61.

not expected to play a dominant role; big guns do not move quickly. But when stalemate descended upon the Western Front, and trenches were dug from Switzerland to the Channel, heavy artillery came into its own. Only high calibre, high explosive shells were even remotely effective against a heavily entrenched enemy. Not only did the army have very limited stocks of these shells (and the guns to fire them), munitions factories at home were ill-equipped to handle the demand for a massive expansion of output. The manufacture of high explosive shells is an extremely dangerous, highly skilled enterprise which could not be entrusted to makeshift factories nor to inexperienced workers.

On 11 February 1915, William Robertson, French's Chief of Staff, warned Haig, the First Army commander, against the prodigious use of shells. The shortage affected tactical planning for the battle of Neuve Chapelle, launched on 10 March, ironically to good effect.[66] After the battle, the artillery was limited to 7 rounds per gun per day, when the optimum figure was at least 30. Haig characteristically blamed the workers' fondness for holidays and drink:

> The best thing, in my opinion, is to punish some of the chief offenders.... Take and shoot two or three of them, and the 'Drink habit' would cease I feel sure. These sub-people don't care what the King or anyone else does – they mean to have their drink.[67]

This was one of the few times during the war when Haig agreed with Lloyd George. 'We are fighting Germans, Austrians and Drink, and so far as I can see the greatest of these deadly foes is Drink', the Chancellor claimed on 29 March.[68] Asquith felt that 'on the question of drink', Lloyd George had 'completely lost his head'.[69] Lloyd George admitted, in a candid moment, that 'The idea that slackness and drink, which some people talk so much about, are the chief causes of delays, is mostly a fudge.'[70] He backed away from state purchase and instead adopted piecemeal measures, which did reduce consumption.[71] There is no doubt that drink was a problem, but the shortage of shells had a great deal more to do with manpower management than with alcohol consumption.

The munitions problem revealed a wayward government at its

---

66 See G. DeGroot, *Douglas Haig, 1861–1928*, pp. 179–83.
67 Haig to Leo Rothschild, 17 April 1915: see DeGroot, *Haig*, p. 184.
68 Wilson, p. 163
69 Jenkins, p. 338.
70 Wilson, p. 163.
71 See Chapter 11, pages 237–9.

worst. On 20 April, Asquith, on information supplied by Kitchener, made the bizarre claim that there was no shortage. Kitchener's subterfuge (if that is what it was: genuine ignorance of the problem seems unthinkable) is understandable given that he bore responsibility for munitions production. Six months into the war, he had become a liability. His recruiting policy had left industry incapable of answering the demands of the massive army he had created. He often admitted that he knew nothing about civilian labour problems, yet he still insisted on War Office control over munitions supply. The Shells Committee met between 12 October 1914 and 1 January 1915, its purpose to provide advice on the munitions problem. It eventually folded because Kitchener was too busy to attend meetings.[72]

Perhaps the burden he shouldered was far too big for any man, in that it combined strategy, manpower and supply in a war larger than any ever encountered. But, if that was the problem, he deserves censure for failing to delegate authority. He ran the War Office like he ran his earlier military campaigns: as an authoritarian surrounded by young sycophants whose primary purpose was to resist interference from outside. A government report later commented:

> There can ... be no doubt that the principle of centralization was pushed to an extreme point by Lord Kitchener. It proved eminently successful during the minor operations in the Soudan which he conducted with conspicuous skill. But it was unsuitable to ... operations on so large a scale as those in which the country has recently been engaged. The result was to throw on the hands of one man an amount of work with which no individual, however capable, could hope to cope successfully.[73]

Kitchener privately confessed that he found it repugnant to discuss military secrets with Cabinet or ministerial colleagues whom he barely knew.[74] He therefore expected blind obedience to his plans, and usually received it. 'The Members of the Cabinet were frankly intimidated by his presence because of his repute and his enormous influence amongst all classes of the people outside', wrote Lloyd George. 'A word from him was decisive, and no one dared to challenge it at a Cabinet meeting.'[75] Kitchener explained his reticence by claiming that all his colleagues repeated military secrets to their

72 Magnus, p. 396.
73 Ibid., p. 378.
74 Ibid., p. 340.
75 Lloyd George, I, p. 298.

wives, with the exception of Asquith, who told them to other people's wives.[76] 'If they will only divorce their wives I will tell them everything!'[77]

By the spring of 1915, the government was in serious disarray. 'Is there any sign', Lord Milner asked Austen Chamberlain in mid-May, 'that the Government have a clear idea what they want to be at, or *by what definite procedure* they hope to achieve victory or even to avert disastrous defeat?'[78] The answer was no. The Dardanelles operation, Churchill's brainchild and the first of many attempts to find an easy way to victory, had settled into embarrassing stalemate. The resultant rows in Cabinet between Churchill and Fisher were rivalled only by those between Lloyd George and Kitchener over munitions. On 14 May, that problem reached a crescendo. *The Times*, acting on information which French supplied to the military correspondent Charles a'Court Repington, wrote of the Festubert operation that 'The need of an unlimited supply of high explosive was a fatal bar to our success. . . . It is certain that we can smash the German crust if we have the means. So the means we must have and as quickly as possible'.[79] On the following day Fisher resigned.[80] Asquith, uncertain that his government would be able to survive increasingly bitter attacks by the opposition and Fleet Street, sensibly chose to form an all-party coalition. There were posts for Tories and, significantly, a few for Labour. But the most significant change was the transfer of munitions production from Kitchener to Lloyd George, now at the head of a new Ministry of Munitions.

The formation of the coalition was undoubtedly significant, but it was not a revolutionary departure from practice. The government's action was in keeping with its response to every previous crisis in this war: the Ministry of Munitions was yet another ad hoc solution devised at the eleventh hour. True, Lloyd George was a dynamic interventionist. But the change was one of personnel not ideology. The government still contained many powerful Liberals who would fight, ditch by ditch, any restrictions upon the freedom of the individual and any expansion of state control. And joining the government were Conservatives by nature suspicious of state intervention,

76 Magnus, p. 345.

77 M. Hankey, *The Supreme Command, 1914–1918*, I, p. 221.

78 D. Dutton, *Austen Chamberlain, Gentleman in Politics*, p. 117.

79 *Times*, 14 May 1915.

80 The issues behind the formation of the first coalition are ably analysed by P. Fraser in 'British War Policy and the Crisis of Liberalism in May 1915', *Journal of Modern History* 54 (1982).

if directed toward the business community. There would be no 'Economic General Staff' equipped to mobilise the entire nation for war and to coordinate the needs of home and fighting fronts.

The War Office, if somewhat attenuated, was still headed by Kitchener, whose immense popularity rendered him unassailable. Angry crowds had burned copies of the *Daily Mail* after the paper blamed him for the shell shortage. And the government was still led by Asquith, who paid the war less than wholehearted attention. 'Mr. Asquith, do you take an interest in the war?', Lady Tree asked the Prime Minister during one of their frequent jolly jaunts into the countryside. Asquith, according to his biographer Roy Jenkins, was 'too eclectic to fill his mind with any single subject and too fastidious to pretend to an enthusiasm which he did not feel'.[81] As long as he remained in power, the government would follow a doctrine of muddle and find virtue in equivocation. 'The real criticism upon the Administration', Walter Long told Asquith on 22 May 1915, 'is to be found in the phrase: "We want to be led; we want to be governed." In other words, it is time for an autocracy, not for constitutional government of the ordinary kind.'[82] The complaint was echoed by Mr Punch, who, in a cartoon, told Mr Asquith 'You'll get all the willing service you need, Sir, if you'll only organise it. Tell each one of us what is wanted of him, and he'll do it.'[83] The government still sought to limit the war's impact upon the population. But, as *The Times* commented, 'the national life, if the Government would only realise it, is being thrown out of gear already to an infinitely greater extent for lack of direction than by any definite action of the State'.[84]

81 Jenkins, p. 348.
82 K. Grieves, *The Politics of Manpower, 1914–1918*, p. 15.
83 *Punch*, 26 May 1915, p. 411.
84 *The Times*, 23 June 1915.

5 WAR BY IMPROVISATION: MONEY, MANPOWER, MUNITIONS AND FOOD

As was discussed in the last chapter, Kitchener intended that the process of wearing down the German army, requiring about two years, would be carried out by France and Russia. Britain would then administer the knockout blow with her new army and emerge from the war the strongest, if not the most heroic, power. Unfortunately it was not within the capability of Britain's allies to withstand, much less wear down, the military might of Germany. A significant contribution from Britain was essential from the earliest stages of the war merely to keep the alliance intact. Kitchener's call for an army of 70 divisions on 7 July 1915 was essentially an admission that his strategy of limited commitment was broken. An army of that size meant only one thing: a long war of attrition with Britain playing a significant and costly part. Casualties would be massive, as would the disruption of the domestic economy.

For all the faults of Business as Usual and of Kitchener's original plan, both at least had a certain coherent logic – albeit misguided. In their place came a strategic vacuum. Although politicians may have realised the scale of the commitment facing Britain, they never fully embraced the idea of total war and instead insisted that mobilising a large army need not imply mobilising the nation. For the rest of the war they preferred to improvise. Within this improvisation lurked elements of Business as Usual and of Kitchener's ideas, and of the sort of war Britain would fight from 1939 to 1945. But no consistent plan emerged. That was the legacy of the May Coalition, a typically Asquithian balancing act between contradictory forces. Interventionists and free marketeers were allowed to remain in a government which resembled Dr Doolittle's Pushme Pullyou.

The war was managed according to the principle of the squeaky wheel. The free market was not interfered with unless production of a commodity fell below desired standards. When the government intervened, it first asked for voluntary compliance with stated goals, then gently cajoled and only regulated as a last resort. This cautious, ad hoc approach meant that coordinated mobilisation was impossible. Wasteful practices easily escaped the government's notice: one factory produced fine, gun metal cigarette cases until late 1917.[1] There were no restrictions (other than those of price and scarcity) upon the voluminous skirts women wore. Advertisers irresponsibly misled customers by claiming the extra material in the skirts would 'encourage our home industries'.[2] Such practices gave civilians the impression that a half-hearted approach to the war was acceptable. In total war the mobilisation of the economy and of civilian morale should go hand in hand. The absence of comprehensive planning caused inequalities of sacrifice among the population, to the detriment of morale.

The name Asquith has often been taken to imply ineffectual, *laissez-faire* war management, that of Lloyd George assertive intervention. In fact the difference between the two is not so distinct. Asquith had his successes, Lloyd George his failures. Asquith occasionally intervened, just as Lloyd George was often content to place his trust in voluntarism. The progress from one war leader to the other was not a radical departure but a slow evolution. Failures evident under Asquith paved the way for remedies proposed by Lloyd George to gain acceptance. Lloyd George did assume a more dynamic approach to the war, but dynamism should not be confused with method. Though he might have believed in coordinated state control, he had to work with colleagues determined to resist state expansion.

In total war, strategy is affected by home front capabilities. The size of a country's military forces is strictly limited: too many soldiers means not enough workers to equip them. If the military grows disproportionately large, weaponry and supplies have to be purchased abroad. But this requires a huge naval commitment to transport those supplies. It also means an automatic balance of payments deficit, financed either by borrowing or by depleting reserves, to dire effect in both cases. It is clearly more appropriate for the size of the military to be determined by what the civilian economy can bear. To bring the discussion closer to home, it was dangerous for Britain to plan for 70 divisions if she was incapable of feeding and equipping an army of that size. Yet this was exactly what transpired; strategic plans were devised not according to what the country could bear but according to the generals' desire for an overwhelmingly powerful force capable of implementing a costly strategy.

1 K. Grieves, *The Politics of Manpower, 1914–1918*, p. 172.
2 *The Times*, 16 March 1915.

ARMS AND THE NATION

By May 1915, the number one priority of British industry was to produce weapons in sufficient quantity to enable British forces to hold their own against the Germans. Hopes of using the war to expand into export markets once dominated by Germany had long since faded. Henceforward, most of what British industry produced would be consumed by Britain or her allies. But producing for an ever-growing army was not simply a matter of expanding output. As the army grew, the problems of equipping it grew exponentially. The original BEF of 120,000 men went to war with 334 lorries, 133 cars, 166 motorcycles, 300 guns and 63 aircraft. Such a force could easily be supplied without seriously disrupting regular industrial production. But by 1918 the BEF numbered nearly 2,500,000 men, who required 31,770 lorries, 7,694 cars, 3,532 ambulances, 14,464 motorcycles, 6,437 guns and 1,782 aircraft. Supplies were exhausted or destroyed at a prodigious rate, especially during gargantuan offensives. One mile of line required 900 miles of barbed wire, 6,000,000 sandbags, 1,000,000 cubic feet of timber and 360,000 square feet of corrugated iron.[3] 'A random selection of statistics', writes Denis Winter, 'shows 6,879 miles of railway specially built in France just for our army; 51,107 rubber stamps to have been issued; 137,224,141 pairs of socks to have been given out; 5,649,797 rabbit skins to have been cleaned and disposed of by the BEF; 30,009 miles of flannelette consumed in the cleaning of rifles.'[4]

The physical plant capable of supplying such a huge army did not exist in 1914. New factories had to be built, supplies of raw materials had to be secured; transport and energy industries had to be coordinated to new production priorities and new sources of essential commodities previously imported from Germany had to be found. This expansion had to come at the expense of other industries, yet no central authority existed to decide where sacrifices would be made. The war also revealed how British industry had failed to stay abreast of foreign competitors. Management was amateurish compared to America, and scientific expertise lagged far behind Germany. The free market was ill-equipped to provide the motivation for expansion and modernisation. Industrialists had to be confident that a secure market existed before they would invest, and rumours of a short war did not inspire confidence. For instance, a Wolver-

3 J. Bourne, *Britain and the Great War, 1914–1918*, pp. 177–8.
4 D. Winter, *Death's Men*, pp. 236–7.

hampton firm complained in May 1915 that it was being asked to risk £150,000 against the slim security of a ten-week War Office contract.[5] While still Chancellor, Lloyd George began to recognise the deficiencies of the free market in wartime. He tried to create the climate for expansion, by removing obstacles to investment, advancing necessary capital and guaranteeing firms against loss in the event of a short war.

The munitions crisis was exacerbated by the nature of this war. Static warfare required much greater use of artillery (particularly heavy artillery) than mobile warfare. The guns also used different ammunition. In a mobile war, shrapnel shells (canisters filled with hundreds of lead balls and an explosive charge) are fired at advancing infantry. But shrapnel was virtually useless in a static war since trenches provided secure protection. The best way to attack an entrenched soldier was to blow up his trench with high explosive shells. But, in order to be effective, these shells had to be accurate to within five yards. Thus, their manufacture required greater expertise than did the more simple shrapnel shells. High explosive shells also had to explode at the right time (in or near a German trench) rather than at the factory or while still in the gun. This was a simple requirement, but not an easy one to ensure.

The War Office initially responded by placing expanded orders with existing armaments firms, on the assumption that they would sub-contract anything beyond their capacity. But this approach had dangerous flaws. Sub-contractors did not always produce the desired quantity or quality of munitions on time. Hastily manufactured shells exploded in the barrels of hastily manufactured guns, or did not explode at all. The Shell Scandal was merely the most potent manifestation of a problem which, had it not been for Kitchener's secretive nature, would probably have become apparent much earlier. The problem was camouflaged by seemingly impressive production figures; during the first six months of the war the supply of munitions increased nineteen-fold. Kitchener boasted that, as a result of his inspiration, munitions factories produced in three days as much ammunition as was produced in a year during peacetime. The ammunition which would be used during the Somme offensive was manufactured under his supervision.[6] Unfortunately, his achievements still fell far short of requirements. In early 1915, there were enough 18

5 C. Wrigley, 'The Ministry of Munitions: An Innovatory Department', in K. Burk, ed., *War and the State*, p. 37.
6 T. Royle, *The Kitchener Enigma*, p. 297.

pdr guns (the workhorse of the army) to equip just 28 divisions, not the 70 Kitchener desired. Sufficient 4.5 and 5 inch howitzers existed for just seventeen divisions and rifles for only 33. The army needed 70,000 hand grenades per day but received just 2,500. Over 26,000 machine-guns were needed, but only 5,500 orders had been filled.[7] Kitchener lacked the capacity to bring about the industrial transformation required to meet these needs. By May 1915, most of the government, encouraged by Lloyd George, had come to view Kitchener as an unfortunate choice as War Minister. But a man promoted as a hero who had so inspired public enthusiasm for the war could not easily be exposed as a failure. Asquith, master of compromise, decided instead to embellish Kitchener's heroic façade while he dismantled the War Minister's power base. The appointment of Lloyd George as Minister of Munitions was based on the hopeful assumption that a quintessential politician would succeed where a quintessential soldier had failed.

The Munitions of War Act, passed by the Commons in July, gave Lloyd George the legal powers to do whatever he deemed necessary to expand production. The Act provided the Munitions Minister with absolute priority over supplies of fuel and power, transportation and over the land on which new factories might be built. The *de facto* nationalisation of the coal and rail industries, begun before Lloyd George took office, was advanced by him. In addition, he established procedures for commandeering stocks of raw materials and made vast forays into the import market, centralising purchase in foreign markets and sending representatives out to develop new supply sources.[8] Lloyd George could also order factories to produce for the government and, where necessary, take them under government control. These 'controlled establishments' eventually numbered in the hundreds. The Ministry set up its own specialised enterprises: four National Cartridge Factories, fifteen National Projectile Factories and an equal number of National Filling Factories. The largest of the latter, at Barnbow near Leeds, had no electricity, water, gas supply, sewerage facilities or road and rail links when construction began in mid-1915. Yet within a year the factory was producing 6,000 shells per day.[9]

The Ministry's impact had less to do with the Act's provisions than with the Minister's character. A marauder and empire-builder,

7 R. J. Q. Adams, *Arms and the Wizard*, pp. 53–4.
8 See *History of the Ministry of Munitions*, VII, especially Part 1.
9 T. Wilson, *The Myriad Faces of War*, p. 237.

he was certain that no industry could be run better than one under his control. When the Ministry was torn from the War Office, the division of responsibilities was neither logical nor efficient. Unhappy with the demarcation, Lloyd George used the emergency and the hopes invested in him to expand his remit. He insisted, soon after becoming Minister, that the Royal Arsenals should come under his control. He then annexed design, on the grounds that the War Office had been dangerously prescriptive in this area, specifically in developing an effective high explosive fuse. Next he took over Kitchener's technical department and set up a Munitions Invention Department (MID) which quickly superseded a rival concern at the War Office. As long as he delivered the goods, his piracy was tolerated. Kitchener grumbled, but remained at his post while it shrank beneath him.

Within one year of the Ministry's existence, its staff numbered 12,000; by the end of the war it had expanded to 25,000 – an indication of the breadth of its concerns.[10] Much of the staff's energy was devoted to research and development. For instance, the Trench Warfare Department was formed to apply technology to the unique problems of a static war. Whilst aiding the development of new weapons, it also adapted old ones, such as mortars and grenades, to new conditions. Both it and the MID were inundated with ideas from soldiers and private citizens. The preposterous (like plans for 'death-ray' machines) grossly outnumbered the practical, but occasionally a weapon (like the Stokes Mortar) was proposed which would make a significant contribution to the war. Factories were encouraged to adopt the latest technologies and management techniques, with the Ministry often providing capital to modernise. Plants which had resisted electrification were forced finally to embrace the twentieth century. In new factories 95 per cent of the machinery was powered by electricity.[11] This forced the electricity industry to modernise; although not strictly speaking nationalised, it did take a much more national approach to generation. Steel mills were likewise encouraged to install Bessemer converters, which increased productivity and allowed much greater use of scrap steel and low grade iron ore than was considered possible before 1914.

Science – under the patronage of the Ministry – made the British better at waging trench warfare but not good enough to escape the trenches. In fact, many of the developments to emerge were responses to or copies of German inventions. Such was the case with the gas

10 Wrigley, 'The Ministry of Munitions', p. 42.
11 Ibid., p. 47.

mask, which had to be continually improved in order to provide protection against ever more deadly gases. Thus, the Ministry enabled Britain to keep pace in a war which steadily escalated in size and ghastliness. Guns available to the BEF increased from 1,173 when Lloyd George entered the Ministry to 3,721 when he left, with a welcome improvement in the ratio of heavy to light. But during that time, the length of the British line increased from 36 miles to 85, and the number of divisions from fourteen to 42.[12]

In June 1916, Kitchener drowned when the *Hampshire*, in which he was travelling to Russia, hit a mine off the coast of Orkney. As the people mourned, many politicians breathed a sigh of relief. Lloyd George took over at the War Ministry, and Montagu replaced him at Munitions. Lloyd George's effect upon arms production had been undeniably impressive. By the time he left in July 1916, manufacture of 18 pdr shells had increased seventeen-fold. A quantity of heavy howitzer ammunition which had previously taken a year to produce now took just four days. During the Ministry's first year, production of guns rose from 1,105 to 5,006, grenades from 68,000 to 27,000,000, machine-guns from 1,486 to 17,679 and trench mortars from 312 to 4,279.[13] But many of the changes which facilitated this enormous explosion of output occurred before the Ministry was created. The problem of poor quality shells (duds) was not solved and may even have been exacerbated in the rush to produce more and more. And hugely impressive short term production figures were achieved at the expense of long term stability. Lloyd George rode roughshod over established labour practices in order to maximise output. Many of these practices were admittedly obstacles to efficiency, but not all deserved destruction. He drove the munitions industry to the point of exhaustion; it needed careful handling to last out the war. Nor was his approach remotely systematic or coordinated. He reacted to perceived emergencies with appropriate alacrity, but left alone those concerns which performed to his satisfaction. A seemingly efficient factory which avoided the Minister's attention operated in a very different world to one which he saw fit to control. This complicated the handling of labour relations and manpower issues.

---

12 Wilson, p. 238.

13 D. Lloyd George, *War Memoirs*, I, pp. 389–90. See also Adams, pp. 172–3, 244–5.

FEEDING THE PEOPLE

The munitions crisis exacerbated but at the same time obscured an equally threatening problem of agricultural production. The calorific value of food produced on British farms slipped from 21.41 billion calories in 1914 to 19.39 billion in 1916.[14] This has commonly been blamed on the fact that farmworkers were unable to resist Kitchener's call or the lure of high wages in munitions factories. In fact, the flight from the land was not as significant as is often assumed. When substitute workers are taken into account, farm labour supply declined by only 7 per cent from 1914 to 1916.[15] But farms did suffer in other ways which, combined, reduced production. For instance, at its peak, the army required over 400,000 horses, mules and donkeys, many commandeered from British farms. The munitions industry had first call on nitrogen and phosphates which previously went into fertilisers.

In August 1916 a report by the Royal Society warned that average per capita food consumption was only 5 per cent above the nutritional minimum, underlining how threatening even a slight drop in supply or a problem of distribution might prove.[16] Yet hard on the heels of the crisis in domestic production came the German resumption of unrestricted submarine warfare on 1 February 1917. Given her dependence upon imported food, this nearly brought Britain to her knees. Her response to the submarine is, thanks to Lloyd George, widely misunderstood.[17] According to myth, he applied the same creativity and dynamism to the U-boat problem as he did to the shell shortage, eventually convincing hidebound admirals to adopt a convoy system.[18] In fact, Lloyd George was slow to recognise the urgency of the problem. As late as 30 March, Maurice Hankey, the Cabinet Secretary, expressed concern about 'the shipping outlook owing to submarines and the inability of the Adty. to deal with it and their general ineptitude. . . . I have many ideas on the matter, but cannot get at Ll. George.'[19] April brought disasters which could

14 P. E. Dewey, 'Food Production and Policy in the United Kingdom, 1914–1918', *Transactions of the Royal Historical Society* Fifth Series, 30 (1980), p. 84.

15 Idem, 'Agricultural Labour Supply in England and Wales During the First World War', *Economic History Review* 28 (1975), pp. 100–9.

16 J. Harris, 'Bureaucrats and Businessmen in British Food Control, 1916–19', in Burk, ed., p. 138.

17 A typically Lloyd George-inspired account can be found in A. J. P. Taylor, *English History 1914–1945*, pp. 122–4.

18 See Lloyd George, I, pp. 617–713.

19 M. Hankey, *The Supreme Command, 1914–1918*, p. 648.

not be ignored. Enemy action sunk 169 British and 204 Allied or neutral vessels – a total of 866,000 tons, or one-quarter of the tonnage which left British harbours.[20] The effects upon the food supply were disastrous; from February to June 1917, 85,000 tons of sugar were lost, at one point reducing the nation to four days' supply. Huge stocks of meat also went down.[21] On 30 April Hankey noted that Lloyd George 'at last . . . has set himself to tackle the submarine question seriously, when it is almost too late'.[22]

The navy understood how to protect its own valuable ships, namely by surrounding them with a cordon of destroyers to serve as a screen for torpedoes and to participate in anti-submarine warfare. But the Admiralty considered it impractical to protect merchant ships in the same way, given the scale of the operation. Impending disaster forced a reconsideration. On 10 May the first convoy of seventeen ships left Gibraltar. All arrived safely in Britain twelve days later. This small success spelt defeat for the submarine campaign. Losses declined steadily for the rest of the year, as ever more ships were convoyed. Before the introduction of convoys, losses caused by submarines averaged 10 per cent, rising to 25 per cent in April 1917. After convoys became the norm, this figure dropped to just 1 per cent.[23] At the same time, destruction of German submarines increased steadily.

Britain also responded to the U-boat with better coordination of shipping. Given the seriousness of the problem and the decentralized nature of the industry, it was perhaps inevitable that action had to come from central government. Yet nothing of substance was done until Lloyd George became Prime Minister. The Ministry of Shipping, with Sir Joseph Maclay at its head, was a welcome if tardy response to a dangerously disorganised industry. Maclay introduced the first comprehensive scheme to coordinate docks and railways in order to relieve congestion and to make the most efficient use of dock labour. The Ministry also assumed powers to requisition shipping at fixed rates and to allocate space. Up until that time, valuable shipping space was often taken by non-essential imports, if a market existed. Maclay, no respecter of established trading relationships, further directed importers to secure goods from the closest supplier in order to reduce shipping times. The reforms were sometimes ridiculously

20 H. Newbolt, *Naval Operations (Official History of the Great War)*, IV, p. 385.
21 Wilson, p. 537.
22 Hankey, p. 650.
23 G. Hardach, *The First World War 1914–1918*, p. 44.

simple: casting aside standard practice, the Ministry ruled that American wheat should be shipped as flour, rather than unmilled, thus reducing shipping space. But only partial success was possible in prioritising ship construction, since the Admiralty was not entirely cooperative. It could not accept that merchant ships were sometimes more essential than warships.

Convoys and a more organised shipping industry could not by themselves solve Britain's food problem. Shipping losses were still greater in 1918 than they were before the commencement of unlimited submarine warfare. And net food imports declined steadily throughout the war, from 34.2 billion calories in 1914 to 31.1 in 1916 and 27.9 in 1918.[24] This meant that the real solution to the food problem had to be found at home. But government intervention in agriculture was highly problematic. This was partly due to the decentralised nature of farming, but more to the traditionally tense relationship between landowners and government. Farmers were by nature suspicious of any change, especially government-inspired. Their conservatism was reinforced by the fact that, in spite of shortages in manpower and raw materials, they stood to gain from the war. Scarcity insured that profits, which stood at £19.6 million in 1913, increased to £100.5 million in 1917. One farmer later reflected: 'it was impossible to lose money at farming then'.[25] Since food shortages were, for most of the war, more a nuisance than a problem, the government was reluctant to confront farmers. It instead preferred cajoling them, employing incentives more readily than regulations.

But some progress was made. Scarcity (of labour and raw materials) acted as a spur to modernisation. Pre-war farming was labour-intensive, wartime and postwar agriculture increasingly mechanised. The government assumed its most active role after December 1916, when food shortages caused by German submarines were at their worst. The Corn Production Act, passed in 1917, guaranteed minimum prices for wheat and oats until at least 1922, thus reassuring farmers who were reluctant to invest in costly modernisation. A wages board was established to administer a minimum wage for farm labourers, and the Board of Agriculture was empowered to see that land was properly cultivated. Substitute labour was made avail-

---

24 Dewey, 'Food Production', p. 81.

25 Idem, 'British Farming Profits and Government Policy During the First World War', *Economic History Review* 37 (1984), pp. 378, 387. See also P. Horn, *Rural Life in England in the First World War*, p. 57.

able, in the form of 84,000 soldiers, 30,000 prisoners of war and 16,000 members of the Women's Land Army. Three million acres formerly devoted to pasture were ploughed up to provide staple crops, mainly grain and potatoes.[26] A total of 7.5 million acres was added to cultivation by the end of the war. This made it possible for the total output of wheat, barley, oats, rye, corn, peas, beans and potatoes to exceed 18 million tons by 1918, up from 14 million in 1914. Or, to put it differently, Britain could feed herself from her own produce an extra 30 days out of the year.[27] But the end result of the government's efforts was to bequeath itself a hostage to fortune in the postwar years: a surplus of home-produced food at protected prices.

Even more promising than shifts in production were changes in food processing, most notably the altering of the composition of bread by using a higher percentage of the raw wheat and by substituting other grains such as barley, maize and potatoes. The inspiration behind these changes came from the Food Production Department (FPD), a sub-department of the Board of Agriculture set up on 1 January 1917. The extraction rate of flour, which was 70 per cent in peacetime, peaked at 91.9 per cent in April 1918. In addition, the flour was stretched by mixing in up to 29 per cent other grains and potatoes.[28] While these changes were encouraging, there were attendant costs. Bread production was more efficient, the bread itself more nutritious, but the people did not care for loaves which seemed as digestible as a howitzer shell and probably as lethal. More importantly, the shift from pasture to arable farming meant a shift from high grade protein from meat and dairy products to low grade protein from cereals and potatoes. Although the calorie level of the average British diet decreased by only 3 per cent from 1914 to 1918, the protein intake declined by about 6 per cent.[29]

Provision of food became a sensitive topic. The real difficulty was distribution, not supply. Food went where money was. The most strident complaints about rising prices came from the workers and the worst queues were in working class areas. Workers were convinced that farmers, wholesalers and retailers were using shortages to extract huge profits from consumers. Anger occasionally boiled

26 A. S. Milward, *The Economic Effects of the Two World Wars Upon Britain*, p. 25.

27 Horn, p. 55. See also Hardach, pp. 126–7.

28 Dewey, 'Food Production', pp. 86–7.

29 Ibid., pp. 72–3.

over into riots and strikes. But because the problem was mainly one of inconvenience rather than imminent starvation, the government was reluctant to regulate. Its first reaction to food shortages was in keeping with its initial response to other problems: it appealed for voluntary action. The public was encouraged to cut consumption through widely promoted economy drives and meatless days. But government appeals for voluntary restraint failed to convince the average middle class person to forgo foodstuffs he had the where-withal to buy. Great emphasis was given to symbolic gestures like the King's decision to convert the flower beds around the Queen Victoria memorial to vegetable cultivation and the dividing of some Royal Parks into allotments.[30] Late in Asquith's ministry the government assumed powers to turn over unoccupied land to allotments, but its lacklustre enforcement of this power is symptomatic of its disinclination to seize private property unless absolutely necessary. This scheme, as with the appointment (by Lloyd George) of the ineffectual Lord Devonport as Food Controller in December 1916, was little more than a sop to an increasingly restless public. The same could be said for the occasional prosecutions of merchants guilty of blatant profiteering and the regulations against wasting and hoarding food.[31] While Devonport concentrated on meatless days, registration of pickled herrings and rules concerning the size of bread rolls, civil servants like William Beveridge grew increasingly frustrated at the government's unwillingness to embrace meaningful regulation. Beveridge was convinced that the distribution of food could not be managed by those who had private interests in the food trade since involvement in one aspect of the industry precluded a proper understanding of its wider problems.[32] Meanwhile, Charles Bathurst, MP, Devonport's spokesman in the Commons, 'told everyone who would listen that he heard very little about his department's policies and disliked most of what he heard'. Devonport's lack of policy was, thought Bathurst, 'nothing less than a crime against the nation'.[33]

In late 1917 the government reluctantly accepted that voluntarism would not by itself avert a crisis. Working class antagonism over food supplies was escalating dangerously, in turn threatening industrial production. At the same time, a poor American harvest, a

---

30 C. Haste, *Keep the Home Fires Burning*, pp. 43–4.

31 These are discussed in Chapters 7 and 10.

32 Harris, 'Bureaucrats and Businessmen', pp. 140, 148.

33 J. Turner, *British Politics and the Great War*, pp. 174, 176.

disappointing domestic potato and cereal crop, and the depredations of submarines rendered food supply precarious. These factors combined to drag the government to the threshold of rationing. Some local authorities in areas where supply problems were most severe had, in an effort to avert serious civil unrest, already introduced limited rationing. A more comprehensive scheme was adopted when Lord Rhondda took over the Ministry of Food in April 1917, after Devonport's resignation. Recognising that bread was the most important staple in the working class diet, he immediately took action to ensure that supplies remained steady and prices did not escalate. Controls introduced in September in fact drove the price of a 4 lb loaf down from 11½d to 9d.[34]

By the end of 1917, the government had in place the machinery for comprehensive control of food distribution under guidelines suggested by Beveridge. Fifteen Divisional Food Committees were given powers to control prices, carry out inspections of processors and distributors and register retailers. But their main purpose was to provide the framework for rationing if and when it became necessary. By the end of the year the first experiments in rationing began, with notable success. Controls continued apace in 1918. By the end of the war, 85 per cent of all food consumed was bought and sold by firms under government control and 94 per cent of all food was subject to price control. In the financial year ending March 1919, the Ministry had a turnover of £900 million. The rationing system was reinforced by 70,000 prosecutions and the levying of £400,000 in fines. By early March the number of people in food queues had fallen from 1,300,000 per week to 200,000.[35] The working class diet improved, wastage was reduced and discontent was alleviated.[36] This success begs the question why controls were not introduced earlier. Lloyd George blamed working class hostility. It was essential, he maintained, 'to approach [rationing] – as had previously been done with compulsory service – along the line of first exhausting the possibilities of voluntary control'.[37] Yet just as there is no real evidence for working class hostility to conscription, so too for rationing. The idea that workers preferred standing in queues to clipping coupons is preposterous. The real reason for delay was that until the

---

34 Horn, p. 50.

35 Harris, 'Bureaucrats and Businessmen', pp. 135, 144.

36 For a further discussion of the implementation of rationing and its effect upon consumers, see Chapter 11.

37 Lloyd George, I, p. 788.

problem became an emergency the government danced to the tune of producers, distributors and retailers, whose hostility to controls was severe and whose power was profound.

THE PROBLEM OF MANPOWER

As the war progressed, the need for labour in Blighty increased at the same time that the supply decreased due to casualties on the Western Front. Kitchener's army competed with industry for the same, limited supply of labour. Blissfully ignorant or hopelessly irresponsible, the government gave its blessing to the army's unfettered expansion. The Treasury Agreement and the Munitions of War Act of 1915, by relaxing restrictive practices, were supposed to ensure a ready supply of labour. Beneath this surface contentment, concern stirred, especially at the War Office. The army had secured 1,342,647 recruits by the end of January 1915, but during February volunteers numbered less than 22,000 per week, a number which it required only a day and a half to collect during September.[38] But if the dwindling volume of volunteers worried Kitchener, he could not voice his concerns since he had yet to explain what he intended to do with all these men and still had far more recruits than he could arm or efficiently train. It was to his advantage to remain vague about requirements. Those on the political right were beginning to demand compulsion, perhaps extending to industrial conscription, but Kitchener did not join this chorus. Not only was he uneasy about the value of conscripts, he still believed that his presence rendered conscription unnecessary. 'I have held up my finger and the men are flocking to me in thousands', he was wont to remark.[39] But he also realised that conscription would force him to show his hand. He would no longer be able to put forward limitless demands and would instead have to balance his needs with those of industry. Thus, though unrestrained volunteering caused domestic havoc, Kitchener was happy for the anarchy to continue.

The destructive yet inconclusive battles of 1915 provided a clue to the level of commitment required for victory to be achieved. Kitchener responded by calling for a 70 division army in July 1915, a demand which seemed to imply conscription. The government came under pressure from two equally diehard groups: those demanding

---

38 I. Beckett, 'The Nation in Arms, 1914–18', in I. Beckett and K. Simpson, eds, *A Nation in Arms*, p. 8.
39 Royle, p. 261.

compulsion immediately and those (mainly Liberals) who considered the choice of whether to die for one's country the last and most important freedom. *The Times* argued on 6 May 1915 that 'The voluntary system has its limits and we are fast approaching them',[40] while one Liberal warned that conscription would strangle civilisation 'in a garotte of steel'.[41] Asquith, wary of the widening rift in his government, was determined that if conscription was to be introduced, its need should first be demonstrated beyond a shadow of a doubt. Toward this end, the government introduced in September the National Register, under which every British subject (male or female) between the ages of 16 and 65 was urged to make themselves known to the government. It revealed that 1,413,000 men in England and Wales (and another 150,000 in Scotland) were still theoretically available for military service, after taking into account those doing essential work at home.[42]

The compilers of the survey stressed that the figure was an upper limit and very rough. No consideration was, for instance, given to the fact that an expanded army meant that more reserved workers would be needed to supply it. Thus, 1.5 million men theoretically available did not mean the army could expand by that number. But that was not how the War Minister saw the matter; he immediately claimed the men for his army. Thus, in August he requested a weekly recruiting level of 35,000 for the rest of the year. Since the flow of volunteers currently ran at 19,000 per week, there seemed little way of reaching this target short of compulsion.[43]

The result was the Derby Scheme. On 5 October 1915, Lord Derby, whose Pals Battalions had earlier proved a boon to volunteering, was appointed Director of Recruiting. 'Perhaps', commented the *Manchester Guardian*, 'in the days to come when the history of the war is written, it will be said that Lord Derby saved the voluntary system.'[44] Derby himself was less sanguine, admitting that he felt like a 'receiver who was put in to wind up a bankrupt concern'.[45] 'For my part', he later wrote, 'though I had always been for compulsory service, I meant to do my very best to make the voluntary system a

40 *The Times*, 6 May 1915.

41 P. Fraser, 'British War Policy and the Crisis of Liberalism in May 1915', *Journal of Modern History* 54 (1982), p. 7.

42 Grieves, p. 21.

43 Ibid., p. 22.

44 *Manchester Guardian*, 7 October 1915.

45 R. J. Q. Adams, 'Asquith's Choice: the May Coalition and the Coming of Conscription, 1915–1916', *Journal of British Studies* 25 (1986), p. 254.

success up to the very end.'[46] Under his scheme, men between the ages of 18 and 41 were encouraged to attest a willingness to volunteer, on the understanding that the youngest men would be taken first and all single men would be taken before any married. It was widely understood that if not enough men attested, compulsion would be introduced. Volunteering was in essence becoming less voluntary; men were encouraged to walk the plank so as to avoid being pushed later. Of the 2.2 million single men of military age, 840,000 attested, of whom 300,000 were rejected on medical grounds. That meant that just over a million ignored Derby's appeal, despite the extension of the deadline by two weeks. Around 1.35 million married men attested, trusting Asquith's promise to call single men first.[47] Shortly afterwards, Derby and Asquith agreed that conscription should be introduced. The government embarked on the road to conscription, but without any systematic accounting of the competing manpower needs of civilian industry, farming, the merchant marine and the Royal Navy. Kitchener blithely argued that since France (which had a smaller population than Britain) maintained an army of 108 divisions, Britain should be able to field 131 divisions.[48] He made no allowance for Britain's unique predicament: her naval role, her dependence upon imported food, and her drastically different economic structure.

'There has been no co-ordination of the different departments', Robertson complained to Haig. 'I have been working up to 70 Divisions. L. George has ordered material for 100 Divisions. The Chancellor of the Exchequer did not till yesterday know either of these things.'[49] Robertson was further perturbed at the way the Chancellor, McKenna, backed by Runciman, President of the Board of Trade, had forced the Cabinet to consider the financial implications of a large army raised via conscription. McKenna argued that even 57 divisions would cost £5 million per day and cause a deficit of £2,000 million by March 1917.[50] Runciman insisted that the men could not be spared from industry. On 12 January 1916, Robertson complained that the

46 R. Churchill, *Lord Derby: King of Lancashire*, p. 193.

47 Turner, p. 73.

48 Grieves, p. 24.

49 Robertson to Haig, 31 December 1915: Haig War Diary, Haig Papers, National Library of Scotland.

50 M. Fry, 'Political Change in Britain, August 1914 to December 1916: Lloyd George Replaces Asquith: The Issues Underlying the Drama', *Historical Journal* 31 (1988), p. 617.

attitude of some ministers is . . . to find out what is the smallest amount of money and the smallest amount of men with which we may hope, some day, to win the war, or rather not to lose it, whereas the proper attitude is to see what is the greatest number of men we can put into the field in the shortest possible period of time.[51]

This 'proper attitude' was shared by Lloyd George, who, in a letter to Austen Chamberlain, argued:

We must win through even though we win in rags. The notion of keeping up our trade as if there were no war is fatal. The single eye always triumphs in the end. Thus Germany fights – her trade gone and her people rationed on potatoes. I implore you not to give assent to the McKenna–Runciman position. If you desert us on this point we shall be baffled and Britain will be beaten.[52]

But even this 'proper attitude' promised chaos unless manpower was better managed. A solution might have been to introduce military *and* industrial conscription, thus enabling the needs of both sectors to be balanced. This seems sensible, but logical manpower planning would have to await another war. Asquith, ideologically opposed to intervention of this magnitude, also understood that it was politically dangerous. Aversion to military conscription was concentrated within Parliament and could be overcome. Opposition to industrial compulsion was rooted within the trade union movement and, as such, was more formidable. It was not known whether the workers would countenance such a profound limitation upon their freedom.

It is perhaps an exaggeration to claim that the Derby Scheme was meant to fail, yet in failing it succeeded. His scheme offered a last opportunity to preserve the voluntarist past, but also indicated a safe path to a conscriptionist future. It is difficult to predict how the public would have reacted to the immediate introduction of conscription, without the cushion of the failed Derby Scheme. But one suspects that opposition was never as powerful as some politicians feared. The group that mattered in the debate were the anti-conscriptionists led by McKenna, Runciman and Sir John Simon, who, if they remained united, had the power to bring the coalition down. By failing, the Derby Scheme fractured that group and ensured that the Military Service Act of January 1916 passed without significant objection in the Commons. Only Simon followed his conscience to the backbenches. McKenna and Runciman were mollified by

51 Grieves, 25.
52 Fry, 'Political Change', p. 617.

Asquith's promise of a Military Finance Committee to study the financial and manpower implications of conscription.

The Act imposed conscription on single men aged 18 to 41, with exemptions for ministers of religion, the medically unfit, the Irish and conscientious objectors. In addition, men employed in essential work could not be conscripted. But, keeping to the decentralised approach, the government left it to local tribunals to decide which workers were essential. This led to great inconsistencies from region to region and hindered a coordinated approach to manpower. Worse still, the Act failed to provide sufficient men to satisfy the army. According to the War Office, too many single men were earning exemptions, without sufficient investigation into the possibility of finding substitute labour among married men or women. In late April, Asquith was forced to concede a second Military Service Act, which extended conscription to married men.

Once in place, conscription brought deep dismay at the Munitions Ministry and the Board of Trade, where it was felt that too many men were being taken from essential jobs. 'The matter is really most serious', complained Montagu in August. 'I do wish the A[djutant] G[eneral]'s Department would indicate a more practical realisation of the state of affairs.' The army either did not care how its exorbitant demands affected the civilian work force, or was determined to ignore the problem. The Adjutant General, Sir Nevil Macready, actually objected to increased artillery production on the grounds that it deprived the army of potential soldiers.[53] Senior officers shared the optimism of the new Commander in Chief, Sir Douglas Haig, who believed that the 1916 offensive on the Somme would break the back of the German army. Thus, planning production for 1917 was pointless since the war would be over by then. Some attempts were made to balance the competing claims of the War Office, Munitions Ministry, Admiralty and Board of Trade, including the setting up of the Cabinet Committee for the Co-ordination of Military and Financial Effort and, subsequently, the Cabinet Committee on the Size of the Army.[54] But both committees lacked the will or political clout to carry through workable solutions. The Man-Power Distribution Board, established on 22 August 1916, was the first concerted effort by government to come to terms with the problem of competing demand.

53 Grieves, pp. 32–3.

54 These were the committees mentioned earlier which were primarily designed to mollify Runciman and McKenna.

Austen Chamberlain became the first chairman of that body. Originally designed to provide the government with objective advice upon balancing manpower needs, the Board quickly fell prey to the rivalry it was intended to mitigate. The War Office and Munitions Ministry did their best to pervert its aims, the former being more successful at doing so. The Board's first report, issued on 30 September 1916, recommended that large orders for munitions should be referred to the Adjutant General, who would comment upon the ramifications for recruiting. The Cabinet's acceptance of this recommendation reinforced the widely held assumption that the War Office had first priority to fit men. The second report, issued on 12 October, advised that badging (the granting of exemptions) should cease until a general review of the situation could be carried out. Montagu feared that the War Office would soon be granted its demand that all badging of men under the age of 30 should cease.

The question of badging caused considerable acrimony between the two sides in the manpower dispute. The War Office was certain that badges were granted indiscriminately, while the Munitions Ministry stubbornly resisted any attempt to review the system. In October 1916 about 1.4 million men were badged, rising to 2 million by April 1917 and to 2.3 million in October 1917.[55] This indicates that the Munitions Ministry was remarkably successful in resisting the depredations upon its work force by the conscription tribunals. A Cabinet Committee on Exemptions was formed to advise upon debadging, but since it had no power to rescind exemptions, the Munitions Ministry freely rejected its advice.

The argument brought to the fore the issue of female labour. Neither the Ministry of Munitions nor the War Office opposed the use of women as substitute labour, but each wanted the other to bear the burden of change. The War Office thought more women should be brought into the factories, and the Munitions Ministry thought the army should introduce women into clerical and administrative positions. Mrs Katherine Furse, who had organised Voluntary Aid Detachments (VADs), proposed a women's auxiliary service for the army, using the VAD as a model. But the army vehemently resisted, the Adjutant General arguing that the manpower problem was not sufficiently serious to warrant such a drastic departure from custom. In contrast, the Munitions Ministry could argue convincingly (if not entirely accurately) that it had been flexible in its attitude to

---

55 P. E. Dewey, 'Military Recruiting and the British Labour Force During the First World War', *Historical Journal* 27 (1984), p. 215.

female labour and that only the most skilled jobs in the factories were performed by badged men.

Meanwhile, increasingly serious food shortages and the expansion of the air war introduced new demands upon the limited labour supply. The Man-Power Board recognised the emergency, but was incapable of suggesting workable solutions. Its last report proposed the formation of local manpower committees but these were in truth little more than a replacement for the existing tribunals which had already proved faulty. Reflecting its War Office bias, it also proposed ending badging of men under 26. Montagu reacted angrily: 'I can't agree to your proposals which will . . . destroy Munitions output just as we are all coming to the conclusion that the war is a war of material.'[56] The Board often failed to appreciate how its proposals would affect the finely balanced domestic labour situation. Threats to badging were, for instance, behind the decision by Sheffield engineers to down tools on 16 November 1916.

Within the Cabinet, there was no such thing as a national view. Chamberlain represented just another sectional interest, yet to be successful he had to bring competing interests into harmony. Asquith's tendency to compartmentalise the war effort encouraged ministers' chauvinism. At times the arguments grew ridiculously petty, for instance when the War Office accused the Munitions Ministry of poaching soldiers on furlough by offering them lucrative factory jobs, while Munitions countered that the army was stealing precious workers with its sweeps upon pubs, betting offices and football grounds.

At the end of 1916 the Army Council calculated that there were still 2,500,000 men of military age in civilian life, and demanded 940,000 of them for the coming year's operations. Despite Haig's failure to achieve a breakthrough on the Somme, the army still claimed first priority over manpower and was becoming increasingly annoyed with Asquith for failing to honour its prerogative. At the same time, Lloyd George, having moved to the War Office and thus to the other side of the manpower debate, harried Asquith incessantly. Strange bedfellows came together to undermine the Prime Minister: Derby, Robertson and Lloyd George manipulated the manpower issue each to his own agenda.

Sensitive to this pressure, Asquith agreed in principle to the adoption of universal compulsory service for all men aged 60 and under. This temporarily quieted Derby and Robertson, but one has

56 Grieves, p. 56.

to wonder whether they fully understood the implications since extending compulsion did not necessarily mean more men for the army, but rather a more coordinated approach to manpower claims. Asquith, hardly committed to the idea, was probably trying to stifle criticism and play for more time. A Civil Committee headed by Lloyd George which included Lord Robert Cecil, Austen Chamberlain, Runciman and Herbert Samuel met to consider the possibilities for National Service, but since these men all approached the problem from very different angles, fundamental agreement was impossible.

Before the Civil Committee could complete any significant work, political crisis intervened. Lloyd George, who had used the manpower problem to undermine Asquith, was eventually able to form a new government because he convinced influential Tories that he would find a solution favourable to the army's interests. His promise to implement National Service proved just the trick for the army and its patrons. But he was not the man they imagined. His idea of National Service was a civilian-directed scheme designed to allow a flexible response to changing manpower demands, not an automatic conveyor belt to transport men into the army. Lloyd George was keenly aware that trade union support was essential to political stability and was not about to endanger that stability by introducing a National Service scheme which alienated workers.

At least as far as manpower was concerned, Lloyd George proved hardly more dynamic than Asquith. Quickly backing away from a compulsory system, he suggested that just as military conscription had been preceded by voluntary enrolment (the Derby Scheme), 'so a similar procedure might be adopted in the present case'.[57] This ran counter to the instincts of Neville Chamberlain, appointed to head the National Service Department. Chamberlain bravely spoke of an industrial army, working under conditions similar to the regular army, which would empower the government to direct labour where it was most needed. But the idea appalled the trade union movement and its new patron on the War Cabinet, Henderson. One suspects that the National Service Department was in truth merely an illusion of action designed to quiet critics. Lloyd George asked the Department to conduct periodic assessments of manpower needs, but did not give Chamberlain the authority which would have made these studies meaningful. Chamberlain, destined to plough the same hopeless furrow as his half-brother Austen (without even the consolation of a seat on the Cabinet), complained:

57 Ibid., p. 73.

> I have never had even a scrap of paper appointing me or giving me any idea of where my duties begin and end. I don't know whether I have Ireland or Scotland as well as England. I don't know whether I have Munitions volunteers. I believe I am to have a salary but I don't know what. I suppose I can be dismissed by someone but I don't know who.[58]

Lloyd George was not about to clarify Chamberlain's confusion, since ambiguity allowed him to please two contradictory groups: those who demanded immediate action and those who feared such action. There was advantage to the Asquithian status quo of allowing the War Office, Munitions, Board of Trade, Admiralty, Air Board and agricultural interests to occupy themselves in fractious rivalry.

As in the past, intervention was agonisingly tentative. The government assumed authority under the Defence of the Realm Act (DORA) to forbid non-essential industries to hire men between the ages of 18 and 60, a seemingly impressive assumption of power, but then stopped short of compelling such industries to release men already working for them. For the moment, the government preferred that male workers should leave these industries voluntarily. Nor was any consideration given to moving children, women and old men from non-essential industries to essential ones. Throughout the war the government ironically had much more authority over the man-power policies of essential industries than it did over non-essential ones. This seems strange given that the non-essential industries were, by definition, not making a significant contribution to the war.

Meanwhile, the army demanded 100,000 men per month for the first four months of 1917, in order to launch a Somme-style offensive in the spring. The virtually autonomous army freely determined its own strategic plans, without taking into consideration the manpower situation. But the worsening food problem meant that farms could no longer be depleted of men to provide new soldiers, though some relief was provided when Home Army soldiers were sent to the farms, thus releasing agricultural labourers for the BEF. In addition, two divisions from the Home Army were sent to the Western Front, much to the disgust of its commander, who argued that 500,000 men were still needed to guard against invasion. The Germans, so the story went, were prepared at any time to release an invasion force of 160,000 men, whose crossing neither the army nor, surprisingly, the Admiralty was confident of being able to prevent. Alarmist

---

58 Ibid., p. 82.

talk of invasion had an ulterior purpose: it pressured the government to release more men from industry.

The National Service Scheme, a civilian variation of the Derby Scheme, was launched on 6 February 1917 at the Central Hall, Westminster. The government asked all males between 18 and 61 to enrol, regardless of whether they were already doing essential work. (Women were not to be enrolled until the scheme for men was up and running.) National Service Committees, formed by local authorities, were given the task of canvassing and publicity, with the actual direction of labour assigned to Employment Exchanges. Enrolled men who were not doing essential work could be moved to another job, perhaps in another area, with travel expenses paid. Wage rates were to reflect local conditions with the minimum set at 25s per week. 'What is less important must give way to what is more important',[59] Chamberlain emphasised.

It was hoped that 500,000 men would be enrolled by 31 March 1917. The actual response was a great embarrassment to the government, though Chamberlain was admittedly never very optimistic about yet another voluntary scheme and had accepted his post with great reluctance.[60] Only 206,000 men enrolled by the target date, of whom 92,489 were subsequently processed by employment exchanges. One-half were already in protected trades, and eventually only 388 men were directed into new employment. In many areas around the country the scheme failed to get off the ground. Lloyd George subsequently confessed that he was 'disgusted'[61] with Chamberlain, criticism only partially justified. Chamberlain's repeated reference to the need for an 'industrial army' alienated workers since it suggested that if voluntarism did not succeed, compulsion would follow hard on its heels. But Lloyd George also deserves criticism; his faith in voluntarism seems strange from a minister who made his reputation by calls for dynamic government intervention. It is difficult to avoid the conclusion that Chamberlain was a convenient scapegoat for a plan never meant to succeed. Lloyd George's close associate Christopher Addison, who had been scathingly critical of Chamberlain's performance, later admitted that the 'job . . . was impossible. . . . He never really had a fair chance.'[62] Since Lloyd George's acceptability as Prime Minister arose precisely

59 Ibid., p. 110.
60 D. Dilks, *Neville Chamberlain*, p. 237.
61 Grieves, p. 113.
62 Dilks, p. 218.

because he offered a refreshing change from Asquithian prevarication, the deception seems all the more cynical.

Chamberlain struggled on at the Department for a further four
months. The huge advertising budget for a scheme which attracted
so few useful recruits was a profound embarrassment to the government, but at least demonstrated that the days when posters of Kitchener could inspire a flood of volunteers were long gone. On 19 July
the War Cabinet accepted a recommendation by a Parliamentary
Select Committee that army recruitment be transferred to a civilian
body. On 8 August Chamberlain, feeling thoroughly swindled,
resigned. Three days later Auckland Geddes took over what now
became a Ministry of National Service, and was given much more
authority than his hapless predecessor had enjoyed. The new ministry
had nothing really to do with National Service, since Chamberlain's
scheme was abandoned, and no one intended putting a compulsory
system in its place. Geddes instead assumed responsibility for army
recruitment and for moving labour to vital war work – or at least
for making suggestions as to where it could be moved. He eventually
assumed power under DORA to close down non-essential industries
and to direct labour from them to essential ones. (It is perhaps
astonishing that it took so long for the government to assume this
power.) A comprehensive List of Reserve Occupations was finally
drawn up and Geddes eventually established a Priority List for
employment exchanges. It weighed manpower demands and was
continually revised according to circumstances. Very good relations
were quickly established with the Ministries of Munitions and
Labour, easing the bitter rivalry which had plagued earlier attempts
to solve the manpower problem.

The rise of the National Service Ministry was paralleled by the
decline of the army's power. Haig and Robertson had promised a
stunning breakthrough on the Western Front once too often. The
muddy disaster at Passchendaele, quickly followed by the cruel
reverse at Cambrai, alienated even loyal friends of the army like
Bonar Law, Derby and Milner, who became much more reticent
whenever demands for recruits were discussed. In a startlingly candid
statement, Lloyd George told the Inter-allied War Council on 12
November, 'We have won great victories. When I look at the appal-
ling casualty lists I sometimes wish it had not been necessary to win
so many.'[63] The Prime Minister wanted the British henceforth to
imitate the 'passive defence' conducted by the French during the

63 *The Times*, 13 December 1917.

latter part of 1917, which he assumed would be much less costly. The Allies would then wait for the Americans to win the war in 1919 or perhaps 1920. But, typical of Lloyd George, he ignored the fact that the French had been able to remain passive only because the British had constantly attacked. However, if his assumptions were wrong, the decisions he drew from them were inescapable. Henceforth the government, though still unable to influence Haig's strategy directly, would do so indirectly by limiting his access to men.

A new War Priorities Committee (of which Geddes was a member) was established, at last allowing a consideration of manpower needs in relation to action on the Western Front. Geddes calculated that of the 3.6 million men of military age in Blighty, only 100,000 could realistically be released to the army. Any more would adversely affect munitions and food production, and ship construction. Around the same time the army put forward its demand of 1,304,000 men for the coming year. The Cabinet Committee on Manpower, formed in December and advised by Geddes, decided in January that the Admiralty would have first call on manpower, followed by ship and tank construction, and only then by the army. Much to its disgust, the army was ordered to effect manpower savings by reducing the Home Army, reorganising into smaller divisions and reducing the number of cavalry units. The latter was particularly painful for Haig, who still dreamt of horsemen galloping to victory. This was an impressively full discussion of manpower needs, unlike any which preceded it. The government was still a long way from a truly coordinated system, since competition between ministries remained intense, but for the first time comprehensive analysis was undertaken. Necessity had finally inspired an assertion of political authority: the army tail no longer wagged the government dog.

Under the terms of the Military Service (No. 1) Act, passed on 6 February 1918, the government assumed the power to cancel certificates of exemption granted on occupational grounds, and also to streamline the enlistment procedure by removing its most aggravating delays. A Revised Schedule of Protected Occupations raised the minimum age of exemption to 23 in protected jobs, and set a series of age limits for non-protected occupations. For the moment, these powers were not exercised, because of the priority given to ship, aeroplane and tank production. But the new measures did enable the government to respond quickly to the emergency of 21 March 1918, when the Germans broke through British lines to a depth of 40 miles on a 43 mile front.

Haig immediately blamed the disaster on Lloyd George, arguing that he had been starved of troops, which was technically true.[64] But he was no innocent victim. During 1916 and 1917 he had vehemently argued that the Germans were on their last legs. It was therefore difficult for him to sound convincing when, in 1918, he suddenly complained that his own army desperately needed reinforcement. Granted, Haig might have been able to foil the German offensive had he been given the men he demanded. But that presumes he would have used the troops wisely, a tenuous assumption. Despite clear warnings that the attack would come on the 5th Army front, Haig left that area the least well defended. Along the entire front the Germans had a six to four advantage, an adequate enough ratio for an effective defence by the British. But on the 5th Army sector the German advantage was five to one.[65] Haig nevertheless claimed on 21 March that 'The enemy's attack seems to be coming exactly against the points on our front which we expected and where we are prepared to meet him.'[66] So confident was he that the Germans would fail, he approved leave for 88,000 men on the eve of the offensive.[67]

But this was no time for recriminations. The army rightfully shot to the top of the Manpower Priority List. The Military Service (No. 2) Act, passed in April, raised the upper age limit to 50 years (55 in the case of doctors), provided closer regulation of appeals tribunals and empowered Geddes to make a clean cut of 23 years in all professions. The government backed away from conscripting ministers of religion, but did pass conscription for Ireland, a measure wisely never enforced. The Revised Schedule of Protected Occupations, passed in January but not implemented until April, released 9,000 recruits per week from munitions work, up from 3,700 in March.[68] But since casualties from 21 March to 9 June averaged over 31,500 per week, these measures did not even allow the army to hold its own.

The emergency did not quell old manpower rivalries. Organised labour, especially engineers, reacted badly to the new measures, as did the Munitions Ministry. The Admiralty baulked at suggestions that more marines should be released for service in France, despite the fact that by no stretch of the imagination were they actively

---

64 See D. Woodward, 'Did Lloyd George Starve the British Army of Men Prior to the German Offensive of March 1918?', *Historical Journal* 27 (1984).

65 G. DeGroot, *Douglas Haig, 1861–1928*, p. 375.

66 Haig to Lady Haig, 21 March 1918: Haig Papers, National Library of Scotland.

67 DeGroot, p. 374.

68 Grieves, p. 192. *History of the Ministry of Munitions*, VI, Part II, pp. 49–50.

employed. Geddes lacked the power to rule upon the use of labour in competing sectors; he could for the most part only exhort colleagues to cooperate. But amidst the incessant grumbling, significant sacrifices were made, as evidenced by a 50 per cent fall in aeroplane and tank production by July.

Starting in April, 100,000 American troops per month began arriving at the front. When the German offensive petered out at the beginning of the summer, the government quickly decided to return priority to munitions, ship and aeroplane production. There matters remained until the end of the war. Haig was particularly perturbed at the government's refusal to increase the troops available to him, despite the stunning success of his offensive which began in early August. But the government, with justification, no longer believed Haig, and was planning for 1919. The sudden victory of Allied forces in November rendered those plans nugatory. Had victory not intervened, 1919 would have been a very lean year for the British. The size of the army would have been drastically reduced and, due to the fall in production during the spring 1918 offensive, a new munitions crisis would have developed.

In the absence of consolidated direction of labour, the government limped from manpower crisis to manpower crisis during the war. Mistaken assumptions about the public's tolerance for compulsion caused excessive caution, but in the main government action was determined by an obsessive desire to preserve the liberal status quo. The government refused to come to terms with total war. At no time did it exercise effective control over the civilian labour force, preferring voluntary appeals and benign exhortations to real management. Whilst it occasionally invoked the rhetoric of an industrial army, it fled in fear from the actuality. No concerted attempt was made until the last year of the war to coordinate manpower needs, which meant that inter-departmental rivalries plagued those given the poisoned chalice of manpower management. During the Second World War, similar manpower problems were avoided by the creation of the Ministry of Labour under the all-powerful Ernest Bevin. Lloyd George did establish such a Ministry, but mainly as a political gesture designed to win Labour Party support. The two Labour ministers, John Hodge and George Roberts, never remotely enjoyed the power assigned Bevin. The Ministry suffered from a lack of effective staff and from rivalries with other ministries and departments, especially the Ministry of National Service. There was no justifiable reason for two separate ministries. 'You are not adding to the efficiency of your organization of the state', MacDonald warned Lloyd George. 'You are simply presenting new points of friction, misunderstanding and trouble.' These rivalries were in part a concerted attempt to limit the Ministry's power, as Conservatives were wary of yielding so much influence to Labour members.[69] In the end Britain found just enough men to squeak through to victory. The manpower problem is perhaps the best example of the British capacity to muddle through. Whether that is a trait worthy of pride or derision remains open to argument.

PAYING FOR THE WAR

Wars cost money as well as lives. Given the emergency, financial questions seem unimportant during a war, but become crucial after it, when future generations bear the budgetary burden. As in other areas of government, measures for financing the British effort were shaped by the prevalent desire to limit the war's impact. Investments in War Savings Certificates and Bonds continued with impressive constancy throughout the war, perhaps because patriotism of this sort was rewarded with interest. From October 1917 to September 1918, war bonds were still bringing in £1,000 million. Sale of war bonds was periodically encouraged through special appeals like Tank Week, War Weapons Week and a Feed the Guns Campaign. War bonds provided protection from wartime inflation and some concessions were given in regard to the payment of death duty after the war. Many workers, particularly those who worked overtime in munitions factories, accumulated considerable savings for the first time in their lives by purchasing bonds.[70]

Because manpower and production policies were chaotic, so too was budgetary policy. Taxation was introduced with the subtlety of a bludgeon. Sudden and drastic increases imposed on a population already wearied by war and struggling to make ends meet caused considerable antagonism. Three War Budgets raised income tax by nearly 150 per cent during the first year of the war. By war's end the standard rate stood at 6s, an eight-fold increase over August 1914. The tax threshold was also lowered which, combined with the fact that incomes rose, meant an extra six million people paid income tax. Aside from the need to raise revenue, lowering the threshold had the broad aim of widening political responsibility, a sentiment

69 R. Lowe, 'The Ministry of Labour, 1916–19: a Still, Small Voice?', in Burk, ed., pp. 111–19.

70 Milward, p. 28.

actually shared by organised labour. Herbert Smith of the Miners' Federation thought it would result in 'more active workers' who would 'know the[ir] position better'.[71] By the end of the war the Treasury was collecting about £8 million per annum from wage earners, or about 4 per cent of the total income tax revenue.[72] But, at the same time, taxation exacerbated existing class antagonisms as the workers, by nature convinced that their world was not fair, were certain that their tax burden was iniquitous. Measures which previously might not have aroused the attention of the average person suddenly became provocative because they affected his wallet. Refusal to pay tax became a new method of working class protest, as was demonstrated in South Wales in mid-1917. But most workers probably agreed with a Scottish miner who, though objecting to the injustice of income tax, was nevertheless prepared to pay it 'when the very existence of the country is at stake'.[73] Few workers realised that supposedly ineffectual excess profits duties raised £200–300 million per year, a quarter of wartime revenue,[74] and that, even though the poorer classes paid tax for the first time, taxation of incomes became more progressive during the war. (Those earning £200 to £1,000 per year gained most from this change.[75])

The average worker paid a great deal more in indirect than in direct taxes. The beauty of this form of taxation was its unobtrusiveness; the steelmaker Sir Hugh Bell argued that 'a tax on commodities is levied without the contributors being aware of its existence and so is levied without much grumbling . . . it is possible in this way to get something towards the maintenance of the state out of the poor and indeed the poorest classes'.[76] During the war, duties, imposts and licences were introduced or increased on beer, spirits, tobacco, matches, admission tickets, sugar, cocoa, coffee, automobiles, motorcycles and cheques. These taxes occasionally reduced consumption, much to the dismay of producers. Brewers complained that output fell by up to 40 per cent due to beer taxes. There was also a surge in home brewing.[77] 'Don't stop smoking because tax on tobacco has increased', a desperate advertisement for Murray's Mellow Mixture

71 R. C. Whiting, 'Taxation and the Working Class, 1915–24', *Historical Journal* 33 (1990), p. 896

72 Ibid., p. 897.

73 Ibid., p. 902.

74 Ibid., pp. 911, 914.

75 Milward, p. 38.

76 Whiting, 'Taxation', p. 908.

77 *The Times*, 6 February 1915.

urged. 'It is your duty to the State to keep on smoking. The Chancellor increased the duty on tobacco to give smokers an opportunity of contributing towards the successful issue of the war.'[78]

Wartime budgetary policy was by necessity reactive: the government decided what it wanted to do and then somehow found the money. The need for victory outweighed fiscal prudence. By 1917, the war was costing £7 million per day. In 1918, costs exceeded £2,500 million, with tax revenues only £900 million.[79] In addition, from mid-1916 Britain financed French overseas purchases and supported the franc against the dollar. Financial support for allies by April 1917 totalled £950 million, around £400 million of it going down the Russian sinkhole. Britain's steadily increasing deficit was paid for by borrowing abroad, through war bonds, or through the sale of overseas assets. The war resulted in the loss of 25 per cent of Britain's real wealth, most of it going to the United States. Some 40 per cent of all British purchases relating to the war were made in North America.[80] Taking into account all these debts, at war's end, Britain owed the US about £1,000 million.[81]

It is easy to be critical of the government's management of the war. There was a great deal of chaos, many avoidable emergencies and some injustice caused by a reluctance to intervene. But no master plan nor great body of experience existed to guide politicians, who were pioneers in the realm of wartime state intervention. If the British record in the Second World War seems more impressive, it is because later generations drew upon the experiences of 1914–1918. Nevertheless, one cannot ignore the sometimes obsessive adherence to outdated values. Change was imposed with great reluctance. Because of the decentralised nature of government, departments competed and did not benefit from each other's experience. Inconsistencies abounded. Voluntarism, for instance, remained a viable alternative in some areas as late as 1918, while its utility elsewhere did not survive past 1915. Asquith was inclined to wait until the last minute before exercising government power, but so too did Lloyd George. He was not the radical dynamo which many have made him. The expansion of the state during the war resembled not a deluge but a slow mountain stream which trickled past boulders of intransigence, its progress slowed by whirlpools of tradition.

78 *The Scotsman*, 13 October 1915.
79 R. Pearce, *Britain: Industrial Relations and the Economy 1900–39*, pp. 35–6.
80 K. Burk, 'The Treasury: From Impotence to Power', in Burk, ed., p. 91.
81 Milward, p. 46.

6 WORKING FOR THE WAR

It is easy to imagine a socialist revolution after six pints at the local. Beer fuels romantic ramblings, and there is great romance in the workers' struggle. The Great War provides a rich seam for bar-room colloquies: cruel betrayals, near victories and martyrdom aplenty. The habit is perfectly harmless, if a shade self-indulgent, at the pub. It is more dangerous when it creeps into serious history. 'During the last weeks of January 1918 it was touch and go whether or not the munitions workers would erupt into political strike, demanding immediate peace negotiations on the Bolshevik terms of no annexations, no indemnities',[1] fantasises James Hinton. Some historians too often allow what they wish had happened to affect their analysis of what did happen. The workers made significant gains during the war: both the trade unions and the Labour Party were stronger in 1918 than they had been in 1914. But these gains were invariably used for pragmatic purposes. The workers wanted better pay and conditions, more secure jobs and steady rents. The unions and the Labour Party wanted a larger part within the political system, not the destruction of that system. Far from bringing Britain close to revolution, the Great War confirmed the unrevolutionary character of the British worker.

By cooperating with the war effort, workers accumulated power which permanently altered their relationship with employers and the government. Three factors worked to their favour. Firstly, the war rendered certain key industries essential to the nation's survival. Secondly, manpower shortages made industrial harmony essential. Thirdly, workers were given the opportunity to demonstrate their patriotism and dependability, unknown quantities before the war. Occasionally shabby treatment did not divert them from the overriding need to win the war. Thus, if industrial harmony was the norm, they deserve the credit. It was precisely because the workers did not

---

1 J. Hinton, *Labour and Socialism*, p. 107. See also idem, *The First Shop Stewards' Movement*, p. 14.

attempt to exploit the nation's predicament for radical purposes that they made modest gains.

COOPERATION AND CONFLICT

It is perhaps understandable that the workers' loyalty was doubted in some quarters. The period since 1910 had witnessed considerable industrial turmoil. But incessant strikes tended to obscure the fact that the trade union movement, despite containing left wing elements, was predominantly reformist and pragmatic. Those characteristics explain its willingness to cooperate with the war effort – first demonstrated by the Trades Union Congress's (TUC's) declaration of an industrial truce shortly after the outbreak of war. Thus, the trade unions immediately surrendered their most effective weapon – the strike – without extracting anything significant in return. The only conceivable explanation for this cooperation is simple patriotism, strengthened by a conviction that a thankful government would reward the workers when peace returned.

The effects of this cooperative mood were immediately evident. At the beginning of August 1914, around 100 strikes were in progress; by month's end just 20. During the second quarter of 1914, 250,000 workers were on strike and 5,000,000 working days were lost. The fourth quarter of 1914 saw just 21,000 strikers and 160,000 days lost.[2] Granted, the first few months of the war were exceptionally harmonious; unions even acted as unofficial recruiting agencies. But even in 1918, the worst year for industrial action, the number of days lost was 5,900,000, which compares favourably with 9,800,000 in 1913, the same in 1914, and 40,900,000 in 1912.[3] Historians too often focus upon the titanic wartime struggles over dilution and manpower controls, which often had political overtones. While they were definitely dramatic, the vast majority of strikes arose over pay and working conditions and were settled relatively easily.[4] During the war over 8,000 awards made by arbitration tribunals were accepted by the workers concerned without further protest.[5]

In November the Crayford Agreement between the Engineering Employers' Federation and the Amalgamated Society of Engineers

2 G. Hardach, *The First World War 1914–1918*, p. 204.

3 C. Cook and J. Stevenson, *The Longman Handbook of Modern British History 1714–1980*, p. 153.

4 N. Whiteside, 'The British Population at War', in J. Turner, ed., *Britain and the First World War*, p. 95.

5 E. L. Woodward, *Great Britain and the War of 1914–1918*, p. 477.

(ASE) established that women could be employed as substitutes for men on machine work previously performed by unskilled or semi-skilled men, as long as the machine was serviced by a skilled mechanic. The Shells and Fuses Agreement, signed in early March 1915 between the engineering unions and the Employers' Federation, continued this trend. The unions accepted dilution (the use of unskilled or semi-skilled workers in jobs hitherto reserved for skilled men), thus surrendering at a stroke the cherished protection gained after decades of struggle. All they received in return were vague promises that skilled workers who remained would not be materially affected; that semi-skilled and unskilled labour would be the first to go when the war ended; that the unions would be consulted in the implementation of dilution; and that old labour practices would be restored when peace came.

Dilution was contentious because it undermined the skill differentials upon which the workers' security was based. These prevented an employer from hiring less skilled workers prepared to accept lower wages. Sidney Webb described how the rules set forth

> what machines should be used for what particular jobs; how the machines should be placed in relation to each other, and the speed at which they should be worked; whether an operative should complete a whole job, or attend only to one machine, or form part of a team of specialised operatives each doing a different process; what wages, if any, should be paid in the intervals between jobs, or whilst waiting for material.[6]

The war gave employers the opportunity to cast aside these barriers and introduce modern production processes. The dilutees were often women – doubly dangerous because they accepted lower wages and were not generally unionised. But, in general, male dilutees aroused much more anger because they constituted a permanent threat to craft privilege, whereas women were considered an aberration confined to the war.[7]

Behind the willingness of trade union leaders to cooperate lay an assumption that the war would be short. Sacrifices, it was thought, would be tolerable because they would be temporary and because enormous rewards would follow. But, on the shop floor, workers bore the costs of cooperation: the erosion of their status and the surrender of their only weapon, the strike. Wage claims due to be pressed in August 1914 were postponed in the interest of industrial

6 S. Webb, *The Restoration of Trade Union Conditions*, pp. 10–11.
7 B. Waites, *A Class Society àt War*, p. 196.

harmony. As a result, by the beginning of 1915, workers were paying dearly for their patriotism. Food prices were 20 per cent higher and general consumer prices 10–15 per cent higher than six months before.[8] A wage rise was warranted, yet difficult to secure because the industrial truce prevented meaningful protest and employers were hardly compassionate.

The situation was most volatile in Glasgow, for a number of reasons. Firstly, a concentration of war-related industries rendered the area extraordinarily important to the war effort. Secondly, the expansion of the munitions and shipbuilding industries led to a massive migration of workers into the Clyde area, aggravating an overstretched housing market. Vacancy of homes was less than 1 per cent in most areas, a figure considerably below the percentage of dwellings deemed technically uninhabitable. Population density was the highest in Britain. Exploitative landlords pulled all too frequently on the ratchet of rent increases. Discontent rose among workers; in February 1915 the newly formed Glasgow Labour Party Housing Committee began to organise disgruntled tenants.[9] A third factor was the ill-feeling dilution inspired among fiercely independent workers. Glasgow engineers were generally more confrontational than those elsewhere.

The first unrest on the Clyde (and the first serious strike of the war) occurred in February 1915; 5,000 engineers at Weir's of Cathcart downed tools when American workers were hired at higher rates of pay. The strike was only partially successful, but more important than its results was the fact that it was initiated by shop stewards without the support of union leaders still wedded to the industrial truce. The rise of shop stewards signalled the shift in union organisation from a craft to a workshop basis. It was, according to G. D. H. Cole, 'a spontaneous growth, the outcome of circumstances common to many different areas rather than the creation of any mind or group which made itself the master of circumstances'.[10] The power of shop stewards was derived from the alienation of rank and file workers toward official union leaders, combined with the involvement of shop stewards in crucial issues like the setting of piece rates, the introduction of new production processes and, especially, the implementation of dilution. The bulk of shop stewards have too often been judged by their militant Clyde colleagues who

8 Hardach, p. 205.
9 I. McLean, *The Legend of Red Clydeside*, pp. 18–20.
10 G. D. H. Cole, *Workshop Organization*, p. xi.

used their power for socialist ends. Yet the vast majority were moderate, unrevolutionary individuals who provided valuable leadership during the unsettling period of transition to new industrial practices.

After the return to work, militant shop stewards formed the Clyde Workers Committee. The CWC's alienation from the official unions became its rallying cry. 'We will support the officials just so long as they rightly represent the workers, but we will act independently immediately they misrepresent them', a pamphlet pledged. 'We . . . represent the true feelings of the workers.'[11] But this was a classic case of militant desperadoes out of touch with their supposed followers. The workers did not agree that the war was a capitalist intrigue; nor did they sympathise with CWC aims to 'maintain the class struggle until the overthrow of the wages system, the freedom of the workers, and the establishment of industrial democracy have been obtained'.[12] Yet, for the moment, an unholy alliance prevailed: 'socialists intent on pursuing the class war to end all privilege allied themselves with members anxious to preserve their ancient privileges against the inroads of machines, piecework and unskilled workers'.[13] The government's big mistake was to assume that leaders and followers espoused the same political agenda.

Hard on the heels of the Clydeside unrest came a further concession by trade unions, namely the Treasury Agreement of March 1915. The unions accepted the introduction of dilution, the suspension of restrictive practices and the enforcement of compulsory arbitration. In return, the government made some hardly burdensome concessions: dilution would pertain only to war work, skilled wages would be maintained even if the work in question was no longer performed by a skilled worker, profits in war industries would be restricted, and peace would bring a restoration of pre-war labour practices.

The agreement was negotiated in the boardroom of the Treasury, where stood a gilt throne once occupied by Queen Anne. Lloyd George was struck by the sight of

> those stalwart artisans leaning against and sitting on the steps of the throne of the dead queen, and on equal terms negotiating conditions

---

11 Hinton, *Labour and Socialism*, p. 106.

12 R. K. Middlemas, *The Clydesiders*, p. 61.

13 H. Clegg, A. Fox and A. F. Thompson, *A History of British Trade Unions Since 1889*, I, p. 297.

with the Government of the day upon a question vitally affecting the conduct of a great war. Queen Anne was indeed dead.[14]

Looking from a much longer perspective, one is impressed not by change but by continuity. The agreement was hardly a radical departure in labour relations, given that the important sacrifices were made by the side accustomed to making them, namely the workers. But one should resist being too scathing. As Henry Phelps Brown has noted, the government did not call employers to the conference, nor warn them of what was likely to transpire; 'it recognized that the power lay with the unions, and dealt with them realistically as "high contracting parties" '.[15]

The Treasury Agreement was a treaty between the unions and the government. It was not law. This deficiency was highlighted by continuing unrest on the Clyde, which the government lacked the legal muscle to control. The passage of the Munitions of War Act in July corrected this problem. Historians disagree about the intent behind the Munitions Act. Hinton believes that it was part of an offensive against the shop stewards movement and 'the nearest approximation that could be devised in the absence of military conscription to the ideal of compulsory national service'.[16] Roger Davidson sees no such sinister intent, arguing that the Act was 'merely a desperate expedient to facilitate labour supply'.[17] Both exaggerate, and both are essentially right. The Act was a response to the manpower shortage, but it was also an attempt to control and discipline labour at a time when scarcity rendered the workers extraordinarily powerful.[18]

For the workers, the most significant provision of the Act was the hated 'leaving certificate' which required a worker to obtain permission from his employer before moving to another job. Failure to comply meant he had to wait at least six weeks before taking up a new job, something few could afford. He might appeal to a Munitions Tribunal, but better pay or conditions were not considered acceptable grounds for changing jobs. This meant that yet another power, the ability to barter labour in a free market, had been surrendered without any significant protest by the official unions. The Act

14 D. Lloyd George, *War Memoirs*, I, p. 177.

15 H. Phelps Brown, *The Origins of Trade Union Power*, p. 79.

16 Hinton, *The First Shop Stewards' Movement*, p. 33.

17 R. Davidson, 'The Myth of the "Servile State" ', *Bulletin of the Society for the Study of Labour History* 29 (1974), p. 65.

18 See G. R. Rubin, *War, Law and Labour*, pp. 7–39.

was a red rag to the CWC bull; David Kirkwood, an activist, argued that it had 'the taint of slavery about it'.[19]

Much had been surrendered, but the workers still possessed the power of their numbers. If thousands of strikers decided to ignore compulsory arbitration, the government could not arrest, prosecute and imprison them since it was desperately addicted to what they supplied. This was demonstrated on 15 July 1915 when 200,000 South Wales miners downed tools in protest over a national pay settlement. The miners' union had not signed the Treasury Agreement and did not feel bound by its terms. Lloyd George confronted the miners head on by declaring the South Wales coalfield a controlled establishment. But the government's legal adviser warned:

> It is of course impossible to summon and try 200,000 men, and only a few can at first be dealt with and the length of time before there can be any real enforcement of the sentence will, I fear, only lead the men generally to regard the Act as ineffective.[20]

Meanwhile Robert Smillie, the miners' leader, threatened a nation-wide strike if South Wales workers were arrested. The government lacked the power to arrest the leaders of a strike, only those who actually downed tools. (This deficiency would soon be corrected.) Recognising a lost cause, Lloyd George promptly conceded the strikers' main demands.

The official historian of wartime labour administration remarked that the South Wales strike 'demonstrated that if a sufficiently large body of men were determined to break the law, they could do so with impunity, as long as public opinion was not strongly against them'.[21] This statement reveals two important limiting factors which acted in the government's favour. Firstly, a strike had to be sufficiently large to prevent effective action against it; secondly, it had to have popular support. If a strike was small or if it lacked local support, the government could apply the law. Fortunately for the government, most strikes were opposed because they violated the populist moral code. It was this code, not the ban, which limited the incidence of strikes. But as the South Wales strike demonstrated, workers could be pushed only so far. A government inquiry concluded that 'the men were driven to strike by the belief... that the owners were "exploiting" the patriotism of the miners, believing it would inevi-

19 Middlemas, p. 63.
20 McLean, p. 30.
21 H. Wolfe, *Labour Supply and Regulation*, p. 127.

tably prevent them from pressing home their claims by actually striking'.[22]

South Wales set a pattern for the settlement of wage disputes in key industries during the war; the government realised that stubborn confrontation was counter-productive. But it grew worried when wage claims seemed part of a wider political agenda, such as in Glasgow where agitation over high rents and the struggle against dilution combined to produce a volatile atmosphere. By November 1915, around 20,000 tenants were participating in a rent strike, mostly in areas housing shipyard workers. When eighteen of them were served summons for non-payment of rent, five shipyards went on strike. On Lloyd George's instigation, the government promptly pushed through a Rent Restrictions Bill which, though it did not completely solve the problem of rising rents, nevertheless represented an important victory for people's politics in Glasgow. But it is significant that Clydeside engineers did not offer their support to the rent strike; theirs was an altogether different argument over dilution.

The government did not realise that it was faced with two distinctly different disputes, an understandable mistake given that they occurred at roughly the same time in the same area. CWC activists exacerbated the confusion by describing their struggle against dilution in Marxist terms more suitable to the rent strike. As a result, when Clydeside engineers grew increasingly militant, the government overreacted to what seemed a burgeoning workers' revolution. Lloyd George rushed to Glasgow on Christmas Day, where he was shouted down by 3,000 angry shop stewards in no mood for patriotic platitudes. The ILP journal *Forward* reported: 'Last Tuesday Mr. Lloyd George, the best paid munitions worker in Britain, came to Glasgow in search of adventure. He got it.' In punishment for its temerity, *Forward* was suppressed, action which Lloyd George felt fully justified under the circumstances. 'D. says the men up there are ripe for revolution', Frances Stevenson, his secretary and mistress, recorded in her diary. '[He] is convinced there is German money up there.'[23]

The CWC demanded what it called co-determination – joint consultation between employers and workers on all production matters. This was not a long way from industrial unionism, under which workers would control the factories. The government was prepared to concede some control over the implementation of dilution, but

---

22 B. Waites, 'The Government of the Home Front and the "Moral Economy" of the Working Class', in P. Liddle, ed., *Home Fires and Foreign Fields*, p. 180.

23 A. J. P. Taylor, ed., *Lloyd George: A Diary by Frances Stevenson*, p. 87.

stopped well short of co-determination. On this issue, the bulk of the Clyde workers were closer to the government than to their shop stewards. Just as the workers had, in early 1915, felt misunderstood by their official unions, alienation which had inspired the formation of the CWC, so now they felt misunderstood by the CWC, whose political agenda was unappealing.

Lloyd George's initial overreaction to the engineers' dispute contrasts markedly with the government's deft handling of it from January to March 1916. Once it realised that the CWC was merely a militant faction, it concentrated on reassuring skilled workers that their jobs were secure and that their power would be restored after the war. That was the carrot. The stick came in the form of a threat to conscript militants. At the same time, tough action was directed against CWC leaders. Literature was suppressed and agitators, charged with sedition, were imprisoned or deported to Edinburgh (harsh punishment for a Glaswegian). This effectively isolated the CWC; it could not mobilise sufficient supporters to protest this treatment. The big difference between the Welsh dispute and the Scottish was that the Welsh strikers were miners, salt of the earth, while in Glasgow the militants were elite engineers for whom the rest of the working class had little sympathy. Socialist romantics have made the CWC rebels into martyrs, but they do not wear this accolade well. This was not a case of workers cruelly crushed, but of a rank and file wisely rejecting misguided leaders.

The Military Service Act which went into effect in March 1916 caused new tensions between workers and government. The workers feared that next would come full industrial conscription. The CWC, for instance, argued that the Act had not been dictated by military necessity, but by the need for 'the military control of industry and consequently the abolition of the functions of our trade unions'.[24] Conscription, many warned, would be used to curb strike activity. But more immediate was the threat posed to men of military age who had so far resisted every encouragement to volunteer and had satisfied their consciences by performing work of national importance. Huge losses on the Somme from July to November 1916, together with improved munitions production (a result of greater efficiency and the flood of female labour), made it increasingly difficult for skilled workers to prove their indispensability. A war of attrition ensued between the government and the unions over the granting of exemptions. Under the Trade Cards Agreement of 18

24 Hinton, *The First Shop Stewards' Movement*, p. 136.

November 1916, engineering unions were at first allowed to determine a worker's qualification for exemption. But this agreement was blamed for a deficit of 148,000 recruits in early 1917 and was rescinded on 3 April 1917.[25]

In 1917, industrial relations worsened, with 5.5 million days lost to strikes – the most since the beginning of the war. The introduction of a new bill extending dilution to private factories, followed by the decision to abolish Trade Cards, prompted the ASE to order a strike in May. It inspired a rather appropriate ditty:

> Don't take me in the Army, George,
> I'm in the ASE.
> Take all the bloody labourers,
> But for God's sake don't take me.
> You want me for a soldier?
> Well that can never be –
> A man of my ability,
> And in the ASE![26]

The ASE's stubborn elitism prevented its opposition to conscription from gaining wider support. As the *Trade Union Worker*, journal of the Workers' Union, commented:

> These people don't care how long the war goes on. They don't care who has got to go in the Army. They have no conscientious objection to manufacturing munitions of war for someone else to use. They are determined to push anyone into the Army; all may go, but not them. Nothing has been more discreditable to the labour movement than the attitude of this section of the alleged skilled men.[27]

Conscription made a mockery of trade union solidarity, since every worker wanted his comrade to be called before him. Witness the response by miners to a comb-out in 1917 which sought 21,000 new recruits from the pits; old-timers were quite ready to sacrifice new miners who had entered pits since the war, because they were not 'bona fide'.[28]

Despite worsening industrial relations, the patriotism of the workers and their devotion to the war effort remained predominant. Most strikes in 1917 and 1918 erupted over the same issues prevalent

---

25 K. Grieves, *The Politics of Manpower, 1914–18*, p. 127.

26 Hinton, *The First Shop Stewards' Movement*, p. 210. Hinton (pp. 196–210) provides a detailed and illuminating discussion of the May strikes.

27 G. Braybon, *Women Workers in the First World War*, p. 69.

28 T. Wilson, *The Myriad Faces of War*, p. 526.

in 1915 and 1916, namely wage claims inspired by steadily escalating prices. Since the cost of living was rising by about 27 per cent per year,[29] the strikes had good cause. The issue of pay became ever more contentious because increasing numbers of workers were subject to income tax. Workers were also troubled by food shortages, which affected them worst. They were convinced, with justification, that some citizens were growing very rich at their expense, by manipulating prices and supplies. Indeed, Lord Devonport, the ineffectual Food Controller, admitted to Lloyd George that 'profiteering is rife in every commodity – bread, meat, tea, butter, and the masses are being exploited right and left'.[30]

There was growing discontent with the government, but few overtly political strikes. Serious strikes in May 1917, involving 200,000 men, resulted in 1,500,000 working days lost.[31] But a Ministry of Labour report on strikes concluded that they had

> obviously . . . not arisen out of any desire to stop the war. . . . On the one hand [the men] were reluctant to hold up the war to the detriment of their relatives in the trenches. On the other hand, it seemed important to them, in their own interests, to keep their trade privileges intact. One has an impression, in short, of unrest paralysed by patriotism – or, it may be, of patriotism paralysed by unrest.[32]

When the Leeds Conference in early June 1917, organised by the ILP and the British Socialist Party, welcomed the Russian revolution and called for the formation of Workers' and Soldiers' Councils, the reaction by the rank and file was decidedly lukewarm. As an indicator of working class opinion, the Leeds Conference was much less significant than the chronic outbursts of anti-German feeling, the support for right wing groups like the British Workers League, and the harassment by workers of pacifist demonstrators.[33] Fifty workers downed tools at a bullet factory when a conscientious objector was promoted to foreman. 'The man was dismissed and the matter settled', commented a report to the government.[34]

In November 1917, 500,000 days were lost due to strikes, but only half that in December and January.[35] A slight calm was appar-

29 Hinton, *Labour and Socialism*, p. 98.

30 Waites, 'Government of the Home Front', p. 17.

31 C. Wrigley, *David Lloyd George and the British Labour Movement*, p. 191.

32 Waites, *A Class Society at War*, p. 208.

33 See Chapter 9 for a discussion of working class patriotism and anti-German riots, Chapter 7 for a discussion of pacifist groups and the reaction to them.

34 Wilson, p. 522.

35 Waites, *A Class Society at War*, p. 232.

ent. The government noticed that, whilst opposition to its new man-power proposals

> was in the first instance extreme, it is now reported that the Clyde Workers Committee have resolved not to strike in protest at the arrangements. As practically all the Workers' Committees look to the Clyde for a lead in the matter, it is clear that no concerted action to 'down tools' need now be expected.[36]

What had caused this calming of labour? During the worst period of 1917 the workers were perhaps annoyed and exhausted, but there was not deep-seated discontent with the war or with the political system – as was demonstrated by how easily anger was quelled. A rudimentary rationing system, tax concessions to married men and a 12.5 per cent pay rise for munitions workers was enough to bring peace to factories, despite the introduction of the unpopular Manpower Bill. A government report accurately described the workers' mood after three and a half years of war as 'loyal and temperamentally conservative'.[37] This was apparent at the Labour Party Conference in January, where pacifists, revolutionaries and ILP members were marginalised in the party's headlong race for mainstream respectability.

The alarmingly successful German spring offensive which began on 20 March inspired among workers a renewed commitment to the war effort and a temporary renunciation of industrial action. Only 15,000 days were lost in April 1918.[38] In other words, when it briefly appeared that the war might actually be lost, patriotism surged and self-interest was temporarily set aside. Even miners and engineers, who had vehemently resisted comb-outs, were unusually cooperative in helping the government find recruits among their numbers. Miners in South Wales often did not even wait for the call up before reporting to induction centres. Among those not called up, there was a corresponding determination to work harder. 'The response to the appeal to munitions workers to work over the Easter holiday was excellent, and indeed almost embarrassing', remarked the Minister of Munitions.[39] This peace lasted approximately four months, ending about the same time the German offensive stalled.

During the final months of war two new phenomena affected industrial relations. Firstly, news that the Hun was on the run

---

36 Wilson, pp. 654–5.
37 Ibid.
38 Waites, *A Class Society at War*, p. 232.
39 Wilson, p. 656.

inspired renewed enthusiasm for the war. Trade unions sent letters of congratulation to Haig and other commanders. This enthusiasm was easily translated into a rabid desire for a punitive peace. Coalition promises to 'Hang the Kaiser' harmonised well with the popular mood. The second phenomenon was organised labour's tendency to prepare for peace by seeking to consolidate power gained during the war. Both the mine and railway unions pressed for radical reorganisation of their industries, leading to nationalisation or at least a national wage system. These two phenomena encapsulate the predominant sentiments of workers throughout the war: steadfast (often jingoistic) support for the war existed alongside a desire to use the opportunities war provided to enhance labour's position within the political structure.

THE STATE AND THE WORKER

War brought profound changes in the relationship between government and the workers. Prior to 1914, the government legislated on labour issues and occasionally arbitrated disputes, but it was not, except in rare circumstances, an employer. During the war this changed radically. The creation of the Ministry of Munitions resulted in the government owning, by March 1918, over 250 factories, mines and quarries, while it exercised authority over a further 20,000 controlled establishments. As one Labour Party activist commented in 1915, the government's definition of munitions was a wide one:

> Tents are munitions; boots are munitions; biscuits and jam are munitions; sacks and ropes are munitions; drugs and bandages are munitions; socks and shirts and uniforms are munitions; all the miscellaneous lists of contracts which fill up three or four pages of the *Board of Trade Gazette*, all, all are munitions.

This meant that by July 1918 nearly 5,000,000 workers were engaged on government contracts, less than half in heavy industry.[40] R. H. Tawney estimated that 'not less than two-thirds of the gainfully employed workers in the country were by 1918 engaged in industries subject to one form or another of war-time regulation'.[41]

---

40 Rubin, p. 17.

41 R. H. Tawney, 'The Abolition of Economic Controls, 1918–1921', *The Economic History Review* 13 (1943), pp. 2–3. P. E. Dewey estimated that out of a male industrial work force of 5,165,000, 61 per cent, or 3,132,500, were engaged in war work in the summer of 1918. Dewey, 'The New Warfare and Economic Mobilization', in Turner, ed., p. 79.

The state's involvement in production brought increased attention to the welfare of the worker. Over 1,000 works canteens were established,[42] 1,000 welfare supervisors were appointed to look after women munitions workers, and another 300 supervised boys in the factories.[43] The connection between war and welfare is long-established, but it must be emphasised that these developments had more to do with efficiency than big-hearted paternalism. A Health of Munitions Workers Committee report stated in 1916 that

> The problem of scientific industrial management, dealing as it must with the human machine, is fundamentally a problem in industrial fatigue. . . . It is therefore the problem of scientific management . . . [to discover] what are the 'maximum efficiency rhythms' for the various faculties of the human machine.[44]

Britain could not afford a work force prone to illness, discontent or bad time-keeping since productivity would suffer. The problem was all the more acute because manpower shortages prevented managers from using threats of redundancy to discipline workers.

The Health of Munitions Workers Committee, created by Lloyd George in September 1915, worked under the proviso that 'without health there is no energy, without energy there is no output'. Its stated aims were:

> To consider and advise on questions of industrial fatigue, hours of labour, and other matters affecting the personal health and physical efficiency of workers in munitions factories and workshops.[45]

Lloyd George commented that it was a 'strange irony, but no small compensation, that the making of weapons of destruction should afford the occasion to humanise industry'.[46] Whether real humanity prevailed is a matter for dispute, but working conditions *did* improve, in the process appeasing workers who might otherwise have been tempted toward radical political solutions to industrial relations problems. It is no surprise that welfare supervisors often clashed with shop stewards over who represented the true interests of rank and file workers. At the same time, managers bitterly resented being told how to run their factories by government-appointed welfare

42 R. Pearce, *Britain: Industrial Relations and the Economy 1900–39*, p. 39.

43 H. Clegg, *The System of Industrial Relations in Britain*, p. 161.

44 J. Melling, ' "Non-Commissioned Officers": British Employers and their Supervisory Workers, 1880–1920', *Social History* 5 (1980), p. 212.

45 N. Whiteside, 'Industrial Welfare and Labour Regulation in Britain at the Time of the First World War', *International Review of Social History* 25 (1980), p. 313.

46 Lloyd George, I, p. 209.

inspectors. This made managers all the more eager for de-control after the war.

The changed role of the state in industrial relations had other important ramifications. Firstly, it meant an automatically adversarial relationship between the government and workers. It was no longer possible for the government to pretend to be an objective arbiter as it had before 1914. Secondly, because of the government's involvement, every labour dispute automatically took on political overtones, even if the workers did not so intend. Thirdly, during the war trade union representatives and ministers negotiated on a technically equal basis, significantly enhancing the former's status. The most profound manifestation of this new status was the inclusion of Labour members in the Coalition governments. The new ministers, among them Henderson, Barnes, Brace, Hodge and Roberts, had all been prominent trade unionists. Finally, war experience convinced workers that government action could alleviate many of the problems afflicting industry. Workers assumed that, once having taken an active role in the economy, the government would not retreat toward passivity. It was from here an easy jump to assume that the government's accumulated gratitude to the workers could be cashed in when peace came and used to buy favourable treatment. The government did not discourage these assumptions, naive though they were.

To what extent was the war responsible for this changed relationship between workers and government? Union membership doubled between 1906 and 1914, then doubled again by 1920, peaking at 8,348,000, or almost half of the working population.[47] Thus, the increasing popularity of the unions (and, by consequence, their growth in power) was a trend not confined to the war. It occurred simultaneously in countries like Sweden, Germany, the United States and France, which all had different war experiences. Phelps Brown argues that the trend can be explained by 'a certain level of industrialization, urbanization and education that promotes militant and massive trade unionism wherever it occurs. . . . [It is] part of the development of western capitalism'.[48] But this steady union growth was complemented by wartime labour scarcity which produced a brief but significant period of trade union power. In other words, massive union membership was not enough on its own to force the state to take notice. What was needed was a crisis when blackleg

47 Cook and Stevenson, p. 153.
48 Phelps Brown, p. 80.

labour was not readily available and when stoppages proved not just inconvenient but potentially disastrous.

And what of class consciousness? It is commonly assumed that the working class emerged from the war more united, which suggests that the war encouraged workers to interpret their predicament in class terms. As Bernard Waites argues, pride in being working class – in struggling through a precarious life whilst maintaining respectability – was strengthened by the war. This solidarity was not antagonistic to working class patriotism; in fact, since the demands of war gave the worker a new importance (whilst increasing the pressures upon him), class consciousness and patriotism fed on each other.[49] But wartime industrial relations could both unite and divide workers, as the issue of pay demonstrates.[50] Wage claims were often expressed in class terms, for instance in response to rising food prices or profiteering, thus encouraging the working class to think and act as a unit. In some cases this unity was imposed, as in the introduction of compulsory collective bargaining and national pay awards. Collective bargaining brought shop stewards into the negotiating process as never before, the effect being to democratise and empower the shop floor. The government found that it could never ignore shop stewards completely and deal only with national union representatives.

On the other hand, competition for wage rises often exacerbated old skill demarcations, causing intra-class rivalry. In September 1915, workers were promised that increased output would not prompt cuts in piecework rates. But automated machinery and other efficiency improvements increased output, benefiting the less skilled workers who often earned more on piece rates than skilled workers on time rates.[51] The Minister of Labour decided in October 1917 to compensate skilled workers with a 12.5 per cent war bonus, but unskilled and semi-skilled workers protested, objections which, given the prevalent ill temper, could not be ignored. The bonus was therefore extended to all munitions workers, much to the disdain of the skilled.[52] In other words, the fact that the unskilled did proportionately better during the war than the skilled may have resulted in working class homogenisation, but not necessarily in harmony.[53]

Localised arguments over pay or dilution often divided the

---

49 Waites, *A Class Society at War*, p. 60.
50 Ibid. p. 217.
51 Whiteside, 'The British Population at War', in Turner, ed., p. 93.
52 Woodward, pp. 475–7.
53 These issues are discussed in greater detail in Chapter 15.

working class, but antagonism over profiteering was universal. This antagonism probably did more to encourage the growth of class consciousness than specific industrial disputes did. Workers were aware that the sacrifices they had made, particularly dilution, when combined with the war's vast increase in demand, enabled employers to amass huge profits. It seemed only fair to restrict profits so that sacrifices would not be confined to one side. Though they won this concession, it was mainly a symbolic victory, since excess profits duties never really solved the problem of excess profits, though they did raise a great deal of revenue.[54] George Askwith, who understood industrial unrest as well as anyone, commented that

> A shipowner who stated that he made profits, was going to make profits, and had a right to make profits, did more harm than a great naval defeat would have done. . . . The profiteer's statement would rouse class against class, and only tend to disruption within the nation itself.[55]

A government report recognised that the profiteering issue had done 'a great deal . . . to destroy the spirit of unity which permeated the country in the early stages of the war'.[56]

Did the working class benefit from the war? On concrete issues of working conditions, income and job stability, one suspects that gains and losses cancelled each other out. Hinton argues that 'On the crudest measure of trade union effectiveness the leadership failed – for most of the war wage rates lagged far behind the rise in prices.'[57] But that is a simplistic judgement, since the leadership is not solely to blame for the failure to press wage claims more vigorously. Patriotism acted as an impediment to strike action, thus preventing the workers from bargaining for better conditions of service. Militant trade unionists remained optimistic that the workers would eventually wake up to their exploitation. 'Daily I see signs amongst the working class', the miners' leader, A. J. Cook, wrote in April 1916,

> of a mighty awakening. The cloroforming pill of patriotism is failing in its power to drug the mind and consciousness of the worker. He is beginning to shudder at his stupidity in allowing himself to become a party to such a catastrophe as we see today.[58]

54 See Chapter 5, pages 72–3.
55 Waites, 'Government of the Home Front', p. 181.
56 Wilson, p. 529.
57 Hinton, *Labour and Socialism*, p. 98.
58 Pearce, p. 38.

But the drug lasted the war. Workers often preferred to work in controlled establishments, for it gave them tangible confirmation of their essential role in the war effort (in turn making them less likely to strike). 'Even the running up of a Union Jack outside the factory was known to have a very salutary effect on morale', writes Waites.[59] The workers sacrificed much for the war effort, but did so willingly. Their cooperation was motivated by patriotism, morality and by a confidence that virtue would be rewarded. A naive sense of justice led to sacrifices made in vain.

Because the workers were prepared to make these sacrifices, industrial relations in Blighty remained impressively harmonious during the war. Little credit seems due the government. Some of its interventions in the labour relations arena were astonishingly clumsy. As was discussed in the last chapter, a more robust and confident Ministry of Labour could perhaps have alleviated manpower problems *and* the unrest they generated. An even bolder move would have been to introduce industrial conscription, but, as one government report reflected after the war, the 'traditional antagonism' to this idea prevented its adoption. Instead, 'A large measure of freedom was left to the worker and such a degree only of regulation was made as was necessarily required by the national interest.'[60] If this was freedom, it was a peculiar variety. One notes with interest that the Munitions of War Act was significantly more stringent than the Auxiliary Service Law passed by 'autocratic' Germany in December 1916.[61]

WORKING WOMEN

The war initially caused significant redundancies in industries dominated by women. Chief among these was the garment industry. The uncertainty of war caused a severe slump in the market for lace, fine needlework, dressmaking and millinery. Restrictions upon the fishing fleet caused redundancies among predominantly female gutters, and the sugar shortage had a similar effect upon the confectionery industry. According to one estimate, 44.4 per cent of all working women were unemployed, for varying periods, in September 1914.[62] As late as April 1915, 89,577 women and 20,815 girls were registered with

59 Waites, *A Class Society at War*, pp. 188–9.
60 Woodward, p. 483.
61 Hardach, p. 189.
62 Braybon, p. 44.

the labour exchanges.[63] In September 1914 *The Times* offered free advertisements to soldiers' and sailors' wives seeking positions in domestic service.[64] The establishment of the Educated Woman's War Emergency Training Fund indicates that hardship was not confined to the lowest classes; women working as governesses and journalists were, for instance, often made redundant.[65] The National Guild of Housecraft endeavoured to teach home-making skills to women from the 'luxury trades' (artists, actresses, musicians, clerks and secretaries) who had been made redundant, so that they might 'become good wives for the men who would return from the front'.[66] So great was the hardship that charities like the Queen Mary's Work For Women Fund were established to find employment for redundant females. Work created through the fund paid below the sweated rate: 'it was felt undesirable', the governing committee argued, 'to fix wages . . . so high as to attract from ordinary employment'.[67] Sylvia Pankhurst called the scheme 'Queen Mary's Sweat-shops' and railed against feminists and women trade unionists who supported it.[68] Yet the scheme did not lack for applicants.

When, in early 1915, Kitchener's call for recruits caused labour shortages, the industrial sector did not immediately look to women. Employers instead called upon the unemployed (an estimated 480,000 men lost jobs at the outbreak of war), the retired, juveniles still in school, or men in non-essential industries. The employment of women was also impeded by their inability to move around the country to take up employment. Activists like Christabel and Emmeline Pankhurst, Mrs Fawcett and Lady Londonderry drew attention to the untapped reservoir of female labour, but they were initially unenthusiastic about factory work for women, feeling instead that more suitable employment existed in clerical and secretarial posts vacated by male volunteers. It is here that the earliest and most significant advancement by women took place. In any case, for women to replace men in the factories first required unions to agree to dilution. Thus, the Shells and Fuses Agreement, the Treasury Agreement, the Munitions of War Act and, indeed, the Shell Scandal were the essential prerequisites to widespread female factory employment.

63 G. D. H. Cole, *Labour in War Time*, p. 229.
64 *The Times*, 18 September 1914.
65 M. Pugh, *Women and the Women's Movement in Britain, 1914–1959*, pp. 18–19.
66 *The Times*, 3 February 1915.
67 Cole, *Labour in War Time*, p. 234.
68 S. Pankhurst, *The Home Front*, p. 54.

It is often carelessly assumed that women did not work before the war. In fact, the female work force increased by approximately 25.5 per cent from 4,934,000 in July 1914 to 6,193,000 four years later. This is significant, but hardly a flood of female workers. Before the war, the largest sector of women's employment was domestic service, with 1,658,000 employed. It fell by 400,000 during the war, but remained top of the list. Textiles, the second most frequent employer, and notorious for its exploitation of women, slipped to third but was still more common in July 1918 than munitions, where, according to myth, women flocked. The greatest numerical increase occurred in banking, finance and commerce, which took on an extra 429,000 women. Across the economy, approximately 962,000 women worked in white collar or service employment during the war, while 697,000 worked in industry, farming or transport.[69] While the distribution was largely determined by demand, female preference did play a part. Of 25,000 women who registered at labour exchanges by March 1915, only 3,600 expressed a wish to be employed on armament work.[70] Thus, most women entered jobs which have since become synonymous with low status female employment: bank tellers, secretaries, low level clerks. They were also more likely to hold onto those jobs after the war than the traditionally male occupations in industry which supposedly provided greater status. 'The development seems likely to be to a great extent permanent', Cole correctly predicted in 1915, 'largely because it is doubtful whether the men will desire to return to their old jobs, but also because women's labour is cheaper.'[71] The fact that the Great War provided better opportunities for women to become secretaries is, one suspects, a bitter pill for present-day feminists to swallow, especially since secretarial posts were more highly prized than those on the factory floor. Contrary to expectation there was no marked increase in women hairdressers or waitresses, as popular prejudice still held that men performed these tasks better.[72]

The war did increase married women's employment significantly. Before the war, a working class woman stayed at a job until she found a man to marry and support her. Since almost all women took jobs out of necessity rather than for fulfilment, very few middle and

[69] Data in this paragraph is taken from Pugh, pp. 19–21, but extrapolations and conclusions are my own.

[70] *The Times*, 30 March 1915.

[71] Cole, *Labour in War Time*, p. 241.

[72] See *The Times*, 8 February, 17 March 1915.

upper class women worked. For a working class woman to continue in employment after marriage was, except in the cotton towns of Lancashire, highly unusual (even more unusual after having children), and in most cases only occurred when a husband was, through illness, redundancy or otherwise, unable to support his family. Only 10 per cent of married women worked outside the home.[73] This changed during the war when, because of propaganda or necessity, married women were tempted back into the work force. The vast majority of the extra 1.25 million women workers during the war were women who had worked before (prior to marriage) or working class girls who entered the work force earlier than normal. Thus, the expansion of female employment drew into the work force few women for whom employment was, or would be, a completely novel experience.

This contradicts the popular assumption that women from all classes were drawn together in the factories – the home front corollary to the myth of class harmony in the trenches. In fact, relatively few middle and upper class women took factory work; if they worked at all, they congregated in white collar and nursing professions. Nor were women from the upper classes always welcomed by male employers or workers since they demanded, and often received, better facilities and treatment. Joan Williams observed:

> I could quite understand the foremen preferring to have real working girls under them to the 'War Workers', who were apt to make much more fuss when displeased and complain to the higher authorities, without being able to be frightened by any threat of dismissal.[74]

Middle and upper class women made up about 9 per cent of munitions workers, being concentrated in skilled and supervisory positions. In other words, the rigid hierarchy of wider society was reproduced in the factory, with fillers at the lowest end of the social scale (their yellow skin a visible manifestation of their inferiority) and inspectors at the top. 'I did not like the look of my companions', Monica Cosens commented. 'They were rough, loud-voiced, and . . . ill-natured.' She found that when a middle class woman like her entered the workplace 'there is a defiance in the air. She is not gently treated.'[75] Perhaps no wonder, if the attitude of Naomi Loughnan was typical of her class:

73 Wilson, p. 716.

74 G. Braybon and P. Summerfield, *Out of the Cage: Women's Experiences in Two World Wars*, p. 76.

75 M. Cosens, *Lloyd George's Munitions Girls*, pp. 17, 108.

The ordinary factory hands ... lack interest in their work because of the undeveloped state of their imaginations. They handle cartridges and shells, and though their eyes may be swollen with weeping for sweethearts and brothers whose names are among the killed and wounded, yet they do not definitely connect the work they are doing with the trenches. One girl, with a face growing sadder and paler as the days went by because no news came from France of her 'boy' who was missing, when gently urged to work harder and not to sleep so often, answered with angry indignation: 'Why should I work any harder? My mother is satisfied with what I takes home on a Saturday.'[76]

After a two-hour shift assembling respirators, Cynthia Asquith concluded:

Any manual labour has great fascination to me and I simply loved it. It is such fun feeling a factory girl and it gave one some idea of how exciting it must be to do piecework for money. ... I must say I hadn't got to do a twelve-hour day – it is quite tiring.[77]

The war was neither long enough nor sufficiently disruptive of social patterns for middle class women to discover the great difference between working for a living and working (temporarily) out of a spirited desire to serve one's country.

When a woman took on factory work, direct substitution was less common than dilution. Substitution meant an unskilled or semi-skilled worker did a job previously performed by a skilled man. Dilution implied the reorganisation of the job, including the introduction of new machinery so that component tasks could be performed by unskilled workers. One industrial study revealed seven trades which women took up for the first time during the war, sixteen in which they had worked before but became more common, and 21 still barred to women. Shell-filling, a common source of employment for women during the war and one which inspired the image of a society in flux, was actually widely performed by women before the war, because it did not require much skill. Barbara Drake, researching the munitions industry for the Fabian Society in 1917, concluded that 'Not one in a thousand of the scores of women introduced into shell and fuse factories proved a claim to take the whole place of a fully skilled tradesman.'[78] According to another estimate, by the end of the war five-sixths of women in industry

76 Braybon, pp. 162–3.
77 S. Hynes, *A War Imagined*, p. 91.
78 B. Drake, *Women in the Engineering Trade*, p. 17.

were doing work which had previously been categorised women's work or which had been restructured to cater to women.[79]

These statistics are, of course, no indication of actual capabilities, but are instead a reflection of societal prejudice. In April 1915, a woman disguised as a man was discovered working in a Barrow shipyard. She explained that she needed money to support her relatives and, as a woman, access to good, well-paying jobs was blocked.[80] Unions, male workers and employers fought a fierce rearguard action against the introduction of women, for the very reason that, given the chance, women could perform as well as men. G. D. H. Cole warned in 1915 that female workers would open up

> difficult problems for the male wage-earner, who may well feel that his job is taken, or his standard of life threatened, by the competition of female labour. He is apt to regard women much as the Australian regards the Chinaman, or as the American regards the East European immigrant, as interlopers, whose different standard of life renders them not only dangerous, but also unfair competitors in the labour market. And the history of women in industry gives some warrant to this attitude.[81]

Transport workers in Hull 'absolutely refused to work with women' and threatened to strike. They were not successful, but in Liverpool, male dockers prevented the employment of women for the entire war. Even the cotton unions, which had a long history of women members, resisted further female incursions in the mills. Male spinners feared that if females were employed 'We shall have the employers saying there is nothing in spinning if a girl can do it, and will pay accordingly.'[82] The worries were real because employers actually did resort to these arguments. Transport workers in Cardiff were especially resistant toward married women whose husbands were employed.[83]

Only when the government stepped in was this resistance broken. The number of women in controlled munitions establishments increased by 300 per cent up to October 1916, but by only 36 per cent in uncontrolled ones.[84] Given proper training, the right conditions and support, women could perform almost any job previously handled by men, except those requiring considerable strength. They

79 Pugh, p. 25.
80 *The Times*, 23 April 1915.
81 Cole, *Labour in War Time*, p. 228.
82 S. Boston, *Women Workers and the Trade Unions*, pp. 112–13, 117.
83 *The Times*, 26 April 1915.
84 Similar figures applied in the chemicals industry: see Pugh, p. 25.

performed better than men in processes requiring great dexterity or in repetition work where pre-war trade practices had placed strict limits on output. Dilution officers visited reluctant factory managers to educate them on the benefits of female employment. But employers who resisted the introduction of women followed a widely accepted logic. As one trade journal commented, 'The prospect to which a man looks forward is to earn enough money to keep a wife; the prospect to which a women looks forward is that *he* may succeed.'[85] The sentiment may seem perverse today, but at the time it was popular, among men *and* women. It therefore made little sense for employers to invest a great deal of time, effort and money into training women who after the war would be more interested in husbands and homes.

Male workers and their trade unions found themselves in a terrible quandary over the issue of women's pay. One woman worker 'sympathised with the way they were torn between not wanting the women to undercut them, and yet hating them to earn as much'.[86] In principle, unions opposed the introduction of women, but at the same time argued that if a woman took a man's job, she should be paid the same. They assumed that if equal pay were the rule, employers would prefer male workers. Some craft unions even campaigned for equal pay in order to block the introduction of women into their industry and to protect men's jobs at the end of the war.[87] Employers, on the other hand, had a ready arsenal of arguments (most of them spurious) to justify lower pay: women produced less, they required more supervision, they needed more costly facilities, etc. One railway employer actually argued that 'A woman ticket collector . . . can never be as successful as a man.'[88] Glasgow tramway supervisors argued that 'it was difficult to get women to realise the importance of time'.[89] Feminists were divided on this subject; some saw equal pay as an important symbol of equality, while others were more pragmatic, fearing that it would block the entrance of women into previously male preserves and prevent them proving their worth.

Lloyd George considered equal pay 'a social revolution which . . . it is undesirable to attempt during war time'.[90] In the government's

---

85 Braybon and Summerfield, p. 50.
86 Braybon, p. 79.
87 Boston, p. 112.
88 Ibid., p. 115.
89 *The Scotsman*, 24 September 1915.
90 H. L. Smith, 'The Issue of "Equal Pay for Equal Work" in Britain, 1914–19', *Societas* 8 (1978), p. 45.

list of priorities, fairness to women ranked well below satisfying
employers, pacifying male workers and maintaining production
levels. A cynical but effective compromise was found. Aware that
employers would be more inclined to take on women if they seemed
a bargain, Lloyd George decided that women should be paid the
same as men on piece rates, but not on time rates. This was not
necessarily unfair to women, since on work requiring dexterity, they
were often more productive than men, and could therefore earn more
on piece rates. But, realising this, employers tended to keep women
out of piecework. On time work they were paid between 50 and 66
per cent of the male rate.[91] They were also subjected to unfair
reductions in their pay (such as if air raids stopped production)
which did not apply to men, and which often reduced pay by as
much as 25 per cent.[92] Nevertheless, in the sorts of jobs women took
up, rates of pay were higher than in those they left. Thus, though
they remained discriminated against in relation to men, they still
made progress.

The introduction of women into factories focused attention on
working conditions. Facilities once suitable for men were considered
unsuitable for women. Washrooms, canteens and toilets had suddenly
to be provided. With purpose-built factories this was not a problem,
but at already established plants, managers were reluctant to provide
for workers who were by definition temporary. The welfare of
women workers was monitored by the Health of Munitions Workers
Committee, the Women's Employment Committee and the War Cabinet Committee on Women in Industry. But these bodies encountered
a serious dilemma: they needed to ensure that factories were safe
and workers healthy (so as to improve efficiency) without seeming
to promote the idea of female industrial labour as a permanent
feature. This dilemma was most acute when it came to crèche provision. One doctor advised the Ministry of Munitions that free
crèches would encourage mothers to take up factory work, yet no
responsible woman would put a child in a crèche. It followed that
since irresponsible women were by definition poor workers, providing crèches would attract the wrong sort of woman and thus reduce
productivity. Against this advice, the government decided that, since
mothers would flock to the factories whether crèches were provided
or not, in the interests of the children childcare should be available.
A compromise between pragmatism and propriety was reached when

91 Pugh, p. 28.
92 Boston, p. 110.

the Ministry decided to sponsor crèches, but only up to 50 per cent of the cost. Availability of places was limited.[93]

The various welfare committees often discovered unsuitable conditions which had existed for a long time, particularly in the textile industry. Though much progress was made, the government was fully aware that excessively high standards limited production. For instance, not a great deal was done to regulate long hours, for obvious reasons. There was, on the other hand, great concern about the poisonous effects of TNT. At Woolwich Arsenal, one study revealed that 37 per cent of woman shell-fillers suffered from abdominal pain, nausea and constipation, 25 per cent had skin problems, and 36 per cent suffered from depression and irritability. During the war there were 349 serious cases of TNT poisoning reported, with 109 deaths.[94] In August 1916, a Ministry of Munitions official warned:

> unless measures are taken to meet this difficulty, serious interference with output may arise as if the operatives become frightened at the number of diseases and deaths of their colleagues, greater difficulty than ever will be experienced in procuring labour.[95]

The government responded by providing sick pay of £1 per week, hospitalisation cover, and eventually a special diet allowance.

The Health of Munitions Workers Committee also recommended that factories should provide welfare supervisors. Class superiority was the essential prerequisite to this managerial function; middle class women, like male subalterns in the trenches, did not require experience (or much training) to supervise their working class charges. The role of supervisor provided many middle class women with the opportunity to pursue a professional career, one in which, as personnel officers, women continued to be prevalent after the war. It was the maternalist nature of the work which seemed to make women perfectly suited to it, but maternalism sometimes conflicted with managerial professionalism.[96] In other words, the interests of the employer and of the worker at times conflicted. Supervisors often interpreted 'welfare' as conditions calculated to make a woman work harder. They not only monitored the behaviour of women at work, but also investigated absenteeism, inspected housing and care of

93 J. Winter, *The Great War and the British People*, pp. 207–8.
94 Braybon and Summerfield, p. 85.
95 Whiteside, 'Industrial Welfare and Labour Regulation', p. 313.
96 See A. Woollacott, 'Maternalism, Professionalism and Industrial Welfare Supervisors in World War I Britain', *Women's History Review* 3 (1994), pp. 29–56.

children and provided education on health, diet and hygiene. Occasionally doubling as personnel officers, they sometimes exhibited a prejudice against hiring married women or those of 'unsuitable' character. Since the war took women away from their home communities and thus, it was thought, cut them off from appropriate moral guardianship, supervisors sought to protect feminine propriety.[97] They maintained constant vigilance against unwholesome entertainments: women workers were reprimanded for spending too much time on the street or for attending the cinema too often. But one positive aspect of the work was that supervisors guarded against sexual harassment on the shop floor. Dark factories provided many opportunities for unwelcome advances; according to Beatrice Webb, 'Foremen . . . have much power in their hands which is not always honourably used.'[98] Women were advised to go to the lavatory in pairs. Some supervisors were well-loved, but most were despised for their intrusiveness. At its 1918 conference the National Federation of Women Workers called for the abolition of welfare supervisors, on the grounds that they replaced organised labour relations with a system of paternalism which undermined trade unions.[99]

But unions were not exactly conspicuous in the attention they paid to the welfare of women workers, the exception being specifically female trade unions. Objections arose not only because women were seen as dangerous competition but also because the principle of female employment undermined a man's claim to be paid a wage sufficient to support his family. Furthermore, each woman was interpreted (wrongly in fact) as having enabled a man to be sent to the front. While the suspicion of women workers was mostly straightforward male chauvinism, it had an indirect justification. Unscrupulous employers *did* exploit women as cheap labour, using them to sidestep sacred union agreements. Thus, women were caught in the crossfire in the battle between capital and labour. Women members were also abhorred because unions, like workingmen's clubs and football teams, were male preserves. 'I have to bear with a woman for 12 hours a day and I will not bear with women for 24', one worker complained.[100] His was a common attitude which applied both to their presence on the shop floor and their membership in unions. Some unions, such as the National Union of Railwaymen,

97 M. McFeely, *Lady Inspectors*, p. 141.
98 Woollacott, 'Maternalism', p. 34.
99 Winter, pp. 207–8.
100 Braybon, p. 90.

which had not accepted women before the war, changed tack. The General Union of Municipal Workers was positively welcoming, accelerating a trend of expanding female membership begun before the war. By the end of the war, 383 unions had women members, another 36 were women-only.[101] But many unions, including the ASE, continued to ban women. Female membership did expand significantly during the war, from 437,000 members in 1914 to a peak of 1,342,000 in 1920.[102] But when peace came, only one out of every six women workers were members.[103] This indicates not only the unwelcoming attitude of the unions, but also that most women saw themselves as temporary employees.

Another persistent myth concerns the popularity of the Women's Land Army. In May 1915, Lord Selborne, the agriculture minister, called upon women to enrol in the Women's Land Service Corps, which became the WLA in January 1917. The image of rosy cheeked maidens in pretty bonnets looking after cows and sheep had immense propaganda value, but in fact the response by women was quite small, as was their contribution. Only 16,000 WLA members assisted with the 1918 harvest.[104] They provided, according to P. E. Dewey, only 8,000 man-units in the production process in 1918. In contrast, the contribution of village women rose steadily throughout the war, totalling 30,000 man-units by 1918.[105] Farming communities were extremely suspicious of female outsiders; rumours of rampant licentiousness abounded. And, no matter how hard they worked, WLA members invariably failed to convince farmers of their worthiness. Cognisant of the prejudice female outsiders would encounter, WLA organisers cautioned them as follows:

> You are doing a man's work and so you are dressed like a man; but remember that just because you wear a smock and breeches you should take care to behave like an English girl who expects chivalry and respect from every one she meets. Noisy or ugly behaviour brings discredit, not only upon yourself but upon the uniform, and the whole Women's Land Army. When people see you pass . . . show them that an English girl who is working for her Country on the land is the best sort of girl.[106]

101 Boston, p. 127.

102 Braybon and Summerfield, p. 73.

103 Pugh, p. 27.

104 C. Dakers, *The Countryside at War*, p. 150.

105 P. E. Dewey, 'Agricultural Labour Supply in England and Wales during the First World War', *Economic History Review* 28 (1975), p. 104. His figures refer to England and Wales only.

106 Dakers, p. 150.

The work was exhausting, dangerous and dirty, with long hours, poor accommodation, strict regimentation and low pay. Most working class women had sufficient sense to realise that money could be made more easily in the cities. Lured by pastoral fantasies, a disproportionate number of middle class women did join the WLA, often giving up well-paying jobs to do so.

British society had an uneasy time coming to terms with changing trends in women's employment. Ray Strachey noted how the press 'began to say that "the nation is grateful to the women" – not realising even yet that the women WERE the nation just as much as the men were'.[107] Government propaganda and the newspapers praised women workers but always stressed that wartime changes were strictly temporary. That eager provider of poetic propaganda, Jessie Pope, conveyed both messages in her 'War Girls':

> There's the girl who clips your ticket for the train,
>   And the girl who speeds the lift from floor to floor,
> There's the girl who does a milk-round in the rain,
>   And the girl who call for orders at your door.
>   Strong, sensible and fit,
>   They're out to show their grit,
>   And tackle jobs with energy and knack.
>   No longer caged and penned up,
>   They're going to keep their end up
> Till the khaki soldier boys come marching back.[108]

'Even if many of the posts formerly held by men which women are now filling are for the duration of the war only, and will have to be yielded up should their original holder return safe and sound', *The Times* wrote optimistically in February 1915, 'they will have tested women's capacity in a way that may have a lasting effect on women's work in the future.'[109]

The increased visibility of women in heretofore unwonted circumstances tested societal tolerance. Since these women were predominantly working class, gender and class prejudices fused. Polite society worried that working class women with surplus income would inevitably get up to mischief. The young, single munitionette, strutting the streets in fancy clothes bought from inflated wages, was

107 R. Strachey, *The Cause*, p. 344.
108 J. Pope, 'War Girls', in C. Reilly, ed., *Scars Upon My Heart*, p. 90.
109 *The Times*, 8 February 1915.

a popular wartime stereotype. Madeline Bedford managed to be both condescending and condemning in 'Munition Wages':

> Earning high wages? Yus,
>   Five quid a week.
> A woman, too, mind you,
>   I calls it dim sweet.
>
> Ye'are asking some questions –
>   But bless yer, here goes:
> I spends the whole racket
>   On good times and clothes.[110]

Female factory workers who appeared ostentatious in their dress or leisure pursuits were frequently suspected of earning money on the 'extra shift' – through prostitution. In fact, very few women earned more than they needed to support themselves.

As one enlightened factory inspector commented in 1916, even the praise of women workers revealed prejudices:

> It is permissible to wonder whether some of the surprise and admiration freely expressed in many quarters over new proofs of women's physical capacity and endurance, is not in part attributable to lack of knowledge or appreciation of the very heavy and strenuous nature of much of normal pre-war work for women, domestic and industrial.[111]

Praise usually went hand in hand with references to femininity, suggesting a desperate hope that women would not be irrevocably hardened by their work. 'Overalled, leather-aproned, capped and goggled – displaying nevertheless woman's genius for making herself attractive in whatsoever working guise'[112] was how the *Daily Mail* referred to one group of factory workers. A famous wartime painting depicted a munitionette in pretty smock and bonnet cradling a shell as she would a baby.

Just as women's war work was presumed to be for the duration only, so too was the praise and gratitude they earned. Any woman who tried to stay in 'man's work' a day past the Armistice was instantly transformed from war hero to selfish bitch.[113] What few in authority understood was that most women, mothers especially, went into the factories not in search of fulfilment but out of necessity. A

---

110 M. I. Bedford, 'Munition Wages', in Reilly, ed., p. 7.
111 Braybon and Summerfield, p. 47.
112 *Daily Mail*, 30 March 1916.
113 This is discussed in detail in Chapters 14 and 16.

study of pre-war female employment compiled by the Fabian Women's Society found that 51 per cent of women workers were supporting someone other than themselves and 80 per cent were entirely self-supporting, leaving a small percentage depending on others for partial support. 'This would seem to prove', concluded *The Times*, 'that in peacetime at least women do not work unless they have to, and that the pocket-money worker ... is largely a myth.'[114] If women were not to work in industry after the war, they would have to work somewhere else. The postwar problem of the 'surplus woman' was recognised as early as February 1915, with possible solutions like emigration to Australia and more extensive training in domestic service discussed.[115] When myths are stripped away, this period no longer seems a golden age of women's emancipation. Women were seen primarily as cheap, easily exploitable labour, useful in a crisis or to break the back of organised labour, but possessing very little value in their own right. On the other hand, perhaps this was the road they had to travel on the arduous journey toward equality. It does them no service to pretend that the road was smooth or that progress was swift.

114 *The Times*, 8 February 1915.
115 Ibid., 17 February 1915.

7 ALIENS, OUTLAWS AND DISSENTERS

THE CRIMINAL ELEMENT

The cataclysm of war made the body politic conventional, loyal and harmonious. Deep patriotism and relative economic stability acted like oil on formerly troubled waters. As a result, the crime rate plummeted. It fell in part because the numbers in poverty declined and because of restrictions upon the sale of alcohol. Furthermore, many of those on the fringes of society, who could not hold down regular jobs and were previously drawn to petty crime, wound up in the military, where their lawless potential was curbed. In February 1915, Montague Sharpe told the Grand Jury that in his opinion crime had dropped by 90 per cent.[1] The one significant exception to this peaceable tendency, anti-German riots, were inspired by the strident nationalism war encouraged. The decline in the crime rate was perhaps fortunate, given that in the first four months of the war, 1,700 Metropolitan Police volunteered for the military and a further 1,000 were deployed around the country to guard military installations.[2]

In December 1914, Mr Robert Wallace, KC, commented upon the markedly decreased workload in the courts. 'The criminal is a patriot', he concluded. 'Like the honest citizen, [he] is impressed by the war conditions, which make it every man's duty to give as little trouble as possible.'[3] There was some truth to this judgement. British society developed a profound contempt for those who strayed from strict definitions of propriety. Since crimes were considered an offence not just against the immediate victim, but also against society, courts took a stiffer line against misdemeanours. Authority became much more intrusive. Welfare supervisors monitored not only the workplace but also people's homes. Over 1,000 women police volunteers

---

1 *The Times*, 8 February 1915.
2 Ibid., 15 January 1915.
3 Ibid., 10 December 1914.

140

patrolled the streets, to curb the 'amateur drift' of women and girls into prostitution.[4]

The Defence of the Realm Act (DORA) severely restricted personal freedom. Its quick passage on 8 August and its all-embracing nature (subsequently extended according to necessity) reveal how determined an otherwise liberal, anti-interventionist government was to secure for itself mechanisms for social control. The crucial part of the Act gave the government the power to 'authorize the trial by courts martial' of any person whose actions were deemed to 'jeopardize the success of the operations of His Majesty's forces or to assist the enemy'.[5] On the surface, this seems to pertain to spies and traitors. In fact, it applied to any action detrimental to the war effort, an application which an ever-vigilant government interpreted widely. An extension of DORA on 28 August created the offence of spreading reports 'likely to cause disaffection or alarm',[6] theoretically entitling the government to quash any dissent. Eventually, the power to ban demonstrations which might make 'undue demands' upon local police forces was added.[7] Wide powers of search were assumed, as was the right to hold suspects without charge. Naval or military authorities could deport from designated areas persons deemed hazardous to the war effort: thus, a militant trade unionist could be banned from the area around a factory.

While ordinary crime declined, the war produced new types of crime. The general uncertainty about the future was a boon to fortune tellers, whose activities were illegal. Arrests multiplied.[8] In time, the authorities clamped down upon citizens who failed to observe the blackout, revellers who built bonfires on Guy Fawkes night, guests who threw rice at weddings, women who passed venereal disease to soldiers, and Londoners who whistled for cabs. In 1917, a baker in Edinburgh was arrested for producing jam tarts on a designated 'sweet-free' day.[9] A butcher from Kensington was fined £50 for selling bad meat to troops.[10] A farmer near Wisbech was fined £140 for selling seed potatoes above the maximum price. A Worksop miller was fined £23 for making white flour instead of the

---

4 P. Levine, ' "Walking the Streets in a Way No Decent Woman Should": Women Police in World War I', *Journal of Modern History* 66 (1994), pp. 43–5.

5 A. Marwick, *The Deluge*, p. 76.

6 S. Pankhurst, *The Home Front*, p. 36.

7 Ibid., p. 375.

8 *The Times*, 26 February, 13 April 1917.

9 *The Scotsman*, 29 March 1917.

10 *The Times*, 6 March 1915.

required wholewheat. A fine of £50 was levied against a Bedfordshire farmer who allowed rats to invade his wheat store.[11] A charge of conspiracy was brought against Ansell John Goudge whose German pianos were 'naturalised' and sold as British.[12]

The war seems to have produced an increase in sex-related crimes and prostitution. Nevertheless, the experience of one Women Police Service member, who detailed 383 cases of prostitution in polite Grantham in 1917, suggests over-zealous policing rather than an extraordinary level of vice.[13] But, as women and girls replaced male workers, they increasingly found themselves in hazardous situations, as the judge at a trial of a shopkeeper accused of molesting a fourteen year old messenger girl observed.[14] Newspapers in 1917 were full of reports of arrests and trials of bigamists. Whether this offence became more common or simply more unacceptable (and therefore visible) is not clear.[15]

Convictions under the Prevention of Corruption Act increased fourfold during the war and in 1916 penalties for bribing public officials had to be strengthened.[16] Christopher Addison complained that munitions contracts attracted 'a singular collection of sharks and adventurers from all parts of the earth'. For instance, a Dundee jute dealer was prosecuted for selling jute for sandbags at three times the normal price.[17] Two Glaswegians who roamed the Scottish countryside masquerading as government agents persuaded farmers to sell horses at greatly reduced prices.[18] Newspaper reports suggest that fraud increased (or became more visible) as con artists preyed on the emotionally vulnerable. 'The professional writer of begging letters has now adapted his whine to a patriotic tune', *The Times* commented.[19] Imposters posing as wounded soldiers frequented railway stations asking for loans of money.[20] Since charitable sentiments reached new heights, so too did the opportunities for trickery. 'The worst class of all' was the impostor who watched casualty lists and

11 P. Horn, *Rural Life in England in the First World War*, pp. 66–7.

12 *The Times*, 21 November 1914.

13 Levine, 'Walking the Streets', p. 54.

14 *The Times*, 9 July 1915.

15 See ibid., 26, 28 February 1917.

16 J. Boswell and B. Johns, 'Patriots or Profiteers? British Businessmen and the First World War', *Journal of European Economic History* 11 (1982), p. 438.

17 Ibid., pp. 428–9.

18 *The Scotsman*, 17 March 1915.

19 *The Times*, 13 February 1915.

20 Ibid., 11 January 1915.

wrote to the relatives of a dead 'comrade' requesting the repayment of an alleged debt.[21]

PERNICIOUS PACIFISTS

Despite the prohibition against spreading dissent, political protest did not disappear. But after 1914, it was carried out mainly by fringe ideologues who maintained a lonely and futile opposition to the government. Their less committed followers took either a pragmatic or patriotic decision to support the war. The pacifists, socialists and feminists who remained were for the most part leaders without followers. They came together in the anti-war movement: pacifists because they believed war was wrong, socialists because it was a consequence of capitalism, and feminists because it was a scourge of patriarchy.

The pacifist movement never lived up to pre-war expectations. On 2 August 1914 a huge peace demonstration took place in Trafalgar Square, addressed by George Lansbury, Arthur Henderson, Keir Hardie and H. M. Hyndman. The crowd affirmed that Britain should remain aloof from the gathering crisis in Europe. Robert Smillie promised that his miners' union would take part in any pan-European effort by trade unionists to bring the war to a halt.[22] But then Germany invaded Belgium and the British embarked upon a moral crusade. The TUC and the Labour Party quickly rallied behind the government, offering their services to the war effort. Arnold Bennett was perhaps typical of the way pacifism dissolved: 'When one sees young men idling in the lanes on Sunday, one thinks: "Why are they not at war?" All one's pacific ideas have been disturbed. One is becoming militarist.'[23]

The group most successful at uniting the diverse disaffected was the Union of Democratic Control, formed by Charles Trevelyan on 5 August 1914.[24] Trevelyan felt that, given the belligerent mood which gripped Europe, direct action to end the war would be futile. The UDC instead concentrated on educating the public on the war's causes, with the aim of eventually establishing mechanisms for peace-

---

21 Ibid., 13 February 1915.
22 F. L. Carsten, *War Against War*, p. 25.
23 A. Bennett, *Journal 1896–1926*, p. 98.
24 See M. Swartz, *The Union of Democratic Control in British Politics During the First World War*, passim.

ful coexistence between nations. The group's Four Points reveal its modest aims:

1. There should be no annexation of territory without the consent of the population involved.
2. Parliament must exercise democratic control over the conduct of foreign policy. Secret diplomacy must be abolished.
3. International disputes should be resolved through the methods of conference and arbitration. A permanent International Council, deliberating in public, should replace balance-of-power diplomacy.
4. National armaments should be limited by mutual agreement, and the pressures of the military-industrial complex regulated by the nationalisation of armaments firms and control over the arms trade.

Prominent members included E. D. Morel, Norman Angell and Arthur Ponsonby. Bertrand Russell, sympathetic to the UDC, nevertheless found its members naively ambitious. When they plotted how to end the war, they seemed 'like eight fleas talking of building a pyramid'.[25]

When Labour joined the coalition in May 1915, some party members took their consciences to the UDC. Feminists, Quakers and other Christians, annoyed by the warmongering of the established churches, also joined. Within a year of its foundation, the UDC had established 50 local organisations and sold 500,000 pamphlets. At its peak it had 100 branches and some 10,000 members.[26] This seems decidedly unimpressive, given the moderate nature of the group's ideals. Since it aimed not to stop the war but to build a peaceful postwar world, it was entirely possible for an individual to support the war and be a loyal UDC member. This moderation frustrated committed pacifists like Ellen Wilkinson of the ILP:

To the ardent pacifist it is a tragedy that the advocacy of the cause of peace should be largely represented in Britain by as cautious a body as the UDC. Its 'four points' are so admirably moderate and remote that no intelligent person, not quite blinded by party, could honestly disagree with them.[27]

The UDC was theoretically non-partisan. Its politics could best be described as 'bourgeois pacifism'; Morel argued that pre-war diplomacy had neglected 'the business interests of the nation'.[28]

25 J. Hinton, *Protests and Visions*, pp. 44–5.
26 Ibid., p. 45.
27 Carsten, p. 54.
28 Hinton, pp. 48–9.

International harmony required a sincere commitment to free trade.

The ILP insisted that only democratic socialism, achieved through the international brotherhood of the working class, would bring lasting peace. But anyone looking for consistency would have fled in frustration from the ILP. As early as 11 August 1914, it sent greetings 'across the roar of the guns' to German comrades.[29] But a few months later some ILP members (including Ramsay MacDonald) issued a joint statement with socialists from Belgium, Britain, France and Russia declaring themselves 'inflexibly resolved to fight until victory is achieved'.[30] Lenin's view that the war would hasten the long-awaited revolution was both enthusiastically received and widely derided by ILP supporters. The party attracted both ardent socialists who supported the war and ardent pacifists lukewarm about the socialist millennium.

MacDonald, who resigned the Labour leadership when the party decided to support the war, admitted: 'Whatever our views may be on the origins of the war, we must go through with it.'[31] His actions may have seemed perfectly logical to him, but they confused those who liked their politics simple. Equally confusing was Keir Hardie. He argued that the nation must be united behind the war, that soldiers 'must not be disheartened by any discordant note at home' and that 'German troops must be thrown back across their own frontier'. Yet what were potential followers to make of his calls for a compromise peace, his denunciation of Russian militarism and his argument that Britain was as guilty of prolonging the war as Germany?[32] When he died in September 1915, the subsequent by-election provided a revealing indicator of working class opinion. The official Labour candidate, James Winstone, identified with the ILP and therefore with Hardie, was defeated by Charles Stanton, a miners' agent allied to the fiercely patriotic Socialist National Defence Committee.[33] Stanton's tirades against the 'brutal butchers of Berlin' impressed the voters, who gave him a majority of 4,000.[34]

Similar divisions existed within feminist ranks. When war broke

29 Ibid., p. 42.
30 Pankhurst, p. 147.
31 Hinton, p. 44.
32 T. Wilson, *The Myriad Faces of War*, p. 155–6.
33 The SNDC eventually became the British Workers' League.
34 B. Doyle, 'Who Paid the Price of Patriotism? The Funding of Charles Stanton during the Merthyr Boroughs By-Election of 1915', *English Historical Review* 109 (1994), p. 1217.

out, not all suffrage campaigners agreed with the precipitous decision of their leaders to support the war. A sense of unease felt by some (mainly younger) members of the Women's Social and Political Union (WSPU) and the National Union of Women's Suffrage Societies (NUWSS), caused them to turn to the UDC. The split among feminists widened when discontented NUWSS members and representatives of Sylvia Pankhurst's militant Women's Suffrage Federation (WSF) announced plans to attend the Women's Congress in The Hague, where delegates from belligerent and neutral nations were to congregate on 27 April 1915. The prospect of British feminists mixing with Germans caused a huge furore at home, the most vocal reaction coming from the suffrage establishment. Mrs Fawcett argued that peace campaigning while German armies still occupied parts of Belgium and France was 'akin to treason'. Emmeline and Christabel Pankhurst maintained that, for suffragettes, the struggle against the Kaiser was 'a thousand times more' important than the fight for votes.[35] They had a point. The pre-war anti-suffrage argument was based heavily on the assumption that women were incapable of service in war. Fawcett and the Pankhursts feared that attendance at The Hague would revive that argument.[36] Many suffragettes who had defected to the WSF because of the WSPU's militant warmongering consequently returned to the fold when Sylvia announced WSF support for the Congress. 'Subscribers are falling off like dead leaves at the end of a season', she complained.[37]

The government played a skilful game of cat and mouse with the 200 British feminists who wanted to go to Holland. McKenna, the Home Secretary, at first announced that no passports would be granted, then relented and approved passage for 20 'women of discretion'. This had the effect (probably intended) of causing a rift between those favoured and those rejected. Crystal MacMillan (who had been selected) lambasted Sylvia Pankhurst (who had not) for referring to the meeting as a Peace Congress: 'To call it a "Peace Congress" gives the impression that its object is to demand peace at any price.'[38] In the end, last-minute obstacles prevented even the small group from sailing. The *Daily Express* commented:

> All Tilbury is laughing at the Peacettes, the misguided Englishwomen who, baggage in hand, are waiting at Tilbury for a boat to take them

35 Pankhurst, p. 149.
36 See M. Pugh, *Women and the Women's Movement in Britain, 1914–1959*, p. 11.
37 Pankhurst, p. 149.
38 Ibid., pp. 150–1.

to Holland, where they are anxious to talk peace with German fraus over the teapot.[39]

Only three British women made it to The Hague, in contrast to 28 from Germany.[40] The Congress inspired the formation of the British section of the Women's International League, which by the end of the war had 50 branches and 3,687 active members, most of them refugees from the NUWSS, and all very moderate pacifists.[41] They linked pacifism to women's emancipation: 'only free women can build up the peace which is to be'.[42] The League was cautious to a fault, even going so far as to exclude British wives of aliens resident in Britain, since to admit them would attract 'a great deal of mud'.[43] One hesitates at giving too much attention to so insignificant a group. Sympathetic historians have written volumes about pacifist women, but very little about the far more numerous and influential female patriots.

Even more moderate than the UDC was the League of Nations Society, formed in May 1915 by the Cambridge classicist Lowes Dickinson, and numbering among its ranks J. A. Hobson and H. N. Brailsford. Though they agreed with the UDC's concentration upon avoiding future war, they objected to its call for a negotiated peace, certain as they were that German belligerence had to be defeated. Though Dickinson was President of the Cambridge Branch of the UDC, he was not optimistic that democratic control over foreign policy would solve the problem of war. He favoured instead a pro-active system of mutual defence against aggression, what Hobson called 'collective security'. This group naturally gravitated toward the United States as the power most capable of leading the world away from anarchy, its sympathy reinforced when President Woodrow Wilson began to promote a League of Nations.

To maintain an even moderately pacifist position in the militantly pro-war atmosphere required a great deal of courage. The patriotic press found pacifists useful for inciting public fury. On the eve of a meeting in the Memorial Hall, the *Daily Express* printed pictures of Morel, Trevelyan and other prominent pacifists and asked: 'Londoners, what do you think of them? Is Germany to hear the wail of peace cranks from the City of the Empire?' Agitated citizens, includ-

39 A. Wiltsher, *Most Dangerous Women*, p. 89.
40 Ibid., p. 96.
41 Pugh, p. 10.
42 Hinton, p. 43.
43 Pankhurst, p. 153.

ing some soldiers, invaded the hall, seized the platform and released stink bombs.[44] Academics who campaigned for a negotiated peace or against conscription were ostracised by colleagues, despite the profound admiration for all things German among British academics before the war. Following his conviction on a charge of making 'statements likely to prejudice the recruiting and discipline of His Majesty's forces', Russell was dismissed from his lectureship at Trinity College, Cambridge, in July 1916.[45] Dickinson, who found that even his moderate pacifism rendered him a pariah at Cambridge ('I lived and ate alone . . . and saw almost nobody'), concluded after Russell's dismissal that universities were 'no place for genuine and independent minds. . . . If you are honest and independent you must be a heretic and an outcast.'[46]

By late summer 1916 the steadily mounting death toll on the Western Front and the slim prospects for victory convinced pacifists that the time was ripe for a negotiated peace. They assumed that feelings of futility amongst the public would increase receptivity to the UDC message. Morel was wildly optimistic about the possibility of attracting trade union support; 'the effect ought to be very great, and combined with the steady operating force of economic factors, casualties, rising prices it might be decisive'.[47] At rallies held throughout Britain, signatures were collected for a petition urging the government to negotiate. The *Manchester Guardian* even lent its weight to the campaign. Given the supposed level of public demoralisation, the total of 200,000 signatures at the end of the campaign seems paltry. Had they been more receptive to the evidence, pacifists might have noticed that support for the war remained solid. Lloyd George's aggressive conduct of the war was very popular, as was the Labour Party's decision to join his government. In contrast, the British Socialist Party (BSP), which alone on the left called for an immediate end to the war, had only 6,435 members in 1917.[48] The decidedly unenthusiastic response to Wilson's January 1917 call for a peace without victory provided yet further proof that the pacifists' hour had not arrived.

The entry of the United States into the war was a mixed blessing for pacifists. Because America seemed untainted by Great Power

44 C. Haste, *Keep the Home Fires Burning*, p. 150.

45 S. Hynes, *A War Imagined*, p. 147.

46 S. Wallace, *War and the Image of Germany*, p. 114.

47 C. Wrigley, *David Lloyd George and the British Labour Movement*, p. 181.

48 Carsten, p. 170.

rivalries, Brailsford and Russell pragmatically decided that it offered the best, if not the most doctrinally pure, hope for peace. But ardent socialists were wary about the prospect of the capitalist USA leading the world toward international harmony. Pacifists derived more hope from the Russian revolution, especially after the Provisional Government backed the Petrograd Soviet's call for peace 'without annexations or indemnities'. Russell thought the revolution 'has stirred men's imaginations everywhere and has made things possible which would have been quite impossible a week ago'. On 3 June the Leeds Convention organised by the ILP and BSP met under the banner 'Follow Russia'. It drew 1,150 representatives from trade unions, socialist organisations, feminist groups and peace societies.[49] One of its resolutions called for the establishment of Workers' and Soldiers' Councils as in Russia. These events failed to excite mainstream labour. Most workers agreed with Ben Tillet, the dockers' leader, who concluded that the conference 'did not represent working class opinion and was rigged by a middle class element more mischievous than important'.[50]

The Labour Party and most trade unions nevertheless supported the revolution, while recognising its precariousness. They argued that a positive response from the allied nations was essential in order to give encouragement to the new Russian government and prevent it signing a separate peace. The international socialist conference scheduled in Stockholm seemed to offer an opportunity for conveying such a response. Henderson, the Labour leader, who had travelled to Petrograd to try to persuade Russian socialists to renew their commitment to the war, was not at first enthusiastic about the conference. He gradually became convinced, however, that an Allied boycott would merely encourage the Bolshevik element in Russia who were pressing for a separate peace. At a special Labour Party conference on 10 August, a large majority approved sending representatives to Stockholm, an idea Lloyd George at first supported. But by the time Henderson returned from Petrograd, the Prime Minister had concluded that, since Russia was a lost cause, attendance would be counter-productive.

Underneath the labour movement's surface enthusiasm for the Stockholm conference lurked profound disagreements. The ILP saw the conference as an opportunity to find a quick end to the war, while the Labour Party hoped it would help Russia renew the fight.

49 Hinton, p. 59.
50 Wilson, p. 522.

At a second party conference on 22 August, support for attendance fell from 1,500,000 to just 3,000. Miners in particular were outspokenly opposed; they sent a delegation to Downing Street to 'proclaim their strong protest against the Stockholm Conference'.[51] More significant was the reaction of Havelock Wilson's Sailors' and Firemen's Union which refused to transport to Stockholm those whose 'sole object . . . is to secure a German peace'.[52] Fortunately for the party, the government's decision to deny passports to British delegates offered an escape from a potentially humiliating débâcle. That Henderson did not have to pay dearly for his poor judgement was due to his subsequent ill-treatment by the Cabinet. He was left waiting outside the Cabinet Office (the infamous 'doormat incident') while colleagues discussed how to discipline him. Called in like a naughty boy to the principal's office, he was sternly reprimanded by the Prime Minister. Aware that no Liberal or Conservative minister would be treated so shabbily, Henderson resigned. But, significantly, he insisted, at the party conference in January 1918, that Labour must remain in the government. To leave would have meant consigning the party to the wilderness and sacrificing all the progress that had been made. The party, preferring pragmatism to pacifist fantasies, backed him by three to one.

Pacifists nevertheless interpreted Henderson's resignation as an assertion of Labour independence. They were also excited by the party's Memorandum of War Aims, released on 28 December, a virtual carbon copy of the UDC's Four Points. By early 1918, pacifists were highly optimistic about the possibilities for a peace campaign organised under the all-embracing banner of the Labour Party. This optimism again proved ill-founded. Pacifists interpreted the widespread public discontent evident in early 1918 as enthusiasm for a negotiated peace. Granted, there was annoyance about the food situation, disappointment at the Cambrai and Passchendaele failures, dismay over new manpower proposals and general exhaustion. But this discontent was by no means the same thing as a groundswell of opposition to the war. Pacifists did not quite understand that massive casualties were as likely to make people more determined to press for the knock-out blow as to convince them of the futility of further offensives. Popular feeling still held that only complete victory would render the accumulated sacrifice worthwhile.

51 Ibid., p. 525.
52 Haste, p. 165. See also J. O. Stubbs, 'Lord Milner and Patriotic Labour', *English Historical Review* 87 (1972), p. 737.

Among the lotus-eaters was John Maclean, prominent Glasgow Marxist and the subject of romantic adulation to this day. He was certain that the combination of stalemate on the front, turmoil at home and revolution in Russia presented a golden opportunity for both peace and the socialist revolution.

> There is a spirit of revolution developing in the workshops. . . . Our unified purpose should be to seize the chance when our enemy at home was weak, to sweep the capitalist class out of the way and bring about peace. We [are] in the rapids of revolution.[53]

The rapids of revolution were in fact a Bolshevik backwater. After the Bolshevik triumph in Russia, few honest socialists in Britain still considered the Russian example worthy of emulation. Even the ILP found Maclean's revolutionary fantasies too frightening to contemplate. Yet despite its relatively moderate evolutionary socialism, by the end of the war the ILP had little more than 35,000 members.[54] Outside Scotland, its number of branches actually declined between 1915 and 1917 from over 600 to less than 500.[55] Peace would not come through a socialist awakening.

Government ministers varied greatly in their reaction to dissidents. Lord Milner was convinced that Britain was riddled with revolutionaries capable of leading innocent workers astray. He sought to establish 'a purely working class movement, which I hope will knock out the "Independent Labour Party" '.[56] With money and support from Milner and other prominent Unionists, the Socialist National Defence Committee (SNDL) was set up in April 1915 by Victor Fisher, one-time Fabian and member of the Social Democratic Federation. 'Governments most frequently do not realize that they are on the brink of a revolution', Fisher warned around the time of the Leeds Convention.[57] The SNDL was intended to act as a counterweight to the 'pernicious and pestilential piffle of Pacifist cranks'.[58] In 1916 it became the British Workers' League and was active in disrupting ILP and UDC meetings. Its newspaper, *The British Citizen*, had an average circulation of 30,000 per week.[59]

---

53 Hinton, p. 69.
54 Carsten, p. 201.
55 Ibid., pp. 170–1.
56 Stubbs, 'Lord Milner and Patriotic Labour', p. 728.
57 Ibid., p. 739.
58 Ibid., p. 718.
59 R. Douglas, 'The National Democratic Party and the British Workers' League', *Historical Journal* 15 (1972), p. 536.

Lloyd George was less alarmed than Fisher or Milner. When Mrs Pankhurst pleaded for the government to 'counteract the pernicious influence of the UDC', he replied that 'the evil effects are for the present confined to a minority'.[60] There was occasional police harassment of UDC speakers and some, including Morel and Russell, were imprisoned for violations under DORA, but in general the government maintained a low profile.[61] The Home Office briefly considered censoring publications produced by the various peace groups, but wisely decided that doing so would draw more attention to pacifists than they would be able to garner on their own. Generally speaking, the government relied on private groups and newspapers to lead the propaganda campaign against pacifist groups. Basil Thomson, head of Scotland Yard, provided the National War Aims Committee, a government-sponsored organisation, with 'early intimation of any pacifist movement' so that it could 'arrange indoor and outdoor meetings as a counterblast'.[62] The police were notoriously slow to respond to violence directed against peace campaigners.

Lloyd George was certain that 'if the workers are convinced that the Government is earnestly and sympathetically seeking a thorough remedy for the evils which undoubtedly exist', they would not be susceptible to the message of dissidents.[63] This was demonstrated by events in late 1917 and early 1918. As was discussed in the last chapter, limited food rationing and a pay rise for munitions workers quelled popular discontent. A declaration of War Aims (delivered, significantly, to a conference of trade unionists) was sufficiently close to Wilsonian ideals (yet without abandoning the knock-out blow) to quiet those who questioned the prolongation of the war. And the German spring offensive quickly put an end to workers grumbling about manpower policies. It was not so much that these developments destroyed the pacifist opportunity but rather that that opportunity never existed. Henry Page Croft, right wing founder of the National Party, condemned pacifists who preyed on 'the feelings of those tired, patriotic people [the workers] in order to get them to turn in the direction of an inconclusive peace'.[64] The description was

---

60 Wrigley, p. 181.
61 Hynes, p. 217.
62 Haste, p. 171.
63 Wrigley, p. 181.
64 Idem, ' "In the Excess of their Patriotism": The National Party and Threats of Subversion', in C. Wrigley, ed., *Warfare, Diplomacy and Politics, Essays in Honour of A. J. P. Taylor*, p. 104.

apt, even if the threat was never as serious as Page Croft and those of his ilk believed.

ANTI-CONSCRIPTIONISTS

Running parallel to the pacifist campaign was the movement against conscription. Though many opposed compulsion, few took up active resistance. Thus, the TUC in September 1915 openly voiced its aversion to the first Military Service Act, but did not press the matter further. Individual trade unions were too busy securing exemptions for their members to devote much energy to a wider campaign against conscription. Three Labour Party ministers tendered their resignations, but all returned to the fold when Asquith assured them that the Act pertained to the duration of the war only, that it would not be extended to industrial conscription, and that tribunals adjudicating on exemptions would be composed of civilian, not military, representatives. At the party conference in January 1916, Labour rank and file protested the ministers' decision to remain in the government, but did not ask them to reverse it. Even the UDC took a fatalistic approach, concluding that conscription, however abhorrent, was inevitable and opposition would be futile.

Active opposition was therefore left to the No Conscription Fellowship, led by the ethical socialist Clifford Allen, and established in December 1914. It campaigned hard against the introduction of conscription, but its main impact came later, in aiding men who resisted the call. The group consisted mainly of young men subject to conscription; half of the approximately 12,000 members served prison sentences during the war.[65] Members included Fenner Brockway, C. H. Norman and Bertrand Russell, who took over leadership when Allen was jailed. Prominent women members included Sylvia Pankhurst, Lydia Smith (who edited the NCF journal *The Tribunal*) and the maternalist pacifist Catherine Marshall, who reckoned that the crimes she committed in aiding conscientious objectors rendered her liable to 2,000 years' imprisonment.[66] Less conspicuous but at least as important were the hundreds of ordinary women who kept the fight going when NCF ranks were depleted due to prison sentences. One NCF member, Mrs Alice Wheeldon, gained unwelcome notoriety when she was tried and convicted (on very suspect

---

65 Carsten, p. 67.
66 Wiltsher, p. 146.

evidence) of plotting to kill Lloyd George and Henderson with poison darts. She was sentenced to ten years' penal servitude.[67]

Allen was optimistic that from the resistance to conscription would grow a wider movement to end the war and, eventually, a more invigorated socialism. 'In so far as we cause the Government to persecute those who believe in peace', he argued, 'so we may . . . stimulate the national consciousness in [the] direction [of peace].'[68] That such a conclusion could have been made amidst the atmosphere of militant patriotism is an indication of either Allen's commitment or his delusion, or both. Unfortunately, he was taken by surprise by the government's flexibility once conscription was introduced. The Military Service Act pulled the rug from under the NCF by enshrining the right of conscientious objection. Rather than accept this as a partial victory, the NCF objected: 'it is not fighting in particular which revolts us, it is war itself that we will not assist'.[69]

Despite the concession to conscientious objection, the NCF still managed to find a role for itself in helping the potential conscientious objector (CO) prove himself before local tribunals. Those tribunals have received a harsh verdict in history's court of justice. In fact, 80 per cent of the men who came before them were granted some form of exemption,[70] which suggests that tribunal members were considerably more open-minded than the general public, which tended to judge COs as traitors, cowards or shirkers. Those who passed the tribunals were enlisted in non-combatant corps: construction crews, grave details, etc. There remained, however, 'absolutists' who refused to undertake any military service. They encountered the particular wrath of tribunals, which were determined to break them. Some were sent forcibly to the front. Among those who maintained their refusal once there, 34 were sentenced to death.

The death sentences were commuted to ten years' penal servitude, but the government still worried about delivering the NCF a public relations bombshell. In May 1916, Army Order X ruled that court-martialled objectors would be turned over to the Home Office, to serve sentences in civilian prisons. Two months later, the government further eased the pressure on itself by setting up the Pelham Committee, which offered a scheme of alternative non-military service. A Central Appeals Tribunal was established to review the

---

67 Marwick, p. 128.
68 Hinton, p. 52.
69 Marwick, pp. 120–1.
70 J. Rae, *Conscience and Politics*, p. 131.

cases of all individuals serving prison sentences to determine whether they qualified for this scheme. Again, rather than claim victory, the NCF objected on the grounds that the new measures merely freed other men to be sent to the front – what it called 'killing by proxy'.[71]

Of the approximately 16,100 conscientious objectors, 3,300 opted for the non-combatant corps, 2,400 worked in ambulances or as stretcher bearers at the front as directed by the tribunals, and 3,964 accepted work at home under Pelham Committee guidelines. Some 6,261 men took their objection with them to prison at least once, of whom approximately 1,350 absolutists refused all offers of compromise and faced a pattern of arrest, trial and imprisonment, during the course of the war and afterward.[72] Those who eventually accepted civilian work were usually employed on road-making, paid at soldier's rates but without separation allowances. The individual's family could apply for Poor Relief, but Poor Law Guardians were never very generous toward a CO's dependants.[73] In all, 71 conscientious objectors died in prison or as a result of injuries received while imprisoned.[74] There were some shameful cases of sadistic treatment. One inmate of Camberwell Prison, told he would be executed, was slowly taken through the motions of an actual execution, to the point of the gun being loaded and pointed at him. Inmates were force-fed, tied into strait-jackets, beaten, kept in filthy cells, fed on bread and water and often tortured. Two of them were kept for 28 hours handcuffed to a bar high over their heads, with a 20 lb weight pulling them down. 'Only those prepared for death could face it', wrote one CO of his prison ordeal.[75]

The ill-treatment of absolutists and their stubborn principles earned them grudging admiration from those otherwise steadfast in their support for the war. Even *The Times* expressed 'considerable sympathy'.[76] But for most people, 'conchies' were easy targets of abuse and even violence. They have since become heroic martyrs. Cases like that of the Quaker Stephen Hobhouse, an absolutist who refused even a medical examination (which he probably would have failed) and went to prison rather than accept any form of alternative service, encourage a tendency to judge all tribunals as villains and

71 Hinton, p. 52.

72 J. Graham, *Conscription and Conscience*, pp. 347–52. Graham's figures do not all add up; one suspects some double-counting.

73 Pankhurst, p. 336.

74 Graham, p. 322.

75 Pankhurst, pp. 314–15.

76 *The Times*, 17 October 1916.

all COs as victims.[77] One nevertheless has to be impressed that the government retained a sufficient sense of justice to protect individuals scorned by the general public.

Opposition to conscription was handled rather adroitly by the government. There was some ill-advised and clumsy repression of the NCF, such as the June 1916 raid on its offices, which had no purpose beyond harassment.[78] But the group was never actually suppressed; members were jailed for resisting the call-up, not because of their affiliation to the group. The government's flexibility forced the NCF into a role it never meant to assume: that of a watchdog ever alert to cruel treatment. 'What had begun as a movement of resistance to the new apparatus of militarism, became itself a tolerated part of that apparatus', wrote Allen. 'The political sting had been drawn from the pacifist witness.'[79] In truth, that sting had never been potent.

The emphasis upon conscription brought the NCF the scorn of philosophical pacifists. Brailsford called it 'a blind alley which won't bring us infinitesimally nearer to peace'. Even Allen, reflecting upon the NCF campaign in 1919, accepted that the absolutist argument had 'repelled' and 'muddled' public opinion. Good pacifists like Lowes Dickinson had trouble deciding who was more worthy of contempt, tribunal members who rejected all exemptions or absolutists who rejected all offers of compromise.[80] Antagonism toward absolutists mushroomed out of proportion to the actual size of the group, in the process creating a large obstacle to the communication of the pacifist message:

> We seemed to wrap ourselves in coil after coil of finely spun logic, to raise our pedestal upon a mountain of phrases and formulas and to be unresponsive to the altered mood of those whose opinions we sought to change.[81]

Allen was perhaps a bit too harsh. The tendency to get tangled in finely spun logic, ignoring the wider public's simple rationality of a just war, was common among dissenters during this war.

77 Wilson, p. 398.
78 Carsten, p. 68.
79 Hinton, p. 53.
80 Wallace, p. 84.
81 Hinton, pp. 53–4.

SPIES AND IMAGINARY SPIES

The treatment of pacifists and anti-conscriptionists might seem evidence of the survival of liberal values. But one should be wary of hasty conclusions. When the government perceived what it thought was a more serious threat to public order, namely that of enemy aliens resident in Britain, it showed no similar liberal tendencies.

Much of the work in controlling the alien 'problem' had been completed before the war, including the compilation of a secret register listing the names and particulars of 28,380 aliens, less than half of whom were German or Austro-Hungarian.[82] On 5 August 1914, McKenna engineered passage of the Alien Restrictions Act. It gave the government the power to restrict the movements of aliens and to remove them from prohibited areas around military installations and ports. A permit was required for an enemy alien to enter or leave the country. All resident aliens were required to register with the police and to notify the authorities if they moved.[83] For instance, on 24 August Karl Kley, a resident alien from London, was sentenced to three months' hard labour for travelling five miles from his place of residence, contrary to the Aliens' Restriction Act.[84] On 9 September 1914, McKenna informed the House that 50,633 Germans and 16,141 Austrians and Hungarians had registered.[85]

Subsequent laws prohibited the posting of letters abroad and the owning of wireless sets, firearms, cameras, military or naval maps, and motor vehicles. Aliens could not assume a new name without the permission of the Home Office. In mid-August, extensive searches were conducted in areas containing aliens, and some arms were discovered.[86] In October 1914, arrests of all unnaturalised male Germans, Austrians and Hungarians of military age began. They were either interned or repatriated. This caused a crisis in the London clothing trade, as so many tailors were German.[87] On 28 November it was decided that all persons, alien or British, moving into hotels or boarding houses had to register with the police. As the war progressed, the government assumed ever greater powers to close down premises, such as restaurants and bars, frequented by aliens.

82 D. French, 'Spy Fever in Britain, 1900–1915', *Historical Journal* 21 (1978), p. 360.
83 P. Panayi, *The Enemy in Our Midst*, pp. 47–8.
84 *The Scotsman*, 24 August 1914.
85 Panayi, p. 50.
86 *The Times*, 12 August 1914.
87 Ibid., 24 October 1914.

The distinction between friendly and enemy aliens became increasingly blurred; regulations were applied regardless of origin. Yet no matter what action was taken, it never satisfied the right wing press, which spread allegations that politicians were protecting a spy ring within Whitehall. By August 1918, the government, under enormous pressure from the right, assumed powers to revoke the citizenship of naturalised Germans and Austrians.

Anti-alien hysteria made it a bad time to be a pigeon in Britain. An over-zealous patriot suggested that citizens should shoot on sight any carrier pigeon rather than attempt to determine whether it was involved in espionage. *The Scotsman* reported on 16 September 1914:

> Already all over the country numbers of birds, the property of innocent owners, have been shot. So serious has the menace become that the National Homing Union have issued a warning to the general public that the shooting of homing pigeons is illegal. A reward of £5 is offered to anyone giving information of such an offence.[88]

DORA outlawed keeping carrier pigeons without a permit. Aliens were, of course, denied permits. Aliens seen in the vicinity of pigeons were immediately suspect. Peter Duhn, a German living in London, was sentenced to six months' imprisonment after a witness testified seeing 'a pigeon on a level with his head about three yards in front of him flying away'. She admitted that although she 'did not actually see the pigeon leave his hand, . . . it must have come from him', and, most crucially, 'it carried a little white paper under its wing'. A search of Duhn's residence revealed no evidence of pigeon-keeping.[89]

Late in September 1914, there were 13,600 enemy aliens in internment camps – 10,500 civilians and the rest prisoners of war.[90] The available facilities for holding them were exhausted and Kitchener's armies had first call on accommodation. The government decided that in future only those aliens who posed an immediate danger would be interned. A wave of anti-German hysteria followed and wholesale internment was resumed.[91] Thereafter, the numbers in internment facilities fluctuated according to public mood. It is at least reassuring that those interned did not generally suffer physically. Food supplies were maintained, though quality was suspect. At the

---

88 *The Scotsman*, 8 September 1914.
89 Ibid., 3 September 1914.
90 Panayi, p. 72.
91 French, 'Spy Fever in Britain', p. 368.

end of the war, internment camps were serving horse meat five days a week and some internees supplemented their diets by eating cats, dogs and seagulls.[92] But only 105 aliens died in camps by April 1917, below the expected actuarial level. At the Knockaloe camp on the Isle of Man the death rate was 2.5 per thousand, while it was 15.7 per thousand for the island generally.[93] Since the policy of internment had little to do with the actual danger aliens posed, one has to marvel at the enormous amount of energy wasted interning them, given the manpower shortage. Many aliens, it must be emphasised, were taken from munitions and other essential work.

Every alien was assumed to be a potential or actual spy. The security services had prepared in advance a list of 22 German agents operating in Blighty. On the outbreak of war, all but one were arrested. After questioning them, the authorities rounded up fourteen more supposed agents.[94] Only one was ever brought to trial.[95] Not satisfied with this effort, Vernon Kell, the paranoid head of MO5g, conducted an intensive campaign to root out 'conspiracies to commit outrage'. The Metropolitan Police during the first month of war investigated nearly 9,000 cases, but no evidence was found 'indicating any combination amongst alien enemies . . . or any kind of military organization among them'.[96] The government's obsession with spies is demonstrated by the expansion of the security services. MI5 was formed in January 1916 from various counter-espionage bodies, the main one being MO5g, which had a staff of twenty before the war. When war ended MI5 had 844 personnel. The other group dealing with aliens, MI9 (formerly MO9), expanded from 170 staff in 1914 to 4,861 at the armistice.[97] In addition, at the outbreak of war the commissioner of police established a special constabulary for London which within three weeks employed 20,000 amateur guards to patrol strategic points like bridges, tunnels, waterworks, gasworks and canals.[98] The results were occasionally tragic. A man loitering near a railway bridge was shot and severely wounded when he failed to answer a challenge from a sentry. Subsequent investi-

---

92 Panayi, pp. 114–15.

93 Ibid., p. 125.

94 N. Hiley, 'The Failure of British Counter-Espionage Against Germany, 1907–1914', *Historical Journal* 28 (1985), p. 858.

95 French, 'Spy Fever in Britain', p. 365.

96 Hiley, 'The Failure of British Counter-Espionage', pp. 858–9.

97 Panayi, p. 181.

98 Hiley, 'The Failure of British Counter-Espionage', p. 859.

gation revealed that the man was stone deaf.[99] These agents were mobilised against a German espionage effort which was poorly organised, unprofessional and limited in scope. The Germans placed little importance on spying. By 1917, 201 people had been arrested for passing information to the enemy and 31 actual agents were arrested, of whom twelve were convicted of serious espionage and executed and another twelve sentenced to varying periods of penal servitude. Few of those arrested were aliens resident in Britain. Most were commercial travellers of various nationalities who entered Britain perfectly legally.[100] Not a single act of sabotage occurred during the war.

POSTSCRIPT

Neither aliens nor dissenters posed any serious threat to public order during the war. The general public's hostility toward both groups (occasionally spilling over into violence) indicates how solid was support for the war. Both groups indirectly helped to sustain morale. The 'enemies in our midst' were a focus for hatred and a stimulus to combative determination. They also provided easy scapegoats if anything went wrong: ships were sunk because of spies; aliens sabotaged shell production; pacifists undermined recruiting efforts. It is not entirely facetious to suggest that the British people needed aliens and dissenters to keep their hatred stoked. Bertrand Russell, Clifford Allen and their comrades probably did more for the cause of war than they ever achieved for the cause of peace.

99 *The Times*, 21 August 1914.
100 Haste, p. 113.

8   LIONS AND DONKEYS

In 1986, the drama series *The Monocled Mutineer*, loosely based on the 'mutiny' at Etaples base in 1917, caused considerable anguish when it was screened in Britain.[1] Viewers objected to the portrayal of a British Army peopled by cruel, sadistic officers and immoral, cowardly, conniving and unpatriotic men. The main character, Percy Topliss, undermined mythical Tommy Atkins, the decent, honest, long-suffering working class soldier who did his duty and survived by sheer pluck. The idea of a Tommy who cheated, lied, fornicated and mutinied was abhorrent.

According to Major General Sir George Younghusband, mythical Tommy was a far cry from reality:

> My early recollections of the British soldier are of a bluff, rather surly person, never the least jocose or light-hearted, except perhaps when he had too much beer. He was brave always, but with a sullen, stubborn bravery. No Tipperary or kicking footballs about it.[2]

Victorian Britain did not have to like soldiers since it could easily ignore them. But when necessity dictated that the army be integrated into society, along came Tommy Atkins. Yet, for the first two months of recruiting, soldiers were drawn from the same groups as before the war: the dregs of society. Thus, once war broke out, respect for the soldier increased even though his character remained unchanged. On the march to barracks during August, Rifleman Percy Jones noticed:

> The people along the line of the route showered things on us and refused to take any money. A gentleman in Watford bought out a whole fruit stall as it stood and told the lucky coster to give us the lot. When we halted people rushed out of their houses to distribute food and drink.

---

1 See D. Gill and G. Dallas, 'Mutiny at Etaples Base in 1917', *Past and Present* 69 (1975), pp. 88–112.

2 G. Younghusband, *A Soldier's Memories*, p. 188.

161

Another young private remarked: 'Up to the war we youths had counted but little in the scheme of the things ... but now we had become knights in shining armour.'[3]

Since the army did not have barracks to house a huge volunteer force, soldiers were billeted during training with civilians, thus ending the segregation of the army from society which had so suited Victorian sensibilities. Despite changing attitudes, some prejudices against soldiers remained. Rifleman Norman Ellison recalled being billeted with a woman who was suspicious and hostile until she summoned the courage to ask: 'Are you volunteers?' On being told they were, she replied with considerable relief, 'Oh, I thought you were common soldiers!' A retired army surgeon agreed to accommodate soldiers 'provided they are clean men who will not spit on the wallpaper'. A soldier in the Gordon Highlanders recalled that the community in which he was billeted 'had visions of all kind of savages armed with claymores descending upon them'. One girl asked 'if I didn't feel the cold at night, on the hills with only my plaid to cover me while sleeping'. Another person assumed that he had never seen, nor indeed used, a bathtub.[4]

Social problems of the parent society were duplicated within the army. Lurking amidst the decent chaps were thieves, villains, cowards and cheats. Oxford-educated J. Staniforth was distressed to find that his unit consisted mostly of 'tramps' who were 'drunk ... seedy, lousy, unshaven' and given to 'smoking, spitting, quarrelling, making water all over the room ... hiccuping and vomiting'.[5] J. B. Priestley concluded that every random group of ten men included one who was 'twisted somewhere inside'.[6] Enlisted men were drawn predominantly from the labouring classes, within which health standards were similar to those we today associate with the Third World. A recruiter in Anglesey estimated that the original height requirement of 5 feet 6 inches (1.68 metres) barred up to 70 per cent of the county's volunteers.[7] Recruits were customarily given a medical examination which placed them into four categories: Grade I consisted of men in satisfactory health, Grade II those with a 'slight' disability. Both were eligible for combat service overseas. Grade III consisted of men with 'marked physical disability', which exempted

---

3 P. Simkins, 'Soldiers and Civilians: Billeting in Britain and France', in I. Beckett and K. Simpson, eds, *A Nation in Arms*, p. 168.

4 Ibid., pp. 172–4.

5 C. Hughes, 'The New Armies', in Beckett and Simpson, eds, p. 104.

6 D. Winter, *Death's Men*, p. 55.

7 Hughes, 'The New Armies', p. 118.

them from combat but not clerical duties. Grade IV were rejected as unfit for any service. As a general rule, middle class men fell into Grades I and II, skilled workers mainly into II and III and unskilled predominantly in III and IV.[8] A pre-war sample of 1,000 Cambridge undergraduates yielded 700 in Grade I, 200 in II, 75 in III and 25 in IV. But for the population as a whole, only 34 per cent made Grade I.[9] Manpower shortages eventually led to less diligent application of health standards, but even in the last year of the war, over one million men were deemed unfit for frontline combat.[10]

For many men, army life represented a more wholesome diet, improved housing, better clothing (especially boots) and more regular medical care than previously experienced. It is therefore no coincidence that many recruits grew a couple of inches and gained considerable weight after taking the King's shilling. Army health standards improved during the course of the war, partly in response to the poor health of its recruits, but also because of greater public scrutiny. The BEF, for example, took no dentists to France in 1914, but four years later 800 were serving with the forces – though they mainly pulled teeth.[11] Men had to be made healthy in order to be able to die for their country. 'If we had been more careful for the last fifty years to prevent the unheeded wastage of human life', a *Daily Telegraph* leader argued with unintentional irony, 'we should have had at least half a million men available for the defence of the country.'[12]

Men used to a life of poverty and monotonous drudgery were a positive asset to the army. The average recruit came from a background of few opportunities and low expectations, in which sudden and premature death was relatively common. In this sense, army life was not radically different. Enlisted men were drawn from the most class conscious society in Europe, and placed in an army which reinforced traditional social hierarchies. They were men who knew their place and fatalistically accepted what their 'betters' told them. Their social background, which better food or housing could not erase, made them ideal soldiers to fight in this sort of war.

When these poor, downtrodden masses joined privileged middle

8 J. Winter, 'Army and Society: The Demographic Context', in Beckett and Simpson, eds, p. 200.

9 Ibid., p. 200.

10 J. Winter, *The Great War and the British People*, pp. 50–3, 59.

11 K. Jeffery, 'The Post-War Army', in Beckett and Simpson, eds, p. 225.

12 N. Whiteside, 'The British Population at War', in J. Turner, ed., *Britain and the First World War*, p. 87.

class officers in the trenches, the universality of experience supposedly encouraged an extraordinary sense of camaraderie, harmony and mutual respect. 'I love all the men', wrote P. Jones, a subaltern in the Tank Corps, 'and simply rejoice to see them going day by day their own jolly selves, building up such a wall of jocundity around me.'[13] For middle class officers, an awakened sense of social responsibility is presumed to have developed.[14] The poet Wilfred Owen, one of the more prominent examples of this enlightenment, wrote:

> I have made fellowships –
>> Untold of happy lovers in old song.
>> For love is not the binding of fair lips
>> With the soft silk of eyes that look and long,
>
> By Joy, whose ribbon slips, –
>> But wound with War's hard wire whose stakes are strong;
>> Bound with the bandage of the arm that drips;
>> Knit in the webbing of the rifle-thong.[15]

Some officers did have their eyes opened by the war, but one should be wary of drawing sweeping conclusions from particular (or indeed peculiar) cases. The myth of trench harmony has arisen because poets like Owen, Sassoon and Graves have been seen as spokesmen for their generation. They were in fact uniquely hyper-sensitive, disillusioned, guilt-ridden individuals. Sensitive poets were ashamed at the way their class treated working class soldiers. Few shared their sensitivity.

According to myth, class antagonism resulted from ignorance, which the trench experience eradicated. Yet it is absolute nonsense to suggest that the middle classes were completely ignorant of workers or vice versa. The middle class supplied society's managers, owners, landlords, bosses. The workers were their drivers, tenants and labourers – the men who cleaned the chimneys, delivered the coal and tended the fields. The very nature of capitalism meant that these two groups constantly interacted. True, the servile relationship of worker to boss was not conducive to real intimacy, but it requires a precarious leap of reason to believe that barriers were broken down in the army, which was even more rigid and hierarchical than

---

13 D. Winter, p. 18.

14 See J. Keegan, *The Face of Battle*, pp. 224–5.

15 W. Owen, 'Apologia Pro Poemate Meo', in J. Silkin, ed., *The Penguin Book of First World War Poetry*, pp. 187–8.

civilian life. Class distinctions were essential to a smooth-functioning army. Army life was merely another form of the manager–worker relationship. This was particularly true in this war, in which the drudgery of trench life had much in common with the monotonous dehumanisation of the factory. War had become work.[16]

To most middle class officers, ordinary soldiers were not only a different class, they were virtually a different species. The ability to lead was, after all, not something one learned, but a product of birth – in the genes. Edward Campion Vaughan wrote of his batman, Dunham: 'He has grown out of the stupidity which caused Hatwell to give him to me, and is now my most valuable possession.'[17] A. A. Hanbury-Sparrow argued that ordinary soldiers were 'definitely inferior beings and you'd no illusions about them'; the idea that officers should be worthy of their men was 'claptrap'.[18] Even Robert Graves complained of the stupidity of his men. Guy Chapman described his men as 'children moving in a haze of their own dreams, unconnected with practical things'.[19] The reference to children was common; a nineteen year old subaltern would refer to a 32 year old private as a 'lad'. Paternalism was much more common than brotherhood.

The army fostered the officer's elite status. Social barriers were carefully buttressed with separate quarters, canteens, cinemas and even brothels. A father whose eight sons were all enlisted men complained bitterly about how officer casualty lists were published within a few days of an action, while those pertaining to men 'are hardly ever available for many weeks, if at all'.[20] In the trenches, the junior officer had his batman who looked after his kit. He ate separately from his men, usually dining on better food, with freer access to alcohol and cigarettes. Upon reaching the front, Graves was shocked to find

> Battalion Headquarters, a dug-out in the reserve line, . . . happened to be unusually comfortable, with an ornamental lamp, a clean cloth, and polished silver on the table. The Colonel, Adjutant, doctor, second-in-command, and signalling officer had just finished dinner: it was civilized cooking – fresh meat and vegetables. Pictures pasted on the papered walls; beds spring-mattressed, a gramophone, easy chairs: we found it

16 I am grateful to my former student Ian Kirby for his impressive insights on this subject.

17 E. C. Vaughan, *Some Desperate Glory*, p. 134.

18 K. Simpson, 'The Officers', in Beckett and Simpson, eds, p. 85.

19 G. Chapman, *A Passionate Prodigality*, p. 58.

20 *The Times*, 5 February 1915.

hard to reconcile these with the accounts we had read of troops waist-deep in mud, and gnawing a biscuit while shells burst all around.[21]

Perhaps the cruellest differentiation came in the treatment of shell shock. Officers were given specialist treatment in comfortable hospitals, an extension of the idea that the mental health of society's elites was better (and therefore more responsive to treatment) than that of workers. In contrast, the ordinary soldier who suffered a breakdown was first assumed to be a shirker who warranted discipline. He was often tried at court martial for cowardice; if found guilty he was sometimes executed. Others were simply sent back to the front, on the assumption that the ailment could be driven from them by exposure to combat. A fortunate few received treatment.

Charles Carrington complained that he 'did not want to belong to a distinct caste', but he was an enlightened exception.[22] Most officers were keen to reinforce distinctions between them and their men. Since 'good form' signified authority, officers worked diligently to look like leaders. At the beginning of the war the uniform was carefully tailored, with rank badges large and conspicuous. Trench life (and the danger of snipers) necessitated greater simplicity and practicality, but, where possible, standards were maintained. Robert Graves recalled how he was sent to riding school *after* his first posting to the trenches – to ride well remained the mark of a gentleman and a potent symbol of authority. The introduction of tin helmets was stubbornly resisted by many officers who worried that they made them look too common and anonymous, besides erasing war's romance. Subtle distinctions became ever more important. Officers carried ornamental sticks instead of populist rifles; others favoured the status of a revolver.[23]

Before the war, even middle class officers were treated with contempt by those from the gentry. War forced the army to lower its standards; by 1917 lower middle class and some respectable workers became officers. There was a great degree of snobbery expressed toward these 'temporary gentlemen' – a term loaded with meaning. These gentlemen were 'temporary' since real status remained a birthright. They had jumped a class, but for the duration of the war only.[24] Elitist oldtimers despaired at new officers who

21 R. Graves, *Goodbye to All That*, p. 97.

22 Simpson, 'The Officers', p. 85.

23 See Keegan, p. 243.

24 See M. Petter, ' "Temporary Gentlemen" in the Aftermath of the Great War: Rank, Status and the Ex-Officer Problem', *Historical Journal* 37 (1994), pp. 127–52.

were incapable of adopting the right form: they were either too familiar with their men or failed to look after them properly.[25] Thus, even if 'temporary gentlemen' were closer in social status to their men than to old officers, they were expected to imitate the latter and make themselves a class apart.

In order for a rigid class system to work harmoniously, those at the bottom must not be unduly aroused by the iniquities of their society. In other words, social harmony requires that workers be not only servile, but docile. The workers in the trenches were certainly that. They failed to experience the slight raising of consciousness which the manpower shortage facilitated among male workers at home – life was too cheap at the front for soldiers to learn self-worth. Historians on the left have had enormous difficulty coming to terms with this image of willing cannon fodder, even though it harmonises well with the submissive character of the British working class and its abhorrence of extremism. To those on the left, Tommy Atkins has been a useful icon of the working class struggle, a man who stoically tolerated the injustices of a class society at war, while he deposited his suffering and humiliation in a bank of consciousness to be drawn upon after the armistice. In truth, the account was virtually empty because few deposits were made.

Ordinary soldiers were more docile *and* more rebellious than the Tommy myth suggests. Most accepted the social order and thus contributed to the smooth working of the system. But there was an outlaw element (the Percy Topliss type) who resented being ordered about by (often younger) officers whose authority stemmed from an accident of birth. Given the rigidly controlled army environment, it was difficult for these men to express their discontent without incurring severe retribution. Nevertheless, one suspects that the Vietnam War was not the first war to be marred by the practice of 'fragging'. Unpopular officers in the Great War were occasionally murdered by their men or left to die in a shellhole when rescue might have been possible.[26]

But the army worked because this sort of rebellion was rare. Deference was the norm. Trench harmony was ensured not because class barriers were broken down, but because they were maintained. An officer was respected and obeyed because he was considered

---

25 Simpson, 'The Officers' p. 78.

26 Julian Putkowski provided evidence to this effect in a panel discussion ('Researching Incidental Drama and Spectacular History') at the 1986 History Workshop conference.

superior. This was true be he a subaltern or a field marshal. There is, for instance, little evidence to support the assumption that senior commanders were deeply despised and that ordinary soldiers lacked confidence about the conduct of the war. One is again reminded of the dangers of taking one's history from the war poets. Sassoon's 'Base Details' castigates the commander who 'speeds glum heroes up the line to death', while he sits 'guzzling and gulping in the best hotel'.[27] The poem is an example of one man's middle class *angst*, not of a widespread contempt for senior commanders. Granted, as the years passed, it became progressively easier to find old soldiers describing commanders, and Haig in particular, as 'butchers'. But that epithet is a by-product of the post-1928 disillusionment with the war.

Serious criticism of the command would, admittedly, have been censored out of letters; therefore the evidence for contempt may have been destroyed. Nor can it be denied that some soldiers felt intense hatred. But what is striking, given the circumstances, are the countless examples of extraordinary reverence felt by soldiers toward senior officers during the war and immediately afterwards. Many examples exist of soldiers feeling extraordinarily fortunate to have caught a glimpse of Haig when his car passed while they were marching. Corporal H. Milward, given some food by Haig when they passed each other (Haig in a car, the soldier on foot), remarked:

> I thought how extraordinary it was that a man with so much responsibility could find time to think of the wants of a humble soldier. To how many men in his position would the thought of my well-being have occurred?
>
> What a contrast there must have been between us. He, handsome, well-groomed, spick and span, smart as a good soldier should be, I dirty, unwashed and wretched . . .[28]

In the army's social order, Haig was almost the equivalent of royalty. Like present-day royals, he was not expected to show humanity or familiarity, therefore the effect was all the greater when he did. Reverence was encouraged by the mystery, pageantry and pomp which senior commanders cultivated. Visual symbols of power reinforced authority: the commander's dress and deportment under-

27 S. Sassoon, 'Base Details', in J. Silkin, ed., *The Penguin Book of First World War Poetry*, p. 131.

28 H. Milward to Lady Haig, 6 June 1929: Haig Papers, National Library of Scotland.

lined his superiority and inspired common soldiers to trust in his leadership. Ordinary soldiers who saw Haig at all saw him on a tall, handsome horse or in an impressive car. His uniform was perfectly appointed and his hat shielded his gaze – thus preventing eye contact and accentuating the distance between him and them. 'I remember being asked on leave what the men thought of Haig', one soldier recalled. 'You might as well have asked the private soldier what he thinks of God. He knows about the same amount on each.'[29] C. E. Carrington, who knew the ordinary soldier well, argued: 'The problem of Haig's personality is not whether his grand tactics . . . were right or wrong; it is how he was able to retain the loyalty of his troops, as he did in 1917, and in 1918, and until his life's end.'[30] Most ex-soldiers heartily welcomed Haig's Honorary Presidency of the British Legion. When Haig died in 1928, the crowds lining the streets of Edinburgh and London as the cortège passed were nearly as large as those for a deceased monarch. Prominent in the crowd were many old soldiers.

Senior officers were under no illusion that this was a democratic war which required them to share the suffering of their men. Along with power went privilege. The fact that his men slept in muddy holes was no reason for Haig to decline a soft bed in a luxurious château. Grouse, salmon, fine wines and the best brandy were sent to him by rich friends at home. Nor did he perceive anything wrong with sending whole lambs and butter from the army stores to his wife so that she would not have to endure food shortages.[31] Luxuries were the confirmation of high authority. In the same sense, extravagant rewards were perfectly justifiable after the war. Already in 1916, Haig assured his wife that 'a grateful nation will not allow me to have a smaller income than I am receiving now! So we will be well enough off to make ourselves comfortable.'[32] Few objections were raised about the luxuries Haig enjoyed during the war, or the rewards he received after it. These were the accepted standards of his class and rank. Greater restraint would have seemed peculiar.

The British class system made things simple for Haig and for the hierarchy of officers below him. His was the most opulent existence, but opulence went with supreme power. Lower down the ladder, the food was less luxurious and the châteaux less grand, but the principle

---

29 D. Winter, pp. 53–4.
30 *Daily Telegraph*, 27 February 1959.
31 G. DeGroot, *Douglas Haig, 1861–1928*, pp. 173, 184, 234–5.
32 DeGroot, p. 277.

– that of authority reinforced by class superiority and the paraphernalia of power – remained the same. The ordinary soldier was a lower form of human being, a man whose responsibility was not to reason why but to do and die. Haig did not therefore perceive a need to cultivate even a superficial familiarity with his men. His authority was reinforced if he remained aloof and mysterious. To discuss the war with an ordinary soldier was about as logical as negotiating the size of a load with one's donkey. Nor was it necessary for Haig to familiarise himself directly with conditions at the front – one had staff officers to do that.[33] After the war, when criticising the senior command became increasingly popular, it was frequently suggested that Haig should have visited front line trenches in order to familiarise himself with the real war. One former soldier replied in *The Scotsman* that the trenches were far too dangerous a place for one so important as Haig.[34] One suspects that this was not an extraordinary sentiment.

The aim of military training is to destroy a man's individuality, so that he acts like a beast in a herd. Charles Hamilton Sorley commented in January 1915 that

> War in England only means putting all men of military age in England into a state of routinal coma, preparatory to getting them killed. You are . . . given six months to become conventional; your peace made with God, you will be sent out and killed.[35]

In the British Army, this group instinct was largely a creation of the regimental system, reinforced by pre-existing loyalties, as in the case of the Pals battalions. 'We all agreed', wrote Graves, 'that regimental pride remained the strongest moral force that kept a battalion going as an effective fighting unit.'[36] This might explain why the British soldier continued to fight for four years without serious mutiny, but it does not sufficiently differentiate him from soldiers in the French, German or Russian armies, who felt similar group instincts, but did mutiny. It is impossible to provide a conclusive explanation for the British exception, something which would require a massive study of national types and their adaptation to combat conditions. There are nevertheless some important differences. British casualties, serious as they were, were significantly lower than those of any other major

---

33 Even if, in his case, they did it very badly.

34 See *The Scotsman*, 13–20 August 1958, for some extraordinary letters in support of Haig written by ex-soldiers.

35 J. Silkin, ed., *The Penguin Book of First World War Prose*, p. 27.

36 Graves, p. 188.

army which did experience mutinies.[37] The British were also better fed and clothed, and the injured had a better chance of survival. In a static war, these differences were enormously important. The continental armies were mainly conscript forces, while the British did not introduce conscription until 1916. Approximately one-half of the total number of men who served during the war were volunteers. (And many who reached military age after 1916 and were conscripted might have volunteered had compulsion not been introduced.) For the entire war, therefore, the proportion of volunteers, men who had essentially chosen their own fate, remained high. But perhaps the most important factor contributing to the resilience of the British soldier was the deference and fatalism of the working class. There was a great deal of passive acceptance of the logic of authority: officers were officers because they deserved to be. Ordinary soldiers were not supposed to question the conduct of war. Even when the war dragged on endlessly, the ordinary soldier, according to C. E. Montague, remained

> unaggressive, unoriginal, anti-extreme, contemptuous of all 'hot-air' and windy ideas. Instead of contracting a violent new sort of heat [he] . . . simply went cold: . . . a Lucifer cold as a moon prompted him listlessly not to passionate efforts of crime, but to self-regarding and indolent apathy.[38]

The compliant character of the British soldier should be no surprise, given that the British working class, in comparison to its European counterparts, has been the least militant, the least revolutionary and the least inclined to make political capital out of labour disputes. No wonder, then, that the experience of war failed to radicalise the ex-soldier. Both the army and society were far too stable for war to be a hothouse for radicalism.

Haig gambled upon the loyalties of these men, but he was a confident gambler. He had little doubt that his men could stand the strains he imposed. In the end, he was correct; while he did not fully understand the nature of British working class loyalty, he correctly gauged its resilience. He did not fear an uprising like that which crippled the French Army in 1917, because he felt that the British were intrinsically superior to the French. What is ironic is that Haig, the man who intentionally remained aloof from his men, had a better understanding of their character than did Lloyd George, who

37 See Keegan, pp. 274–84.
38 C. E. Montague, *Disenchantment*, p. 142.

considered himself their champion. Lloyd George feared that the slaughter of thousands of British soldiers would encourage a Russian-style working class rebellion. For this reason, he desperately sought a less costly way to wage war and also tried to bring Haig under control – succeeding in neither area. Haig, in contrast, believed that his men could take it and Haig was right. His conception of the working class as solid, simple and overwhelmingly obedient was fundamentally correct.

Within the army, there were occasional disturbances to the calm, but they are the exceptions which prove the rule. There were 169,040 courts martial in the British Army during the war, but if one takes into account the extraordinary circumstances of war and an army obsessed with discipline, the figure does not suggest a crime rate significantly higher than would be expected in peacetime civilian society. Courts martial could pertain to relatively minor offences like drunkenness. Those pertaining to mutiny, cowardice and self-inflicted wounds together account for less than 1 per cent of the total number of fighting men.[39] The most famous example of unrest within the army was the Etaples 'mutiny', which shared six basic characteristics with similar, but less striking, disturbances. Firstly, these incidents were connected to a specific grievance, such as ill treatment by a commandant, insufficient supplies or unwholesome food. They could, for instance, occasionally be triggered by something seemingly trivial like a shortage of jam. Secondly, the disturbances almost always occurred behind the lines, where there often lurked a large concentration of 'professional malingerers and shirkers'.[40] Thirdly, they were generally non-violent. Fourthly, the incidents were often perpetrated by regular soldiers rather than conscripts – an indication perhaps that conscription, by widening the pool of recruits, meant a lower proportion of social deviants. Fifthly, the army usually reacted to these disturbances with remarkable restraint, handling them not unlike peacetime industrial action.[41] Finally, and most importantly, the disturbances were not inspired by opposition to the war and were therefore not mutinies in the conventional sense.[42] The little mutinies were essentially variations upon traditional British labour disputes. Interesting as they may be, one must resist the historian's

39 J. Ellis, *Eye-Deep in Hell*, p. 185.

40 D. Englander and J. Osborne, 'Jack, Tommy and Henry Dubb: The Armed Forces and the Working Class', *Historical Journal* 21 (1978), p. 598.

41 Gill and Dallas, 'Mutiny at Etaples Base', pp. 103–4.

42 See R. Holmes, *Firing Line*, p. 44, and G. Dallas and D. Gill, *The Unknown Army*, passim.

tendency to exaggerate the extraordinary. Granted, small disturbances occurred relatively often, but they had absolutely no bearing upon the army's effectiveness. By their triviality, they demonstrate how cohesive, stable and smooth-functioning the army was.

The German commander Erich Ludendorff is reputed to have described the British Army as lions led by donkeys. The aphorism misses the mark. A lion is supposed to symbolise bravery, but is he really brave, or merely dominant? A donkey symbolises stupidity, but is he really stupid, or merely submissive, downtrodden and dominated? In other words, it is perhaps more appropriate to describe the British Army as donkeys led by lions. Officers and commanders were very lion-like: dominant, domineering, selfish and preoccupied with the preservation of their world. With no disrespect intended, the working class soldier was a beast of burden, a man caged by a life of drudgery, squalor, powerlessness and social stasis. As such, he made the perfect soldier.

9 MOBILISING MINDS

As has been seen, the British government relied heavily upon the voluntarist spirit during the war. But, occasionally, people needed persuading before that spirit overwhelmed them. Yet who was to do the persuading if the government instinctively abstained from interfering in the lives of citizens? Who would volunteer to encourage volunteers? A typically British solution was found. Mobilisation of public spirit was performed largely by private bodies, encouraged and guided by government. Direct government intervention occurred as a last resort, in a limited and surreptitious fashion.

There were distinct advantages to this approach. The British were wary of a government which presumed to tell them how to think. The government was equally convinced that good causes should not require advertisement. Therefore, persuasion originating from private sources was more acceptable and more likely to be effective. Also, the approach allowed the government to divorce itself from propaganda's ugly side. Appeals to base instincts were left to newspapers and fringe organisations.

There were also distinct disadvantages to this approach. With no real propaganda programme, private bodies acted in conflict, neutralising each other. For instance, a patriotic newspaper might assure its readers that all was well at the front, in the process undermining a private recruiting committee's efforts to secure volunteers for the army. By failing to manage the news, the government allowed newspapers to create a hero of Kitchener, thus rendering it impossible to get rid of 'Lord K of Chaos' when his deficiencies became apparent. But disorganisation was a cost the government willingly paid in order to preserve the voluntarist principle. In the process, it left itself prey to the spirit it refused to control. Emotions were given free rein and irrationality was often encouraged. The sleep of reason produced monsters.

PROPAGANDA

On the home front, an ad hoc, decentralised and ultimately chaotic approach to propaganda reigned until the last year of the war. Most of the morale-boosting was carried out unconsciously by ordinary citizens. Even at the worst of times, the vast majority of the population wanted to believe that the war was proceeding well. The most popular rumours were those which inspired optimism, such as stories of an angel strengthening the British line at Mons, and of Russian soldiers (still with snow on their boots) seen throughout Britain in August 1914, travelling in the direction of the Western Front. One popular story concerned the alleged madness of the Kaiser, whose ear trouble 'seriously distempers and heats the brain'.[1] Even the more frightening rumours, such as the supposed arrest of five aliens for attempting to poison Chingford reservoir, acted as a spur to vigilance and resolve.[2] The willingness to believe these rumours, as with the keen interest in German atrocity tales, meant that public spirit remained steadfast.

But patriotic individuals were always ready to give public spirit a boost. Until late 1917, when war weariness grew, the government was satisfied to leave propaganda to inspired amateurs in organisations like the Cobden Club, the United Workers, the Atlantic Union and the Victoria League. Through these groups, authors used their skills to patriotic effect. The Fight for Right Movement included among its members John Buchan, Sir Henry Newbolt, Thomas Hardy and Gilbert Murray. According to its manifesto:

> the spirit of the Movement is essentially the spirit of Faith: Faith in the good of man; Faith therefore in ourselves, Faith in the righteousness of our Cause, Faith in the ultimate triumph of Right; but with this Faith the understanding that Right will only win through the purification, the efforts and the sacrifices of men and women who mean to *make* it prevail.[3]

The reference to faith, purification and sacrifice was common: the war was widely seen as an opportunity for spiritual purgation. Churches especially stressed this message. Some sermons were frankly grotesque; P. M. Yearsley, a Wimbledon clergyman, cautioned parishioners that the Germans 'intended, in the event of a successful invasion of England, to destroy every male child'.[4] Other sermons,

---

1 C. Haste, *Keep the Home Fires Burning*, p. 105.
2 T. Wilson, *The Myriad Faces of War*, p. 170.
3 Haste, p. 25.
4 Wilson, p. 740.

if not outright lies, were hardly appropriate to the pulpit: the Bishop of London's recruiting efforts incurred the censure of many colleagues but were undoubtedly successful. Other clergymen were less blatantly jingoistic, but references to the virtue of sacrifice were intentionally unsubtle.

Public taste limited government action. The MP Stanley Baldwin admitted that 'Propaganda is not a word that has a pleasant sound in English ears. . . . The Englishman dislikes talking about himself and dislikes advertising what he has done.' Government advertisement, a wartime memo commented, 'was thought to be the work of the vulgarian; it was also thought useless'.[5] Though the employment of the popular novelist Buchan and the press barons Beaverbrook and Northcliffe to boost morale suggests a wholesale abandonment of such scruples, diehard principles remained strong. In a very hostile Commons debate in August 1918 on the subject of propaganda, one MP objected

> to the assumption that . . . the influencing of thought and opinion amongst civilized nations, is a thing to be carried on in the spirit of a successful commercial traveller, and that the kind of thing that constitutes good advertising for business is the kind of thing that constitutes good advertising in the case of a great nation and a real war.[6]

The government had to promise that all propaganda bodies would be disbanded immediately after the armistice. Aside from the assumed vulgarity of this sort of advertisement, many feared that propaganda might be used to sustain in power an unpopular government.

Much propaganda in the first three years of the war was designed to encourage voluntarism and thus to avoid the necessity for government intervention. Nearly 2.5 million copies of 110 different posters on a multitude of themes were issued in the first year of the war,[7] produced either by a relevant ministry, by quasi-governmental bodies like the Parliamentary Recruiting Committee or by private groups. Nearly every government initiative had its attendant voluntary organisation to urge public support. This pattern began early in the war with the large number of groups formed to persuade the faint-hearted to join Kitchener's army, among them the Order of the White Feather. Later, government bodies like the Ministry of National Service and the National War Savings Committee were aided by a plethora of

5 B. Waites, 'The Government of the Home Front and the "Moral Economy" of the Working Class', in P. Liddle, ed., *Home Fires and Foreign Fields*, p. 191.

6 *Hansard*, 5 August 1918.

7 Wilson, p. 734.

voluntary groups which organised meetings and recruitment drives and, in the case of the Ministry of Food, instituted campaigns to encourage food economy. The novelist Sarah MacNaughten noticed a 'peculiar brutality' in supposedly well-meaning people prodding others to contribute to the war effort. 'I am reminded of birds on a small ledge pushing each other into the sea. The big bird that pushed another one over goes to sleep comfortably.'[8]

One of the biggest birds, both literally and figuratively, was the publicist, newspaper proprietor and one-time MP Horatio Bottomley. He appealed to the population's coarser instincts in a way no self-respecting minister could, such as when he acted as prosecutor in a mock trial of the Kaiser in Bournemouth. Bottomley's populist tactics were enormously influential in motivating the common man to contribute to the war effort, especially early in the war when his recruitment drives produced undeniable surges of commitment. No mainstream politician rivalled him in the crowds he attracted, nor in his ability to rouse working class bigotry. But promotion of the war effort and self-aggrandisement overlapped. 'I sell myself to the man with the most money', he admitted. Recruitment speeches were given free, but at all other patriotic lectures (he gave some 340 during the war) he claimed between 65 and 85 per cent of the proceeds.[9] A highly successful scheme for selling War Savings Certificates and Victory Bonds, advertised in Bottomley's *John Bull*, was eventually discovered fraudulent, resulting in his conviction and imprisonment in 1921.[10]

Early in the war, the most influential voluntary group was the Central Committee for National Patriotic Organizations (CCNPO), formed in August 1914. In theory an educational body, its remit was in truth propagandistic. The presence of eminent political figures in senior, albeit largely titular, positions (Asquith was president, Balfour and Rosebery vice presidents) allowed groups like the CCNPO to claim political legitimacy without having to bear political responsibility. A similar pattern was followed by the Parliamentary Recruiting Committee – the model for quasi-governmental propaganda efforts. Though it had government backing, took advice from the War Office and cooperated with the Ministry of Munitions and the Home Office, it was not strictly speaking an official government body. Great

8 Haste, p. 59.

9 G. S. Messinger, *Propaganda and the State in the First World War*, pp. 208–9.

10 See A. Hyman, *The Rise and Fall of Horatio Bottomley*, and G. Rawlings, 'Swindler of the Century', *History Today* 43 (July 1993), pp. 42–8.

efforts were made to maintain an illusion of voluntarism. Funding came from private sources and, though senior political figures headed the organisation, they did so as private citizens free of party ties. The very nature of the PRC was a propaganda message: its non-partisan structure suggested a spirit of cooperation while its private façade reinforced the voluntarist ethic.

It was not until February 1917, and the establishment of the Department of Information, that the government openly acknowledged involvement in home front propaganda. Lloyd George felt that, after two and a half years of consistently gloomy news, a more dynamic approach was needed. But the semblance of voluntarism was not entirely abandoned. The National War Aims Committee (NWAC), which Buchan's Department of Information established in May 1917, imitated the voluntary, non-partisan character of the PRC. The NWAC, which eventually absorbed the CCNPO, continued its technique of shaping propaganda messages to local conditions. By early 1918 it was active in 345 parliamentary constituencies.[11] During one fortnight in 1917, 899 meetings were organised.[12]

The government's closer supervision of propaganda is demonstrated by the fact that, from August 1917, the Department of Information and the NWAC were both headed by the same man, Sir Edward Carson. Though it was at first dependent upon donations from party funds, this changed in November 1917 when £240,000 was allotted from the Treasury, the largest single sum the government spent on home front propaganda. The NWAC, according to its charter, was designed to 'counteract and render nugatory the insidious and specious propaganda of the pacifist publications' and to encourage the 'inflexible determination to continue to a victorious end the struggle in maintenance of those ideals of Liberty and Justice which are the common and sacred cause of the allies'.[13] (Whether the pacifists deserved such serious attention is open to doubt.) Since women seemed more susceptible to war weariness than men, special attention was given them. As with the government, NWAC volunteers had difficulty distinguishing between genuine pacifism and more general discontent arising from labour problems, inflation or food shortages. Efforts by largely middle class volunteers to encourage renewed sacrifice from mainly working class audiences often annoyed the latter.

11 M. Sanders and P. Taylor, *British Propaganda during the First World War*, p. 68.
12 Messinger, p. 130.
13 Haste, pp. 40–1.

As time wore on, the definition of war aims widened and the scope of NWAC activity broadened. By March 1918 it effectively controlled all home front propaganda. Like the PRC, it concentrated on organising public meetings and producing pamphlets and posters, distribution of which was voluntarily taken on by the newsagents W. H. Smith from October 1917. From August to October 1917, some 3,192 meetings were organised.[14] At large public rallies a brass band would play and often a tank or other impressive weapon of war would be present. The tactic of dropping leaflets from an aeroplane was occasionally employed, as during the Birmingham 'Win the War Day' on 21 September 1918. Great use was made of film, but since cinema space could not always be secured, the NWAC fitted out five motorised cinema vans which toured the country showing films outdoors on gable ends.

One should not infer from the existence of the NWAC that the government engaged in an honest and open discussion of war aims with its citizenry. 'Once it was known we were discussing these questions', a Cabinet document warned, 'the effective prosecution of the war might be rendered more difficult.'[15] But in 1917 a number of incidents dented the popular belief in a just and noble cause. On 19 July the Reichstag passed a resolution calling for a negotiated peace. Scorned by Lloyd George, it was nevertheless welcomed by a small but significant group of MPs. The publication of the Secret Treaties (after Russia's withdrawal from the war) exposed the rather embarrassing territorial claims of the Allies. These events rendered the NWAC's work much more difficult. In the absence of a clearly defined statement of aims, the NWAC instead tried to explain what was happening in the war, in a manner calculated to encourage support for the Allied effort. This included peripheral information on all the belligerent countries and the nature of their governments – rather like a modern studies seminar. Fearing that Bolshevism might be contagious, the NWAC prepared material and speeches directed specifically at the working classes. Pamphlets by prominent trade unionists like Ben Tillet explained why peace on German terms was out of the question. Audiences and readers were told that Prussian militarism had yet to be defeated and that an incomplete peace would only leave it ripe for resurgence. The incurable barbarism of the Teutonic race was a common theme.

Lloyd George finally issued a statement of war aims to a meeting

14 Sanders and Taylor, p. 105.
15 Ibid., p. 68.

of trade unionists on 5 January 1918. Not yet pandering to the public's hunger for revenge, he emphasised that Britain had no intention of destroying Germany or even of imposing democracy upon her. Instead, Britain aimed to defeat Germany's army unconditionally and to use victory for positive ends. These included the restoration of Belgium, the return of Alsace-Lorraine to France, self-determination for other conquered countries, reparations to the victims of German oppression, and the establishment of an international organisation to arbitrate disputes and control arms. Yet one doubts that the statement did much to spur British resolve. By this stage, fatalism had set in: the war was there and it had to be won. Given this fatalism, there was little positive that propaganda could achieve. In March, the government learned a lesson about the manipulation of morale. After four years of trying to convince the public that the Germans were on the brink of defeat, it had to admit that the enemy could still achieve a sizeable victory. Yet strikes stopped, recruiting offices were again crowded and production increased. Contrary to expectations, the public could handle bad news.

Much praise has been given to British propaganda for its contribution to victory, but one doubts that it was instrumental in convincing neutrals to join the cause or in exhorting people at home toward greater effort. The most valuable propaganda work was done inadvertently by the Germans. Their conception of total war was too advanced for British tastes. They were very good at appearing evil, a fact which impressed the British people more than the incessant messages about the worthiness of their own cause. The execution of the nurse Edith Cavell is a case in point. In a strictly legal sense, her assistance to British soldiers stranded behind German lines was indeed espionage. But the Germans failed to understand that their cause would be better served by showing mercy than by the strict application of law.[16] The U-boat war, the shelling of Eastbourne and the bombing of London arose from Germany's acceptance that in modern war all civilians are combatants. Britain and the rest of the 'civilised' world were still a generation away from a similar acceptance.

CENSORSHIP AND THE PRESS

Much of the propaganda work on behalf of the British war effort was performed voluntarily by the patriotic press, and all major newspapers were patriotic. Many had originally opposed the war, shifting

16 H. Lasswell, *Propaganda Technique in the World War*, p. 32.

to a pained acceptance of it after 4 August and, after the German invasion of Belgium, to strident belligerence. The British, enthusiastic newspaper readers, enjoyed a wide variety of papers. Sixteen daily newspapers served London alone.[17] Newspapers not only knew how to reach the ordinary citizen, they knew how to communicate with him – skills which the government did not have. Witness, for instance, the massive circulation of the letter from 'A Little Mother', published in the *Morning Post* in 1916, with its exhortation to women to 'pass on the human ammunition of "only sons" to fill the gaps'. The letter was subsequently made into a pamphlet which sold 75,000 copies in less than a week,[18] a far more impressive circulation than anything produced by the CCNPO, PRC or NWAC. It is ironic that the government and the military were so suspicious of the fourth estate, placing ridiculous obstacles in the way of reporters who were, on the whole, extremely loyal.

An uneasy relationship existed between government and the press. On the one hand, most newspaper proprietors rose from the same stock and belonged to the same clubs as politicians. But they were still a breed apart, rather like eccentric and mischievous cousins who refused to conform to an established code of behaviour. The responsibility of journalists to criticise government was accepted in theory by both sides but caused conflict in practice, especially since during wartime criticism was easily confused with disloyalty. Ministers expected that they should be able to sit down with press lords and decide, over cold salmon and champagne, what the people should know. Most of the time this arrangement worked. C. P. Scott, editor of the *Manchester Guardian*, decided not to publish a letter received from a corporal who described how the British had shelled their own troops at Loos, because it would be 'too damaging' to morale.[19] But occasionally newspapers acted too independently for the government's liking, which caused some politicians to demand stiff curbs on the press. Because press lords felt their loyalty was beyond question, they resented regulation. Those who were chummy with ministers were given special favours, those who were not suffered unfairly. A 'network of uneasy and transitory relationships' developed between politicians and newspapermen eager to use each other for their own purposes.[20]

17 Haste, p. 29.
18 Wilson, p. 402.
19 T. Wilson, ed., *The Political Diaries of C. P. Scott*, p. 142.
20 S. Koss, *The Rise and Fall of the Political Press*, p. 249.

A paranoid government feared that spies lurked in every corner ready to exploit careless leaks of information. Some regulations were ridiculous: weather reports were banned from newspapers on the grounds that they were useful to the enemy, and the publication of chess problems (suspected of being a conduit for secret messages) ceased. More serious were the controls imposed by the Press Bureau, headed by F. E. Smith. It was established on 6 August by the First Lord, Winston Churchill, acting in cooperation with Kitchener. The Bureau, according to Churchill, would ensure that 'a steady stream of trustworthy information supplied both by the War Office and the Admiralty can be given to the press'.[21] In fact, the stream was hardly steady and the information it carried seldom trustworthy. Journalists quickly discovered that the Press Bureau's function, contrary to Smith's claims, was not publicity but censorship. They renamed it the *Sup*press Bureau. Smith did not last long, being replaced at the Bureau by Sir Stanley Buckmaster on 30 September 1914. He demanded sweeping powers to 'punish as well as threaten the press', but the government wisely decided that further restrictions were unnecessary.[22] He subsequently complained that cosy relationships between ministers and certain press lords 'rendered the proper execution of my duties extremely difficult'. There were occasions, he claimed,

> when strong measures should have been taken with papers like *The Times* and the *Daily Mail* [but] my efforts to exercise against them the powers conferred by the Defence of the Realm Act were defeated from within [the government].[23]

By November 1914 Bonar Law was questioning whether 'the Press is more muzzled than is necessary for military reasons'.[24]

Censorship came in two forms. The information journalists received was strictly controlled; banned from close proximity to the fighting forces, they had to rely on government briefings. Had Kitchener had his way, the army would have operated in total secrecy. But since he could not be that restrictive, he instead advised that 'it is not always easy to decide what information may or may not be dangerous, and whenever there is any doubt we do not hesitate to prevent publication'.[25] The army spokesman, Colonel Sir Ernest

21 Sanders and Taylor, p. 20.
22 N. Hiley, ' "Lord Kitchener Resigns": The Suppression of the *Globe* in 1915', *Journal of Newspaper and Periodical History* 8 (1992), p. 27.
23 Koss, p. 245.
24 Haste, p. 37.
25 Sanders and Taylor, p. 23.

Swinton, endeavoured to 'tell as much of the truth as was compatible with safety, to guard against depression and pessimism, and to check unjustified optimism which might lead to a relaxation of effort'.[26] As his statement attests, censorship was intended both to prevent valuable information from getting into enemy hands and to keep the public ignorant lest its morale prove precarious. Buckmaster sought to control information which would 'unduly depress our people', a policy which prompted one irate citizen to remark: 'It seems incredible that an official in such a capacity could so entirely be a stranger to the sentiment and character of our British race as to think such a course advisable.'[27] Mr Punch felt 'a certain envy of the Americans. Even their provincial organs often contain important and cheering news of the doings of the British Army many days before the Censor releases the information in England.'[28] Asquith noted as early as September 1914 that 'The papers are complaining, not without reason, that we keep them on a starvation diet.' But instead of improving the supply of information, he urged Churchill to add 'such a seasoning of condiments as your well-skilled hand can supply'.[29]

The second form of censorship was the control exercised over what journalists wrote. The pre-war practice of voluntary censorship was continued; editors submitted to the Bureau any material felt to be sensitive, but were not required to do so. The Bureau regularly issued 'D' notices designed to warn editors about topics they should avoid. Though some editors complained that the system was open to exploitation by the unscrupulous, self censorship worked because the government could impose heavy penalties under DORA against those who transgressed. The most notable example was the two-week suppression of the *Globe* after it published stories in November 1915 that Kitchener was being forced to resign. The story originated from within the government and was essentially true – a fact which did not prevent the paper's punishment under DRR27 of DORA, which rendered it unlawful to 'spread false reports or make false statements'.[30] Editors could be prosecuted for publishing anything deemed valuable to the enemy, even if the information originated from an official source like the Press Bureau. Furthermore, though the Bureau operated under the auspices of the Home Office, it was

26 Haste, p. 32.
27 *The Times*, 16 November 1914.
28 Wilson, *Myriad Faces*, p. 195.
29 Haste, p. 34.
30 Hiley, ' "Lord Kitchener Resigns" ', p. 33.

not its agent. Thus, an article passed by Bureau censors might still invite Home Office prosecution.[31]

For most of the war, but particularly in the first crucial year, the government failed abysmally to manage the news. The Bureau did not confirm the embarkation of the BEF until three days after it arrived in France, thus annoying reporters who felt that not only did the public have a right to know, but that knowledge of how smoothly the action had been executed would have been a boon to morale. Given a loyal press, it would have made more sense for the Bureau to have assumed a public relations function rather than a regulatory one. But what was perhaps most annoying was the lack of consistent guidelines governing what could and could not be reported. *The Times*, commenting on the *Globe* affair, remarked how the government had 'not for the first time ... missed a golden opportunity of working with the press instead of attempting to mystify it, feed it with half-truths and finally to penalise it'.[32] No restrictions were imposed on reporting the retreat from Mons, a setback the government should presumably have kept under wraps.[33] In contrast, the sinking of the battleship *Audacious* on 27 October 1914 was kept secret for the entire war, much to the annoyance of Rear-Admiral Sir Douglas Brownrigg, the Royal Navy's Chief Censor, who felt that the decision 'cost us the confidence of the public both here and abroad'.[34] Obsessive secrecy convinced some journalists, in particular *The Times* military correspondent, Charles a'Court Repington, that censorship was 'a cloak to cover all political, naval and military mistakes'[35] and that journalists consequently had a duty to expose them. But most reporters patiently tolerated restrictions.

In the absence of real news, it is no wonder that the press exaggerated relatively insignificant events, such as air raids. These provided exciting stories (unlike the Western Front) and conveniently underlined the barbarism of the Hun. The stories also escaped the jurisdiction of the Censor, since they concerned information in the public domain. But they spread fear throughout Britain, even in places where German bombers could not possibly reach. Press Bureau appeals to newspapers to 'refrain from publishing further articles which may add to the feeling of apprehension ... already

---

31 Sanders and Taylor, pp. 21–2.
32 *The Times*, 8 November 1915.
33 Sanders and Taylor, p. 24.
34 Messinger, p. 115.
35 Sanders and Taylor, p. 24.

prevalent specially among the poorest and most ignorant classes'[36] had little effect. Sensational reporting reinforced the view that all journalists could not be trusted. Yet the government had only itself to blame; a more cooperative policy would have permitted more effective control over stories deemed inconvenient. The massive gulf between the home front and the fighting front, about which almost every soldier complained, was widened by the difficulty even the most sincere civilians experienced in trying to learn legitimate news of the war.

Lord Robert Cecil, Parliamentary Under Secretary at the Foreign Office, began a personal campaign in mid-1915 to convince the government that strict secrecy was alienating an important ally, the press. Restrictions impeded propaganda efforts in neutral countries. Some journalists found that the more liberal Foreign Office would release information banned by the Bureau. Cecil's campaign was moderately successful; by 20 December 1915 all restrictions on material relating to foreign affairs were abolished.[37] But policies toward the press still differed from ministry to ministry and often contradicted each other.

Meanwhile the Press Bureau, under its new co-directors, E. T. Cook and Frank Swettenham, grew slowly more accommodating toward journalists. Weekly ministerial press conferences organised by the Newspaper Proprietors Association began in February 1915. Finally, in May 1915, restrictions barring correspondents from the front were lifted. Also, on Foreign Office instigation, senior army and naval officers gave regular weekly briefings to journalists. The establishment of MI7 within the War Office in early 1916 improved the handling of information with better recognition of how censorship could serve propaganda. These changes did not, however, immediately improve the accuracy of reporting, since the high command, still deeply suspicious of the press, imposed strict restrictions on where correspondents could go. Reporters were carefully provided a 'headquarters view' which reflected prevalent optimism. At Haig's GHQ, intelligence, censorship and propaganda were all handled by Brigadier General John Charteris who tended to confuse his various functions. On one occasion reporters were shown debilitated German prisoners as proof that attrition was proceeding inexorably. But in order to drive home this message, Charteris removed able-bodied

---

36 Wilson, *Myriad Faces*, p. 510.
37 Sanders and Taylor, p. 29.

prisoners before the inspection. Patriotic reporters further embellished Charteris's already well-embroidered information.

The press willingly cooperated in the collective effort to pull the wool over the public's eyes. Ponsonby felt that there was 'no more discreditable period in the history of journalism'.[38] Since the army and navy provided few actual tales of heroism, desperate and unscrupulous correspondents occasionally made them up. Haig's horses may have stood unemployed in army stables, but magazines and newspapers reported dramatic cavalry charges. As Lord Rothermere admitted to J. L. Garvin, 'We're telling lies, we know we're telling lies, we daren't tell the truth.'[39] One of the more honest war correspondents, Philip Gibbs, commented candidly on the elusive nature of truth:

> My dispatches tell the truth. There is not a word, I vow, of conscious falsehood in them . . . but they do not tell all the truth. I have had to spare the feelings of the men and women who have sons and husbands still fighting in France. I have not told all there is to tell about the agonies of this war, nor given in full realism the horrors that are inevitable in such fighting. It is perhaps better not to do so, here and now, although it is a moral cowardice which makes many people shut their eyes to the shambles, comforting their soul with fine phrases about the beauty of sacrifice.[40]

Throughout the war, prosecution of newspapers was remarkably rare – evidence of their willingness to cooperate. The Press Bureau did admonish editors sometimes as often as three times a week,[41] but admonishments predominantly arose from indiscretions born of over-enthusiasm, not from wilful attempts to undermine the war effort or to criticise the government or the forces. Granted, there were times when the government was criticised, most notably during the Shell Scandal. Northcliffe was notably successful in undermining the authority of Asquith. But criticisms of the government were designed to encourage a more dynamic war effort. And, though the press misled the public, the patriotic public appears to have preferred it that way. When the *Daily Mail* rightly blamed the shell shortage on Kitchener, a huge public outcry ensued. Advertisers cancelled contracts and circulation plummeted by over a million.

---

38 Ibid., p. 30.

39 L. Masterman, *C. F. G. Masterman*, p. 296. The quotation is admittedly third hand, coming via Lucy Masterman's husband.

40 Haste, pp. 68–9.

41 Ibid., p. 31.

Though relations between press and government improved during the war, improvement came on the latter's terms. Government gradually realised that journalists were both willing and well-suited to perform a valuable propaganda function. Emphasis shifted from controlling the press to playing upon journalists' egos. Poachers were promoted to gamekeepers, as for instance in the appointment of George Riddell as a government adviser early in the war, and later in the drafting of Beaverbrook, Rothermere and Northcliffe into the Cabinet. Lower down the scale, journalists were kept sweet with minor posts in the Press Bureau, exclusive access to military sources or by strategic use of the honours system. It was not a proud period for British journalism. The Harlot of Fleet Street sold herself cheaply.

GERMAN ATROCITIES

Widespread circulation of German atrocity stories from the first weeks of the war has led conspiracy theorists to suspect a government plot, planned in advance of war's outbreak. This idea was popular during the 1930s for two reasons. Firstly, those inclined to be charitable toward Germany sensed an orchestrated campaign of black propaganda against her during and after the war.[42] Secondly, pacifists, astonished at the way the British people participated so willingly in the war, assumed they must have been duped. But it seems unlikely that a government so naive about propaganda and generally ill-prepared for war could have planned such a campaign. Nor did a government body capable of doing so exist before August 1914. Yet before the war was a week old, atrocity stories were in circulation and reported in newspapers. One has to conclude that the wide dissemination of these stories arose from a 'political and cultural self-mobilisation'[43] – people, government and press all suffered the same hysteria.

Popular fears encouraged a tendency to believe the worst about the enemy and to make up or pass on stories which reinforced cultural stereotypes. Severed hand stories, which had many variations, are deeply symbolic. The victims were usually innocent children or young (virginal) women, or members of the clergy or nuns, suggesting religious martyrdom. Many atrocity stories had sexual/sado-masochistic themes; Nurse Hume, it was alleged, had her

42 See, for instance, A. Ponsonby, *Falsehood in War-Time*.
43 I am grateful to John Horne who, by delightful coincidence, happened to give a paper at St Andrews on the subject of atrocities while I was preparing this chapter.

breasts cut off by a German soldier. Without going too deeply into psychological explanations for the public's fascination, one suspects that the stories allowed the discussion of topics ordinarily considered taboo.[44] 'A young woman ravished by the enemy', wrote Harold Lasswell, 'yields secret satisfaction to a host of vicarious ravishers on the other side.'[45]

Myths and gossip aside, many atrocities actually did occur. During the advance through Belgium (the period from which most stories emerged), the enormous pressure upon the mainly conscript German army left soldiers prey to collective hysteria. When Belgians resisted the invaders, sometimes viciously, German officers ordered their men to respond with brutality. Hostages were taken, human shields were used and rape was widely committed. One study of the invasion has recorded in excess of 100 incidents in which more than ten civilians were killed. An estimated 20,000 to 30,000 buildings were destroyed, not as a result of fighting between armies, but from malicious burning. The Germans did not deny their part in these reprisals, but were surprised when they were labelled atrocities by Entente authorities keen to exploit the propaganda value.[46]

Real events combined with civilian fantasy to produce powerful myths. The fear and excitement of autumn 1914 rendered the British susceptible to fantastic atrocity stories. The highly charged atmosphere was further enhanced by Belgian refugees who were readily available to confirm stories. Since the stories were by definition sensational, they made good newspaper copy, better than anything emanating from the front. In newspaper caricatures, German soldiers were drawn as murderers, rapists, sadists and arsonists.[47] It was only natural that newspapers occasionally fabricated stories which were felt to be true but for which there was no hard evidence. For instance, a pre-war photograph showing three German soldiers holding trophies won in an athletics contest was recaptioned by the *Daily Mirror* as 'three German cavalrymen loaded with gold and silver loot'.[48] A

44 Haste, p. 85.

45 Lasswell, p. 82.

46 See J. Horne and A. Kramer, 'German "Atrocities" and Franco-German Opinion, 1914: The Evidence of German Soldiers' Diaries', *Journal of Modern History* 66 (1994), pp. 4–32.

47 See E. Demm, 'Propaganda and Caricature in the First World War', *Journal of Contemporary History* 28 (1993), pp. 163–92.

48 Haste, p. 88.

picture of a Russian pogrom against Jews in 1905 was reprinted in British papers as evidence of German atrocities in Belgium.[49]

The public's appetite was limitless, yet so was the German ability to provide raw material for propaganda machines. Factual German atrocities were almost as shocking as imagined ones. After the 'rape' of Belgium came the use of poison gas, Zeppelin raids and unrestricted submarine warfare. The shelling of Scarborough and Hartlepool in December 1914 resulted in over 700 casualties, with 137 people killed. The fact that a party of schoolchildren was hit reinforced prevalent conceptions about German barbarity. Since the raid had no military justification, its only significant effect was to render the British more worried about invasion and thus more determined to resist. The coining of the *Lusitania* medal, a clumsy bit of satire, likewise demonstrated the German tendency to score own goals. The medal was actually an attempt to draw attention to British hypocrisy by pointing out that the *Lusitania* had indeed carried arms and that German warnings to such ships had been ignored. Yet it was too easily confused with a medal congratulating the successful U-boat crew, a judgement encouraged by British propaganda. Fed a steady diet of tales which had a factual basis, the public naturally tended to believe occasional stories which were totally fabricated, such as rumours which circulated in 1917 about German corpse conversion factories.

The government was not above adding grist to the atrocity mill. In October 1914, Asquith derided German 'hordes who leave behind them at every stage of their progress a dismal trail of savagery, of devastation and of desecration worthy of the blackest annals of the history of barbarism'.[50] The NWAC published a 'German Crimes Calendar' listing a separate atrocity for each month, the specific date of the crime circled in red. A more sustained effort to make use of atrocities came with the Bryce Report, formally titled *Report of the Committee on Alleged German Outrages*. The report was aimed at neutral countries, particularly the United States. Its release one week after the *Lusitania* sinking was a lucky coincidence which magnified its impact in America. But it also had an enormous effect at home, where it sold for 1d, the price of a newspaper. The 360-page report (with an evidentiary appendix another 300 pages long) seemed by its very bulk to confirm German wrongdoing. It also helped that

49 A. G. Marquis, 'Words as Weapons: Propaganda in Britain and Germany During the First World War', *Journal of Contemporary History* 13 (1978), p. 487.

50 Haste, pp. 22–3.

Lord Bryce, formerly Ambassador to Washington, had impeccable credentials for honesty and objectivity and was, rather conveniently, an admitted Germanophile who had, until the invasion of Belgium, opposed British involvement in the war. In the introduction he explained how his doubts had been overwhelmed by 'this concurrence of testimony, this convergence upon what were substantially the same broad facts, . . . the truth of these broad facts stood out beyond question'.[51] The evidence convinced Bryce that Germany was guilty of 'murder, lust and pillage . . . on a scale unparalleled in any war between civilized nations during the last three centuries'. Crimes had been committed not because of poor discipline but as part of 'a system and in pursuance of a set purpose'.[52]

The Bryce Committee was hardly a model of judicial rectitude. Depositions were not taken under oath and, as the Home Secretary, Sir John Simon, admitted, the committee passed judgement 'without themselves undertaking the work of interrogation'.[53] Evidence which questioned the legitimacy of atrocity claims, such as the fact that no actual victims of hand amputation could be found, did not make it into the report. When one committee member, Harold Cox, expressed a desire to investigate the reliability of evidence, he was discouraged from doing so. One of the more malleable (and mainstream) members of the committee, Sir Kenelm Digby, who admitted that there was 'probably a good deal of exaggeration and inaccuracy' to the evidence, nevertheless advanced the concept of 'general truth' – while all the specific events might not be true, the tendencies they indicated were. 'We ought as much as possible to avoid the appearance of relying on individual cases', he wrote, 'and rest on the broader facts where you have concurrent testimony.'[54] But, as Cox pointed out, the broader facts were all based on individual cases, therefore if the latter were suspect so too were the former. His reservations had little impact on the committee or the report. One wonders how a man of such seemingly impeccable honesty as Bryce was led astray. Perhaps his loyalty to a greater truth convinced him of the necessity of telling lesser lies. In his mind Germany was evil and Britain's cause just. To question individual

---

51 Sanders and Taylor, p. 143.

52 Wilson, *Myriad Faces*, p. 189.

53 T. Wilson, 'Lord Bryce's Investigation into Alleged German Atrocities in Belgium, 1914–15', *Journal of Contemporary History* 14 (1979), p. 373.

54 Ibid., pp. 374–5.

cases of atrocities threatened to bring the entire edifice of Germany's evil tumbling down.[55]

THE ENEMY WITHIN

Alleged German atrocities fired latent anti-German animosity. The victims of this epidemic of hatred were those of German origin living in Britain. Pre-war invasion literature had prepared the ground for this surge of anti-alien paranoia. The Hun invasion would be facilitated, so the stories went, by thousands of German bakers, barbers, butchers and waiters who were quietly awaiting the opportunity to assist the Fatherland. Thus, when war broke out, a gullible, frightened public assumed that every innocent German shopkeeper or tradesman was an enemy agent. Stories circulated about German waiters and butchers poisoning food, German watchmakers constructing bombs, German barbers cutting customers' throats.

Newspapers, chief among them the *Daily Mail* and *John Bull*, warned against the 'enemy in our midst'. Early in the war the former demanded a boycott of restaurants employing Germans:

> REFUSE TO BE SERVED BY A GERMAN WAITER. IF YOUR WAITER SAYS HE IS SWISS, ASK TO SEE HIS PASSPORT. THE NATURALIZATION FORM IS JUST A SCRAP OF PAPER. ONCE A GERMAN ALWAYS A GERMAN.[56]

'I call for a vendetta', wrote Bottomley,

> a vendetta against every German in Britain – whether 'naturalised' or not. As I have said before, you cannot naturalise an unnatural abortion, a hellish freak. But you can exterminate it. And now the time has come.[57]

John Bull carried out a vicious assault upon politicians with supposedly German connections, such as those with German-sounding names (like Sir Edgar Speyer) or with pre-war business interests in Germany. The First Sea Lord, Prince Louis of Battenberg, born in Austria to a German prince, was by any reasonable assessment a loyal and trustworthy public servant. But this was wartime, and the public far from reasonable. He was hounded from office in October 1914 and later resorted to changing his name to Mountbatten. The politician who suffered most was Haldane, who had done so much

55 See ibid., pp. 379–82.
56 Haste, p. 113.
57 P. Panayi, *The Enemy in Our Midst*, p. 233.

to prepare Britain for war. Two days into the war the *Daily Express* complained pointedly of the presence within the government of 'elderly doctrinaire lawyers with German sympathies'.[58] *John Bull* made much of the fact that Haldane's dog was named Kaiser. 'Every kind of ridiculous legend about me was circulated', Haldane recalled,

> I had a German wife; I was an illegitimate brother of the Kaiser; I had been in secret correspondence with the German government; I had been aware that they intended war and withheld this from my colleagues; I had delayed the dispatch and mobilisation of the expeditionary force.[59]

It was no coincidence that, when the first coalition was established in May 1915, a wary Asquith could find no room for Haldane.

The Royal Automobile Club and the Stock Exchange banned members of German origin for the duration of the war. Even the UDC decided that 'persons of enemy alien nationality should not be enrolled'.[60] Demands for a boycott of German or any foreign goods naturally benefited companies able to prove undiluted British pedigree. Dunlop Tyres made much of its British origin, forcing its main competitor, Michelin, to insist that it had 'contributed more to the war than any other tyre company'.[61] De Reszke cigarettes insisted that its products 'are British-made and all the shares in the company are held by British subjects. Mr. Millhoff, the managing director, is a Russian by birth'.[62] The drinks manufacturer Schweppes had a difficult time convincing the public that it was originally a Swiss firm, now manufacturing exclusively in Great Britain.[63] An advertisement by Onoto pens sought to inform the British public that 'the Waterman Pen is sold in this country through the Austrian-controlled firm L. and C. Hardmuth. . . . Every Waterman Pen sold therefore . . . means profit to the King's enemies.'[64] British flower bulb growers made much of the fact that Dutch growers were still trading with the enemy.[65] 'Are you drinking German waters?' one advertisement ran, 'Apollinaris comes from Germany. Perrier comes from France. Perrier – the table water of the Allies.'[66]

The reaction by aliens, the vast majority of whom were entirely

58 Wilson, *Myriad Faces*, p. 198.
59 Haste, p. 125.
60 Panayi, pp. 199–200.
61 *The Scotsman*, 16 September 1915.
62 *The Times*, 2 September 1914.
63 Ibid., 2 October 1914.
64 *The Scotsman*, 12 November 1914.
65 Ibid., 8 October 1915.
66 Ibid., 7 January 1915.

innocent and loyal, was so desperate as to be pathetic. German commodities like liverwurst were given anglicised names, as were Turkish baths. Union Jacks were prominent in shops. A Kentish Town barber displayed in his window the notice: 'THIS IS A INGEL-ISCHE SCHOPP'. A baker, apparently unaware of the nuances of alliances in mid-August 1914, adorned his van with signs which read: 'We beg to inform the public that we are Italian bakers, fighting side by side with the English.'[67] But these efforts seldom deterred irrational crowds. Aliens and anyone of German origin suffered terribly. Despite the labour shortage, it became extremely difficult for them to find work.

Aliens were suspected not only of espionage but also of a concerted campaign of moral corruption. In the *Imperialist*, Captain Harold Spencer warned on 26 January 1918 that 'agents so vile [were] spreading debauchery of such lasciviousness as only German minds could conceive and only German bodies execute'.[68] He and Pemberton Billing MP claimed access to a 'Black Book' compiled by German agents which named 47,000 Britons, including 'Privy Councillors, youths of the chorus, wives of Cabinet Ministers, dancing girls, even Cabinet Ministers themselves . . . diplomats, poets, bankers, editors, newspaper proprietors, and members of His Majesty's household', who had engaged in 'the propagation of evils which all decent men thought had perished in Sodom and Lesbia'.[69] (If only German bodies were capable of these perversions, one wonders how the 47,000 managed to learn.) The Commissioner of the Metropolitan Police, Sir Edward Henry, began an investigation in 1916 of 28 coffeehouses and cafés owned or frequented by Belgian refugees which were havens for 'prostitutes and other undesirables' including spies.[70] The logic was clear: since perversion is foreign, most foreigners are perverts, and those perverted must be under foreign influence. According to popular prejudice, sexual deviancy and espionage were connected; aliens used their deviant ways to weaken Britain. Combating spies therefore helped to purify Britain.

The outpouring of hatred, sanctioned by government and press, erupted into mob violence whenever a highly visible German 'atrocity' occurred. 'No immigrant community in twentieth-century

---

67 *The Times*, 17 August 1914.
68 Panayi, p. 176.
69 P. Barker, *The Eye in the Door*, pp. 154–5.
70 Wilson, *Myriad Faces*, pp. 402–3.

Britain', Panayi argues, 'has endured violence on such a scale.'[71] The worst riots occurred in May 1915, prompted by news of the German use of gas on the Western Front and by the *Lusitania* sinking. At least seven deaths were recorded. In Liverpool, an estimated £40,000 worth of damage was caused and 200 buildings were 'gutted'.[72] Of the 21 Metropolitan Police districts, only two were free of disorder.[73] In East London, Sylvia Pankhurst watched in horror as a crowd knocked a woman to the ground and kicked her until she was unconscious.

Those on the political fringe benefited from the tide of hatred. Bizarre racialist creeds suddenly became acceptable. Disappointed by government inaction, Admiral Charles Beresford called for full internment of enemy aliens and advocated the establishment of vigilante teams to search out foreign traitors. Dr Ellis Powell, editor of the *Financial News*, attracted huge crowds to his speeches about the German-inspired 'Unseen Hand' – 'a magnetic and dexterous personality . . . at work permeating every department of our public life, rewarding subservience, and penalising independence'.[74] The Anti-German League, which became the British Empire Union after 1915, counted among its ranks Beresford, Havelock Wilson, Powell and the future Home Secretary William Joynson-Hicks. It was yet another privately organised propaganda body, dedicated to spreading hatred of all things German. The group produced the 1918 film *Once a Hun, Always a Hun*, which advocated a ban on trading with Germany after the war. In August 1917, Brigadier General Henry Page Croft took racism into parliamentary politics with the establishment of the National Party. After the war he attracted considerable support with his demands that 'no one not born a British subject and son of a British father' should be eligible for any government service and that all Germans should be banned from living in Britain for ten years.[75]

The shock and disappointment which followed the German spring offensive in 1918 prompted fresh outbreaks of anti-alien feeling, extending even to Belgian and French residents. Spy stories

---

71 Panayi, p. 257.
72 *The Times*, 12 May 1915.
73 Panayi, p. 243.
74 See *The Times*, 9 February, 5 March 1917.
75 C. Wrigley, ' "In the Excess of their Patriotism": The National Party and Threats of Subversion', in Wrigley, ed., *Warfare, Diplomacy and Politics, Essays in Honour of A. J. P. Taylor*, p. 104. See also W. D. Rubinstein, 'Henry Page Croft and the National Party 1917–22', *Journal of Contemporary History* 9 (1974), pp. 129–48.

provided convenient explanations for the successful assault. The British Empire Union and the British Empire League sponsored rallies in London and around the country calling for concerted action against aliens. A rally on 13 July was, according to *The Times*, 'the biggest crowd seen in [Trafalgar] Square since the outbreak of the war'. In August, an anti-alien petition bearing 1.25 million signatures was delivered to Downing Street. In the following month, over 1,000 demonstrators picketed the residence of the Foreign Office official Sir Eyre Crowe, whose misfortune it was to have been born in Germany to a German mother. By no stretch of the imagination were his pre-war actions even remotely pro-German.[76]

D. H. Lawrence, himself a victim of irrational prejudice (his wife was a German), described how 'a wave of criminal lust rose and possessed England'. Pressure from 'indecent bullies like Bottomley of *John Bull* and other bottom-dog members of the House of Commons . . . was steadily applied . . . to break the independent soul in any man who would not hunt with the criminal mob'. Yet even Lawrence wrote, after the *Lusitania* sinking, that he was 'mad with rage. . . . I would like to kill a million Germans – two millions.'[77] Panayi rightly argues that though latent anti-alienism existed, the fierce hostility toward Germans arose more from 'the weight of immediate influences'.[78] 'Alas, poor Patriotism, what foolish cruelties are committed in thy Name!' Pankhurst concluded.[79]

POSTSCRIPT

British propaganda during the war was characterised by terrible chaos and lack of direction. The early reliance upon voluntary bodies made it impossible for any cohesion to be developed. When the government began to intervene more actively, it did so on a piecemeal basis, such that contradictory policies were pursued by competing departments. The establishment of a Ministry of Information improved matters, but Beaverbrook still found that 'the sphere of the Ministry's work was not defined with sufficient clearness. No charter of rights and duties [was] drawn up.'[80] Given these deficiencies, one doubts that propaganda made a significant contribution to

---

76 Wilson, *Myriad Faces*, p. 643.
77 Panayi, p. 286.
78 Ibid., p. 291.
79 Wilson, *Myriad Faces*, pp. 160–1.
80 Sanders and Taylor, p. 86.

maintaining home front morale. Even the best propagandist would have had difficulty putting a gloss on such a static and costly war. For the first four years of the war the British people had little reason to feel cheerful, yet their morale held. They were not duped by their government; a propaganda effort so chaotic could not have contributed to mass mind control. The steadfast patriotism of the British people and their unquenchable faith in eventual victory instead arose from within themselves.

10 HOUSES, HOMES AND HEALTH

A chapter on British home life during the Great War by necessity focuses upon women. This does not 'ghettoize' women's history but rather emphasises contributions frequently unrecognised. Even feminist historians have tended to concentrate on women's work outside the home, especially in jobs previously performed by men – thus perpetuating a male-orientated standard of achievement. Yet whatever else women did during the war, they also managed homes and held families together. Since many carried out these functions in addition to full-time employment, their achievement is all the more impressive. The maternalist pacifist Catherine Marshall warned that

> War is pre-eminently an outrage on motherhood and all that mother-hood means; the destruction of life and the breaking-up of homes is the undoing of women's work as life-givers and home-makers.[1]

British society survived the war intact largely because women, despite all the pressures upon them, continued to be wives and mothers.

HOUSING

In poorer tenements before the Great War, conditions were often atrocious – cramped, ill-heated, damp and vermin-infested. For the working class housewife, maintaining the home meant cooking, cleaning and washing without any of the labour-saving devices taken for granted today. Homes were not only harder to clean, they became dirty easier, due to the more squalid environment and the scarcity of clean water. A 1901 Rowntree survey found only 19 per cent of houses in York had a separate water supply. Even fewer had baths or indoor toilets.[2] Water had to be carried up flights of stairs, with waste water carried down. Local authorities were technically respons-ible for improving the housing stock, but slum clearance was impeded

---

1 J. Hinton, *Protests and Visions*, p. 44.
2 A. Marwick, *The Deluge*, p. 65.

by lack of funds. Private landlords, tempted by other attractive investments, only reluctantly spent money on improvements.

During the war, the Royal Commission on Housing in Scotland described 'dark, narrow and foul-smelling' tenements where the stairs are 'filthy and evil-smelling, and foul water run[s] down the stairs, sickly cats everywhere spread . . . disease'. Another study of housing in Wales revealed

> The towns and villages are ugly and overcrowded; houses are scarce and rents increasing, and the surroundings unsanitary and depressing. The scenery is disfigured by unsightly refuse tips, the atmosphere polluted by coal dust and smoke and the rivers spoilt by liquid refuse from works and factories. Facilities for education and recreation are inadequate and opportunities for the wise use of leisure are few.[3]

Overcrowding was rife. The average pre-war family had 4.6 children; 71 per cent had four or more, 41 per cent seven or more.[4] In 1911, more than 30 per cent of the population lived in conditions of more than three persons to two rooms. Between 1911 and 1915, more houses were demolished in London than built.[5] Nation-wide, construction virtually ground to a halt once war began, since manpower and raw materials were more urgently needed elsewhere. The number of families sharing a dwelling increased from 15.7 per cent in 1914 to 20 per cent by war's end.[6] The proportion of uninhabited to inhabited dwellings dropped significantly, which implies that the desperate took up residence in houses previously deemed unfit for human habitation.[7] By the end of the war, the shortage of homes was estimated at 600,000.[8] Yet large houses in the cities often stood vacant, temporarily abandoned by the wealthy who could no longer find servants to maintain them.

The only significant building programmes carried out during the war were organised by the government to house munitions workers. By the end of the war, the Ministry of Munitions had spent £4.3 million housing its workers. From 1915 to 1916, over 12,000 rooms at Woolwich and Greenwich were provided; in the same period only 30 private houses were built in all of London.[9] Approximately 2,800

---

3 Ibid., pp. 244–5.
4 G. Braybon and P. Summerfield, *Out of the Cage: Women's Experiences in Two World Wars*, p. 23.
5 J. Burnett, *A Social History of Housing 1815–1970*, p. 217.
6 Braybon and Summerfield, p. 98.
7 J. Winter, *The Great War and the British People*, p. 243.
8 M. Bowley, *Housing and the State 1919–1941*, p. 12.
9 Winter, p. 243.

temporary cottages and 10,000 houses were built by the Ministry on 38 separate estates during the war. While the emphasis was at first on temporary accommodation, some impressive permanent houses were built, such as Well Hall Estate, near Woolwich. But approximately 20,000 munitions workers lived in hostels, usually converted schools or church halls which offered a barrack-like existence, with unappetising food and poor heating.

Increased demand for homes combined with static supply meant galloping rent inflation, a problem especially acute where war industries attracted workers from around the country. Unscrupulous landlords (they were common) often raised the rents of sitting tenants to intolerable levels in order to make way for more affluent immigrant workers. Box and Cox arrangements were not unknown: lodgings were rented to one group of workers by day, another by night. Given its liberal inclinations, the government would ordinarily have been inclined to stay out of the housing quagmire, but when landlords took out eviction orders, the police became involved and so too, by association, did the government. By autumn 1915, unrest was occurring in Birmingham, Luton, Manchester, Glasgow and London. An extended strike in Glasgow which began when some 5,000 people, mainly women, came out in support of an impoverished soldier's wife (and mother of seven) who faced eviction, finally inspired government action. The Increase of Rent and Mortgage Interest (Rent Restriction) Act, introduced in Parliament on 25 November 1915, pegged rents for working class dwellings at pre-war levels and stipulated that mortgages were not to be foreclosed nor interest rates increased. The first rent restriction act passed in British history, it exceeded the protesters' demands. Since rents were set at 1914 levels, with no account for wartime inflation, landlords were transformed overnight from profiteers to dispossessed. They reacted, quite naturally, by neglecting maintenance.

Housing was occasionally made worse by enemy action. In December 1914, German cruisers shelled East Coast towns, causing minor damage and some 700 casualties. But far more frightening were Zeppelin raids, which began in January 1915 and continued sporadically into 1916. Ordinary citizens were bewildered at the arrival of war on their doorstep:

> Who would think that vault benign
>   God's last area free from vice,
> Initiates the aerial mine,
>   With babes below as sacrifice.[10]

10 V. Verne, 'Kensington Gardens', in C. Reilly, ed., *Scars Upon My Heart*, p. 120.

After a raid on Hull, an angry crowd stoned a Royal Flying Corps vehicle, on the assumption that the airmen were to blame for inadequate protection.[11] The British did their best to adjust: lighting restrictions were instituted in London and along the East Coast (later spread further afield), air raid shelters were constructed, a primitive early warning system was developed, and crews of night fighters gradually perfected a defensive screen. *The Times* commented that one advantage of the blackout was that stars were now visible: 'London moves under a vaster and steadier horizon.'[12] The makers of Hall's Wine, a nerve tonic, boasted that their product 'worked wonders when administered to the ladies, and prevented the nervous collapse of several when the bombs were dropping and the strain on the nerves was at its worst'.[13]

By the end of 1916, the Zeppelin was beaten. But then came the even more fearsome Gotha bombers. Their first raid on London resulted in 162 deaths and 432 injuries, mainly around Liverpool Street Station.[14] In all, 51 Zeppelin raids and 57 aeroplane raids resulted in 1,413 people killed during the war and 3,407 injured.[15] In terms of their actual effect, the air raids certainly never deserved the emphasis given them by newspapers at the time. Their propaganda value to the British heavily outweighed their strategic value to the Germans.

The war, because it focused attention on the value of human life, increased awareness of living standards. The astonishing number of men deemed unfit for military service highlighted the squalid conditions from which they came. It was widely held that men prepared to sacrifice their lives for their country deserved better. The Conservative MP Walter Long argued: 'To let them come home from horrible, waterlogged trenches to something little better than a pigsty here would, indeed, be criminal . . . and a negation of all we have said during the war, that we can never repay those men for what they have done for us.'[16] This sympathy inspired the 'Homes Fit for Heroes' ideal trumpeted during the 1918 election. But since landlords were even less likely than before to invest in new housing, or repair the old, only the government seemed capable of constructing the

11 T. Wilson, *The Myriad Faces of War*, p. 390.
12 *The Times*, 4 January 1915.
13 Ibid., 7 June 1915.
14 Wilson, p. 509.
15 Marwick, p. 238; Braybon and Summerfield, p. 97. Winter, p. 71) provides a slightly lower figure of 1,266.
16 R. Reiss, *The Home I Want*, p. 3.

number and quality of homes required. Whether it was prepared, ideologically and financially, to take on this burden, remained to be seen.

FOOD AND HOUSEHOLD NECESSITIES

For the average working class family, one-fifth of total food expenditure went on bread and flour. Six months into the war, the cost of wheat had risen by 72 per cent, barley by 40 per cent, and oats by 34 per cent.[17] A bumper harvest caused a fall in prices in spring 1915, but by the end of 1916 the standard 4 lb loaf cost 10d, up 4d from two years before. In autumn 1917 the government finally stepped in, pegging the price at the 1916 level. At various times butter, margarine, sugar, bacon and cheese prices were also fixed. Sugar prices rose most drastically – 163 per cent in the first two years of the war.[18] Potatoes, another working class staple, were steady during the first eighteen months of the war, then doubled in price due to a bad harvest.[19] The poorest cuts of meat, which workers had once found affordable, appeared on market stalls at double their pre-war price. Milk and butter also doubled during 1916, though they were not standard commodities in the working class diet. 'Everyone has less money to spend on food', went one advertisement. 'The wise ones make nourishing Quaker Oats the stand-by.... Your family won't miss expensive bacon and eggs if you serve delicious Quaker Oats.'[20]

Food shortages had a more widespread effect upon civilian morale than price rises. People of all classes blamed shortages on poor administration and on unscrupulous shopkeepers. The middle and upper classes were not accustomed to being denied commodities which they had the money to buy. Luxury items often disappeared completely and uncertain supplies of meat wreaked havoc upon dinner party plans. But the working class suffered the most, since they had less time to waste in queues and did not have the spare cash which occasionally provided a way around shortages. 'Anyone who penetrated the poorer neighbourhoods became familiar with the queue', commented Mrs C. S. Peel.[21] In December 1917, *The Times*

---

17 Wilson, p. 150.
18 A. Marwick, *Women at War*, p. 137.
19 Wilson, pp. 404–5.
20 *The Times*, 18 November 1914.
21 C. S. Peel, *How We Lived Then*, pp. 96–7.

reported food queues of more than 1,000 persons in some parts of London.[22] The Society for the Prevention of Cruelty to Children sought to remedy the problem of young children waiting in the early hours of winter mornings to buy bread.[23] Ugly scenes, usually directed against shopkeepers, occurred regularly. In January 1918, the military was brought in to control munitions workers in Leytonstone who looted shops after their wives had been unable to secure food. Much to the government's annoyance, workers increasingly took time off to relieve their wives in queues. As has been seen, the government responded halfheartedly to popular demands for the regulation of supplies. Lord Devonport's voluntary rationing scheme of February 1917 urged each citizen to restrict himself to 4 pounds of bread, 2½ pounds of meat and 12 ounces of sugar per week. This was a calculated attempt to shift consumption from grain, a mainly imported commodity, to meat, a mainly home-produced one.[24] But it demonstrated a remarkable ignorance of the working class diet: since the poor could not afford that much meat, they required much more bread.

A general reluctance to change eating patterns exacerbated shortages. Substitute commodities were seldom enthusiastically received by consumers. Supplies of tinned fish were more dependable than those of fresh, but some consumers baulked at the price, others at the taste. Margarine consumption did more than quadruple during the war,[25] but attempts to popularise horse meat and eels were not conspicuously successful.[26] The poet Aelfrida Tillyard poked fun at measures adopted to stretch the limited supply of food:

Here is a plate of cabbage soup,
    With caterpillars in,
How good they taste! (Avoid all waste
    If you the war would win.)

Now, will you have a minnow, love,
    Or half an inch of eel?
A stickleback, a slice of jack,
    Shall grace our festive meal.

We've no unpatriotic joint,
    No sugar and no bread.

22 Marwick, *Women at War*, p. 141.
23 *The Times*, 15 January 1915.
24 G. Hardach, *The First World War 1914–1918*, p. 128.
25 *The Times*, 9 January 1919.
26 Ibid., 12 July, 14 August 1915.

Eat nothing sweet, no rolls, no meat,
    The Food Controller said.

But would you like some sparrow pie,
    To counteract the eel?
A slice of swede is what you need,
    And please don't leave the peel.

But there's dessert for you, my love,
    Some glucose stewed with sloes.
And now good-night – your dreams be bright!
    (Perhaps they will – who knows?)[27]

Bread could not be substituted, but it could be doctored. The milling process was altered, transforming the loaf into what would today be called 'wholewheat'. Other grains and even potato flour were added. The result was more nutritious, but less desirable for consumers who believed that bread should be white. They complained, but still ate the bread; consumption was higher in 1917 than in pre-war years. In order to reduce consumption, authorities forbade the sale of bread not less than twelve hours old.

In February 1918, the Ministry of Food, now led by the more dynamic Lord Rhondda, finally instituted a rationing system in London and the Home Counties. Queues virtually disappeared. By mid-July a more comprehensive system was introduced throughout the country. The system even extended to restaurants, with customers having to surrender coupons with their order. Each household registered with a retailer, who was then supplied according to the needs of his registered customers. Weekly allowances stipulated 1½ pounds of meat per person, 4 ounces of butter or margarine, and 8 ounces of sugar. The bread allowance was 4 pounds for women and 7 pounds for men.[28] Children under six were given half the meat ration, while adolescent males and men working on heavy jobs received a supplemental allowance. But this allowance was not always taken up, since, as the Board of Trade admitted, 'a certain part of the population, especially in Scotland and in some country districts . . . could not afford to purchase the full amount to which their ration entitled them'.[29]

By the end of the war, thanks to a more interventionist government, power had shifted slightly from retailers to consumers. Shop-

27 A. Tilyard, 'Invitation Au Festin', in Reilly, ed., p. 113.
28 Braybon and Summerfield, p. 103.
29 Marwick, *The Deluge*, p. 239.

keepers were fined for hoarding food, for selling it above prescribed prices, and for refusing to sell to customers who were not regulars. But consumers were also snared by the long arm of the law. According to William Beveridge:

> it became a crime for a workman to leave a loaf behind on the kitchen shelf of the cottage from which he was moving (£2 fine), for a maiden lady at Dover to keep fourteen dogs and give them bread and milk to eat (£5), for another lady in Wales to give meat to a St. Bernard (£20), for a furnaceman dissatisfied with his dinner to throw chip potatoes on the fire (£10), and for a lady displeased with her husband to burn stale bread upon her lawn (£5).[30]

In 1918, a Mitcham man was charged with shooting a deer at Morden Hall Park. He admitted the offence, but argued, 'It's a job to live on these meat rations, I must have something for my children.' In the same month, an inquest into the deaths of survivors of a shipwreck found that when the unlucky sailors were taken ashore they were only served coffee, due to the 'too literal regard for food restrictions' among the local people.[31]

In the first six months of the war, labour shortages (so many miners volunteered for the army) and disruption on the rail network wreaked havoc upon the coal supply. Coal prices rose by about 20 per cent, and supplies remained precarious throughout 1915 and 1916, especially in large urban areas. The need to conserve fuel led to a DORA regulation banning Guy Fawkes bonfires from 1916. By spring 1917 the problem reached crisis proportions, with police regulating crowds at railway distribution points. With winter came coal rationing in London; allocations were determined according to the number of rooms in each house. Shortages hit the middle classes proportionally harder than the workers. The affluent could no longer secure the supplies necessary to keep large homes heated at pre-war standards of comfort. The poor, in contrast, had never enjoyed the luxury of warm homes. In fact, with many workers enjoying increased income, heating became one of war's benefits. Thus, rationing of coal did not decrease consumption, since workers bought up supplies denied to the middle class. Shortages also affected retailers; shops were forced to close earlier during winter to save on heating and lighting, thus making life even more difficult for already harried housewives.

The food bill rose by 60 per cent during the war, to about £2

---

30 W. Beveridge, *British Food Control*, pp. 238–9.
31 *The Times*, 12 March 1918.

per week for the average working class family.[32] Rent and rates rose until the Rent and Mortgage Interest Act came into force. Fuel cost increases added another 2s to the budget. Clothing rises added 3s or 4s, but this is not an accurate index of the steep increase in costs since the total amount spent was limited as much by scarcity as by price. As for alcohol, a report released in 1917 revealed that consumption declined by 16 per cent from 1914 to 1916, but expenditure (due to taxes and inflation) rose by 24 per cent.[33] Tobacco consumption rose, with expenditure rising even faster. New taxes also affected family budgets. McKenna's first budget of September 1915 rendered those in the £130–£160 per annum income range liable to tax. By the end of the war, 32 per cent of workers in this band paid tax, the rest avoiding it because of various allowances. In addition, the average family paid 10 per cent of income in indirect taxes, up from 6 per cent in 1913.[34] All this meant that weekly wages had to rise by about 22s to compensate for inflation and taxes during the war.[35]

Taking inflation into account, the real value of household incomes among the working classes remained steady or improved slightly during the war. Since it was legal for a child to be employed at fourteen (many took jobs even earlier), a family with older children often found that the war provided more than one steady income. Anecdotal evidence demonstrates that wage rises, abundant overtime and a competitive labour market often brought unaccustomed prosperity. Charities found little to do; by pre-war standards there were few genuinely needy people. Tramps were much less common on the streets and convictions for theft and vagrancy declined significantly. In December 1914, the Salvation Army reported that no more than 200 persons per night were using its shelters, less than a tenth of pre-war numbers.[36] In January 1915 there were 70,596 people in London workhouses and 30,394 on the outdoor list. This represented a decrease of 4,045 on the previous year.[37] But improvements were not enjoyed equally throughout society, nor were they immediate. The earlier part of the war brought considerable hardship since wage rises did not at first keep pace with price inflation. In June 1916,

32 Winter, p. 215.

33 *The Times*, 28 February 1917.

34 R. C. Whiting, 'Taxation and the Working Class, 1915–24', *Historical Journal* 33 (1990), pp. 897, 908. See also Chapter 5, pp. 106–8.

35 Winter, pp. 229–31.

36 *The Times*, 16 December 1914.

37 Ibid., 26 January 1915.

food prices were 61 per cent higher than in July 1914, while wages had risen by under 20 per cent.[38]

Military service often entailed financial hardship. The government wisely realised that, in order to maintain civilian morale, it could not allow the wives and families of servicemen to be forced onto the Poor Law. Separation allowances were therefore paid from the beginning, calculated according to the husband's rank. The wife of a private with one child received 15s; inflationary increases meant she received 23s by the end of the war. Extra increments were paid for each additional child. By the end of the war, nearly £420 million had been doled out to 1.5 million wives and their children.[39] In cases where the husband had, before the war, been in irregular or poorly paid employment, these allowances could result in an improvement of family circumstances. 'It seems too good to be true', one soldier's wife remarked, 'a pound a week and my husband away.'[40] But no woman got rich off the state's largesse; allowances in reality covered only one-half of family expenditure.[41]

Living together out of wedlock was more common than is often presumed. After much agonising, the authorities decided that allowances would still be paid even if a marriage licence could not be produced. The decision angered religious groups worried about the implied threat to the sanctity of the marriage vow.[42] But if the policy seems progressive, in other ways the administration of allowances maintained the British tradition of mixing morality with social welfare. Allowances could be terminated on grounds of infidelity or immoral behaviour. The government assumed that 'the woman by her infidelity has forfeited the right to be supported by her husband', and therefore 'there is no obligation on the State to continue this payment if the husband would no longer be under a duty to maintain her if he were now in civil life'. In October 1914 an Army Council Memorandum on the 'Cessation of Separation Allowances and Allotments to the Unworthy' called upon police to monitor whether allowances were spent wisely. The chief commissioner of the Metropolitan Police objected; he could not 'understand why anybody should assume that the wife of a soldier is necessarily a person who required the police to look after her'. Nevertheless, women discovered drunk

---

38 Hardach, p. 124.

39 S. Pedersen, 'Gender, Welfare, and Citizenship in Britain during the Great War', *American Historical Review* 95 (1990), p. 990.

40 Ibid., p. 1003.

41 Winter, p. 241.

42 *The Times*, 23 November 1914.

or those who frequented pubs too regularly often found their allowances terminated. In all, 16,000 women, 2 per cent of claimants, had their allowances withdrawn because of allegedly immoral behaviour.[43] These rulings reflected a prevalent attitude that women on their own with money to spare could not be trusted. 'No greater slander has ever been circulated', judged the NSPCC, 'than the assertion that soldiers' wives as a class were lacking in the spirit of self-restraint.'[44]

It is difficult to estimate the number of those who suffered a decline in living standards as a result of the war. Most of those associated with the war economy gained, and the majority of the working population was engaged in war-related work. But those outside the mainstream war economy did suffer. A government investigation in 1915 revealed that

> cotton operatives and certain classes of day-wage workers and labourers – are hard-pressed by the rise in prices, and actually have to curtail their consumption. . . . Many people in receipt of small fixed incomes necessarily also feel the pressure; and it is obvious that . . . a family . . . in which the children are within school age may suffer exceptionally.[45]

Sylvia Pankhurst, working among the distressed in London's East End, found that

> Even the women who had received the full separation allowances promised, were in sad case. The wife of a Territorial, with two young children and expecting a third, got 1s 5d a day from the War Office. Having moved into London when her husband was called up, she got no London allowance. Her rent was 6s a week. She wept with despair at finding herself with only 3s 11d a week for food, fuel, light, and all the needs of her family![46]

Some hardship was avoidable. The government was, for instance, notoriously slow paying disability allowances to injured soldiers returning from the front. Both army pay and separation allowance ceased during the sometimes interminable period it took for disability to be assessed.[47] Since so many soldiers came from heavy jobs in civilian life, even a relatively minor disability could prevent a return to pre-war occupations.

The National Food Economy League published guides on house-

---

43 H. Jones, *Health and Society in Twentieth-Century Britain*, p. 35.
44 Pedersen, 'Gender, Welfare, and Citizenship', pp. 997–9.
45 Marwick, *Women at War*, p. 137.
46 S. Pankhurst, *The Home Front*, p. 28.
47 Pedersen, 'Gender, Welfare, and Citizenship', p. 993.

hold management carefully calculated to suit the various classes. Titles included *Housekeeping on Twenty-Five Shillings a Week, or under, for a Family of Five* (price 1d), *Patriotic Food Economy for the Well-to-Do* (6d) and *War-time Recipes for Households where Servants are Employed* (6d). Readers of *The Times* were advised to 'instruct your keeper to cease feeding your pheasants with maize and corn'. The birds would not suffer and might even 'afford better sport'.[48] Another article advised 'the better class' to save tea leaves from the first brew, dry them and send them for distribution to the poor or to the troops.[49] 'The woman who would feed her family well and yet reduce expenses must first of all learn to cook, so that she may instruct her cook in the best and cheapest methods of preparing food.'[50] The *Win the War Cookery Book* advised house-wives that

> The British fighting line shifts and extends and now *you* are in it. The struggle is not only on land and sea; it is in *your* larder, *your* kitchen, and *your* dining room. Every meal *you* serve is now literally a battle.[51]

'The great fault in English cookery', argued *The Times*, 'has hitherto been the extraordinary wastefulness, and servants are the great bar-rier to all reform.'[52] A leaflet was prepared advising servants how they could help their employers effect economies. 'Let us remember that the wealthy have much to do with their wealth', it ran. 'War to-day is very costly, and if it should last long, it is the wealthies who rightly will have to part with the most – at all events in the way of money.' Servants were advised to prepare themselves for wage cuts, which should be borne with equanimity.[53]

Government controls and food campaigns revealed a remarkable insensitivity to working class life. Recipes for 'patriotic' haricot bean fritters, barley rissoles and nut rolls were more relevant to those of the middle class who had the time and expertise to enable their preparation. Frequent 'thrift' campaigns (usually accompanied by fresh exhortations to buy war bonds) were likewise inappropriate. 'I must say I was surprised to read last month of women ... being advised to lead the way in *thrift*', one housewife remarked. 'Take

48 *The Times*, 8 August 1914.
49 Ibid., 14 August 1914.
50 Ibid., 6 July 1915.
51 M. Pugh, *Women and the Women's Movement in Britain, 1914–1959*, p. 13.
52 *The Times*, 25 August 1915.
53 Ibid., 9 January 1915.

the lead, Ye Gods! To advise us working women to be thrifty is about the limit!'[54]

Many professional families found that fixed incomes failed to keep pace with inflation. Most did not suffer, but they still felt aggrieved. When Vera Brittain's parents complained about the short-age of servants and good chocolate, they would not have been con-soled by the fact that the poor had never enjoyed those luxuries, war or not. Nina Macdonald referred lightheartedly to middle class privation in her poem 'Sing a Song of War-time':

Sing a song of War-time,
Soldiers marching by,
Crowds of people standing,
Waving them 'Good-bye'.
When the crowds are over,
Home we go to tea,
Bread and margarine to eat,
War Economy!

If I ask for a cake, or
Jam of any sort,
Nurse says, 'What! in War-time?
Archie, certainly not!'
Life's not very funny
Now, for little boys,
Haven't any money,
Can't buy any toys.

Mummie does the house-work,
Can't get any maid,
Gone to make munitions,
'Cause they're better paid,
Nurse is always busy,
Never time to play,
Sewing shirts for soldiers,
Nearly ev'ry day.[55]

Two charitable agencies, the Professional Classes War Relief Commit-tee and the Professional Classes Special Aid Society, were formed to look after those forced, as one spokesman commented, 'to live the "simple life" with a vengeance'. This meant 'a smaller house, less

54 Braybon and Summerfield, p. 99.
55 N. Macdonald, 'Sing a Song of War-time', in Reilly, ed., p. 69.

food and clothing, fewer servants and cheaper education for our children'.[56]

As for the wealthy, they generally maintained pre-war standards. In December 1916 the first Public Meals Order limited day meals to two courses and those in the evening to three, but restaurateurs found clever ways round the ruling. Petrol rationing did curb motoring for pure pleasure, but other luxuries were hardly affected. The consumption of sparkling wine, champagne and port increased massively; the latter became the favoured tipple of white collar workers during the war.[57] Readers of *The Times* were assured that stocks of champagne in France were safe and that 1914 would be a very good year, similar to 1870, the year of the Franco-Prussian War.[58] 'Today the true patriot who can afford it will eat asparagus, not potatoes', the government advised.[59] Potatoes, in other words, should be left to the poor. There was no apparent fall in the wearing or buying of jewellery, and dress sales actually increased between 1915 and 1917. Nor did theatre attendances fall markedly.[60] Siegfried Sassoon was ashamed at the sight of 'old men with their noses in their plates guzzling for all they're worth' at the Formby Golf Club. There were 'enormous cold joints and geese and turkeys and a suckling pig and God knows what'.[61] If, as Marwick suggests, the war created 'a strong breeze of egalitarianism',[62] many were able to shelter from the wind.

THE NATION'S HEALTH

War is supposed to be dangerous to the health not only of soldiers but also of civilians. One would expect poor diet and hard work, exacerbated by constant anxiety, loneliness and stress, to exact a physical toll. In fact, health standards did not decline at all and, in many ways, they improved. This is what Jay Winter calls the 'paradox of the Great War'. He has discovered that life expectancy for men in England and Wales rose from 49 to 56 years and for women from 53 to 60 years between 1911 and 1921, an *acceleration* of the

56 B. Waites, *A Class Society at War*, p. 51.
57 J. Harris, 'Bureaucrats and Businessmen in British Food Control, 1916–19', in K. Burk, ed., *War and the State*, p. 138.
58 *The Times*, 16 October 1914.
59 Pugh, p. 14.
60 Marwick, *The Deluge*, p. 240.
61 Wilson, p. 405.
62 Marwick, *The Deluge*, p. 242.

generally improving trend evident in the first three decades of the century. Those who avoided the fighting were healthier because of the war than they would have been without it.[63]

> For almost every category of death, significant declines were registered in these years. Some of these could not have occurred had the population been increasingly malnourished or deprived of other essential goods and services in wartime.[64]

To extend the paradox even further: 'The lower down the "pay ladder" you were, the greater were your chances of improving your life expectancy during the war.'[65] Infant mortality rates, the most sensitive gauge of changing social conditions, improved significantly in England and Wales (on average 8 per cent during the war years), while they remained constant in Germany and worsened dramatically in France, Italy and Austria. The rate declined fastest among the working class in manufacturing cities like Manchester, Birmingham and Sheffield – a trend mirrored in Scotland. In other words, the decline was more impressive in areas with high female employment than in areas unaffected by the rush of women into the factories.[66]

Winter's findings are open to dispute. He relies heavily on Prudential life insurance statistics as a basis for mortality rates; since those statistics pertain mainly to skilled and semi-skilled workers, the 'underclass' are often under-represented.[67] Though female health generally improved, death rates for women aged 10–29 and 75–9 rose during the war.[68] Female mortality rates from tuberculosis, pneumonia, bronchitis and influenza were higher in every war year than in the years immediately preceding 1914, even when the effects of the 1917–18 influenza epidemic are taken into account. Winter blames this on the decline in housing standards and the movement of rural dwellers to urban areas where overcrowding and bad air exacerbated respiratory conditions.[69] Starting from a different (and

63 Winter, p. 105.

64 Ibid., p. 117.

65 Ibid., p. 106.

66 J. Winter, 'Aspects of the Impact of the First World War on Infant Mortality in Britain', *Journal of European Economic History* 11 (1982), p. 718.

67 See L. Bryder, 'The First World War: Healthy or Hungry?', *History Workshop Journal* 24 (1987), p. 143.

68 B. Harris, 'The Demographic Impact of the First World War: An Anthropometric Perspective', *Journal of the Society for the Social History of Medicine* 6 (1993), p. 349.

69 J. Winter, 'Public Health and the Political Economy of War: A Reply to Linda Bryder', *History Workshop Journal* 26 (1988), p. 168. See Bryder, 'The First World War', pp. 146–9, for another opinion.

supposedly more reliable) set of statistics, including evidence on children's heights, Bernard Harris disputes Winter's infant mortality data, arguing that 'there is little to suggest that the war had any great effect upon what was already a well-established trend'.[70] Nor does he agree that the poorer classes experienced the greatest improvement. 'The overall impression is one of continuity rather than discontinuity during the war years.'[71]

But Harris's continuity, if less impressive than Winter's improvement, is still striking, particularly during a time of chaos, destruction and privation. This is especially true since civilian access to medical care was severely restricted due to the army's demand for doctors. At the front each doctor looked after on average 376 soldiers, while at home each had 2,344 civilian patients.[72] The military took proportionately more doctors from the poor than from the better off since panel doctors and those from urban areas were ranked higher on the scale of dispensability than private doctors and those from rural areas.[73] Some districts in Glasgow had more than 5,000 patients for every doctor. (The present-day ratio varies between 500:1 and 800:1.) A Croydon doctor stopped for a traffic offence in 1918 told police he hoped they would send him to prison, as it was the only way he could get a rest.[74] Winter reckons that during the war, 20 per cent of the population was without adequate medical coverage (defined as more than 4,000 patients per doctor).[75] Yet in areas like Shoreditch and Bethnal Green, 'which were depleted of medical care by anybody's standards', health standards improved.[76] This is perhaps understandable, since most of the population was unaccustomed to regular medical attention. The National Insurance Act of 1913 had not by this stage had a profound effect upon civilian health. Furthermore, before the age of antibiotics, there was not a great deal a doctor could do to combat the major diseases which ravaged the poor. One study in fact reveals that women were more likely to die in childbirth if a doctor was present. In other words, middle class women were often more at risk because they could afford a doctor.[77]

70 Harris, 'The Demographic Impact', p. 350.

71 Ibid., p. 351.

72 Winter, *The Great War and the British People*, p. 170.

73 Ibid., p. 161.

74 *The Times*, 6 November 1918.

75 Winter, *The Great War and the British People*, p. 179.

76 Ibid., p. 186.

77 I. Loudon, 'Deaths in Childbed from the Eighteenth Century to 1935', *Medical History* 30 (1986), pp. 27–41.

The significant fall in the number of deaths due to diarrhoeal disease and the fall (or at least stabilisation) in the mortality rate due to pregnancy and childbirth would not have been possible had nutrition standards declined during the war. It is difficult to comment with any precision on the wartime working class diet, since wide variations between geographical areas and income groups make a mockery of averages. But some wartime effects are obvious: the decline in sugar and alcohol consumption must have had positive effects upon civilian health. While sugar, butter and meat consumption declined significantly (the latter compensated somewhat by greater consumption of bacon), that of bread and potatoes was maintained or rose. This suggests that the working class diet became more starchy, but calorie levels were maintained. 'The chief hardship suffered by the population was that of a less attractive, rather than an inadequate diet', writes one expert.[78] But since available figures pertain to households not to individuals, two qualifications are essential. Firstly, during the war, the birth rate declined and families were smaller. Fewer people meant bigger portions and a higher calorie intake. Secondly, and even more importantly, over six million men were fed, for varying lengths of time, by the army. Since adult men previously received the lion's share at mealtime, during the war the rest of the family (especially the mother) ate better.

Thus, civilian diets seem to have improved despite inflated food prices. This could be explained by increases in family income, which were most pronounced among the poorer classes, who, Winter argues, not coincidentally enjoyed the greatest improvement in health standards. More money was spent on food than before the war, and the food itself was nutritionally better. The establishment of industrial canteens, increased provision of school meals, and the extension of health insurance and disability pensions also had positive effects.[79] The Liverpool Women's Industrial Council found 'preponderating evidence that the effect of separation allowances has been good, especially as regards the health and general well-being of the children'.[80] Factory welfare supervisors may have been motivated more by industrial efficiency than by human kindness, but they did help to improve the health of workers. For instance, they discouraged

[78] P. Dewey, 'Food Production and Policy in the United Kingdom, 1914–1918', *Transactions of the Royal Historical Society*, Fifth Series, 30 (1980), pp. 73, 78.

[79] Winter, 'Aspects', pp. 728–9.

[80] Pedersen, 'Gender, Welfare, and Citizenship', p. 1002.

213

workers from bringing insubstantial or unhealthy dinners to work, urging them instead to use the canteens.[81]

One must resist being blinded by Winter's statistics. As with income rises, so too with health, war's benefits were not equally shared. Young, single women who worked long hours in draughty factories and went home to damp, cold lodgings were particularly susceptible to tuberculosis. 'It is not only her health she is risking, but her youth as well', one male worker observed. 'It makes me sad to see the young girls here; they come in fresh and rosy cheeked, and before a month has passed they are pale and careworn.'[82] Better income did not always bring better health. And medical statistics provide little illumination of war's most common ailment, grief. A woman who lost a husband or son would have derived little consolation from the fact that the war had improved her diet.

CHILDREN

Ubiquitous death meant greater value placed upon life. Babies were the chief beneficiaries of this wartime sentiment. They came to be seen as a generation of hope poised to replace the shattered and demoralised. This did not mean that more babies were born; the birth rate in fact declined from 23.9 per 1,000 population in 1914 to 19.4 in 1918. But every baby was more highly valued. 'While nine soldiers died every hour in 1915, twelve babies died every hour, so that it was more dangerous to be a baby than a soldier', argued the Bishop of London. 'The loss of life in this war has made every baby's life doubly precious.'[83] Even the NUWSS grew concerned that wider employment opportunities for women posed problems for children. Mrs Fawcett reassured mothers who stayed at home that 'the care of infant life, saving the children, and protecting their welfare was as true a service to the country as that which men were rendering by going into the armies'.[84]

This 'cult of the child' inspired various pro-natalism campaigns. 'The noble sacrifices in the battlefield, in the air and on the sea must not be made in vain', argued the Babies of the Empire Society. 'Every effort must be directed to securing the future of the

81 A. Woollacott, 'Maternalism, Professionalism and Industrial Welfare Supervisors in World War I Britain', *Women's History Review* 3 (1994), p. 33.

82 Braybon and Summerfield, p. 83.

83 *Daily Telegraph*, 2, 18 July 1917. See also J. Lewis, *The Politics of Motherhood*, p. 29.

84 M. Fawcett, *What I Remember*, p. 218.

214

race.'[85] National Baby Weeks of 1917 and 1918 sought to 'save every savable child'.[86] Concern even extended to those who had once been pariahs. The National Council for the Unmarried Mother drew attention to the high mortality rates among illegitimate children and the Conservative MP Ronald McNeill urged that the unfortunate mothers, 'both for the children's sake and for their own, should be saved from the degradation which too often follows a single lapse of virtue'.[87] To this suggestion, *The Times* commented that 'The real stigma of bastardy is social, and it cannot be removed by any legislative declaration, as some people seem to suppose.'[88]

A report entitled *The National Care of Maternity in Time of War* argued that it was 'increasingly incumbent upon the nation to assist mothers and to render the conditions of childbirth as favourable as possible'.[89] The report demanded better medical provision, more and better-trained midwives, and more attention to pre- and post-natal diet. A government investigation of factory conditions warned that

> the overstrain of industrial work immediately before or after childbirth involves the risk of grave injury to women and child alike . . . the strain of long-standing or continuous overwork in girlhood and later . . . may have far-reaching effects on the birth-rate and the degeneration of the race.[90]

Needless to say, such profound attention to the welfare of children would have been no less appropriate in peacetime. And amid all the strident demands for more babies, few paused to consider the consequences. George Newman, Chief Medical Officer to the Ministry of Health, regretted how 'we are sometimes apt to forget or ignore the heavy burden which a family of children near together in age places upon the working class mother'.[91] Birth control remained a sensitive subject, firstly because it supposedly threatened racial decline (especially since the middle class were more knowledgeable about it) and secondly because it implied that intercourse could have a purpose beyond procreation. The National Birthrate Commission

---

85 Jones, p. 40.
86 Braybon and Summerfield, p. 107.
87 Pugh, pp. 18–19.
88 *The Times*, 21 April 1915.
89 G. Braybon, *Women Workers in the First World War*, p. 117.
90 N. Whiteside, 'Industrial Welfare and Labour Regulation in Britain at the Time of the First World War', *International Review of Social History* 25 (1980), p. 315.
91 Lewis, p. 202.

found that doctors advised patients to space out their births, but refused to tell them how. This was a selfish hoarding of knowledge since, according to the 1911 census, doctors had the smallest families of all categories of occupations.[92]

The Women's Labour League and the War Emergency Workers National Committee quickly jumped on the child welfare bandwagon. Feminists noted for their militancy before the war campaigned hard for measures to reduce the infant mortality rate, in the process emphasising maternalist conceptions of womanhood which they suddenly found empowering.[93] Maude Royden argued:

> The State wants children, and to give them is a service both dangerous and honourable. Like the soldier, the mother takes a risk and gives a devotion for which no money can pay; but, like the soldier, she should not, therefore, be made 'economically dependent'.[94]

Campaigns for family allowances, or the endowment of motherhood, gathered pace. Mary Stocks, editor of the *Woman's Leader*, defended the allowances as 'the conscious allocation to mothers *qua* mothers of resources adequate for the proper performance of their function'.[95]

Many of the campaigns had racialist and eugenist overtones. The need for white British babies to populate the Empire was widely accepted. Some campaigners pointed out that better pre- and post-natal care was advantageous in that it would allow more male children to survive. (The male infant mortality rate was higher than the female.[96]) The fact that the birth rate had plummeted most markedly among the middle class disturbed many. The 'particular and peculiar duty' of respectable women to bear children was frequently stressed,[97] and some eugenists (of the 'better dead' school) actually warned that better health provision worked against natural selection by allowing those of poorer stock to survive.[98]

More common, however, was the reminder to all mothers of

---

92 J. Weeks, *Sex, Politics and Society*, p. 45.

93 See S. Koven and S. Michel, 'Womanly Duties: Maternalist Politics and the Origins of Welfare States in France, Germany, Great Britain and the United States, 1880–1920', *American Historical Review* 95 (1990), pp. 1076–108.

94 S. Pedersen, 'The Failure of Feminism in the Making of the British Welfare State', *Radical History Review* 43 (1989), p. 91.

95 S. K. Kent, 'The Politics of Sexual Difference: World War I and the Demise of British Feminism', *Journal of British Studies* 27 (1988), p. 241.

96 Lewis, p. 29.

97 Braybon, pp. 124–5.

98 Lewis, p. 29.

their 'duty to the State to care for the babies that belong to the State as well as to themselves'. Authorities were confident that better training alone, rather than material improvements in living standards, could improve the lot of the child. 'Efficient housewives are more important than bricks and mortar to the making of healthy homes', wrote one self-important (male) social commentator. Girls were therefore to be given a 'thorough training in cooking, housework, laundry work and needle work [which] leads up naturally to mother-craft'.[99] Rebecca West was not alone in suspecting (with good reason) that the training was in truth designed to prepare young women for a return to domestic service.[100]

As Winter points out, the 'Mothercraft' debate was characterised by the 'relatively ineffective, if not pointless exercise of men telling other men how women ought to behave'.[101] All of the top posts on the National Baby Week Council were occupied by men.[102] Bizarre but still topical was the advice given by Captain Sir William Wiseman, who advised mothers 'not to reprove, but to encourage' children who fought in the nursery. That experience, he argued, had rendered the British superior to the Germans at hand-to-hand combat. 'In a rough and tumble with Tommy Atkins [Germans] always went off in the opposite direction.'[103] But women 'experts' could be equally absurd. *Labour Woman*, the Labour Party-sponsored journal, argued that the best mothers were those who strove to become 'thinking citizens'. Enlightenment would come through a system of 'co-operative housekeeping': cooking, cleaning, washing and mending would be done according to an efficient division of labour. 'Each woman . . . set free from the incubus of home slavery, would be able to follow the work for which she is best fitted by temperament and training.'[104] The writer, a woman, did not explain how these itinerant menders, cookers, cleaners and washers would, at the same time, provide a stable home life for children.

Pro-natalism inspired concrete improvements in the provision of health visitors and clinics for women and children. Organisers of the Children's Jewel Fund, under the slogan 'a jewel for a baby's life', called for donations of money and jewellery to finance infant welfare centres. By the time the fund was wound up in 1920, £700,000 had

---

99 Braybon, pp. 124–5.
100 Lewis, p. 93.
101 Winter, *The Great War and the British People*, p. 189.
102 Jones, p. 41.
103 *The Times*, 8 September 1915.
104 Braybon, p. 126.

been collected.[105] (The Duchess of Marlborough gave a £5,000 pearl necklace.[106]) But this was one area in which the government was not prepared to leave matters to the vagaries of voluntarism. The Care of Mothers and Young Children Act of 1915 empowered local authorities to set up facilities 'for the purpose of the care of expectant mothers, nursing mothers, and young children', with subsidies of up to 50 per cent provided by the Local Government Board. By 1917, 446 infant welfare centres were operated by voluntary bodies, with another 396 centres administered by local authorities.[107] The number of full-time health visitors in England and Wales rose from 600 in 1914 to 1,355 in 1918. On the other hand, some local authorities resisted the move to set up centres on the grounds that they undermined individual responsibility – the first step down the slippery slope toward the nanny state.[108]

Sylvia Pankhurst felt that 'in spite of all the purse-proud patronage and snobbery which has been displayed in connection with them, maternal and infant centres are proving a great boon to numbers of women'.[109] This was perhaps an over-optimistic assessment. At the clinics, middle class women dispensed advice formulated by middle class men to working class mothers. A clash of cultures inevitably developed, limiting the extent of improvement. Health visitors were prone to assume that the primary cause of infant illness was fecklessness or ignorance on the part of mothers. As one commentator explained: 'In searching for the cause of a polluted stream one naturally traces it backwards and towards its source.'[110] Quite typical was the Middlesbrough Medical Officer of Health, who blamed poor child health standards on the 'shiftless, careless, and dirty . . . habits' of mothers.[111] But middle class mothers were also criticised, in particular those who refused to breast feed. The eugenist C. W. Saleeby argued that such women should be 'ashamed to look a tabby cat in the face.'[112] But though middle class women were the most avid readers of the many and varied family care manuals, they did not have access to the same welfare network as was provided for working class mothers. On the other hand, the latter were understandably

105 Lewis, p. 34.
106 Winter, *The Great War and the British People*, p. 192.
107 Lewis, p. 96.
108 Jones, p. 41.
109 Lewis, p. 100.
110 Ibid., p. 30.
111 Winter, *The Great War and the British People*, pp. 203–4.
112 Lewis, p. 69.

reluctant to take advantage of the services provided and were wary of allowing 'intruders' into their homes. As a result, the real potential of the clinics was not realised until well after the war. The significant fall in infant mortality rates cannot be attributed to them.

Children benefited indirectly from wartime regulations regarding the consumption of alcohol. Drunkenness was reduced, which increased domestic harmony. Getting drunk was not only more difficult but also more socially unacceptable. Intoxicated men or women were seen as unpatriotic – selfishly withholding labour from the state. In December 1914 *The Times* commented upon the fact that early closing of pubs had resulted in fewer children on the streets after 10:00 p.m. 'The child's bed time often synchronizes with the public house closing hour. At last his poor, stunted body has the chance of getting an hour or two's "beauty sleep".'[113] But perhaps the most striking effect of the control of the drink trade was the fall in the number of infant deaths registered at weekends. A tragic scenario had been all too common: excessive Friday or Saturday night drinking led to 'overlaying' – babies sharing beds with parents being smothered by a drunken mother or father. After the introduction of drink controls, the weekend blip in the statistics disappeared.[114]

Concern for children extended to new interest in education. Prior to the war, 75 per cent of children left school by age fourteen. The financing of education was precarious; since funds came from local rates, poorer areas naturally had the worst schools. But even the wealthy public schools had serious problems, though these were not universally recognised. Overemphasis upon Classics and games, to the detriment of science, left Britain's 'elites' ill-prepared for the emerging age of technology. The war focused attention on this deficiency – hardly a week passed without an agonised letter in *The Times* on the neglect of science – but not on its cause.

At first, the manpower problem militated against progress in education. In the first year of the war, the number of children attending secondary school fell by 1,000. But the autumn 1915 intake was up by 3,000 and that of 1916 by 9,000.[115] There were twice as many working class children in secondary school in 1921 as in 1913.[116] This enthusiasm was further demonstrated by impressive working

---

113 *The Times*, 14 December 1914.

114 Winter, *The Great War and the British People*, p. 210. See Lewis, p. 76, for another explanation.

115 Wilson, p. 815.

116 Waites, p. 266.

class attendance at rallies held round the country by the Education Minister, H. A. L. Fisher. Educational issues were prominent on the agenda of TUC and Labour Party conferences. But all this enthusiasm was held in check by the rightward shift in British politics. Action did not keep pace with progressive talk. Fisher's maiden speech in the Commons called for improved pay for teachers, more nursery schools and better medical services at school. But administration and financing would remain in the hands of local authorities, thus perpetuating vast inequalities in provision. Fisher expressed a hope that the school leaving age of fourteen would henceforward be more strictly enforced, but he stopped well short of universal secondary education. As regards the curriculum, the government seemed more concerned with preserving the civilising influences of classical studies than with closing the technology gap.

Before the war, a hodgepodge of laws governed the employment of children, with wide variations from region to region. A child was technically supposed to stay in school until fourteen, but those with good attendance records could leave a year earlier. Factory work was not allowed until the required schooling was completed, but 'half-timers' could, from age twelve, work up to 33 hours a week, as long as they still attended school half time. Street hawkers had to be at least eleven, and boys could not work in mines until they were fourteen.[117] During the war, the manpower shortage led to increased pressure upon local authorities to relax restrictions. In August 1915, the Headmistresses' Association approached the Home Secretary about the huge increase in girls as young as twelve employed in street-selling.[118] Factory inspectors were reasonably successful at preventing the exploitation of juvenile workers, but they could not possibly stop every abuse. Cases of children working over 100 hours a week or 35 hours continuously were not unknown. A firm that worked a girl for 30 hours at a stretch was prosecuted when the situation came to the attention of a factory inspector. The counsel for the defence, arguing that 'Now is not the time to talk about Factory Acts', suggested that the Home Office 'ought to have struck a special medal' for the girl, instead of wasting its time in the 'fatuous folly' of prosecuting the employer. The latter was placed on probation.[119]

In August 1917, Fisher admitted that 600,000 children had been

117 Marwick, *The Deluge*, pp. 156–7.
118 *The Times*, 6 August 1915.
119 Jones, p. 45.

put 'prematurely' to work during the first three years of the war.[120] The pull of extra money was difficult for children and their families to resist. By the end of the war, girls and boys were earning up to £2 per week in munitions factories. 'Parental control, so far as it formerly existed, has been relaxed through the absence of families from their homes', a governmental committee reported in 1917. 'The withdrawal of influences making for the social improvement of boys and girls has in many districts been followed by a noticeable deterioration in behaviour and morality.'[121] One needs to be very suspicious of the judgements of middle class investigators, whose disapproval of working class habits was notorious. Nevertheless, some alarming changes in behaviour were evident. With fathers fighting abroad and mothers often working, children (especially boys) who earned undreamt-of levels of income were often tempted into delinquency. While the general crime rate fell, offences committed by juveniles rose. Authorities in Bath noted a 284 per cent rise in juvenile crime between 1914 and 1918.[122] Nor did middle class mothers escape condemnation. A correspondent to *The Times* wrote of households where the children 'rarely see [their] "war mamma" ' who is involved in every worthy cause. 'They run wild, unobserved, for even nurse is war-working, and absorbed in knitting projects of a complicated kind.'[123]

The need for women's labour meant inevitable neglect of children, even by the most conscientious mothers. While most women workers were single and childless, the vast expansion of the female labour force was made possible by the willingness of wives and mothers to work. The state was relatively quick to accept the necessity of female labour, but slow to recognise the consequent need for childcare. Mothers made do as best they could: of 129 munitions workers' children in Leeds under school age in 1916, 83 were left with grandmothers or other family, 42 with neighbours, one with a landlady, one with a day nursery and one boarded out.[124] Some mothers went home at midday to feed children, much to the regret of employers. For the state to provide childcare was considered a dangerous precedent, since mothers of young children were not under

120 Marwick, *Women at War*, pp. 143–4.
121 Idem, *The Deluge*, p. 159.
122 *The Times*, 12 March 1918.
123 Ibid., 23 April 1915.
124 Braybon and Summerfield, pp. 100–1.

normal circumstances supposed to work. As *The Times* commented in 1916:

> It would be deplorable if the measures taken to preserve the health of girls and mothers in the war factories led married women definitely to abandon their homes for industrial work. If their incursion into skilled labour is to be permanent, then we have paid infinitely too high for any advantage to our arms.[125]

Necessity forced a gradual recognition of the state's role in the provision of childcare. From 1917 the government agreed to pay 75 per cent of the cost of crèche facilities, to a maximum of 7d per child. But crèches were slow to materialise. Leeds had none until 1918, a not untypical case. At the large government-owned munitions factories, only 108 day nurseries catering to just 4,000 children existed by 1917.[126] As *The Times* quotation above indicates, crèches were seen as a necessary evil. This explains why government provision was limited to munitions factories; other mothers, no matter how important their work, were left to their own devices. Even the supposedly enlightened *Labour Women* found it necessary to stress that 'No creches, etc. can ever make up to children for the mother's love. Whatever a childless woman may do for the community is nothing to the service rendered by her [sic] who gives it healthy and good children.'[127] But a note of reality was injected into the debate when a woman writing to *Reynolds Newspaper* challenged the President of the Local Government Board, an ardent opponent of working mothers: 'If the Rt. Hon. John Burns will show me a way out of the difficulty [poverty] I shall be delighted, but it seems to me that until then I must work.'[128] Few were courageous enough to suggest that working mothers might be a lesser evil than poverty-stricken children.

Mothers bore the greatest burden of blame for the erosion of family stability. Official responses to war's disruption were often either feeble, inappropriate or insensitive. At large munitions factories welfare supervisors were given wide latitude to inspect workers' homes to check on cleanliness and the care of children. For many of the supervisors, this would have been their first exposure to workers' homes. Substandard conditions were often blamed on slovenliness rather than on low family income. It was a no-win situation for

125 *The Times*, 24 June 1916.
126 Braybon and Summerfield, p. 106.
127 Braybon, p. 124.
128 Lewis, pp. 79–80.

working mothers. If they neglected their homes in order to be good workers, they were cursed by society for being poor mothers. Yet if they took time off work to look after their family, they were criticised for being unreliable and unpatriotic workers. As one factory manager remarked, 'A day's washing may be a very serious thing for a woman, but to stay away and leave her machine idle for a day's wash does not appear to be anything but trivial to her employer.'[129]

HOLDING IT ALL TOGETHER

The Great War generation of women has been consistently misunderstood. The dominant images have been those of young women factory workers earning unaccustomed wages and finding a freer life of short skirts, cigarettes and less inhibited love. Icons like Vera Brittain commemorate female success in a man's world. Yet if she had been typical, it is difficult to see how British society could have held together. There were undoubtedly liberating forces at work, but one suspects that most women did not recognise them as such, seeing the changes instead as curious and enjoyable anomalies which would not alter the status quo. The vast majority of women during the war did what women always do: they raised children, fed families and maintained the home. Home fires were kept burning because British women dutifully kept furnaces stoked.

The role of housewife had to be performed under enormous strain. Improvements in living standards and health did not necessarily mean an easier life. Food queues and price rises caused endless consternation. The quality of housing stock declined, if not by bombs then by neglectful landlords. It was a thankless task trying to balance the roles of mother and factory worker. Misplaced patriotism and social do-goodery shed light on the ideals of 'mothercraft', which meant that mothers were judged according to ever more rigorous standards. Children had to be looked after, often without the help of a father, at a time when they were more easily led into temptation. Changes which improved a family's material fortunes often disrupted family harmony. A woman with a husband in France might have found that, with her wages and his separation allowance (not to mention one less mouth to feed), household income was steadier and more substantial than before the war. But she would still have to deal with the pain of separation and the hollow ache of loss, while trying to balance family demands with those made by her employer.

129 Braybon and Summerfield, p. 105.

Regardless of her class, a woman in 1914 was defined in terms of a man. She was someone's wife, sister, daughter, mother or sweetheart. The war did little to alter this association other than to make it more precarious. It is perhaps impossible for a later generation (men *or* women) entirely to understand how vulnerable these women must have felt when their men went off to war and they were left to cope alone in what remained a man's world. For some, the experience was undoubtedly enervating. Many found that patriarchy was built on a foundation of sand. They discovered they could do nearly everything that men once did. Some even enjoyed being freed from boorish or bullying husbands. The war's been a "appy time for us' one mother told Mrs Peel. 'It's the only time since I've been married as I and the children's 'ad peace.'[130] But no matter how unequal marital relations may have been in the Great War era, it is difficult to believe that this comment was typical. Most women found the absence of a man, especially if he was in danger, virtually intolerable.

Because mourning is by nature an individual act in Western societies, we know little of how women in Britain coped with separation and death. Each persevered in her own unique way. Some were bewildered, some stunned. Some grieved loudly and uncontrollably, others in stoical silence. Those who seemed on the surface unaffected hid inside a soul which would remain forever a vacuum. Some women went blatantly mad. A survey conducted after the war found that 12 per cent of widows died within a year, 14 per cent reported seeing the ghost of a deceased loved one and 39 per cent felt his presence.[131] As Vera Brittain wrote after the loss of her fiancé Roland Leighton:

> But, though kind Time may many joys renew,
>   There is one greatest joy I shall not know
> Again, because my heart for loss of You
>   Was broken, long ago.[132]

Out of disruption and death, a desire to rebuild arose. During and immediately after the war, 'experts' reminded women, a shade condescendingly, of their value to society: 'Home and motherhood remain woman's great and unique work', *The Times* stressed.[133] In 1917, the feminist Catherine Gasquoine (who had once dreamed of a

---

130 Peel, p. 172.
131 Winter, *The Great War and the British People*, p. 257.
132 V. Brittain, 'Perhaps', in Reilly, ed., p. 15.
133 *The Times*, 5 October 1916.

'golden age which was to come with the self-assertion of women') gave a hint of the 'new feminist' line popular after the war:

> with the outbreak of war we women were brought back to the primitive conception of the relative position of the two sexes. . . . Again man was the fighter, the protector of woman and the home. And at once his power became a reality.[134]

The Countess of Warwick wrote that 'my own dream and my own vision are of woman as the saviour of the race. I see her fruitful womb replenish the wasted ranks, I hear her wise counsels making irresistibly attractive the flower-strewn ways of peace.'[135] Most women would not have expressed this sentiment so floridly, but one suspects they would have agreed nonetheless. Moralising propaganda for mothercraft and pro-natalism reflected a popular will, it did not create that will. As Claire Tylee has written,

> the pattern . . . of emotional depth and resurrection, did not usually lead to a sense of 'common sisterhood' or to a political new life as in [Vera] Brittain's case, but to a more traditional 'new life' of motherhood. A child was a new beginning, a commitment to the future.[136]

Rather than encouraging women out of the home, war's greatest effect was to draw them back.

134 Kent, 'The Politics of Sexual Difference', p. 245.
135 Braybon, p. 166.
136 C. Tylee, *The Great War and Women's Consciousness*, p. 229.

11 'ARE YOU FORGETTING THERE'S A WAR ON?'

No matter how catastrophic and tragic the war was, the British still managed occasionally to enjoy themselves. The ways they did so, and the reactions which leisure pursuits provoked, reveal much about the divisions and stresses in Blighty during the Great War.

Since leisure is by nature an extravagance, of time or money, those both idle and rich had the most opportunity for enjoyment. The greater one's wealth, the easier it was to keep war's privations at bay. Diaries and letters indicate that life was no less lavish after August 1914; in fact, opportunities for excitement increased. There was always a dear friend whose departure for the front had to be celebrated at the Ritz or Savoy. War news brought spice to dinner conversation; good gossip traded at inflated wartime prices. 'Some of these women', Maurice Hankey complained after lunch at Ciro's (the 'latest fashion freak restaurant'), 'talk too much *and* know too much.' Others purposefully tried to ignore the war and had the means to do so. The Bloomsbury group, much admired for its erudition but seldom ridiculed for its silliness, found parties a handy escape. 'Ottoline [Morrell] . . . took it upon herself to keep us all merry & gave a party every week', wrote Vanessa Bell. She did her bit to pull 'all the celebrities of the day' out of the gloom by providing a steady regime of good food, clever capers and pompous conversation. Occasionally, they escaped to a 'funny little house by the sea . . . [where] we live without newspapers . . . & no horrors of any kinds'.[1]

A visit to London by two Serb diplomats, concerned for their starving people, included, rather inappropriately, dinner at the Carlton. 'It was . . . rather terrible to those Servians [sic] to see hundreds of people eating oysters and drinking champagne',[2] wrote Lady Scott. Quick to criticise such lavish displays, she could never quite resist them. On 6 May 1916, she dined 'at the Piccadilly of all

---

1 T. Wilson, *The Myriad Faces of War*, pp. 164–5.
2 Ibid., p. 164.

awful places. I was shocked to death to see the extravagance of the women's dress – & we eat foie gras, I eat it too with a feeling of disgust at the gaudy brilliantly lighted place.'[3] The military correspondent Colonel Charles a'Court Repington admitted a similar guilty indulgence:

> Lady Ridley and I discussed what posterity would think of us in England. We agreed that we should be considered rather callous to go on with our usual life when we were reading of 3,000 to 4,000 casualties a day.... she supposed that things around us explained the French Revolution and the behaviour of the French nobility.[4]

Everyone is entitled to an escape from war's cruel realities, but among the rich, moderation was rare and hypocrisy ran deep. While they indulged, they expected others to maintain a Spartan approach to war. Government ministers enjoyed the luxuries of high office and lectured the public on the need for austerity. Even *The Times* felt a democratic disgust: 'there are whole circles of society in which the spirit of sacrifice is unknown', it remarked in 1917. 'There should be no exceptions to the rigorous rule of self-denial which has been willingly undertaken by the great mass of our people.'[5]

Perhaps the most blatant hypocrisy came in the reaction to football, the working man's game. Middle class critics condemned the way professional matches continued as if nothing had happened. Complaining loudly about the 'scandal of professional football... with the huge "gates" of loafing lads', Sir George Young concluded that 'among the poor and ignorant, the uprising of the proper spirit is slow work'.[6] *The Times* responded poetically:

> Come, leave the lure of the football field
> With its fame so lightly won,
> And take your place in a greater game
> Where worthier deeds are done.
> No game is this where thousands watch
> The play of a chosen few;
> But rally all! if you're men at all,
> There's room in the team for you.
> . . .
> Then leave for a while the football field
> And the lure of the flying ball

3 Ibid., p. 405.
4 C. Repington, *The First World War 1914–1918*, 2, p. 3.
5 J. Walvin, *Leisure and Society 1830–1950*, p. 130.
6 Wilson, p. 164.

Lest it dull your ear to the voice you hear
When your King and country call.
Come join the ranks of our hero sons
In the wider field of fame,
Where the God of Right will watch the fight
And referee the game.[7]

Devotees of less plebeian games delighted in parading their patriotism. A rather too smug MCC secretary remarked that cricketers
'now look for their heroes on the great field of battle'.[8] Philip Collins
of the Hockey Association claimed that abandonment of all football
matches would release 40,000 men for the armed services, and the
cricketer W. G. Grace joined the chorus of disapproval. A St Andrews
University rugby player turned soldier wrote in *College Echoes*:

There's not much good in grousing,
    Work lies here to be done;
'Varsity days are sweetest,
    Though soldiering's just A1.
So we'll have a good go at the Germans,
    An', by conch, won't we make 'em run![9]

Rugby clubs in Kent cancelled fixtures, and the Rugby Football
Union formed a Pals battalion of player volunteers.

The Football Association, keen to improve its image, allowed
recruiting campaigns at league grounds. Supporters were bombarded
by messages like 'Are You Forgetting There's a War On?' and the
ubiquitous 'Your Country Needs You.'[10] Posters sought to turn team
loyalty into battalion solidarity:

MEN OF MILLWALL
Hundreds of Football Enthusiasts
are joining the Army daily.
Don't be left behind.
Let the Enemy hear the 'LION'S ROAR.'
Join and be in at
THE FINAL
and give them a
KICK OFF
THE EARTH

---

7 *The Times*, 24 November 1914.

8 Walvin, p. 129.

9 'The Subaltern' (by O. N. E. More), *College Echoes* (St Andrews), 30 October
1914. I am grateful to Corinna Peniston-Bird for locating this reference.

10 A. Marwick, *The Deluge*, p. 90.

But the FA remained 'even more decidedly of the opinion that in the interests of the people of this country, football ought to be continued'. Meanwhile, the numbers volunteering at matches dwindled as the year ended, which was interpreted as further evidence that football fans were unpatriotic. Of the 16,450 attestation cards distributed by Lord Derby at a Liverpool–Everton match in January 1915, only 1,034 were returned, and of those only 206 expressed a willingness to enlist.[11] The response at Arsenal, wrote *The Times*, 'contrasts strongly with the wholesale volunteering which has distinguished the performers and devotees of other forms of sport. Rugby Union clubs, cricket elevens, and rowing clubs throughout the kingdom have poured men into the ranks.'[12] In fact, as has been seen, by this stage the volunteer spirit was in decline across the nation. It was unfortunately not generally acknowledged that, of the nearly 1.2 million men who had volunteered by the end of 1914, nearly 500,000 had come forward through footballing organisations.[13]

Greatest scorn was reserved for the teams themselves. 'From the very nature of their trade they are in the prime of manhood, more qualified to pass any test of age and health, and physically the flower of our potential recruits.' Managers were condemned for 'virtually bribing [the players] away from their country's service'.[14] But, according to the FA, only 5,000 players were professionals, among whom 2,000 had already volunteered and another 2,400 were married. That left only 600 men who could remotely be considered 'shirkers'. The *Athletic News* recognised that

> The whole agitation is nothing less than an attempt by the classes to stop the recreation on one day in the week of the masses . . . what do they care for the poor man's sport? The poor are giving their lives for this country in thousands. In many cases they have nothing else . . . there are those who could bear arms, but who have to stay at home and work for the Army's requirements, and the country's needs. These should, according to a small clique of virulent snobs, be deprived of the one distraction that they have . . .[15]

The masses were fighting a losing battle. Heavyweight newspapers heaped scorn on players and fans. The FA eventually surrendered; League football was stopped after the spring of 1915.

---

11 *The Scotsman*, 5 January 1915.
12 *The Times*, 23 November 1914.
13 Walvin, p. 129.
14 *The Times*, 25 November 1914.
15 C. Veitch, ' "Play Up!, Play Up! and win the War!" Football, the Nation and the First World War 1914–15', *Journal of Contemporary History* 20 (1985), p. 375.

Meanwhile, football fans retaliated by pointing out, as one angry supporter commented, that 'Amongst the most vigorous critics of football are numberless racecourse frequenters, fox hunters, and golfers.'[16] Enjoying sport became a precarious pastime. *The Times* commented:

> It would not be easy to imagine a more infuriating sight, in the present state of the public temper, than that of a young man in flannels carrying a racket. A year ago, if he attracted notice at all, he suggested one blamelessly bent on healthful exercise tempered by flirtation. Now he would be regarded as a double-dyed traitor. It would be said of him that not only was he not at the front, but that he was wanting in the sense of right conduct at home.[17]

The Boat Race was abandoned for the first time since it became an annual event in 1856. Racing enthusiasts claimed that their sport 'employs many people unfitted for other work' (namely short jockeys), while it preserved English bloodstock.[18] But they eventually bowed to pressure. With the exception of Newmarket, all racing ceased at the end of May 1915. In March 1918, golfers in Eastbourne were fined for illegally using petrol to get to the course.[19] Only boxing appeared to thrive, for understandable reasons. 'Here are something of the ingredients of war – blood and sweat and struggle, the cunning manoeuvring for blows and the taking of them cheerfully', wrote *The Times*. 'We are filled with admiration for sheer courage above all qualities and here is the courage of the battle in miniature.'[20]

The country never quite decided upon the proper way to act during wartime. Many a newspaper editorial urged citizens to 'do their part by setting an example of seriousness and self-denial'.[21] The Temperance campaign increased in popularity, adding among its number those who thought making beer was wasteful of resources[22] and those who associated alcohol with enjoyment, something inappropriate to war. On the opposite side were those who recognised the occasional need to escape the war, by whatever means. For instance, despite the difficulties of train travel and the ravages of German artillery, seaside holidays remained popu-

16 *The Times*, 26 November 1914.
17 Ibid., 26 May 1915.
18 Ibid., 4 March 1915.
19 Ibid., 9 March 1918.
20 Ibid., 26 January 1915.
21 Ibid., 13 September 1915.
22 See ibid., 26 January 1917.

lar.[23] Resorts marketed themselves as suitable substitutes for German and French spas. 'Visit St. Andrews', went one advertisement in English papers. 'The picturesque old city. Beautiful Scenery, Sea bathing, &c. Specially Excellent Golf. Everything Quite Normal.'[24]

Yet the well-heeled who allowed themselves a week amidst the charms of the Old Course could still criticise workers who enjoyed themselves in their own way. If the worker happened to be a woman, animosity ran deeper. There was a panicked reaction to strange invaders on hallowed ground; men did not appreciate women in *their* pubs and restaurants. Some single women undoubtedly found unaccustomed enjoyment during the war. They frequented cheaper restaurants, dance halls and cinemas. They spent spare cash on clothes, and sometimes even splashed out on a fur coat (though invariably a fake one[25]). But neither their health nor their purse would have permitted the sybaritic life which myths suggested.

Welfare supervisors attached to factories kept close watch on the leisure activities of young female workers. It was confidently assumed that the girls' mothers would appreciate

> that someone will support her daughter in her effort not to succumb to evil talk and foul insinuation, to the temptation to join in drinking parties or in pleasures that look harmless to the high spirited girl and are full of peril.[26]

In October 1914, *The Times* summarised the serious problem facing British society:

> Little imagination is needed to picture the evils which may arise when a young girl in a state of mental restlessness produced by the war finds herself at once unemployed, with such free time on her hands, with a sudden and absorbing interest thrust upon her through the presence of a large number of troops stationed in her town, and with a desire to help with no ability to do so.[27]

The enthusiasm which many young women felt toward men in uniform was indisputable; one commentator reported seeing 'some young Colonials running for their very lives to escape a little company of girls. One might have thought, to see them, that they had

23 See ibid., 31 July 1915.

24 Ibid., 15 July 1915.

25 G. Braybon and P. Summerfield, *Out of the Cage: Women's Experiences in Two World Wars*, p. 71.

26 Ibid., p. 90.

27 *The Times*, 13 October 1914.

tigresses at their heels.'[28] Whether this constituted a threat to society was open to argument. Milicent Fawcett felt that the desire of girls to visit the camps was 'quite natural and wholesome', but 'in the absence of proper control it certainly leads in very many cases to deplorable consequences'.[29] When one substitutes rock stars for soldiers in this equation, the phenomenon described acquires a present-day relevance, as does the reaction to it.

Khaki fever did not last much longer than the rush to the colours. But the fall-out from it continued for the rest of the war. According to Sylvia Pankhurst:

> War-time hysterics gave currency to fabulous rumour. From press and pulpit stories ran rampant of drunkenness and depravity amongst the women of the masses. Alarmist morality mongers conceived most monstrous visions of girls and women, freed from the control of fathers and husbands who had hitherto compelled them to industry, chastity and sobriety, now neglecting their homes, plunging into excesses, and burdening the country with swarms of illegitimate children.[30]

It was feared that a large army would encourage an 'amateur drift' of otherwise decent women into prostitution. Munitionettes with spare cash were often cruelly assumed to be making money on the side by immoral means. In Cardiff, women were banned from pubs between 7:00 p.m. and 6:00 a.m. and from the streets between 7:00 p.m. and 8:00 a.m. But, according to a Women's Police Patrol member, a similar measure in Grantham forced genuine prostitutes to entertain men 'in their houses instead of being out on the streets', which did 'more harm than if the women had actually been in the public houses and in the streets where people could see them'.[31]

Fears of an epidemic of immorality prompted the formation of the Women Patrols Committee and the Women Police Service. These were voluntary groups, the inspiration of feminists worried that the 'foolish, giddy, irresponsible conduct . . . of the young girls might . . . [lead] them into grave moral danger'. The women police, by patrolling cinemas, ports, camps, parks and any areas where soldiers congregated, aimed to save girls 'from their own folly'.[32] The Home Office, which supported the schemes, made it clear that 'the women

---

28 A Woollacott, 'Khaki Fever and Its Control: Gender, Class, Age and Sexual Morality on the British Homefront in the First World War', *Journal of Contemporary History* 29 (1994), p. 331.

29 Ibid., p. 329.

30 S. Pankhurst, *The Home Front*, p. 98.

31 Braybon and Summerfield, pp. 108–9.

32 M. Pugh, *Women and the Women's Movement in Britain, 1914–1959*, p. 32.

patrols ... are being organised primarily with a view to the care of girls and women who are not prostitutes and would not ordinarily come under the notice of the police ... their object is mainly preventive'.[33] One pamphlet produced by the WPC warned that 'Often girls sink so low in their sin that they can never rise again, but sink lower and lower until they die a lonely and terrible death.'[34] But, lest there be misunderstanding, there was also considerable concern for the welfare of men:

> there is a great danger of the men being damaged and made unfit for the hard and awful work in front of them unless parents and employers try to prevent the girls from getting excited, running wild in the evenings and forgetting their honour, their purity, their self-respect. ... It is terrible to think that the folly and sin of any of the women and girls should make these men *less* fit to die and send them away with a guilty conscience.[35]

'There is an identifiable parallel between the women patrols and the young women they sought to control', writes one historian. 'They were both out after dark, roaming the streets, both enjoying a new, wartime freedom and imbibing the excitement of the times.'[36] But the differences between the two groups are much more important. The women police were almost without exception middle aged and middle class, whereas the women they monitored were predominantly young and working class. The two groups followed very different moral codes, which inevitably led to conflict. Perfectly innocent behaviour, such as a married couple fondling in a park, could attract the officious attention of prudish policewomen. They performed a valuable function, especially when they rescued girls from what amounted to rape. But there is no doubt that voyeurs and prying busybodies were attracted to the calling and revelled in their new legitimacy.

War can be erotic. Its effect upon the libido has been grossly exaggerated, but, as with any myth, this one has a basis in fact. Take a man in uniform with leather, throw in the machismo of fighting and guns, add a woman susceptible to romance and excitement, bring them together in the urgency of a 48-hour leave, and the result can be explosive. If sexual activity did increase, it was because there

---

33 P. Levine, ' "Walking the Streets in a Way No Decent Woman Should": Women Police in World War I', *Journal of Modern History* 66 (1994), p. 44.

34 Ibid., p. 49.

35 H. Jones, *Health and Society in Twentieth-Century Britain*, p. 36.

36 Woollacott, 'Khaki Fever', p. 336.

was more opportunity: greater mixing of the sexes, more of a tendency to throw caution to the wind, less of the censure and control which tightly knit communities once exercised. As Mary Agnes Hamilton recognised:

> Life was less than cheap; it was thrown away. . . . All moral standards were held for a short moment and irretrievably lost. Little wonder that the old ideals of chastity and self-control in sex were, for many, also lost. . . . How and why refuse appeals, backed up by the hot beating of your own heart, or what at the moment you thought to be your heart, which were put with passion and even pathos by a hero here today and gone tomorrow?[37]

The relaxation of inhibitions was not necessarily good for women; a moment's weakness often meant years of woe. The pressure upon 'decent' women was tremendous; when intercourse occurred, women were not always willing partners. Charles Cain was shocked at the behaviour of his fellow soldiers:

> The men I was with were rough with women, boasted of their conquests, many of whom were actually raped, but there were no prosecutions to my knowledge. Suffice it to say that ten soldiers were billeted on one woman who had three teenage daughters, and the mother and all the daughters finished up in the family way.[38]

One suspects that the weight of public scorn fell on the women, not the soldiers. The old double standard still applied: a woman who surrendered to male pressure or to her own desires was automatically deemed 'not the right sort'. Quite typical was the reaction of an officer to news that his occasional sexual partner was pregnant:

> I met her in the latter end of January and kept company with her for about six weeks . . . she is not the class of girl for me. . . . I am shortly leaving for the Front, and am putting the affair in my mother's hands. She is in possession of all the dates, and should they tally with the birth of the child, I have instructed her to make a small allowance for the maintenance of the child.[39]

According to Jeffrey Weeks, the centuries-old tradition of humiliating unwed mothers by serenading them with 'rough music' continued in parts of Cambridgeshire during the Great War.[40]

In April 1915, the Tory MP Ronald McNeill spread fears of a

37 M. A. Hamilton, *Our Freedom*, p. 251.

38 P. Simkins, 'Soldiers and Civilians: Billeting in Britain and France', in I. Beckett and K. Simpson, eds, *A Nation in Arms*, pp. 175–6.

39 Pankhurst, p. 182.

40 J. Weeks, *Sex, Politics and Society*, p. 60.

population explosion of 'war babies' around military camps.[41] Two sets of values collided: an old one which abhorred illegitimacy and a new one which treasured every newborn baby. 'No one wants to mete out and apportion blame in this matter', complained *The Times*, 'but it is an even worse mistake to begin to glorify human frailty as though it were praiseworthy.'[42] The sheer volume of newspaper articles on the subject demonstrates an advanced obsession with the problem of war babies. Eventually, an official inquiry concluded in June 1915 that 'the rumours which have circulated have been proved beyond doubt to have no foundation in fact'.[43] The proportion of illegitimate births did rise by 30 per cent during the war. But since the overall birth rate fell, the actual number of illegitimate births declined.[44]

Venereal disease, on the other hand, was a serious problem, with 32 out of every 1,000 soldiers afflicted in 1917.[45] Though medical checks at brothels near the front were frequent, frenetic activity rendered the problem difficult to control. The implications were serious, firstly for manpower and secondly for the spread of the disease at home. The Royal Commission on Venereal Diseases, reporting in 1916, estimated that in working class areas of London, 8–12 per cent of men and 3–7 per cent of women suffered from syphilis, with the figures higher for gonorrhoea.[46] The Commission recommended 'a franker attitude toward these diseases',[47] but feminists criticised its failure to provide guidance on prevention. The 1916 Public Health (Venereal Diseases) Regulation Act did establish a network of clinics offering free confidential diagnosis and treatment. But, whereas the Edwardians had viewed VD as something which men gave to helpless women, now the disease was seen as a scourge inflicted upon innocent Tommies by lascivious harlots. Regulation 40D of DORA, passed in March 1918, made it illegal for a woman afflicted with VD to have intercourse with a serviceman. After March 1918 a woman suffering from VD could be arrested for having sex with her husband, even if he had infected her in the first place.[48]

The acquittal of Pemberton Billing in the libel action raised by

41 Simkins, 'Soldiers and Civilians', p. 176.
42 *The Times*, 21 April 1915.
43 Ibid., 18 June 1915.
44 Jones, p. 36.
45 Simkins, 'Soldiers and Civilians', p. 185.
46 Weeks, p. 215.
47 Marwick, p. 150.
48 Jones, p. 37; Weeks, p. 216.

the dancer Maud Allan (he had alleged, in essence, that she was a lesbian) might be interpreted as an endorsement of his allegations that Britain was riddled with sexual deviancy.[49] Yet one suspects that debauchery was less common than gossip suggested. All societies have a love–hate relationship with sex: decent people despise licentiousness but delight in hearing about it. The London Public Morality Council went to great lengths investigating sexual activity in parks like Hampstead Heath and Clapham Common. The Assistant Commissioner of Police, on receipt of the report, pointedly remarked that the Council might 'bear in mind that the conduct of which they complain only constitutes an offence when committed within the view of the public'.[50]

According to Marwick, the war 'spread promiscuity upwards and birth control downwards',[51] a claim more lyrical than logical since it reinforces stereotypes of a lusty working class and overstates the dissemination of contraceptives. Condoms were more widely available by the end of the war, but mainly as a measure to control VD. Despite the near epidemic of VD, there was still heated debate about whether promoting condom usage encouraged immorality. The increased use of contraceptives amongst middle class married couples does nevertheless suggest wider acceptance of sex for enjoyment rather than merely for procreation. *Married Love*, the hugely influential work by Marie Stopes published in March 1918, sold 2,000 copies in its first fortnight and by 1924 had undergone 22 reprints.[52] But Stopes, as the title of her book suggests, was concerned about sex within marriage; widespread use of contraceptives for premarital sex was at least another generation away. For the working class, solid conclusions about something as private as sex are difficult. Cutting through the gossip, one imagines that the war stimulated the heart more than it activated the libido; there was more romance than intercourse. A 1918 Commission of Inquiry investigating fears that licentious WAACs were corrupting innocent Tommies[53] could 'find no justification of any kind for the vague accusations of immoral conduct on a large scale which have been circulated'.[54]

Fears about women overcome by carnal desire were only slightly

49 See Chapter 9, page 193.
50 Weeks, p. 214.
51 Marwick, p. 147.
52 Weeks, pp. 187–8.
53 Wilson, p. 724.
54 Braybon and Summerfield, p. 113. M. Eksteins (*Rites of Spring* pp. 224–5) is also susceptible to the myth of free love.

more hysterical than those about women intoxicated by alcohol. 'Unhappily there is no reason to doubt that drinking among the poorest classes of women has increased considerably since the outbreak of the war', wrote *The Times*.[55] Social workers wrote to *The Times* in October 1914 complaining that women who insisted their children were starving were 'all the time puffing into our faces fumes of whisky, gin and the like'.[56] The Women's Advisory Committee of the Liquor Control Board cited excessive drinking among soldier's wives as the cause of a rise in crime, 'reckless procreation', infidelity, 'feeble-mindedness' and improvidence, all leading to 'race suicide'.[57] Yet the NSPCC found that female drunkenness actually declined. Women interviewed by Braybon confirmed these findings, claiming that they seldom went to pubs during the war, and almost never alone.[58]

Blighty did have a drink problem, though it was never confined to the working class. Rubber-legged workers spilling out of pubs at all hours were more visible than soused gentlemen in clubland. But, prior to the war, most pubs in London opened at 5:00 a.m. and closed at 12:30 a.m. Factory hands did drink before and during work. The Intoxicating Liquor (Temporary Restriction) Act, passed on 31 August 1914, addressed this problem by giving licensing authorities the power to restrict opening hours. The new regulations (imposing a closing as early as 9:00 p.m.) were first applied to munitions areas, but gradually became more general. A government report released on 29 April 1915 directly linked poor production at factories in Barrow with workplace intoxication. Scotsmen who had moved to the area for war work were blamed – a cheap shot, one suspects. In response, the government used DORA to establish on 10 June a Central Control Board to regulate liquor sales in areas important to the war effort. Fourteen areas were initially named, in which the sale of alcohol (both on premises and off-sales) was restricted to as little as $4\frac{1}{2}$ hours per day. As the war progressed, the number of areas increased, such that by 1917 the Board held jurisdiction over the drinking habits of 93 per cent of the population. The government, through the Board, also encouraged the establishment of model pubs designed to clean up the drink trade at the same time

---

55 *The Times*, 14 December 1914.

56 Ibid., 3 October 1914.

57 S. Pedersen, 'Gender, Welfare, and Citizenship in Britain during the Great War', *American Historical Review* 95 (1990), p. 998.

58 Braybon and Summerfield, p. 70.

that they controlled consumption. Cheap restaurants and canteens were established as an alternative to disreputable drinking dens.

Other regulations included the banning of spirit bottles smaller than quarts (less easy to consume quickly and less transportable), restrictions upon the simultaneous purchase of spirits and a beer 'chaser', and the prohibition of spirit sales (by the bottle) on Saturday and Sunday. One of the more ingenious measures (or iniquitous, depending upon one's point of view) was the banning of 'treating' – buying a drink for another individual. This was specifically designed to cut down on drunkenness among soldiers, who found that wearing a uniform to a pub virtually guaranteed a night of free drinking. The government progressively lowered the permitted alcohol content of beers and pegged the potency of spirits at 70 per cent proof. Weaker beer, universally derided, not only curbed drunkenness, it also helped to conserve food supplies and farm labour. Liquor duties further reduced consumption and raised revenue. The price of a pint rose from 3d in 1914 to as high as 10d by the end of the war, due mostly to taxation.

State action did reduce consumption. Convictions for drunkenness and assault, which stood at 62,882 in 1908, were down to 1,670 by 1918. A study released in 1917 revealed that arrests for drunkenness among women decreased from 40,815 in 1914 to 24,206 in 1916. 'There has never been so great a reduction spread over so large a population in the same space of time',[59] remarked an amazed and chastened *Times*, one of the leading contributors to the myth of rampant female drunkenness. The *New Survey of London Life and Labour* commented favourably on the

> decrease in the amount of drinking per head ... and the decreased extent to which actual excess, and the economic effects of excess are found. The social status of drunkenness has steadily fallen in the eyes of the working-class population. Where once frequent drunkenness was half admired as a sign of virility, it is now regarded as, on the whole, rather squalid and ridiculous.[60]

The *Brewer's Gazette* commented how 'great traffic centres, like the Elephant and Castle, at which immense crowds usually lounge about until 1 o'clock in the morning, have suddenly become peaceful and respectable'.[61] If drinking had become socially unacceptable, the middle class could at least turn to another handy drug to deaden

59 *The Times*, 13 March 1917.
60 Marwick, p. 345.
61 Ibid., p. 104.

the pain of war. Cocaine usage increased to such an extent that the government eventually had to prohibit its importation, except under licence. Possession and consumption remained legal. 'The apostle of the cocaine cult finds many disciples', wrote *The Times*, 'for he offers a new release from time and circumstance.'[62]

While the popularity of pubs declined, other forms of entertainment boomed. Nightclubs, symbolic of the roaring twenties, were almost exclusively the preserve of the wealthy during the war, especially since drinks were exorbitantly priced and gambling involved relatively high stakes. They ranged in quality from swank to downright seedy, yet even the best had a hedonistic air. Scantily clad dancing girls, bawdy songs and sluttish waitresses provided the opportunity to sample what passed for immorality during the war. Dance halls were slightly more acceptable, though self-appointed moral guardians campaigned vigorously against them. Dancing itself, other than the folk variety, was initially an entertainment for the prosperous classes, but during the war class barriers fell. American ragtime and jazz, and the dancing styles they inspired (such as the foxtrot and Charleston), raised fears of cultural pollution, especially given their identification with blacks.

If a lovelorn couple wanted a few private hours together, where better than a dark cinema? Before the war, most cinema houses had staff specifically employed to reprimand and remove viewers more interested in fondling than the film. The manpower shortage rendered these monitors a luxury, much to the dismay of the National Council of Public Morals which warned of widespread depravity. A representative of the London Cinema Exhibitors replied that 'When investigation is made, it is usually found that the alleged misconduct is nothing more than the privileged manifestation of affection between the sexes.'[63] One suspects that, since cinemas were enormously popular among the working class, the moral censure was yet another manifestation of class prejudice: just as workers could not be trusted with drink, so too they could not be trusted to behave themselves in the dark. But no amount of moral censure could stop the cinema's growth in popularity; audiences of around 20 million per week attended 3,000 cinemas in 1914.

Perhaps because of its image as a cheap imitation of the theatre (anything so popular *must* be of low quality), the cinema was at first eschewed by the better off. But its popularity widened during the war,

---

62 *The Times*, 16 December 1918.
63 Marwick, p. 181.

partly because newsreels offered 'authentic' scenes from the front. Going to the cinema became patriotic: a way to participate in the war effort. An advertisement for the film of the Battle of the Ancre maintained that *'It is your duty and your privilege to see it.'*[64] Quite by accident, and somewhat late in the day, the government discovered that it was not necessarily wise to keep the public completely ignorant of the horrors of the war. *Battle of the Somme*, released in September 1916, allowed Frances Stevenson, whose brother was killed on the Somme, 'to understand what Paul's last hours were: I have often tried to imagine to myself what he went through, but now I *know*: and I shall never forget'.[65] A correspondent to *The Times* wrote: 'I have already lost two near relatives, yet I never understood their sacrifice until I had seen this film.'[66] But war scenes had to be handled with great care, according to Geoffrey Malins, the official director of newsreels:

> You must not leave the public with a bitter taste in their mouth at the end. The film takes you to the grave, but it must not leave you there; it shows you death in all its grim nakedness, but after that it is essential that you should be restored to a sense of cheerfulness and joy. That joy comes out of the knowledge that in all this whirlpool of horrors our Lads continue to smile the smile of victory.[67]

Battle of the Somme demonstrates the successful achievement of this aim. Though the film was unusual in its depiction of British soldiers being killed, viewers still, according to the *St. Andrews Citizen*, felt 'a thrill of pride in the British race as [they saw] the long column of Tommies bravely marching to the attack. There is no air of despondency about them; they look like heroes going to conquer.'[68] *The Times* reviewer was 'more convinced than ever of the invincible spirit of [his] fellow countrymen in France'.[69] The film was, however, not without its critics. The Dean of Durham expressed dismay about the crowds who felt 'no scruple at feasting their eyes on pictures which present the passion and death of British soldiers'.[70]

Since the war was an integral part of everyone's life, almost any representation of it was automatically popular. *Battle of the Somme*

64 *The Times*, 13 January 1917.
65 A. J. P. Taylor, ed., *Lloyd George: A Diary by Frances Stevenson*, p. 112.
66 *The Times*, 2 September 1916.
67 G. Mosse, *Fallen Soldiers*, p. 149.
68 *St. Andrews Citizen*, 14 October 1916.
69 *The Times*, 5 September 1916. I am grateful to my former student Luke Yates who provided much valuable research on this subject.
70 *The Times*, 1 September 1916.

had 2,000 bookings in its first two months, with profits of £30,000.[71] A film could be deadly boring and still attract huge audiences, and huge profits for cinema owners. The stodgy and humdrum *Britain Prepared*, a three-hour epic which one dispassionate American critic judged 'as uninspired as a hardware catalogue',[72] left a more subjective English critic at a loss for words: 'To say that [it] is marvellous, wonderful, stupendous, magnificent and so on would fall very short of the real truth.'[73] Cinema audiences, eager to watch almost anything, were sitting targets for propagandists. But, to the credit of the government, the importance of film as a provider of news was not completely overwhelmed by its value as a propaganda vehicle. Most of the 700 'propaganda' films were realistic portrayals of a nation at war. Inappropriate material may have been edited out but fictitious scenes were generally not edited in. Trench footage in *Battle of the Somme* was staged, but the aim was not to lie but to recreate the truth when the real truth could not, given the limitations of the medium, be filmed. 'I have tried to make my pictures actual and reliable', Malins wrote. 'Above all I have striven to catch the atmosphere of the battlefield.'[74]

Private producers had fewer scruples when it came to the truth. Effective propaganda was produced voluntarily by filmmakers who recognised that war provided the conditions for huge profits: action, melodrama, romance aplenty *and* audiences automatically attracted to patriotic themes. D. W. Griffith is a case in point. His *Intolerance* (1916), though a recognised classic, was a box office flop because of its pacifist theme. Brought to Britain in 1917 to make war films, he was not above pandering to popular belligerence. *The Great Love* and *Heart of the World*, generally recognised as lesser achievements, were very popular and, as such, effective propaganda. The latter, which includes a scene in which Lillian Gish is nearly raped by a cruel German officer, combined everything calculated to please a wartime audience: action, romance, a hated villain, sex and a happy ending. 'The tried and popular elements of drama have not been swept away by a wave of militarism, but have been ingeniously adapted to a new state of things', one critic wrote.[75] But not all films concentrated upon war themes. Some were unashamedly escapist,

71 N. Reeves, 'Film Propaganda and Its Audience: The Example of Britain's Official Films During the First World War', *Journal of Contemporary History* 18 (1983), p. 472. See also C. Haste, *Keep the Home Fires Burning*, p. 45.

72 Wilson, p. 738.

73 Reeves, 'Film Propaganda', p. 480.

74 Ibid., p. 465.

75 *The Times*, 23 January 1915.

such as those of Charlie Chaplin and his myriad, less memorable, copiers. Chaplin's ability to act as a tonic for the soul eventually outweighed the ill-feeling which arose because he was 'not doing his bit'.[76] Even frivolous films, by distracting attention from the war, had a positive effect. The cinema drew people out of their homes, where they might otherwise mire in gloom. The group dynamics of cinema-going proved an immense boon to morale. When fire broke out in the Lanark Picture House, the pianist had the presence of mind to strike up 'It's a Long Way to Tipperary'. The audience joined in, thus cooling nerves, which allowed an ordered exit.[77]

Escapism perhaps explains the continued popularity of music halls. Largely the preserve of the better off working class, they were by their very nature perfectly suited to wartime, since they catered to the peculiar British tendency to confront adversity by resorting to song. Routines were essentially crude political cartoons put to music. Fat German soldiers, with sausages hanging from their pockets, were a rich source of musical ridicule. London County Council liberally granted full music licences to picture palace managers who wanted to include patriotic singing on their programmes.[78] An astute piano supplier recognised the lucrative opportunities for recreating the music hall atmosphere at home: 'The "Pianola" piano enables you to celebrate good news fittingly', went one ad. It was 'always ready to play the music that expresses your present mood'.[79]

Mainly middle class before 1914, theatres were democratised during the war. In cities across Britain, drama companies enjoyed packed houses and extended runs. This popularity was achieved in part by diluting the highbrow content, much to the consternation of traditionalists. Theatre managers, like film producers, understood the marketability of war. A steady fare of crudely patriotic dramas were offered which usually included opportunities for audiences to join actors in rousing song. At the same time, managers recognised a popular need, especially among soldiers, to escape the war. 'The great charm of *Peter Pan* is that it enables the onlooker to forget for a few hours the worries of everyday life', wrote *The Times* critic. 'It was a real joy at the Duke of York's theatre to leave the thoughts of European war outside.'[80] Another critic commented:

76 Walvin, p. 133.
77 *The Scotsman*, 21 October 1914.
78 *The Times*, 25 January 1915.
79 Ibid., 27 February 1915.
80 Ibid., 26 December 1914.

It would probably be found that those who read their newspapers most and with most lively imagination want no war in the theatre, while for the rest the theatre is the force which crystallizes the ambient rumour. And thus, between the desire to learn about the war and the desire to forget about the war, we have the crowded houses which puzzle our foreign friends.[81]

The London Palladium put on 1,043 performances in 1916, which drew three million people. The audience was composed of 61 per cent women, 8 per cent children and 31 per cent men, 46 per cent of the latter in uniform.[82]

High culture still managed to survive the war. An increased sensitivity to the preciousness of life inspired a thirst for the sublime. According to Sir Thomas Beecham:

In wartime the temper of a section of the people for a while becomes graver, simpler, and more concentrated. The opportunities for recreation and amusement are more restricted, transport is limited, and the thoughtful intelligence craves and seeks these antidotes to a troubled conscience of which great music is perhaps the most potent.[83]

Tastes in classical music nevertheless reflected the war mood. Audiences became familiar as never before with the Russian and Japanese national anthems. German music declined in popularity, while pieces which reflected the martial mood (like the *1812 Overture*) became favourites.

The visual arts were not without their attraction. Early in the war, attendances at the National Gallery declined slightly, which convinced an economy-minded government that it would be acceptable to close galleries. The angry protest in the press which followed ensured that the policy was quickly reversed (though hours were restricted). By war's end, the crush of eager art lovers at times became unbearable. Museums were also a popular diversion, with exhibits often taking on a war theme. Perhaps the most bizarre was the fly exhibition at the Scottish Zoological Park, the feature of which was an exhibit of the 'body louse which has been a source of great pain and annoyance to the troops at the front'.[84]

One might be inclined to explain the enormous and profound poetic output during the Great War as a symptom of Beecham's thirst for the sublime, but some qualifications are necessary. Modern-

---

81 Ibid., 5 February 1915.
82 Ibid., 22 January 1917.
83 Marwick, p. 185.
84 *The Scotsman*, 1 October 1915.

ist literature and painting were not invented in the trenches. Both existed before the war: in other words, Rupert Brooke's romantic poetry was already old-fashioned at the time it was written. But modernism's stark realism was particularly appropriate for conveying the horrors of industrialised war, particularly a war which so lacked the heroic themes upon which romanticism depended. Nevertheless, though modernists found a rich vein to tap, one should not assume that their poetry was popular. The poems of Wilfred Owen and Siegfried Sassoon (or the paintings of Paul Nash and Muirhead Bone) have been admired by subsequent generations because they conform to and reinforce *ex post facto* images of the Great War. Though the Great War generation was a poetic one, the vast majority of poetry read and written was of a type characterised by tortured rhyme, sugar-sweet romanticism and an overwhelming evocation of noble, patriotic war. A stanza from 'To a Soldier in a Hospital' reveals that this sort of poetry could even be written after the carnage of the Somme:

> So when you went to play another game
>   You could not but be brave:
> An Empire's team, a rougher football field
>   The end – perhaps your grave.[85]

There were still romantics aplenty in 1916. An excessively confident St Andrews student gave the following advice to mothers who had lost sons:

> Why would ye mourn and be of heavy heart
> Ye who have lost your children in the fight?
> Rather rejoice that they should play their part
> And fall so nobly in the cause of right.[86]

We may revere Owen, but the Great War generation preferred Jessie Pope. As for the visual representation of the war, the populist sketches of Bruce Bairnsfather were more widely favoured than the shattered landscapes of Nash. This does not mean that a generation should be judged solely by its popular art. But that art is a useful indicator of how the common people viewed the war. The popular culture of 1914–18 suggests that the public wanted to be amused, diverted, uplifted and persuaded that the war was noble and right.

85 Anonymous, 'To a Soldier in a Hospital', *The Spectator*, 12 August 1916.
86 *College Echoes* (St Andrews), 12 February 1916.

The fact that the people at home wanted to believe in a 'good war' made life easy for propagandists and profitable for entertainment entrepreneurs, but it widened the gulf between home and fighting fronts. No matter how real some of the newsreels and films were, they could never be real enough. Therefore, the longer the war lasted, the wider this gulf became and the more scornful were soldiers of civilians. 'I was thoroughly "fed up" with the attitude of most of the people I met on leave', wrote the poet Herbert Read in 1917. 'They simply have no conception whatever of what war really is like and don't seem concerned about it at all.'[87] When asked whether he had told his wife while on leave about conditions at the front, an English soldier replied, 'I didn't get a chance, she was so busy tellin' me all the news about Mrs. Bally's cat killin' Mrs. Smith's bird, Mrs. Cramp's sister's new dress, and how Jimmy Murphy's dog chewed up Annie Allen's doll.'[88] The stubbornly mundane nature of home front life fuelled the bitterness of war poets like Sassoon and of shame-ridden civilians like Edith Sitwell. Her poem 'The Dancers' is a strident attack upon wartime merriment:

The music has grown numb with death –
But we will suck their dying breath,
The whispered name they breathed to chance,
To swell our music, make it loud
That we may dance, – may dance.

We are the dull blind carrion-fly
That dance and batten. Though God die
Mad from the horror of the light –
The light is mad, too, flecked with blood, –
We dance, we dance, each night.[89]

The condemnation heaped upon the home front, though understandable, is not entirely fair. There was insensitivity and hypocrisy in this war, but the fighting front did not have a monopoly on virtue. The Great War revealed that, in the interests of morale, leisure pursuits should carry on as closely as possible to normal. A collapse of morale on the home front would have ended the war much more quickly than a German breakthrough on the Western Front. Dancing and

87 H. Read, 'War Diary', in J. Silkin, ed., *The Penguin Book of First World War Prose*, p. 289.
88 Eksteins, p. 229.
89 E. Sitwell, 'The Dancers', in C. Reilly, ed., *Scars Upon My Heart*, p. 100.

drinking, watching Chaplin or supporting Wolverhampton Wanderers enabled one to cope. Enjoying oneself in boisterous company
was much better than grieving in silent solitude.

12 DENOUEMENT: 1918

On 31 December 1917, New Year celebrations in Blighty were decidedly muted. The past year had been the worst of the war. The Passchendaele offensive had repeated the Somme's ghastliness. Action at Cambrai in late November seemed to promise a bright future with technology taking the place of raw manpower on the battlefield. Church bells celebrated the stunning advance. But then the British, weakened by months of costly fighting, were pushed past their original line by a massive German counterattack. Politicians and generals engaged in an ugly orgy of blame. Elsewhere, the news was equally bleak. An armistice on 17 December between the Central Powers and Russia cleared the way for the transfer of German troops to the West. In late October, the Italians were routed at Caporetto. Why, ordinary people wondered, was an enemy supposedly on the brink of defeat capable of such impressive victories? The year had provided only two causes for optimism. The first, the declaration of war by the United States, lost much of its lustre when the Americans proved slow to mobilise. The second, Allenby's capture of Jerusalem, merely indicated how desperate the British were for something, anything, to lift their spirits. As everyone realised, the real war was on the Western Front. From that vantage point, only a fool would have predicted victory in 1918.

At home, the war intruded in ways never imagined. More dynamic government meant greater limitations on the freedom of every citizen, be it in the ability to travel, access to basic commodities, or the choice whether to serve in the military. Gotha bombers – a horror much greater than Zeppelins – attacked in earnest. The rail system finally reached breaking point: services were cancelled at short notice and trains were stuffed with tired and harassed passengers. There were shortages of coal, paper and especially food. Queues outside shops grew, as did resentment towards profiteers who capitalised on the public's misery. On the streets, the constant presence of severely disabled ex-soldiers was an unavoidable reminder of war's cruelty. To the miseries of war were added the scourge of disease. The influenza epidemic which began in the latter half of the year was surprisingly democratic in its effects; it attacked young and old, rich and poor without distinction. Before it ran its course in the spring of 1919, it claimed approximately 200,000 lives.

Against this backdrop, the new year seemed to promise even worse anguish and privation. But neither disease nor countless casualties, shortages, taxes, nor harsh regulations broke the British spirit. The giddy belligerence of 1914 had long dissipated, replaced by grim determination to see the war through. The stunning success of the German March offensive made the British more resolute, not less. *The Times* captured the mood with advice to citizens:

> Be cheerful, face facts and work; attend volunteer drills regularly; cultivate your allotment; don't exceed your rations; don't repeat foolish gossip; don't listen to idle rumours and don't think you know better than Haig.[1]

The flurry of recriminations which followed the March setback revealed that the political and military establishment was far less united than its citizenry. While Haig grumbled about being starved of troops, Lloyd George went public with claims that the British Army was numerically stronger in January 1918 than in January 1917. Whilst technically correct, this was in fact an attempt to hoodwink Parliament and the public, a fact pointed out by General Frederick Maurice in an accusatory letter in the press on 7 May.[2] That letter provoked an acrimonious debate in the Commons – one of the few times during the war when Parliament provided real drama. Lloyd George, employing all his skills of manipulation and evasion, totally out-manoeuvred a hapless Asquith and emerged with his power more secure than ever. But, as Trevor Wilson has shown, it is easy to exaggerate the importance of the Maurice debate, and dangerous to do so.[3] The debate is important because it was not important. As with the March offensive itself, it did not dent the British public's determination to carry on with the war, nor did it destabilise the political status quo.

By the time the turbulence from the Maurice debate had settled, the German offensive was spent and fortunes had shifted decisively toward the Allies. But this in no sense signalled an early end to the war. The British felt confident that they had absorbed the worst the Germans could deliver, but still expected a long and costly effort

1 D. Winter, *Death's Men*, p. 245.
2 D. Woodward, *Lloyd George and the Generals*, chapter 12 and p. 238.
3 T. Wilson, *The Myriad Faces of War*, pp. 573–5.

to dislodge them from France and Belgium. The heavily fortified Hindenburg Line seemed impregnable. The Germans, so the scenario went, would rest out the winter, replenish their forces with a new call-up in 1919 and resume the bitter fight. The British Cabinet made war plans for 1919 and 1920. Since British factories had been depleted of manpower in the aftermath of the March offensive, supplies of munitions were dangerously low. A new shell crisis seemed imminent.

But Haig's determination, which in 1916 and 1917 had seemed misplaced, was suddenly appropriate. Victory piled upon victory. The French Army, inspired by the turn of events, discovered an untapped reserve of strength and resumed the attack. Even the Americans began to pull their weight. September and October brought fresh cause for optimism: an Austrian peace effort, the signing of an armistice by Bulgaria and Turkey, a German peace note.

And then, quite suddenly, it was all over. On the morning of Monday 11 November, engineers were hastened to the Tower of Parliament to reactivate the striking mechanism of Big Ben. The big clock would strike at 11:00 a.m., the first time since August 1914. At 10:55 Lloyd George made a short statement outside Downing Street: 'At eleven o'clock this war will be over. We have won a great victory and we are entitled to a bit of shouting.'[4]

Shout they did. When Big Ben tolled, echoed by church bells round the country and by the cacophonous firing of guns, a massive release of emotion occurred. Victory had 'rushed on us with the speed and impact of a comet', wrote Osbert Sitwell.

> That night it was impossible to drive through Trafalgar Square: because the crowd danced under lights turned up for the first time for four years – danced so thickly that the heads, the faces, were like a field of golden corn moving in a dark wind. The last occasion I had seen the London crowd was when it had cheered for its own death outside Buckingham Palace on the evening of 4th of August 1914; most of the men who had composed it were now dead. Their heirs were dancing because life had been given back to them. They revolved and whirled their partners round with rapture, almost with abandon, yet, too, with solemnity, with a kind of religious fervour, as if it were a duty.[5]

Crowds gathering at Buckingham Palace chanted 'We want the King! We want the King!' He duly appeared, waved to the vast crowd then quickly disappeared inside. Some time later, he ended his wartime

---

4 S. Weintraub, *A Stillness Heard Round the World*, p. 252.
5 O. Sitwell, *Laughter in the Next Room*, pp. 1, 3–4.

abstinence by breaking open a bottle of brandy originally laid down by the Prince Regent to celebrate victory at Waterloo. It tasted 'very musty'.[6]

At the front, the end had a distinctly bizarre quality. The official announcement that the war would end went round the units on the morning of the 11th. One soldier recalled:

> On the morning of the 11th ... there were rumours of an Armistice, but we did not attach much importance to them. At about 10:45 we were in action against the Germans, east of Mons, and one of our troops had just charged some German machine-guns. A private soldier came galloping towards us; he was much excited, had lost his cap, and could not stop his horse. As he passed us he shouted: 'The war's over! The war's over!' We thought, undoubtedly, the poor fellow was suffering from shell-shock.[7]

Artillery logs record firing right up to 11:00. Last-minute raids caused inevitable fatalities. Then all went quiet. Action ceased as if a referee had blown a whistle. 'The match was over and it had been a damned bad game', recalled one officer. Soldiers reacted differently to the end of the war: some engaged in a frenzy of celebration, others expressed their happiness with greater restraint. But most celebrated survival, not victory. Many cried, not always in joy. One soldier, overcome by the weight of conflicting emotions, wrote of his 'worst ever depression'.[8] 'We were very old, very tired, and now very wise', thought Guy Chapman.[9] 'What a victory it might have been – the real, the Winged Victory, chivalric, whole and unstained!' wrote C. E. Montague. 'The bride that our feckless wooing had sought and not won in the generous youth of the war had come to us now: an old woman, or dead, she no longer refused us.'[10]

In most cities and towns, massive street parties erupted. They lasted for hours, in places for days. The end of the war was excuse enough to kiss (a) any soldier and (b) any young woman. By the end of the day, even these qualifications ceased to apply: everyone was kissing everyone else in decidedly un-British fashion. 'Custom and convention melted away as if a new world had indeed dawned', recalled Caroline Playne.[11] High spirits inevitably gave way to low behaviour: excessive drinking, vandalism, violence, thievery, etc.

6 Weintraub, p. 263.
7 G. Chapman, ed., *Vain Glory*, p. 705.
8 Winter, p. 235.
9 Chapman, p. 707.
10 C. E. Montague, *Disenchantment*, p. 129.
11 Chapman, ed., p. 706.

Oswald Mosley recalled seeing his future wife Cimmie Curzon draped in a Union Jack singing patriotic songs at the Ritz. Later she 'tore around Trafalgar Square with the great crowd setting fire to old cars and trucks'.[12] A throng of Sandhurst cadets emerged from the gates of the college and jumped on an old horse-drawn coach waiting for customers. 'The ancient vehicle collapsed under the weight and the old cabbie was left, clay pipe in hand, surveying the wreck whilst cadets rushed along the Great Southwest Road.' Weintraub concludes that 'It was almost a metaphor for what had happened to the Old Order in Europe.'[13] A more sensitive examination would conclude that it was a metaphor for what had not happened to the British social order: it remained perfectly acceptable for patricians to treat plebs with disdain.

Many, unable to forget the ubiquitous tragedy of the war, found it impossible to share in celebration. Victoria Smith remembered her school being let out at the sound of the bells. As the children rushed out, she saw 'amidst the empty desks ... the geography mistress, head in hands, quietly but copiously crying. She had been widowed by the war.'[14] Vera Brittain, who had lost her brother, her fiancé and two close friends, concluded that peace had 'come too late for me'. 'All those with whom I had really been intimate were gone: not one remained to share with me the heights and depths of my memories.'[15] 'I keep seeing all these horrors, bathing in them again and again', wrote Katherine Mansfield, 'and then my mind fills with the wretched little picture I have of my brother's grave. What is the meaning of it all?'[16]

One who could justifiably question the meaning was Wilfred Owen's mother. The war had been officially over for an hour when a War Office messenger delivered the telegram informing her of her son's death a week earlier during action on the Sambre.

> 'Strange friend', I said, 'here is no cause to mourn.'
> 'None', said the other, 'save the undone years,
> The hopelessness. Whatever hope is yours,
> Was my life also; I went hunting wild
> After the wildest beauty in the world,
> Which lies not calm in eyes or braided hair,

12 N. Mosley, *Rules of the Game*, p. 19.
13 Weintraub, p. 261.
14 Ibid., p. 257.
15 V. Brittain, *Testament of Youth*, pp. 327–8.
16 P. Vansittart, *Voices from the Great War*, p. 253.

But mocks the steady running of the hour,
And if it grieves, grieves richlier than here.
For by my glee might many men have laughed,
And of my weeping something had been left,
Which must die now. I mean the truth untold,
The pity of war, the pity war distilled.[17]

17 Wilfred Owen, 'Strange Meeting', in J. Silkin, ed., *The Penguin Book of First World War Poetry*, p. 197.

13 COMING HOME

SLIPS AND CIVVIE SUITS

In confronting the problem of what to do with 3,750,000 soldiers, sailors and airmen, the government had two basic concerns: the first was to avoid mass unemployment resulting from a tide of released veterans with no secure promise of employment, the second to avoid runaway inflation resulting from industry's inability to convert to peacetime production quickly enough to meet a flood of pent-up demand. The solution seemed to lie in controlled demobilisation based upon the labour needs of industry. Thus, those with assured employment would have precedence over those without. In other words, economic stability would take precedence over social justice.

Demobilisation plans were established well before the armistice. Military personnel were to be divided into five groups. The first and smallest group was the 'demobilisers', those men (mainly civil servants) who would administer the demobilisation process. 'Pivotal men', the second group, consisted of those considered job creators, men whose return to civilian life would expand opportunities for those who followed. They might, for instance, be highly skilled engineers essential to the transition of an industry to peacetime production. An authority within each industry was appointed to dole out the strictly limited number of pivotal places. Both the demobilisers and the pivotal men were to be released before the commencement of general mobilisation.

'Slip men', the third group, were those already guaranteed jobs at home. (The 'slip' referred to the section torn off from the civil employment form which the individual presented to his commanding officer, confirming that he had been promised employment.) These men were to be released in a controlled fashion after the beginning of general mobilisation, according to a priority based on the importance of their occupation to reconstruction. Thus, a man guaranteed a job in a coal mine would take priority over one promised work as an insurance clerk. The remaining 'nonslip men', those without guaranteed employment, were divided into two groups: the first had skills likely to land them immediate employment in industries vital to recovery, and the second had no such prospects.[1]

The lucky possessor of a slip would be sent to a camp behind the lines and then to one of 26 dispersal stations where he would be processed within 24 hours and released on a 28-day furlough, after which he would be formally demobilised. At the dispersal station he would be given a railway warrant, ration book, pay for the period of the furlough and either an allowance of 52s 6d for the purchase of civilian clothes, or a demob suit. (The government had stockpiled huge quantities of grade three standard cloth for suits.) He would be allowed to keep his uniform and his helmet. Greatcoats could be retained or sold back to the government for £1 at any railway station. He would also receive unemployment insurance, worth 29s per week for himself, 6s for his first child and 3s for each additional child, up to a limit of twenty weeks.[2]

Within each category, further priority would be calculated on the basis of marital status, length of service, and time spent in the front line. Men already at home were to be treated the same as those stationed abroad, thus ruling out the possibility of unfair advantage being given those on leave. But this was as far as the government was willing to go toward fairness. The system was logical but remarkably unjust. It was slanted in favour of those with short service records, since they were most likely to retain close ties with employers. Thus, a single man conscripted in 1917 who never saw active service but who had been promised a job could easily be given priority over a volunteer of 1914 with wound stripes, a wife and children but no promise of employment. The overriding principle was 'last in, first out'.

The government, preoccupied with the election campaign and the peace negotiations, failed to anticipate the fallout from a system so iniquitous. *The Herald* commented sarcastically:

> We leave the matter of finding him employment to the owners and we present him with cash and promises, which work out to an average of about 9s a week for fifty-two weeks, provided he is unemployed for twenty of them. It is superb, immense. None but an imperial people,

---

1 Details of the demobilisation scheme and its subsequent history can be found in S. R. Graubard, 'Military Demobilization in Great Britain Following the First World War', *Journal of Modern History* 19 (1947), pp. 297–311.

2 Ibid., p. 299; G. Coppard, *With a Machine Gun to Cambrai*, p. 133; D. Winter, *Death's Men*, p. 239.

victorious against its enemies, but overcome with emotion and thankfulness before its returning heroes, could have done it.

Because of the rather ambiguous end to the war (an armistice, not a surrender), release of demobilisers and pivotal men did not begin until 9 December. Industrialists, keen to begin the transformation to peacetime production, but prevented from doing so by the labour shortage, grew increasingly strident in their criticism. By 7 December *The Herald* had given up on irony:

> Send the boys home. Why in the world the delay? The war is not officially 'over', but everyone knows that in fact it is over. Munitionmaking has stopped; motorists can joy ride; the King has had a drink; society has had its victory ball and is settling down. . . . Danger of too rapid demobilization? Bunkum! There are thousands of men for whom jobs are waiting, but the Army won't let them go. And – even if a man hasn't a job – why not let him go home at once?[3]

In response to this criticism, the government began tinkering with the system. On 13 December, it unveiled a 'contract system' whereby a serviceman on leave could be demobilised if he was able to secure an offer from a pre-war employer. Six days later, Lloyd George, under increasing pressure, appointed Sir Eric Geddes to coordinate the work of the fourteen separate departments concerned with demobilisation. On the same day, the government began paying out gratuities according to a scale agreed by the Commons on 20 November. At the top of the list, Field Marshal Haig and Admiral Beatty were granted £100,000. (Haig at first asked for £250,000.[4]) Lower down the scale, lieutenants were allotted as much as £226; corporals £28 and privates £20.[5] The gross inequality of the rewards may seem striking today, but at the time most veterans were impressed by the government's generosity.[6]

The changes did not stifle discontent. On 3 January 10,000 soldiers protested at Folkestone by refusing to board ships back to France. Another 2,000 demonstrated at Dover and 8,000 at Brighton. But the most embarrassing incident was a relatively small one centred on Whitehall. Arriving in lorries, soldiers picketed government offices with signs like 'WE WON THE WAR, GIVE US OUR TICKETS'; 'GET A MOVE ON, GEDDES'; 'NO MORE RED TAPE'; 'WE WANT CIVVIE SUITS' and 'PROMISES ARE NOT PIE

---

3 Graubard, p. 301.
4 G. DeGroot, *Douglas Haig, 1861–1928*, p. 399.
5 Winter, p. 240.
6 Coppard, p. 134.

CRUST'.[7] The militancy was all the more shocking given that nothing remotely similar had occurred during the worst periods of trench warfare. The combativeness of the protesters arose in part from fears that they would be sent to Russia to fight the Bolsheviks (20,000 had already been sent), but more specifically from a desire to extend leaves so as to benefit from the contract system. Realising its mistake, the government on 7 January suspended the contract system and, aware of the potentially explosive nature of the demonstrations, wisely decided not to take action against the participants. Lloyd George meanwhile reminded the country that the war was not yet officially over and that in any case 300,000 men had already been demobilised, arguments which contradicted each other.

After the election, Churchill took over the War Ministry with a mission to sort out demobilisation. After consulting Haig and Geddes, he devised Army Orders 54 and 55 which, despite claims to the contrary, signalled a complete abandonment of the old system in favour of one based on age, length of service, and combat experience – basically 'first in, first out'. Under the new system, any soldier who had enlisted before 31 December 1915, or who was over 37, or who had three wound stripes, would be released immediately. Some 1,300,000 men satisfied none of these criteria. From that number, 400,000 were to be released as pivotal men or on hardship grounds, leaving 900,000 to guard the Rhine bridgeheads or to serve as a home force. To pacify them, pay was nearly doubled, bringing it closer to comparable civilian rates.

While a much better system, Churchill's scheme depended upon quick implementation. The need for haste was underlined when soldiers returning to Calais from leave refused to return to their units – the largest protest to date.[8] Haig's determination to take a tough line against the Calais protesters exacerbated the problem. Though he had openly criticised the original demobilisation plans, he was certain that the rioters were 'led astray by Bolshevist agitators' and ordered that

> If men start disturbances in Calais or elsewhere, *the disturbances are to be quelled at all costs, and as soon as possible. Discipline must be maintained*, and rioters if they cannot be arrested must be shot.

Order was quickly restored, whereupon the matter of punishment

---

7 Graubard, p. 303.

8 See G. Dallas and D. Gill, *The Unknown Army*, chapters 8–12. The authors give the protests more importance than they perhaps deserve.

arose. Haig insisted that the ringleaders should be shot in order to maintain army discipline. Churchill demanded leniency. Haig, disgusted, continued to insist upon his sovereign right to shoot rioters, but in practice obeyed Churchill's wishes.[9]

Quick implementation of the Churchill scheme prevented further serious disturbances. Men were released, according to Churchill, 'at the enormous rate of 13,000 or 14,000 daily'.[10] Within ten weeks, 56 per cent of eligible officers and 78 per cent of eligible men had been demobilised. The process was applied equally smoothly to the Royal Navy and the RAF. After one year, only 125,000 eligible men in the army awaited release. By that stage, the army had shrunk to 381,056 men, mainly volunteers. (The requirement of 900,000 was abandoned after the Versailles Treaty was signed in June 1919.) This was, by any reckoning, an enormously impressive achievement. The government's initial concern that mobilisation had to be slow and controlled in order to avoid unemployment and economic disruption seemed unfounded. In 1919 and 1920, the average annual rate of unemployment was 2.7 per cent, virtually the same as in 1913.[11] But perhaps a more relevant year for comparison is 1921, when the total unemployed topped one million, above which it remained until 1940. It is nevertheless difficult to imagine, in light of the disturbances which took place, that the government would have been able to retain men in the services for two or three years after the war in order to manipulate the labour supply more efficaciously.

PENSIONS AND REHABILITATION

Roughly 25 per cent of veterans who returned to Blighty suffered some form of disability. The government began to study this problem in May 1916, when the War Injury Pensions Committee was formed. Much to the annoyance of those concerned, pensions were not made a statutory right; instead the traditional system of Royal Warrants was maintained. If pensions were determined by parliamentary statute, ministers argued, political parties might attempt to 'buy' the votes of ex-servicemen with unscrupulous promises to raise pensions. The full disablement pension was eventually set at 25s per week, with an extra 2s 6d for each child. This was a pitifully small amount,

9 DeGroot, pp. 401–2.

10 K. Jeffery, 'The Post-War Army', in I. Beckett and K. Simpson, eds, *A Nation in Arms*, p. 213.

11 Graubard, p. 311.

about what an unskilled labourer earned. The pension was then reduced according to scales of disability: for instance, a man missing an entire arm would get 16s; if the loss was above the elbow, 14s, below the elbow, 11s 6d. The left arm was valued less generously, unless the veteran was left-handed. According to the Disabled Society, 41,050 ex-servicemen had at least one limb amputated.[12] Rates were also determined according to the rank of the person concerned.[13]

Disablement pensions inspired nearly universal scorn. Haig delayed acceptance of a peerage in an effort to embarrass the government into reconsideration. The government believed that, as in the past, the disabled should rely in part upon charity. But Haig, recognising that conditions were altogether different, insisted that 'Officers and their wives . . . will not, and ought not to be asked to, accept *Charity*.'[14] (It is not clear whether he thought it still acceptable for ordinary soldiers to do so.) The pressure forced the government to pass the Great War Pensions Act of 1921, making pensions a statutory right. The full pension rate was increased to £2 per week and 26s 8d for a widow. In March 1921, 1,187,450 pensions were granted in nine categories of disability. Nearly 40,000 totally disabled received the full amount. In addition, 192,678 widows' pensions (covering, in addition, 344,606 children) were granted. Another 10,605 separate orphans' pensions were awarded.[15] Despite the fact that pensions were still low, officials feared that amputees would attract 'an undesirable class of women . . . seek[ing] to entrap the soldiers for the sake of their monetary value'. In response, the Eugenics Society suggested that entitlement to pensions be linked to maternity not matrimony.[16]

Article 5 of the Pensions Act stipulated that claims had to be made within seven years of the date of discharge, effectively excluding those who developed complications from wounds (both physical and psychological) long after the war. The act also specified that rates could be revised downwards if the cost of living fell. Pensioners feared that they would be the first victims of cost-cutting efforts by the Exchequer. This sort of parsimony roused the ire of John Gals-

---

12 S. Koven, 'Remembering and Dismemberment: Crippled Children, Wounded Soldiers, and the Great War in Britain', *American Historical Review* 99 (1994), p. 1185.

13 Winter, p. 253.

14 DeGroot, p. 398.

15 J. Winter, *The Great War and the British People*, pp. 273–6.

16 Koven, 'Remembering and Dismemberment', p. 1191.

worthy who edited a Ministry of Pensions journal for and about disabled ex-servicemen:

> The State, like the humblest citizen, cannot have it both ways. If it talks – as talk it does, with the mouth of every public man who speaks on this subject – of heroes, and of doing all it can for them, then it must not cheese-pare as well, for that makes it ridiculous. Britain has climbed the high moral horse – as usual – over the great question of our disabled; she cannot stay in that saddle if she rides like a slippery lawyer.[17]

In fact, rates were never reduced, but the clause continued to annoy. In 1929, a final award was made to all veterans with disability no greater than 20 per cent. This still left 229,034 in receipt of pensions. Again, anomalies were revealed, since there was nothing to protect the unfortunate ex-serviceman removed from the pension rolls in 1929 whose disability subsequently worsened.

On pension boards, budgetary prudence often took precedence over humanity. Under the seven-year rule, widows were denied pensions because their husbands died just weeks after the deadline had passed. An embarrassed government eventually abandoned this stipulation in 1924. A particularly heartless case of officiousness arose when a woman was denied a widow's pension because she had married her husband after he had received his eventually fatal war injuries. She apparently should have realised that she was marrying a damaged bridegroom.[18] Cases involving loss of limbs were usually straightforward, but others, such as those concerning respiratory diseases or mental disability, were open to wide, and often unfair, interpretation. Instances abound of men who had been perfectly healthy before 1914 suffering from respiratory diseases which pensions boards refused to accept were war-related. According to Ministry records, approximately 80,000 men died of war-related illnesses or injury after the war.[19] A more liberal interpretation of the definition of 'war-related' would obviously have yielded a much higher figure. Cases of what would now be called post-traumatic stress disorder (some leading to suicide) were denied compensation on the grounds that the condition had not been apparent during the war. Under pressure from the British Legion, the government in 1938 investigated whether war service caused a generally higher propensity toward illness, premature ageing and early death. Though the evidence is compelling, the official actuary advised that such a propen-

17 Ibid., p. 1201.
18 J. Winter, p. 265.
19 Ibid., p. 276.

sity would be impossible to determine conclusively. The government therefore decided that it had no legal responsibility to provide compensation.[20] Yet half a century after the war, war service (and particularly the effects of gas) was still being listed as a contributory cause of death on coroners' reports.[21]

Little rehabilitation or retraining was provided for the disabled. Ignoring Legion demands for a law obliging employers to take on a small percentage of disabled veterans, the government instead insisted upon a voluntary programme. The King's National Roll scheme encouraged employers to take on disabled ex-servicemen to a minimum of 5 per cent of their work force. By 1926, 28,000 firms were participating, employing 365,000 disabled men. But 'disabled' in this case might mean something as minor as a missing finger. The seriously disabled did not benefit significantly from the scheme. And, when unemployment became widespread, the disabled could not compete on equal terms with able-bodied men for an ever-shrinking pool of jobs. 'They have the greatest claim on the country, and yet many able to do a day's work are not able to get it', one sympathetic critic wrote. 'Who can blame them if, instead of being honoured and contented, they become broken wanderers with curses on their lips?'[22]

The government's record in preparing the able-bodied for peacetime was hardly better. George Coppard expressed a common bitterness at his treatment after demobilisation:

> Although an expert machine gunner, I was a numbskull so far as any trade or craft was concerned. Lloyd George and company had been full of big talk about making the country fit for heroes to live in, but it was just so much hot air. No practical steps were taken to rehabilitate the broad mass of demobbed men, and I joined the queues for jobs as messengers, window cleaners and scullions. It was a complete let-down for thousands like me... there were no jobs for the 'heroes' who haunted the billiard halls as I did.[23]

Coppard's recollections demonstrate how memory often compresses: the problems he described are accurate, but for the period after 1920, not for the short boom which immediately followed the war. That boom actually worked to the detriment of ex-servicemen, since it convinced the government that re-employment of veterans could

20 See ibid., pp. 273–8.
21 H. Jones, *Health and Society in Twentieth-Century Britain*, p. 52.
22 Koven, 'Remembering and Dismemberment', p. 1200.
23 Coppard, p. 133.

be safely left to market forces. But between 1921 and 1939, the number of unemployed ex-servicemen averaged around 500,000, with peaks over 700,000. What especially irked veterans was that their war service often rendered them less employable than those who had not served. Positions on apprenticeships or courses went to younger men, old jobs had disappeared or were already filled, and business opportunities had evaporated. The problem was toughest for those who had joined up at eighteen (or younger), before starting out on an apprenticeship or in higher education. In 1922 there were 300,000 ex-servicemen under age 30 without formal skills or training. Nor had they much prospect, once the recession began, of receiving the training they desperately needed. The government might have wanted to help, but it was convinced it did not have the resources. Some concession was granted in 1922 when it was stipulated that 75 per cent of men employed on public works projects funded by the Unemployment Grants Committee had to be ex-servicemen. But since such projects were relatively rare, the measure had little effect upon veteran unemployment.

Ex-officers were not immune from joblessness. Coppard recalled that 'It was a common sight in London to see ex-officers with barrel-organs, endeavouring to earn a living as beggars.'[24] The phenomenon became something of a cliché in novels of the inter-war period, among them D. H. Lawrence's *Lady Chatterley's Lover.*[25] The problem was especially acute for the 'temporary gentlemen' who had become accustomed to the standards of an elevated class, but now could no longer afford those standards. Because officers had traditionally been gentlemen of private means, it was not thought necessary to make provision for postwar poverty. Officers, unlike rankers, were not entitled to free unemployment compensation, nor were they allowed to use the labour exchange. 'When it is borne in mind that in a very large number of cases this class of officer did not ask for a commission but was nominated by his Commanding Officer', wrote one critic, 'the fact that he should be worse treated on discharge than if he had remained in the ranks seems almost impossible to defend.'[26]

24 Ibid.

25 M. Petter, ' "Temporary Gentlemen" in the Aftermath of the Great War: Rank, Status and the Ex-Officer Problem', *Historical Journal* 37 (1994), p. 129.

26 Ibid., p. 150.

DEMOBILISED WOMEN

Demobilisation meant not just releasing men from the military, but also releasing women from their war service. By the end of 1918, an estimated 750,000 women had been made redundant. By 1919, only 200,000 women workers remained in engineering, just 30,000 more than pre-war figures.[27] Within the Ministry of Reconstruction, two bodies, the Civil War Workers Committee and the Women's Employment Committee, anticipated the problems which changes in patterns of employment would mean. The aim was to return as smoothly as possible to the status quo ante-bellum. Women who had been told that it was their patriotic duty to join the work force were now told that it was unpatriotic to hang onto a job rightfully belonging to an ex-serviceman. The ASE, in a spirit of vindictiveness, used the courts to force the pace of female redundancies, under the terms of the Restoration of Pre-War Practices Act of 1919.[28] The largest union representing women, the National Federation of Women Workers, benignly accepted a moral obligation to give way to men.

Women workers on government contracts received two weeks' pay in lieu of notice and a free rail pass home. They were also covered by an 'out of work donation' of 20s per week for the first thirteen weeks, 15s for the next thirteen weeks, whereupon it ceased altogether.[29] Women in receipt of benefit were subject to virulent scorn; newspapers derided the 'dodgers' and 'loafers' 'taking a holiday at the public expense'.[30] The *Daily Telegraph* commented:

> a little investigation (at the labour exchange) showed that since they have 'been in munitions' women have acquired to a remarkable extent a taste for factory life. Many of them of course, might return at once to the domestic service from which they came, but, for the moment at any rate, they literally scoff at the idea.[31]

Eventually the government denied benefit to any woman who refused to take a job offered her. (A man was only denied benefit if he refused an offer in his specific trade.) At one employment exchange, an official

27 G. Rubin, 'Law as a Bargaining Weapon: British Labour and the Restoration of Pre-War Practices Act 1919', *Historical Journal* 32 (1989), p. 933.
28 Ibid., pp. 936–7.
29 G. Braybon, *Women Workers in the First World War*, p. 179.
30 G. Braybon and P. Summerfield, *Out of the Cage: Women's Experiences in Two World Wars*, pp. 122–3.
31 Braybon, p. 187.

entered a room in which 40 women were waiting for offers of employment and asked 'Who is for domestic service?' As no one replied, each one was handed the usual form and told she was not entitled to benefit.[32]

This effectively depressed wage rates in traditionally female areas of employment since unscrupulous employers could force a woman to take a job which paid well below the benefit rate simply by threatening to report her to the labour exchange if she refused the offer. At the same time, a determined push to improve the image of domestic service began. Potential servants were promised better pay and conditions and greater consideration by the mistress of the house. The various tactics were effective: in March 1919 there were 494,000 women registered unemployed, two-thirds of the total. Eight months later the figure had fallen to 29,000, the result of women being forced back into domestic service or removing themselves from the unemployment register.[33]

Women workers had become pariahs. They were simultaneously criticised for accepting unemployment benefit rather than taking up work and for refusing to give up jobs rightfully belonging to men. The latter complaint was especially common in 1920, when most servicemen had been demobilised and unemployment began to rise. 'The girls were clinging to their jobs, would not let go of the pocket-money which they had spent on frocks', complained the war correspondent Philip Gibbs.[34] Typical was the attitude of the *Southampton Times*:

> While it would be a shame to turn women out of their jobs at short notice in cases where such a procedure would mean absolute hardship, and, perhaps, starvation, there is no reason to feel sympathetic towards the young person who has been earning 'pin money' while the men have been fighting, nor the girls who left women's work, to which they could return without difficulty . . .[35]

The *Daily Sketch* on 28 June 1919 wrote of the 'Scandal of the Proposed Retention of Flappers while Ex-Soldiers Cannot Find Jobs'.[36] It became so objectionable to employ women in 'men's work' that women were often displaced by men who had avoided military service. Before long, critics began to discredit the contribution made

---

32 S. Boston, *Women Workers and the Trade Unions*, p. 151.

33 Braybon and Summerfield, p. 121.

34 S. K. Kent, 'The Politics of Sexual Difference: World War I and the Demise of British Feminism', *Journal of British Studies* 27 (1988), p. 238.

35 Braybon, p. 189.

36 M. Pugh, *Women and the Women's Movement in Britain 1914–1959*, p. 82.

by women during the war. A *Leeds Mercury* journalist welcomed the dismissal of female bus conductors:

> Their record of duty well done is seriously blemished by their habitual and aggressive incivility, and a callous disregard for the welfare of passengers. Their shrewish behaviour will remain one of the unpleasant memories of the war's vicissitudes.[37]

The effort to force women out of employment was so successful that in July 1921 just 30.8 per cent of women were employed, down from 32.3 per cent ten years earlier.[38]

Married women workers were treated especially harshly. It was assumed that, since a husband must be supporting them, they were simply greedy. The *Edinburgh Evening News* demanded the sacking of 'this class of social scrounger'.[39] Few paused to consider whether a woman calling herself 'Mrs' was perhaps divorced, separated or widowed, and therefore in need of work. Once the out of work donation ceased, unemployed married women often found themselves ineligible for benefit as they had not paid the requisite stamps prior to 1914. In 1922 the government, keen to reduce social welfare costs, ruled that married women were ineligible for the dole unless total family income was less than 10s per week.[40] When unemployment began to rise, employers came under increasing pressure to lay off the few remaining married women workers so as to free jobs for men. In 1921, London County Council made all married women staff (excluding doctors and teachers) redundant. Married women were also ineligible for the few government-sponsored training schemes organised for women. The one exception was a course in 'home arts', which offered wives 'an opportunity to perfect themselves in household accomplishment which will make the home fit for the ideal family life'.[41]

Women who remained in work after the war did so largely by returning to pre-war patterns of employment. Labour exchanges reported that placements in domestic occupations increased by 40 per cent in 1919 compared to 1918.[42] Those few who remained in industry usually had to accept menial jobs at lower pay. Almost all women bus conductors and railway guards lost their jobs; those who stayed usually became booking clerks. The only areas in which

37 Braybon, p. 189.
38 Kent, 'The Politics of Sexual Difference', p. 238.
39 Pugh, p. 81.
40 Ibid., p. 82.
41 *The Times*, 18 December 1918.
42 Braybon and Summerfield, p. 120.

women were conspicuously successful at retaining jobs were in office and shop work – the one significant change in the pattern of employment to result from the war. But since these had always been low status jobs for men, the change hardly seems significant.

Women workers in traditionally male industries were 'temporary men', useful only for the duration of the war. When peace came, a return to normality was widely welcomed (by men *and* women) because it implied that society had not been fundamentally altered by the employment of women in men's jobs. Only those women who enjoyed the changed circumstances of war regretted this return to normal. Some women did protest – 6,000 marched on Parliament in 1919 – but more typical was the entirely peaceful exodus of 1,500 women per week from Woolwich Arsenal.[43] Those who were reluctant to leave factories did not feel factory work was inherently better or more rewarding than domestic service or the millinery trades. Factory work was monotonous, dangerous, dirty and often demeaning. It appealed because it was man's work and thus provided higher status and better pay. But women did not gain status by moving into men's jobs. As the example of clerical work demonstrates, when a man's job is taken over by women, its status declines.

'STANDING STOUTLY TOGETHER'

Even if the government had been more sympathetic to women workers, it could not ignore the demands of returning soldiers. Fears of angry mobs of ex-servicemen had preoccupied Whitehall since conscription had been introduced. Conscription implied a two-way bargain; men taken against their will expected something in return when peace came. The relationship between the soldier and the state had been altered, but so too had the nature of the soldier himself – or so it was feared. Concerns expressed by Haig were quite widespread:

> Under the Military Service Act a leaven of men whose desire to serve their country is negligible has permeated the ranks. The influence of these men and their antecedents generally are not such as to foster any spirit but that of unrest and discontent, they come forward under compulsion and they will depart from the Army with relief. Men of this stamp are not satisfied with remaining quiet, they come from a class which like to air real or fancied grievances.[44]

43 Pugh, p. 81.
44 Haig to Lord Derby, 3 October 1917: Haig War Diary, National Library of Scotland.

Memories of pre-war strikes and fears of Bolshevism combined to produce a rampant paranoia. The image of loyal, patriotic Tommy Atkins quickly faded, replaced by that of a greedy, ruthless, violent worker-revolutionary bent on claiming exorbitant reward for his service. Fears were exacerbated by the uncomfortable knowledge that for the past four years these workers had been taught to resolve disputes violently. A worried Home Office agent noted that 'in the event of rioting, for the first time in history, the rioters will be better trained than the troops'.[45]

The government was especially worried by the proliferation of ex-servicemen's associations which agitated on issues like pensions and employment. The National Association of Discharged Soldiers and Sailors was established in September 1916, followed in 1917 by the National Federation of Discharged and Demobilised Soldiers and Sailors and by the Comrades of the Great War. The Association had basically Liberal sympathies, while the Federation had links with the Labour Party. Both were keen to work within the political system and were in no sense revolutionary. The Comrades, formed by Lord Derby and linked to the Conservative Party, was intentionally designed to provide a countervailing force to these groups. It tended to attract right wing thugs malevolently inclined toward labourist politics.[46]

Despite their rather tame nature, the government was suspicious of any attempt by the Association and the Federation to organise ex-servicemen. The airing of legitimate grievances was easily confused with revolutionary activity. Basil Thomson, head of Special Branch, was ordered to infiltrate the groups. Beginning in spring 1918, weekly reports on their activities were produced. Try as he might, Thomson found it hard to discover any remotely threatening activities. A report submitted in October depended on rather desperate conjecture:

> there is a determined attempt among extremists to capture the Discharged Soldiers' Federation, and the demand for better allowances should be carefully watched for if they succeed in getting the soldiers and their wives to back them, they will be a very numerous and dangerous body.[47]

45 S. R. Ward, 'Intelligence Surveillance of British Ex-Servicemen, 1918–20', *Historical Journal* 16 (1973), p. 179.

46 D. Englander and J. Osborne, 'Jack, Tommy and Henry Dubb: The Armed Forces and the Working Class', *Historical Journal* 21 (1978), p. 619.

47 Ward, 'Intelligence Surveillance', p. 182.

Special Branch infiltrators had to justify their existence, therefore they could never entirely discount the threat of revolution. But the predominant characteristic of ex-servicemen's groups was their willingness to act within the political system, as evidenced by their fielding 29 entirely respectable candidates in the 1918 election. Nor, for that matter, did the voting tendencies of ex-soldiers in the election provide much reason to fear Bolshevik belligerence.

A potentially more serious threat arose in February 1919. The Soldiers', Sailors' and Airmen's Union aimed specifically to stir up discontent among servicemen awaiting demobilisation. It also actively opposed intervention in Russia. In March the SSAU attracted a prominent recruit in the form of Lieutenant-Commander J. M. Kenworthy RN. But Special Branch was not unduly worried, as the report of one meeting indicates:

> Plans for a *coup d'état* of a very childish description were discussed, and Kenworthy is asserted to have declared that the navy was ripe for mutiny. Other speakers talked of arms and bombs being secretly stored and of soldiers who were ready to join them in establishing a republic. There is no cause for alarm in this, for such talk is the stock in trade of these extremists when they get together . . .[48]

According to the original terms of the Derby Scheme, men who enlisted could be retained no more than six months after the termination of hostilities. The SSAU, deciding that the government had no legal jurisdiction over these men after 11 May 1919, urged them to leave of their own accord. At the same time, sailors were urged to capture ports and join in a general strike. All this was tantamount to inciting mutiny. Special Branch took this threat seriously and on 8 May raided Union headquarters, seizing records. But it was working class complaisance, not alert policing, which forestalled mass mutiny. The British soldier was simply not the raw material of which revolutions were made.

The fortunes of two avowedly radical ex-servicemen's associations formed after the armistice, the National Union of Ex-Servicemen (NUX) and the International Union of Ex-Servicemen (IUX), provide further proof of this fact. Both campaigned for a profound transformation of society, the IUX being slightly more extremist than the NUX. Like the SSAU, they provoked considerable alarm within the government but eventually demonstrated, by their ignominious failure, the predominantly moderate nature of ex-servicemen. At its

---

48 Ibid., 184.

height the IUX attracted only 7,000 members. The NUX, more mainstream, was slightly more successful.[49]

The demise of the IUX and the NUX coincided with the rise of the British Legion, an amalgamation of the Comrades, Federation, Association and the more recently formed Officers Association. Haig, by insisting that one united ex-servicemen's association would have greater impact upon government policy, was instrumental in bringing the groups together. That was a logical aim, but Haig was also keen to steer ex-servicemen away from left wing politics. Immediately after the armistice, he warned that his men

> are still soldiers though without arms, and no doubt will go in for fresh groupings for new objectives, hitherto unthought of by the present race of politicians! Above all, they will take vigorous action to right any real or supposed wrong! All this seems to me to make for trouble unless our Government is alert and tactful.[50]

According to Haig, the British Legion, by reproducing the camaraderie of the trenches, would buttress the social order during these turbulent times. As he explained in 1922:

> Subversive tendencies are still at work, short cuts to anarchy are still the fool's talk of unstable intellectuals. There is all the greater need for men of all ranks who are determined ... to stand stoutly together. A rallying ground for such men is offered by the Legion. It appeals to all who have worn the King's uniform, and who, therefore, realise the nobility of service, to enrol themselves to win the peace, even as they won the war.[51]

Though Haig claimed to have in mind an entirely democratic organisation, without privilege of rank, he confessed privately that he was against a separate officers' group because it would 'withdraw the real leaders from the ex-servicemen'. The potentially disruptive tendencies of ex-servicemen would be further harnessed by directing their attention outward: the Legion would 'foster the spirit of self-sacrifice which inspired ex-servicemen to subordinate their individual welfare to the interests of the Commonwealth'. This meant steering clear of domestic politics: 'I think our politics should be Imperial and in no sense partisan.'[52] In this context, to be apolitical meant in fact to be Conservative.

Haig was successful in creating one ex-servicemen's association,

---

49 See Englander and Osborne, 'Jack, Tommy and Henry Dubb', p. 619.
50 DeGroot, pp. 403–4.
51 N. Barr, 'Service not Self: The British Legion 1921–1939', p. 112.
52 DeGroot, p. 404.

but less successful in making it popular. Its membership never exceeded 500,000, rather small when one considers the total number of veterans. (Over 3,000,000 men joined a similar organisation in France.[53]) The Legion's lack of appeal remains a mystery, but may be due to the characteristics Haig deemed essential: namely the abhorrence of politics and the tendency of ex-officers to dominate the leadership. The Legion eventually became, as Haig intended, a bastion of traditional values. As for its record in campaigning for ex-servicemen's interests, it fails to impress. The Legion was not conspicuously successful in its campaign against the seven-year rule governing disability claims, nor did it do much to aid the cause of unemployed ex-servicemen. It was Legion policy to remain aloof from politics. Honorary Presidents, like Haig and Jellicoe, were establishment figures reluctant to confront Conservative-dominated governments. But by divorcing itself from politics, the Legion ended up being easily manipulated by politicians.

By 1921, ex-servicemen had been effectively tamed. They were never an opponent worthy of the government's power. Romantic historians on the left look back at the period 1918–20 and marvel at a would-be revolution. Walter Kendall, for instance, claims that the prospects for revolution 'were probably the most serious since the time of the Chartists'.[54] But that is hardly cause for a sharp intake of breath. Historians are supposed to analyse not fantasise:

> if socialist influence had existed within any of the services, if there had been, for example, a common front between soldiers and sailors in 1918–19, if the soldiers had launched a co-ordinated movement, or established links with any of the trade union struggles pending, then the whole future of the state might well have been called into question.[55]

The above seems as pathetic as the pipe dreams of Kenworthy and the SSAU. There was very little revolutionary raw material within the services. The question remains: were these men cajoled, manipulated and finally forced into cooperating with an unjust system, or were they merely sheep? Given their passivity during the war, their willingness to accept an iniquitous system of pensions, their tolerance of an unfair distribution of gratuities and their acquiescence in the placid British Legion, one is inclined to believe that they were, in fact, sheep.

The government never quite understood that the vast majority

---

53 Barr, 'Service not Self', pp. 91–2.
54 W. Kendall, *The Revolutionary Movement in Great Britain*, p. 187.
55 Ibid., p. 194.

of ex-servicemen were merely interested in a quiet life after the war. They wanted to return to their homes, find a job and do what is now understood to be a phenomenon of twentieth-century total war: namely start a baby boom. The popularity of domesticity can be seen as further proof of the widespread desire to return to normality. In 1917, a wedding ring maker applied for exemption from conscription on the grounds that his firm was doing an enormous trade and the work was of national importance.[56] He had a point, even if the tribunal did not agree. The family was, as one author has described, 'a haven in a heartless world'.[57] Political grievances were aired only when this haven seemed threatened, in particular by poverty. It is a pity that the government saw every ex-serviceman as a potential Bolshevik and thus failed to understand just how moderate were his desires and how cheap was the price of the social harmony he craved.

56 *The Times*, 15 March 1917.
57 J. Winter, p. 264.

14 THE DEAD, THE LIVING AND THE LIVING DEAD

Until recently, the tendency of old women to outnumber old men on the streets of Britain was commonly blamed on the Great War: husbands or potential husbands were killed on the battlefields of France and Flanders.[1] The disparity still exists, yet the explanation is no longer credible since the war was too long ago. (The women are old but not *that* old.) The real reason for the maldistribution of the sexes on the streets of Britain is more prosaic. Britain was and remains a patriarchal society; husbands wait at home while wives do the shopping. And, if there is a surplus of widows, it is because women live longer than men.

Yet the image of the war as a demographic disaster stubbornly persists. It is commonly held that the war resulted in a Lost Generation – defined either as all the dead or, specifically, as those educated elites who would otherwise have become postwar leaders. The uninterrupted decline of Britain since 1918 has been blamed on the loss of these men of promise. Britain, so the argument goes, was henceforth ruled by 'pygmies'.[2] As will be seen, there is little evidence to support a demographic disaster. Many very promising men died in the war, but to blame the dull decades of the twenties and thirties on their absence is to engage in a futile exercise in counterfactual reasoning. The Lost Generation is important only as a myth, a popular explanation for the course history took.

The myth customarily refers to those who died. Perhaps instead the lost generation was those condemned to go on living, shouldering the tragedy and loss which the Great War caused – a fate described by Margaret Postgate Cole:

But we are young, and our friends are dead
Suddenly, and our quick love is torn in two;

---

1 An explanation I was given upon arrival in Edinburgh as a graduate student in 1980.

2 C. L. Mowat, *Britain Between the Wars*, p. 142.

So our memories are only hopes that came to nothing.
We are left alone like old men; we should be dead
– But there are years and years in which we shall still be young.[3]

'I had great ambitions', wrote Storm Jameson after the war. 'I have none now . . . very little in me is real except the absolute need, intellectual and spiritual, for withdrawal.'[4]

THE DEAD

Estimates of British deaths in the Great War range from around 550,000 to over twice that number.[5] Figures vary according to the purposes of those who cite them: there was, for instance, a tendency to underestimate the dead in official reports released immediately after the war. On the other hand, Denis Winter, keen to emphasise the war's destruction, puts the number at precisely 1,104,890, a figure provided without explanation or footnote.[6]

For the purposes of this study, we will rely on data supplied by Jay Winter, which, given his exhaustive investigations, are probably the most reliable. He claims the total military dead numbered 722,785. This does not include 15,000 fatalities in the merchant navy and fishing fleets as a result of enemy action, nor 1,266 civilian deaths caused by bombing or bombardment,[7] nor the victims of munitions factory explosions, nor the suicides brought on by grief and despair. But by whatever reckoning, the mortality figures seem sufficiently large to justify talk of a lost generation. Over 514,000 men under the age of 30 lost their lives in the war,[8] a loss which would presumably take decades to replace. But in strictly demographic terms there was no net loss. In the period 1911–14, migration to and from Britain resulted in a net population loss of over one million people. During the war, emigration stopped. In fact, expatriates rushing back to defend the mother country resulted in a net gain of 100,000 people in 1914. Presuming that pre-war migration trends would have continued had war not intervened, Britain would

3 M. P. Cole, 'Preaematuri', in C. Reilly, ed., *Scars Upon My Heart*, p. 22.
4 M. S. Jameson, *No Time Like the Present*, p. 179.
5 See J. Winter, *The Great War and the British People*, pp. 68–9.
6 D. Winter, *Death's Men*, p. 261.
7 J. Winter, pp. 72–3.
8 Ibid., p. 81.

have lost over one million people.[9] Instead, as a result of the war, she lost around 725,000, a net gain of over a quarter of a million. Those who left Britain before the war were predominantly single males between eighteen and 30, the same group from which soldiers were predominantly drawn. Thus, neither the size nor the social structure of the British population was fundamentally altered by the war. After the war, a sharp rise in the birth rate and better civilian health caused population to increase further. Thus, the war resulted in a small but significant population explosion. In demographic terms, the Lost Generation myth has no foundation.

But what of a lost generation of elites? Examining the numbers of officer casualties relative to other ranks reveals that the middle class suffered proportionately higher casualties than the working class. (Though not all middle class men became officers, the vast majority of officers were middle or upper class.)

Distribution of war losses between officers and men[10]

	Officers			Other Ranks		
	Served	Killed	%	Served	Killed	%
Army	247,061	37,484	15.2	4,968,101	635,891	12.8
Navy	55,377	2,937	5.3	584,860	40,307	6.9
RFC/RAF	27,333	4,579	16.8	326,842	1,587	0.5
Total	329,771	45,000	13.6	5,879,803	677,785	11.5

Granted, senior officers and their staff encountered very little danger. But junior officers in the trenches (because they led assaults) suffered the highest risks of all military personnel. The disproportionate death rate among junior officers is revealed in fatality rates (numbers killed relative to numbers enlisted) for members of Oxford and Cambridge Universities. Since members of these universities were thought to have the most leadership potential, they had the greatest chance of becoming officers and therefore the greatest likelihood of dying. (Only 3 per cent of nearly 1,000 Balliol men who enlisted served in the ranks.) Bearing in mind that the death rate for all the forces was 11.5 per cent, that for Oxford was 19.2 per cent and for Cambridge 18.0 per cent. For those who matriculated between 1910 and 1914 (those most likely to become junior officers), the figures climb to 29.3 per cent killed for Oxford and 26.1 per cent for Cambridge.

9 Ibid., pp. 266–70.
10 Ibid., p. 91. The figures have been taken from Winter, however some totals and percentages have been corrected.

Similarly high figures can be derived from the rolls of honour of elite public schools. Approximately 19 per cent of peers under age 50 who served were killed.[11]

None of this is intended to discount the sacrifices of the working classes. Fully 96 per cent of infantry casualties came from the ranks.[12] But the above figures do suggest a statistical justification for a lost generation of elites. The middle class male was more likely to volunteer, partly for cultural reasons, but more importantly because he would not have been troubled by the financial implications of doing so. He was also more likely to be passed fit and less likely to be engaged in a reserve occupation. Finally, given the strong possibility that he would be made an officer, he was more likely to be killed. The knowledge (or intuition) that the middle and upper classes experienced a disproportionately high mortality rate prompted the Bishop of Malvern to contend that the loss of public schoolboys 'can only be described as the wiping out of a generation'.[13] Many similar claims have been made, but seldom so vehemently than by J. B. Priestley: 'nobody, nothing will shift me from the belief which I shall take to the grave that the generation to which I belonged, destroyed between 1914 and 1918, was a great generation, marvellous in its promise'.[14]

But it is impossible to measure accurately the promise of one generation against another. Those who believe in the idea of a lost generation of elites cite noteworthy individual deaths like that of Raymond Asquith, described by A. D. Lindsay as the most brilliant man he had ever known, or the promising poets killed in the war, among them Wilfred Owen. Tragic as the losses were, in order to thrive in the postwar world, Britain needed not more poets and classical scholars, but scientists, technicians and engineers – types abhorred by that gloriously aesthete Edwardian generation. Some promising scientists were killed, among them H. G. J. Moseley, the gifted disciple of Ernest Rutherford,[15] but he was perhaps typical of the British tendency to produce individual geniuses in theoretical science while neglecting to train solid technicians good at applied science. This tendency persisted after the war.

It could be argued that, since previous generations of politicians arose from the crop of classical scholars produced at the good public

---

11 Ibid., pp. 92–3.
12 Ibid., p. 84.
13 Ibid., p. 98.
14 D. Winter, p. 254.
15 T. Wilson, *The Myriad Faces of War*, p. 752.

schools, the war deprived Britain of promising political leaders. But if the men in question were members of an elite, it was an elite based upon social standing, not merit. Had they lived, these lost elites would have grabbed the baton passed by their fathers, the same fathers who had presided over a society in which talent was abominably wasted and an economy left in a persistent state of decline. It requires an impressive act of faith to presume that the 1914 generation, had they survived, would have embarked on a fundamentally different course. In other words, the leadership potential of those lost is dubious. And, it must be remembered, Britain's European rivals, against whom her decline is unfavourably measured, also suffered gargantuan losses, yet somehow found leaders to inspire recovery.

Vera Brittain, egotist, elitist, mistress of self-pity and principal spokeswoman for the Lost Generation, described male survivors of the war as 'fussy, futile, avid, ineffectual'. They 'wallowed in nauseating sentimentality and hadn't the brains of an earwig – simply provided one proof after another that the best of their sex had disappeared from a whole generation'.[16] (As regards sentimentality, one can only conclude that this is a fine example of a pot calling a kettle black.) The Lost Generation myth is traditional, prescriptive, mysogynist and anti-democratic. It ties the destiny of Britain to a 'few good men', ignoring the potential contribution of men from outside the elite and from all women.

SURVIVING

A better way of looking at the Lost Generation is brought to mind by C. E. Montague:

> So we had failed – had won the fight and lost the prize; the garland of war was withered before it was gained. The lost years, the broken youth, the dead friends, the women's overshadowed lives at home, the agony and bloody sweat – all had gone to darken the stains which most of us had thought to scour out of the world that our children would live in. Many men felt, and said to each other, that they had been fooled.[17]

'It is easy to be dead', wrote the poet Charles Hamilton Sorley.[18]

---

16 V. Brittain, *Testament of Youth*, p. 428.

17 C. E. Montague, *Disenchantment*, p. 136.

18 C. H. Sorley, 'Two Sonnets', in J. Silkin, ed., *The Penguin Book of First World War Poetry*, p. 89.

The lost were not those who died, but those condemned to go on living in horror, grief and guilt. After the armistice, each survivor – civilian and combatant, male and female – had to shoulder an individual anguish. Some adjusted, others never did.

Soldiers who fought felt emotions more intense than most men would ever experience in peacetime. 'How', asks the protagonist in *Last Men in London*, 'can things be so wrong, so meaningless, so filthy; and yet also so right, so overwhelmingly significant, so exquisite?'[19] Soldiers felt greater fear, grief, disgust, but also love. As Guy Chapman confirmed, love for one's comrades was often deeper than that felt for anyone:

> I found that this body of men had become so much a part of me that its disintegration would tear away something I cared for more dearly than I could have believed. I was it, and it was I.

> My love is of a birth as rare
> As 'tis for object strange and high:
> It was begotten by Despair
> Upon Impossibility.[20]

To have the object of such love destroyed was more than some could handle. Witness Ivor Gurney's grief in 'To His Love':

> He's gone, and all our plans
>   Are useless indeed.
> We'll walk no more on Cotswold
>   Where the sheep feed
>   Quietly and take no heed.

> His body that was so quick
>   Is not as you
> Knew it, on Severn river
>   Under the blue
>   Driving our small boat through.

> You would not know him now . . .
>   But still he died
> Nobly, so cover him over
>   With violets of pride
>   Purple from Severn side.

> Cover him, cover him soon!
>   And with thick-set

19 O. Stapledon, *Last Men in London*, p. 225.
20 G. Chapman, *A Passionate Prodigality*, p. 276.

> Masses of memoried flowers –
>   Hide that red wet
>   Thing I must somehow forget.[21]

It is no surprise that those who suffered this profound and unique grief often considered themselves a race apart, and felt more affinity with one-time enemies than with those at home. 'The man who really endured the war at its worst was everlastingly differentiated from everyone except his fellow soldiers', argued Sassoon.[22] In 1968 Charles Carrington wrote:

> We are still an initiate generation, possessing a secret that can never be communicated.... Our characteristic is that we were all put to the same test; all exposed our strength and weakness to the same public gaze; all, when young, rejected the illusions about life and death that some men nourish in old age. Twenty million of us ... shared the experience with one another but with no one else, and are what we are because, in that war, we were soldiers.[23]

Ford Madox Ford complained of the 'slight nausea that in those days you felt at contact with the civilian who knew none of your thoughts, phrases, or preoccupations'.[24] The war experience was a fully laden pack which the ex-soldier could not discard, even had he so desired. The archaeologist and ex-soldier Stanley Casson thought that he had 'put the war into the category of forgotten things', but eventually found that 'The war's baneful influence controlled still all our thoughts and acts, directly or indirectly.'[25] Sassoon complained:

> The rank stench of those bodies haunts me still,
> And I remember things I'd best forget.[26]

For Guy Chapman, 'England had vanished over the horizon of the mind. I did not want to see it.'[27] He instead volunteered for the Allied Army of Occupation. Captain Frederick Osborne could not bear to leave dead comrades and chose instead to spend the rest of his life

21 I. Gurney, 'To His Love', in Silkin, ed., p. 115.
22 S. Sassoon, *Memoirs of an Infantry Officer*, p. 280.
23 C. E. Carrington, 'Some Soldiers', in G. A. Panichas, ed., *Promise of Greatness*, p. 157.
24 F. M. Ford, *Parade's End*, p. 181.
25 P. Fussell, *The Great War and Modern Memory*, p. 325.
26 S. Sassoon, 'The rank stench of those bodies haunts me still', in Silkin, ed., p. 124.
27 Chapman, p. 346.

tending their graves in Belgium.[28] Another veteran quickly returned to France to live the life of a peasant: 'I realised that this was what I needed. Silence. Isolation. Now that I could let go, I broke down, avoided strangers, cried easily and had terrible nightmares.'[29] But these were extraordinary reactions; the great majority returned with their heavy burden of memories to a now alien home. Some were driven mad remembering. Others wrote memoirs or poetry in an ambitious, but usually futile, effort at purgation. Many simply reminisced with other old soldiers, in pubs or British Legion clubs. Coppard was delighted to find a member of his old Division living close by: 'My heart leaps when I spot him walking up the road. We never miss a natter, and his eyes shine as we go over the umpteenth episode of our war experiences.'[30] Some men considered the war the best years of their lives and felt bittersweet regret upon demobilisation. Others despised the war, but hated the staid complacency of the home front even more and could not bear to part with comrades. For many, therefore, peace brought a terrible loneliness, an emotional vacuum which stretched indefinitely into the future.

Some men could not excise the horror of war; it consumed them like a relentless cancer. Forty-eight special hospitals were established to handle emotional casualties of the war.[31] In 1922, 65,000 shell-shock victims were receiving disability pensions and 9,000 were still hospitalised.[32] Not all had received treatment before the armistice; instead, they tried for a time to hold back the terror, finally succumbing to its overwhelming power. In the first ten years of peace, 114,600 men applied for pensions for mental disorders:[33]

– These are men whose minds the Dead have ravished.
Memory fingers in their hair of murders,
Multitudinous murders they once witnessed.
Wading sloughs of flesh these helpless wander,
Treading blood from lungs that had loved laughter.
Always they must see these things and hear them,
Batter of guns and shatter of flying muscles,

28 D. Winter, pp. 262–3.
29 Ibid., p. 243.
30 G. Coppard, *With a Machine Gun to Cambrai*, pp. 134–5.
31 D. Winter, p. 252.
32 S. Hynes, *A War Imagined*, p. 307. See also D. Englander and J. Osborne, 'Jack, Tommy and Henry Dubb: The Armed Forces and the Working Class', *Historical Journal* 21 (1978), p. 599.
33 H. Jones, *Health and Society in Twentieth-Century Britain*, p. 51.

Carnage incomparable, and human squander
Rucked too thick for these men's extrication.[34]

Many existed in limbo between madness and sanity, suffering from what would today be called post-traumatic stress, but suffering alone, unaware and without assistance. Around three million men witnessed at first hand the horror of trench warfare and rare was the soldier who did not witness death. 'All was not right with the spirit of the men who came back', wrote Philip Gibbs,

> They were subject to queer moods, queer tempers, fits of profound depression alternating with a restless desire for pleasure. Many of them were easily moved to passion when they lost control of themselves. Many were bitter in their speech, violent in opinion, frightening. . . . Something seemed to have snapped in them.[35]

'When I was demobbed', one veteran recalled, 'I used to have bad nightmares. I used to wake up in the middle of the night bathed in perspiration.' Haunted by the vivid memory of killing a wounded and unarmed German who had dragged himself into a pillbox, a British ex-soldier found that, twelve years after the war, 'still at night comes a sweat that wakes me by its deadly chill to hear again that creeping, creeping'.[36] Smells, sounds, faces, would suddenly bring to the surface long forgotten horrors. The worst tragedies of the Great War were not those marked by little white stones in France and Flanders.

And then there were those whose bodies would forever bear the scars of war.

> Crippled for life at seventeen,
> His great eyes seem to question why:
> With both legs smashed it might have been
> Better in that grim trench to die
> Than drag maimed years out helplessly.[37]

A network of hospitals was established to deal with war's ravages:

> By 1920 there were 113 special hospitals, with 18,603 beds, dealing with the most severely disabled and supplemented by 319 separate surgical clinics, thirty-six ear clinics, twenty-four eye clinics, nineteen heart centres. . . . One hospital specializing in the removal of steel between April 1919 and March 1925 treated 771 officers and 22,641

---

34 W. Owen, 'Mental Cases', in Silkin, ed., p. 195.
35 P. Gibbs, *Now It Can Be Told*, pp. 547–8.
36 D. Winter, p. 248.
37 E. Dobell, 'Pluck', in Reilly, ed., p. 31.

men surgically. Queen Mary's hospital, Sidcup, which touched only facial injuries, in the same period operated on 2,944 men.

As with mental cases, many physical injuries were slow to materialise. In 1928, 5,205 artificial legs, 1,106 arms and 4,574 eyes were issued for the first time. Eye ulceration resulted in 33 new cases of blindness in 1933.[38] The imagination of weapons designers caused unimaginable agonies. Trooper Samuel Rolfe had nearly all his skin removed by mustard gas. Contact with air was excruciatingly painful. Dressing him in clothes saturated with Vaseline provided little relief. Doctors eventually immersed him in a perpetual bath until 1925, when death finally freed him from war's torture.[39]

The Times insisted that the war disabled 'bear the heritage of all our endeavours since we became a people. The qualities they incarnate are those that have upheld our name in strength and honour. . . . They must be won back from despondency and incapacity, restored to independence and usefulness.'[40] An agency was established to find them wives; to father children would, it was felt, restore their manhood and make them vicariously whole. 'Does it matter? – losing your legs', a bitter Sassoon wrote, 'For people will always be kind.'[41] The line between kindness and condescension was exceedingly fine. Time nurtured contempt, born of the guilt and embarrassment which the disabled innocently inspired.

Many of those who escaped death or serious injury were haunted with guilt at being singled out to survive. Death had been bizarre, mysterious, inexplicable; to go on living seemed a capricious injustice. In *Death of a Hero*, the protagonist admits to a vendetta against the living:

> What right have I to live? . . . When I meet an unmaimed man of my generation, I want to shout at him: 'How did you escape? How did you dodge it? What dirty trick did you play? Why are you not dead, trickster?' It is dreadful to have outlived your life, shirked your fate, overspent your welcome. . . . You, the war dead, I think you died in vain, I think you died for nothing, for a blast of wind, a blather, a humbug, a politician's ramp. But at least you died. You did not reject the sharp, sweet shock of bullets, the sudden smash of a shell-burst, the insinuating agony of poison gas. You got rid of it all. You chose

38 D. Winter, pp. 251–2.

39 A. Gregory, *The Silence of Memory*, p. 52.

40 S. Koven, 'Remembering and Dismemberment: Crippled Children, Wounded Soldiers, and the Great War in Great Britain', *American Historical Review* 99 (1994), p. 1188.

41 S. Sassoon, 'Does it Matter?', in Silkin, ed., p. 131.

the better part. . . . But why weren't we one of them! What right have we to live?[42]

No wonder that men like Aldington, Sassoon and Carrington felt that those who did not serve (men or women) could never properly remember those who did. They could not possibly understand 'the hell where youth and laughter go'. The inappropriateness of remembering was touched upon by Sorley:

> When you see the millions of mouthless dead
> Across your dreams in pale battalions go,
> Say not soft things as other men have said,
> That you'll remember. For you need not so.
> Give them not praise. For, deaf, how should they know
> It is not curses heaped on each gashed head?
> Nor tears. Their blind eyes see not your tears flow.
> Nor honour. It is easy to be dead.
> Say only this, 'They are dead.' Then add thereto,
> 'Yet many a better one has died before.'
> Then, scanning all o'ercrowded mass, should you
> Perceive one face that you loved heretofore,
> It is a spook. None wears the face you knew.
> Great death has made all his for evermore.[43]

Sorley's sense of futility is understandable, but so is the desperation of those civilians intent upon remembering that 'one face'. Coming to terms with the war often meant honouring the lost loved one as a hero whose cause was worthy. Death had to have justification, for futility combined with loss was too much to bear. Immediate postwar evocations of the conflict bear a striking resemblance to perceptions of it in August 1914. The war was a 'great triumph and a great deliverance', the *Daily Mail* commented on Armistice Day 1919; 'how great will only be realised in days to come . . . though our hearts may swell with the legitimate pride of victory, our minds should dwell on the sacrifices of success and on the burdens it has laid upon our shoulders'.[44] 'The ability to transmute suffering into "sacrifice" was largely unimpaired', writes Adrian Gregory.[45]

Around three million Britons lost a close relative in the war.[46] 'I

42 R. Aldington, *Death of a Hero*, p. 201.

43 C. H. Sorley, 'When you see the millions of mouthless dead', in Silkin, ed., pp. 89–90.

44 *Daily Express*, 11 November 1919.

45 Gregory, p. 34.

46 Ibid., p. 19.

am beginning to rub my eyes at the prospect of peace', wrote Cynthia Asquith in October 1918. 'I think it will require more courage than anything that has gone before . . . one will at last fully recognize that the dead are not only dead for the duration of the war.'[47] Whereas the literature of those who fought evokes the memories of the 'pale battalions' who forged a brotherhood of suffering, that of civilians is more particular. Those at home might have been unable to comprehend the millions of mouthless dead, but they had no difficulty comprehending an empty chair at dinner. Civilians who grieved, grieved alone over a very personal loss.[48]

The loneliness of bereavement was described by Harry Lauder, who lost his son John:

> My only son. The only child that God had given us. . . . For a time I was quite numb. Then came a great pain and I whispered to myself over and over again the one terrible word 'dead'. It seemed that for me the board of life was blank and black. For me there was no past and there would be no future. Everything had been swept away by one sweep of the hand of fate. . . . I was beyond the power of human words to comfort.[49]

Mr Thomas Shaw lost five sons in the war, as did Mrs Fraser of Edinburgh.[50] It seems pointless to compare their suffering with that of the men who fought. On the death of his son, Asquith wrote: 'Whatever pride I had in the past, and whatever hope I had for the far future, by much the largest part of both was invested in him. Now all that is gone.'[51] One of the most poignant examples of emotional desolation is that of Rudyard Kipling, who did so much to inspire militant patriotism before 1914. 'What stands if Freedom fall?' he wrote. 'Who dies if England live?'[52] Suitably inspired by his father's stirring words, John Kipling cajoled his way into the army at age seventeen. After John's death at Loos in September 1915, Kipling was never the same again. On the one hand he felt a most intense grief:

> My son was killed while laughing at some jest. I would I knew
> What it was, and it might serve me in a time when jests are few.

47 Wilson, p. 751.

48 C. Tylee, *The Great War and Women's Consciousness*, p. 229.

49 H. Lauder, *Roamin' in the Gloamin'*, pp. 184–5.

50 D. Winter, p. 255; Gregory, p. 39.

51 Oxford and Asquith, *Memories and Reflections*, 2, pp. 158–9.

52 R. Kipling, 'For all We Have and Are', in *The Oxford Dictionary of Quotations*, 3rd edn, p. 299.

On the other hand he was extremely bitter toward those deemed responsible:

> If any question why we died
> Tell them, because our fathers lied.[53]

The lying fathers were British politicians, the Pope, the German enemy, et al.[54] But who is to say if, in his darkest moments, Kipling did not include himself among the guilty?

Because of the taboo against women soldiers, hardly any woman of the time could have first-hand experience of the strain of battle, the sight of comrades being blown apart and the savagery of becoming themselves killers. But those closed areas of experience (for most people, anyway) were mutual; for, just as women did not kill, men do not give birth. No soldier, no matter how seasoned, could have understood the grief of Mrs Fraser mentioned above or of Mrs Coster who lost four of five sons, the last a few days before the armistice.[55] A mother (signing herself 'Hope') who lost two sons, one at sea, in 1919 made a desperate plea to the government to conduct a search of islands in the Mediterranean and Indian Ocean for survivors of torpedoed ships who might 'have no possible chance of sending home news of their escape'.[56] Jeremy Seabrook recalls how, when he was growing up in Leicester, a woman in his block would every night call her three sons in from play. All three had died on the Somme.[57]

It is perhaps understandable that women outnumbered men at Remembrance Day ceremonies in the interwar period.[58] 'How should you leave me, having loved me so?' asked Marian Allen in 'The Wind on the Downs':

> I think of you the same and always shall.
> We thought of many things and spoke of few,
> And life lay all uncertainly before,
> And now I walk alone and think of you,
> And wonder what new kingdoms you explore.
> Over the railway line, across the grass,
> While up above the golden wings are spread,

53 R. Kipling, 'Epitaphs of the War', in Silkin, ed., pp. 135–6.
54 Wilson, p. 753.
55 D. Winter, p. 255.
56 *The Times*, 3 January 1919.
57 D. Winter, p. 258.
58 Gregory, pp. 32–3.

Flying, ever flying overhead,
Here still I see your khaki figure pass,
And when I leave the meadow, almost wait
That you should open first the wooden gate.[59]

One can be reasonably confident that Allen is unique only in her eloquence; the desolation she felt was shared by many women. Trevor Wilson mentions a woman who remarked as late as 1975 that she lost her sweetheart at Loos.[60] Never subsequently married, she would undoubtedly have sympathised with the following from Olive Lindsay:

The best of me died at Bapaume
    When the world went up in fire,
And the soul that was mine deserted
    And left me, a thing in the mire,
With a madden'd and dim remembrance
Of a time when my life was whole.[61]

'She lies with Raymond's two last letters in her hand, doesn't care to see the children [and is] utterly distraught', remarked Asquith of his daughter-in-law.[62] It is no wonder that in the years following the war, there was a marked rise in the popularity of spiritualism and seances, as mourners attempted by whatever means to communicate with lost loved ones. The great problem was to pay homage to the past without being tormented by it. 'Though we cannot forget the dead', wrote Brittain, 'we must not remember them at the expense of the living.'[63] It was sound advice not always successfully observed.

THE RITUAL OF REMEMBRANCE

Much of the ritual surrounding the burial of the war dead was new, devised to suit an extraordinary war. In the Napoleonic War, the dead were often burned or buried in mass graves to prevent the spread of disease. Instead of being collected together in their own cemeteries, they were honoured (if at all) with a monument or a plaque in a regimental church. Specifically military cemeteries only began to

---

59 M. Allen, 'The Wind on the Downs', in Reilly, ed., pp. 1–2.
60 Wilson, p. 753.
61 O. Lindsay, 'Despair', in Reilly, ed., p. 64.
62 Wilson, p. 753.
63 V. Brittain, *Testament of Experience*, p. 92.

appear with the advent of mass industrialised war.[64] But it was only after the Great War that these cemeteries gave separate recognition to each individual soldier.[65] The cemeteries impose identity and individualism upon a vast, depersonalised war. According to psychologists who specialise in bereavement, publicly naming the dead is an important stage in the process of recovery.[66]

Early in the war, the dead were usually buried near where they fell, the graves marked with temporary wooden crosses. If the ground was fought over for considerable time, these could be destroyed and the bodies themselves disinterred. In 1917, in keeping with the meticulous organisation of huge offensives, long trenches were dug beforehand and filled as the fighting progressed. The graves were still marked with wooden crosses, each labelled with a metal strip. In 1916 officials decided that since it was not practical to bring all the bodies home for burial, it was only fair that none should return. They were therefore disinterred from temporary graves and placed in graveyards located close to where the deaths had occurred. Germans and English, often buried side by side in temporary graves, were removed to separate cemeteries. The wooden crosses were shipped home, and sometimes buried in churchyards, acquiring status similar to religious relics.[67]

British cemeteries were deeded in perpetuity to Great Britain. Care of the 500 grounds was given to the Imperial War Graves Commission in 1921. By that time, agreement had been reached upon a uniform pattern for cemeteries. In most there is a Stone of Remembrance with the inscription 'Their name liveth for evermore', taken from Ecclesiasticus and suggested by Kipling. Occasionally a small chapel contains a list of those buried in the cemetery and a symbol of the resurrection. The uniform gravestones are arrayed in neat, evenly spaced rows, suggesting military order but also symbolising equality of sacrifice. Between 1920 and 1923 the shipment of headstones from Britain averaged 4,000 per week.[68] Each man whose body had been found was allotted a stone inscribed with a cross, Star of David, crescent or other relevant symbol. Above it went the name, rank, regiment and date of death. Below might go an inscription chosen by the widow or parents, finances permitting.

---

64 G. Mosse, *Fallen Soldiers*, p. 45.
65 Ibid., p. 50.
66 Gregory, p. 23.
67 Mosse, p. 91; Hynes, p. 271.
68 M. Eksteins, *Rites of Spring*, p. 255.

The Rosenbergs were charged 3s 3d to have Isaac memorialised as a poet and artist.[69] Cemeteries were carefully landscaped; each had its own full-time gardener. Where possible, flowers and shrubs readily identifiable as English were planted. 'There is much to be said for the occasional introduction of the English yew (where soil permits) from its association with our own country churchyards', a War Graves Commission document advised.[70] One is inevitably reminded of Rupert Brooke: 'If I should die, think only this of me: / That there's some corner of a foreign field / That is forever England.'[71] The green pastures and pretty flowers evoke a preindustrial idyll, a far cry from the urban wasteland whence most of the dead came.

Those whose bodies were not found were usually commemorated on a plaque in the cemetery. A considerable effort was nevertheless devoted to finding as many as possible. Beginning in 1920, search parties consisting of 4,000 men scoured battlefields looking for corpses. Some 30,000 were found by 1928, but only one-quarter of these could be identified. French and Belgian farmers were paid a bounty for every body uncovered. Ploughing still brings them to the surface to this day.[72]

Beginning in 1920, pilgrimages to the graveyards in France and Belgium were organised. The word 'pilgrimage' (as they were officially called) was particularly apt. The visits proved very popular; cemeteries became, as they were intended, shrines of remembrance. The first to organise trips was the Young Men's Christian Association (YMCA), followed soon after by the British Legion, Red Cross and other charitable groups. The cost – £6 in 1920 – was kept as low as possible, but still ruled out the very poor. Before long, sensing a market, the travel agent Thomas Cook began to organise tours and advise on suitable hotel accommodation. Cars could be rented at railway stations and maps to cemeteries supplied. French and Belgian entrepreneurs conducted tours of battlefields, complete with real trenches.

> Ladies and gentlemen, this is High Wood,
> Called by the French, Bois des Fourneaux,
> The famous spot which in Nineteen-Sixteen,
> July, August and September was the scene
> Of long and bitterly contested strife,

69 D. Winter, pp. 259–60.
70 Mosse, p. 84.
71 R. Brooke, '1914', in Silkin, ed., p. 81.
72 D. Winter, pp. 260–1.

By reason of its high commanding site.
Observe the effect of shell-fire in the trees
Standing and fallen; here is wire; this trench
For months inhabited, twelve times changed hands;
(They soon fall in), used later as a grave.
It has been said on good authority
That in the fighting for this patch of wood
Were killed somewhere above eight thousand men,
Of whom the greater part were buried here,
This mound on which you stand being . . .
                                        Madam, please
You are requested kindly not to touch
Or take away the Company's property
As souvenirs; you'll find we have on sale
A large variety, all guaranteed.
As I was saying, all is as it was,
This is an unknown British officer,
The tunic having lately rotted off.
Please follow me – this way . . . the *path*, sir *please*,
The ground which was secured at great expense
The company keeps absolutely untouched,
And in that dugout (genuine) we provide
Refreshments at a reasonable rate.
You are requested not to leave about
Paper, or ginger-beer bottles, or orange-peel,
There are waste paper baskets at the gate.[73]

Since not everyone could go on these pilgrimages, the cemeteries were inappropriate as national shrines. A desire for a shrine in Britain inpired the commissioning of the Tomb of the Unknown Warrior and the Cenotaph. In 1920 an unidentified corpse was exhumed and brought across the channel in the French destroyer *Verdun*. The Unknown Warrior (note the romantic use of 'warrior', not 'soldier') was placed in a coffin made of oak from the Royal Palace at Hampton Court, in which was also placed a helmet, a khaki belt and a Crusader's sword. The coffin was then buried in Westminster Abbey on the same day that the Cenotaph was unveiled. Within a week, nearly one million people came to pay homage at the tomb. For each grieving relative of a missing son or husband, the tomb provided a point of focus:

There was a woman carrying a bunch of white heather tied with a tartan knot who had been journeying since the early hours of the morning from a homestead on the slopes of the Pentlands. Her man

---

73 P. Johnstone, 'High Wood', in G. Chapman, ed., *Vain Glory*, pp. 710–11.

was one of the 'missing' and in her heart was the thought that he might be the 'unknown'.[74]

In its first three days, the Cenotaph, designed by Sir Edwin Lutyens, attracted over 400,000 solemn visitors.[75] It became the spiritual centre of remembrance. On 15 November 1920 the *Daily Mirror* reported a seven-mile queue of mourners waiting to place wreaths at the Cenotaph.[76] Each year on Remembrance Day, an ever-declining number of soldiers marched in formation to pay homage at the symbol of the collective dead. Those who could not travel to London took part in similar processions to war memorials erected in the early 1920s in villages, towns and cities across Britain. These memorials evoke traditions and values which the British felt they had fought to preserve. Classical designs were very popular. If the human form was employed it was often as a saint or angel, such as St George. If soldiers were depicted, they were presented in a non-threatening manner, often with swords instead of guns. Equally symbolic was the use of poppies in wreaths and in the lapel buttons sold by the British Legion. They brought to mind not only the flower which grew on the battlefield, but also, more symbolically, the blood of sacrifice.

The ceremony inevitably inspires patriotism, but it is above all a ritual of remembrance, not a celebration of victory. It was, granted, not for everyone. Some preferred their own private forms of mourning.

> May I remember you
> And murmur with serenity,
> Without intensity,
> Without virulence[77]

wrote Ursula Roberts in her poem berating the crowds mobbing the Cenotaph. Some soldiers vowed to have nothing to do with remembrance ceremonies and avoided them for the remainder of their lives. But for most the ritual was, and remains, an essential part of the process of coming to terms with the war without forgetting it. Many former soldiers, including those deeply embittered by the war, took part. That they did so surely suggests they perceived it a fitting

---

74 Gregory, p. 27.
75 Mosse, pp. 95–6.
76 Gregory, p. 26; Eksteins, p. 255.
77 U. Roberts, 'The Cenotaph', in Reilly, ed., pp. 93–4.

way to honour comrades. For one day at least, the ritual brought together the living – both veteran and civilian – in solemn homage to the dead.

15 THE SOCIAL LEGACY OF THE WAR: THREE STEPS FORWARD, TWO BACK

On 29 November 1917, Lord Lansdowne openly called for a negotiated peace in the letter columns of the *Daily Telegraph*. To push on to victory would, he maintained, 'spell ruin to the civilised world'. All that had made Britain great would be destroyed; 'we are slowly killing off the best of the male population of these islands'.[1] Lansdowne was not a pacifist, but an elitist who feared that, with the best men slaughtered, England would drift rudderless into democracy, republicanism, socialism and decline. He was scorned during the war, but his ideas afterwards resurfaced in more palatable form as the Lost Generation myth. Continued fascination for the Great War derives in part from its imagined status as a catastrophic event which swept away all that was noble and great and replaced it with drabness, disillusion and strife.

There are two problems with this scenario. Firstly, it implies a pre-war England reminiscent of a J. M. W. Turner painting – a prelapsarian idyll devoid of social discord, industrial unrest, poverty or class conflict. Gentle workers tug forelocks, summers are long and warm, and there is 'honey still for tea'.[2] That England is, and was, a myth. Secondly, Lansdowne and his disciples ignored the extraordinary capacity of their society to accommodate social change within a pastoral English ethos. The mighty British Empire was built on Sheffield steel, Newcastle coal and Clydeside engineering, yet the prevalent images of Britain remain those of stately homes, cottage gardens, Henley regattas and strawberries at Wimbledon. Social strife did not suddenly arise during the Great War. That men like Lansdowne could convince themselves it did demonstrates how well progress had been contained and values preserved since the Industrial Revolution. Nor was this process of containment an elitist con-

---

1 *Daily Telegraph*, 29 November 1917.
2 Rupert Brooke, 'The Old Vicarage, Grantchester', in T. Cross, ed., *The Lost Voices of World War I*, pp. 56–7.

spiracy; some of the greatest admirers of 'Merrie England' were the workers who never enjoyed its luxuries.

The war was insufficiently cataclysmic to destroy this fundamentally stable social system. Granted, social change did result. The workers' experiences did alter their world view and their position within society. The same could be said for the middle and upper classes. Likewise, the relationship between men and women and the role of the latter within society evolved. But, looking back from the vantage point of the approaching millennium, what is striking is how much of pre-war society survived. The war was not a deluge which swept all before it, but at best a winter storm which swelled the rivers of change. And, just as it (like all wars) provided opportunities for positive change, so too it stimulated conservatism and counter-reaction, rendering progress erratic and limited.

CONSCIOUSNESS AND CONFLICT

A noticeable redistribution of income occurred during the war. Tax increases, death duties and rent controls rendered the very wealthy worse off in 1925 than ten years earlier.[3] Inflation plagued those who derived their income from investments. Landowners who made their money from produce did well, but those (the majority) who lived off rents suffered. In contrast, workers, because of the manpower shortage, commanded higher wages as the war progressed, allowing most of them to stay just ahead of inflation. But this redistribution of income should not be confused with an erosion of class barriers and a widening of opportunity. The gains and losses of various groups instead led to heightened awareness among all classes.[4] Resultant conflict inhibited progress for society as a whole.

The social impact of the war is best examined by looking at the classes separately. The upper class, depending on one's point of view, either declined drastically or expanded during the war. Since membership in the upper class is theoretically defined by birth, one can appreciate that its ranks were depleted by a disproportionately high casualty rate. In addition, wartime budgetary measures forced the sale of many estates and left others financially precarious. Taxes introduced during the war remained in force after it, as governments quickly found new uses for the revenue. F. M. L. Thompson, studying two representative estates, found that whereas tax claimed 4 per cent

3 B. Waites, *A Class Society at War*, p. 88.
4 Ibid., p. 98.

of gross rental income in 1914, it took 25 per cent in 1919.[5] But these taxes, though mildly redistributive, did not lessen class distinctions. The wealthy felt greater animosity toward those, namely the working class, assumed to be the winners in this redistribution.

Old estates were thrice cursed: firstly by additional financial burdens; secondly by being deprived of the next generation of young men capable of providing essential management; and thirdly by the postwar agricultural depression.[6] But though times were hard, real penury was a long way off. Archibald Sinclair, Baronet of Ulbster in Caithness, warned his new wife in 1918 that

> Large theatre and dinner parties, a big London house, quantities of dresses and jewels, shooting parties . . . on the pre-war scale, these things we cannot aspire to and must dismiss altogether from our minds.[7]

The family could nevertheless afford (in addition to the Caithness estate) a medium-sized London house with full retinue of servants, including butler, cook and parlour-maid, nurse for the children, chauffeur and a groom for four polo ponies.[8] Shooting parties were not as grand as those before the war, but were still grand enough to attract glamorous guests. One suspects that Sinclair's experience was not atypical. In hard times the fittest survived: the more dynamic members of the upper class diversified their portfolios, often selling land to finance more lucrative investments.

If we include in the upper class those with the means to mimic its ways, we can see how the class expanded during the war. A significant number of men made vast fortunes. Lloyd George's tendency to draft business leaders into politics gave them the essential ingredient of service to the state which had always distinguished members of the upper class. After the war, their new status was symbolically confirmed by an unorthodox distribution of honours and peerages. This illustrates the fundamental flexibility of British society, even in its most traditional enclaves. The composition of the upper class changed, but its essential nature, its position in society and its power remained fundamentally intact.

The composition of the middle class also changed during the war era. White collar workers increased by over a million between 1911 and 1921, rising from 12 to 22 per cent of the working

5 T. Wilson, *The Myriad Faces of War*, p. 772.

6 N. Whiteside, 'The British Population at War', in J. Turner, ed., *Britain and the First World War*, p. 97.

7 A. Sinclair to M. Sinclair, 5 September 1918, personal collection.

8 G. DeGroot, *Liberal Crusader: The Life of Sir Archibald Sinclair*, p. 54.

population.[9] Some sections of the middle class did well out of the war; others suffered. The law profession was healthier in 1918 than in 1914, if only for the fact that war casualties reduced the supply of lawyers. Shopkeepers also generally did well, especially those catering to groups who enjoyed a rise in income. For instance, women's clothiers had a good war, since many women earned unaccustomedly high wages.[10] In January 1917, the Forestreet Warehouse Co., drapers, announced that 1916 profits had increased by 58 per cent over 1914.[11] According to Auckland Geddes, 'quite small persons' who amassed huge profits in the haberdashery trade purchased 'estates of several hundred acres in the country'.[12] But inflation was particularly hard on landlords, on those dependent on fixed incomes, and on those whose occupations were not sufficiently important to earn them salary rises. Small businessmen in non-essential industries found it difficult to keep skilled (or any) labour, with disastrous effects upon production and profits. The highest paid industrial workers often earned more than the lowest paid white collar workers. In 1917, a middle class Yorkshireman complained bitterly about how the workers had unlimited access to food, coal, beer and entertainment. 'The war instead of being a terror has almost come to be regarded as a blessing in disguise, and our people continue to live in a fool's paradise regardless of the future.' Afraid of the social disintegration which would result from this condition of plenty, he warned that 'our rulers ... will only have themselves to blame for the results which must inevitably follow'.[13]

Because the middle class volunteered for the army more readily than any other group, it suffered proportionately higher casualties. Losses were keenly felt. Before the war, birth control had allowed many families to stretch limited incomes. According to Masterman:

> The 'only child' or 'only son' which was before the war the sole luxury permitted to so many ... has perished in the ultimate and fierce demands of war. He went out – in the great majority of cases – a volunteer. Every spare farthing had been spent on his upbringing from babyhood. He was to be the pride and assistance of his parents when they attained old age.[14]

9 Whiteside, 'The British Population at War', p. 97.

10 Wilson, p. 773.

11 *The Times*, 30 January 1917.

12 J. Boswell and B. Johns, 'Patriots or Profiteers? British Businessmen and the First World War', *Journal of European Economic History* 11 (1982), p. 432.

13 *The Times*, 21 February 1917.

14 C. Masterman, *England After the War*, p. 79.

Suitably alarmed, the eugenist Dean Inge warned that racial deterioration would result; the 'best sort' would be inclined to have smaller families. Somewhat less apocalyptic, Masterman complained that 'the Middle Class . . . is being harassed out of existence by the financial after consequences of the war'.[15] In truth, the middle class was being harassed *into* existence. Charities and special interest groups like the Professional Classes War Relief Committee encouraged class solidarity. Newspaper editorials moaned about the 'New Poor' who suffered a peculiar martyrdom in which servants were unavailable or unaffordable, laundry was no longer sent out and clothes were mended, then mended again. 'Doing without' became the shibboleth of a group previously unaccustomed to economising. Adversity encouraged homogenisation; a middle class sense of identity was felt even among those who did not suffer. A bunker mentality developed which was both anti-labour and anti-capitalist; the enemies were overpaid, lazy workers and unscrupulous profiteers, both of whom cheated honest taxpayers. These antagonisms inspired the formation of the Middle Class Union, the anti-waste campaigns of the 1920s, the aggressive response to the 1926 General Strike and the postwar protests against high taxation. When circumstances improved in the interwar period, most middle class families found themselves better off than they had been in 1913. Deflation was a welcome boon, housing was cheap and readily available, new consumer goods flooded the markets, female unemployment provided cheap servants and jobless rates were consistently below those of the working class. But class solidarity, formed in adversity, survived the return of good fortune.

The working class changed most significantly during the war. Again, a process of homogenisation occurred. Substitution, dilution and the replacement of previously manual tasks with machine work blurred once-distinct status, skill and income differentials. Unskilled workers made proportionately greater gains than skilled craftsmen, so that the entire class became more cohesive. As G. D. H. Cole observed:

> The skilled worker can no longer think of the less skilled workers as he was apt to think of them before the War, and the less skilled worker will no longer be conscious of the same subordination to the skilled worker . . . the fundamental effect is to draw the two groups more closely together.[16]

15 Ibid., p. 34.
16 G. Cole, *Trade Unionism and Munitions*, p. 4.

A crafts union spokesman expressed a common but futile desire when he asked Lloyd George to 'devise ways and means of eliminating the skilled knowledge which the semi-skilled men will have acquired'.[17] Some feared that the decline of skilled trades would weaken trade unionism. But in 1920 a Ministry of Labour spokesman found that ' "class consciousness" is obliterating the distinctions between those who follow different occupations in the same works'. This contributed to an 'increasing tendency for the trade unionists of one shop, works or small district, to act together, irrespective of their divisions into crafts or occupations'.[18]

But divisions within the working class did not entirely disappear.[19] Workers before the war were rigidly arranged into a social hierarchy of Babylonian complexity. The war erased some of the myriad distinctions, but skill differentials – real or imagined – were still cherished and never surrendered willingly. The war also added new points of tension. Under dilution, skilled workers were increasingly placed in supervisory positions, overseeing the work of unskilled dilutees. The friction which resulted was exacerbated by resentment among skilled workers who did not feel that their pay sufficiently reflected their new status.[20] Furthermore, the widening of the tax base created antagonism between those who paid and those who did not. According to the government, this was a beneficial side-effect of new revenue measures – a fragmented working class was more malleable.[21] Finally, considerable friction existed between those workers who fought in the trenches and those who avoided service. Antagonism arose not only because of the greater danger war service implied. As one contemporary journalist observed:

> Whilst Mrs Jack Tar or Mrs Tommy Atkins have found it a tight squeeze to stretch the money far enough to cover ordinary necessities, Mrs Nouveau-Riche of munition fame, and Mrs Dockyard Matey have been able to indulge in finery that never came their way before 1914.[22]

But though internal divisions remained strong, the working class

17 Waites, p. 195.

18 Wilson, p. 770.

19 See A. Reid, 'The Impact of the First World War upon British Workers', in R. Wall and J. Winter, eds, *The Upheaval of War*, passim.

20 J. Melling, ' "Non-Commissioned Officers": British Employers and their Supervisory Workers, 1880–1920', *Social History 5* (1980), p. 213.

21 R. Whiting, 'Taxation and the Working Class 1915–24', *Historical Journal* 33 (1990), p. 904.

22 D. Englander and J. Osborne, 'Jack, Tommy and Henry Dubb: The Armed Forces and the Working Class', *Historical Journal* 21 (1978), p. 615.

presented a more united front externally. Class identity was reinforced by workers' pride in their contribution to the war and by growing antagonism toward other classes. During the war, social inequalities were made apparent in previously unaccustomed ways. Class antagonism is always greatest during periods of high inflation, since workers find more points of conflict with landlords, management or, in this case, government. Workers could not help but notice that their contribution to the war effort often involved considerable financial sacrifice. In contrast, businessmen managed to be both wealthy and patriotic, as James Lithgow candidly admitted to his brother:

> Put bluntly it does not matter a damn to us selfishly how deep in the soup [the country] gets as it will be all the more profitable to pull it out, but both of us can lay definite claim to having been guided by better motives in all we have done since this trouble arose.[23]

A Cabinet paper regretted the fact that 'abuses of profit-making has . . . contributed to bring profit into wider disrepute'.[24] There were numerous other flashpoints. Food queues were always worst in working class areas. Unfair landlords preyed upon the defenceless poor. Finally, the government seemed more inclined to regulate and control the worker's life (leaving certificates, conscription, outlawing strikes, etc.) than that of the capitalist. Though this was hardly the worker's first encounter with injustice, the iniquities were all the more galling because they contradicted rhetoric about a nation united in struggle. Workers in consequence became more assertive. A railway clerk confessed how, before the war, going on strike produced 'a sense of personal degradation'. He and his fellow workers 'had a childlike belief in the good intentions of the companies'. But, as a result of the war, 'this state of confidence has given way to an attitude of deep distrust and in many instances of grave suspicion'.[25]

Arthur Gleason, an American who studied British society immediately after the war, observed:

> An old Oxford friend said sadly to me: 'Ten years ago, when I came into a crowded bus, a working-man would rise and touch his cap and give me his seat. I am sorry to see that spirit dying out.'[26]

The anecdote indicates that workers had become less reverential, but

23 Boswell and Johns, 'Patriots or Profiteers?', p. 442.
24 Whiting, 'Taxation', p. 912.
25 Waites, pp. 256–7.
26 A. Gleason, *What the Workers Want*, p. 250.

it does not necessarily follow that society became more equal. Gleason's middle class friend still perceived class distinctions and felt them worthy of preservation. Likewise, the worker's refusal to touch his cap and surrender his seat is as significant an indicator of class barriers as was his willingness to do so before the war. His actions should not be confused with an assumption of equality, but are instead an assertion of hostility toward someone once respected, now scorned, but still distinctly different.

And what of the effect of the war upon the social consciousness of the more than five million men who served in the armed forces? The highly traditional, heavily authoritarian military quarantined men from the social changes which occurred on the home front. Thus, Tommy Atkins did not experience the same awakening of working class awareness which occurred at home.[27] One persistent myth, encouraged by the war poetry, is that camaraderie between the classes in the trenches produced an atmosphere of mutual respect which survived into the postwar years. Granted, junior officers felt a resurgence of the old *noblesse oblige* which had declined during the previous generation of industrial unrest. But the old social hierarchy remained intact, as an officer in Christopher Stone's *The Valley of Indecision* confirms:

> And what have the officer class learned? . . . To manage men. How? By example, partly. By setting themselves a higher example than they expect of their subordinates. And by looking after their men: thinking of their men's comfort, mark you, before their own.[28]

This paternalism should not be confused with intimacy, or with equality. A similar paternalism (or, rather, maternalism) was evident in the factories where 'lady superintendents' looked after the welfare of the working class women they supervised.[29] But, as Ernest Bevin remarked in 1919:

> my experience with all this good feeling, . . . is that the leopard has not changed his spots. It is as big an effort now to get a bob or two a week for your work-people as ever it was . . .[30]

Concern for survival as a nation may have camouflaged class divi-

27 See Englander and Osborne, 'Jack, Tommy and Henry Dubb', pp. 602–3.
28 G. Sheffield, 'The Effect of the Great War on Class Relations in Great Britain: The Career of Major Christopher Stone DSO MC', *War and Society* 7 (1989), p. 98.
29 See A. Woollacott, 'Maternalism, Professionalism and Industrial Welfare Supervisors in World War I Britain', *Women's History Review* 3 (1994).
30 Wilson, p. 769.

sions, but it did not in any sense wipe them out. Class antagonism quickly resurfaced after the war. Noble Tommy Atkins, removed from his trench and shed of his uniform, became a lazy, selfish, grasping proto-Bolshevik, much derided and feared by the middle class.

The prescriptive forces at work in society are evident in the experiences of the 'temporary gentlemen' – men from humble backgrounds who, out of necessity, became officers. These men attracted a good deal of antagonism during the war from the 'genuine articles'. Wilfred Owen remarked derisively upon the presence in his unit of 'privates and sergeants in masquerade'. 'Two at least of the officers are quite temporary gentlemen', he told his mother. 'I'd prefer to be among honest privates than these snobs.' 'I felt the bottom of the barrel had been scraped for officer material', concluded the novelist Stuart Cloete. Alfred Burrage was alarmed to find his favourite West End haunt full of these interlopers. 'Judging by the manners and accents . . . they were nearly all "Smiffs", late of Little Buggington Grammar School, who had been "clurks" in civil life.' These attitudes contradict the optimism of propagandists who judged the development a 'splendid signpost to the future. When the job is done, we shall settle down more friendlily, without the class distinctions and the horrible class war that were the curse of this country prior to 1914.' Those who earned the distinction 'temporary gentleman' had few such illusions. A former salesman remarked:

> I try hard to remind myself that the three stars which I now wear are only the temporary marks of proficiency that the war will, in ending, wipe out, and that I will step back into that drab old life . . .

Many found that their wartime status provided little advantage after 1918. One ex-captain complained:

> We have got to wipe this 'war record' clear off our minds, drop the 'captain' and 'lieutenant' off the advertisements, and regard ourselves as fit young civilians who have had a 'jolly fine holiday for four years'.

R. H. Mottram referred to a process of being 'de-officered' which, for him, meant the added indignity of 'finding our earning capacity lower in the peacetime jobs to which we thankfully returned'.[31]

Before the war, working class assertiveness was constrained by fatalism, by deep divisions within the class, by precarious employment and by limited opportunities to express discontent. The war

---

31 M. Petter, ' "Temporary Gentlemen" in the Aftermath of the Great War: Rank, Status and the Ex-Officer Problem', *Historical Journal* 37 (1994), pp. 130–43.

rendered the working class more homogenised and more inclined to interpret problems in class terms. Thus, society as a whole became less harmonious and the working class stronger. But the growth of working class solidarity did not destroy the social order, as Lansdowne feared. As Waites argues,

> there took place between 1914 and 1924 a concatenation of changes in English society which altered the specific form of the class structure but did not fundamentally disturb those processes of social differentiation which are generic to a capitalist market society.[32]

A more assertive working class was matched by more assertive middle and upper classes, each prepared to defend its interests more aggressively. New mechanisms for the control and containment of the working class were introduced. The Munitions of War Act restricted labour's freedom of action by making industrial action an offence against the state. Workers were also encouraged to feel a moral duty not to strike. Industrial welfare supervisors had long term implications for labour management: not only did they increase discipline, but by making the workplace more attractive, they reduced working class discontent and limited the appeal of radical unionism.[33] One government memorandum postulated that careful industrial management would render a new generation of workers 'more malleable and . . . more easily influenced . . . they will provide for the future a more capable and reasonable body of adult labour'.[34] In similar ways, female industrial supervisors curbed both class *and* gender assertiveness.

In *Military Organization and Society*, Stefan Andreski proposed that the greater society's participation in a war, the more comprehensive the consequent social change. But there are a number of problems with the notion of a 'military participation ratio'.[35] Participation meant improved income for many, but, as we have seen, income levels and social status are not directly related. Class differences are based on deep-seated cultural characteristics which cannot be erased by better employment opportunities alone. But the biggest problem with the idea of progress through participation is that it fails to

32 Waites, p. 279.

33 See Melling, 'Non-Commissioned Officers', p. 214.

34 N. Whiteside, 'Industrial Welfare and Labour Regulation in Britain at the Time of the First World War', *International Review of Social History* 25 (1980), p. 318.

35 S. Andreski, *Military Organization and Society*. P. Abrams argues that the failure of reconstruction after 1918 is proof that the military participation ratio is a fallacy: see 'The Failure of Social Reform: 1918–1920', *Past and Present* 24 (1963), pp. 43–64.

acknowledge the precariousness of the workers' wartime gains. However well they may have done during the war, they were ill-equipped to weather the economic storms of the 1920s and 1930s. The repetitive labour which the unskilled worker took on during the war was harder to find in peacetime and, with manpower suddenly plentiful, did not pay as well. Granted, most unskilled labourers were better off without a job in 1923 than they were with one in 1913, but this was economic progress, not social.

Class awareness, even if strategically directed, is never enough on its own to achieve greater status or mobility. Awareness may make possible an assertion of class identity, but raw power is also essential. For workers this power has traditionally been derived from real or manipulated scarcity of labour. That power was in short supply after the war. Class solidarity survived and was perhaps even enhanced by the shared suffering of mass unemployment. But solidarity on its own was not enough; workers could command very little power in a period of surplus labour.

An awakening of working class identity should not be confused with class conflict or even with radical politics.[36] The miners were slow to embrace the Labour Party and were suspicious of socialism, yet they hardly lacked a sense of identity. In the 1918 election a rise in working class awareness co-existed with resounding support for the Tories. Yet this is not as contradictory as it may at first seem. During the war, the workers were among the most patriotic in society and vigorously supported the conflict. In the 1918 election, the Tories presented the image of toughness and resolution which harmonised best with working class patriotism. Belligerent Tory promises of revenge upon Germany dovetailed well with the prevalent xenophobia. The Tories also presented a patriotic national image which neither the divided Liberals nor sectionalist Labour could establish with conviction. The Conservative-dominated coalition seemed the best prospect for achieving the 'land fit for heroes' which workers coveted. Thus, Tory-voting workers were neither misguided nor unaware; they simply saw their interests best represented by the Conservatives. Finally, class awareness can imply an assumption of inferiority: many workers sincerely believed that the Tories had a natural fitness to govern.[37] 'The war made plutocratic reality some-

36 See Waites, p. 22, for an extensive discussion of this point.

37 Studies conducted in 1960 found deference voting still very prominent among the working class. See R. Samuel, 'The Deference Voter', *New Left Review* (January 1960), pp. 9–13.

what more visible', argues Waites, 'but it remained a peculiarity of
the English to defer to government by Old Etonians.'[38]

A LAND FIT FOR HEROES?

In previous chapters, we have seen how some significant improvements in the condition of the poor occurred during the war. These
improvements generally survived the armistice. There were fewer
people in poverty, the result partly of wartime redistribution of
income, but also of decreasing family size. Meagre incomes did not
have to stretch as far. Food was more affordable, health care more
accessible and health standards consequently better. Government
spending on social services, which stood at 4 per cent in 1914,
hovered around 8 per cent between the wars. Unemployment benefit
was available to 2,250,000 workers before the war and 12,000,000
after the passage of the Unemployment Insurance Act of 1920.[39] The
increased attention to social services can be explained by two factors
connected with the war. Firstly, the war broke down resistance to
higher taxation. Secondly, war revealed the extent of social distress
and encouraged a desire to alleviate it. Thus the Coalition's promises
of 'a fit land for heroes to live in' during the 1918 election campaign
struck a popular chord. But this sense of goodwill was not universally
felt, nor did altruism survive long past the armistice. Many agreed
that social welfare was desirable, but little consensus existed on how
to finance it.

There were strict limits on postwar social progress. The eight-
hour day and 48-hour week became standard, with few exceptions,
after the war. This brought increased opportunities for leisure and
relaxation, but poverty prevented their fullest exploitation. Unemployment benefit covered short term emergencies, but was inadequate
during long term joblessness – a depressing feature of the interwar
period. Expanded union membership and increased confidence on
the part of the working class rendered the workers better equipped
to demand improvements, but union power and worker confidence
quickly diminished when unemployment rose. The redistribution of
income apparent between 1913 and 1924 did not continue into the
next decade. Despite the general improvement in the lot of the very
poor, in rural areas, malnourishment actually increased during the
1920s.

38 Waites, p. 116.
39 Wilson, p. 800.

Limited social progress strengthened the class system. Social mobility remained extremely difficult, but quality of life did improve. Life became more tolerable for those on its lowest rungs, rendering them more accepting of its iniquities. Though the desire for an improvement in the lot of the poor was widely felt, very few demanded, as a corollary, a social revolution. Rich and poor, privileged and downtrodden, shared a fundamental conservatism when it came to social change. The extreme patriotism of workers during the war, and their consistent antagonism towards socialist (as opposed to labourist) politics, suggest that most workers linked the continuation of British greatness with a preservation of her social system. There is little evidence that, even in the lowest trough of the slump, they wanted anything more radical than an amelioration of their plight.

There was little enthusiasm for creating the mechanisms to facilitate social mobility or, better still, a breakdown of the class system. For example, concern about poor working class housing inspired the Addison Housing Act of 1919, which was designed to enable the building of 500,000 homes in three years and, as a corollary, revive the construction industry. *The Times* commented in April 1919 that there was 'no doubt that the country regards this as far and away the most important Bill in the government's programme of social reconstruction'.[40] Houses, it was hoped, would wean the poor from radical politics. 'One of the great difficulties of the future will be unrest', commented the Opposition Leader Donald Maclean, 'and one of the best ways of mitigating it is to let people see that we are in earnest on this question.'[41] But real commitment, financial and emotional, was lacking. Within two years Addison was out, the victim of Conservative-inspired parsimony and a growing abhorrence of policies which smacked of egalitarianism. Many Tories sheltered behind the principle that house construction was not a justified area for state intervention. Welcoming the government's change of heart, *The Times* commented in June 1921 that the Addison plans had been 'ill-advised . . . at a time when the whole reaction of men's minds was against over-government and towards individualism and freedom of personal enterprise'.[42] When the building trade eventually revived it did so because of the boom in privately financed suburban construction for the expanding middle class. Local councils, when they could scrape together the money, built simple houses for the

---

40 *The Times*, 2 April 1919.
41 M. Swenarton, *Homes Fit for Heroes*, pp. 85–6.
42 *The Times*, 21 June 1921.

workers which were an improvement on the slum, but a long way from homes fit for heroes.

Education reforms were even more disappointing. Progress here would presumably have provided the best opportunities for social mobility. The Fisher Education Act of 1918 raised the school leaving age from twelve to fourteen, with 'continuation classes' of eight hours per week for those leaving early to take up employment. Local authorities were encouraged (not required) to provide more nursery places and better medical care in schools. Similar reforms were passed for the separate Scottish system. But the Act did not attack the traditionalism and elitism of the old system. There was no acknowledgement of the need for universal secondary education and no fundamental reform of the curriculum. And, in the end, even Fisher's modest reform proposals were not fully implemented. Continuation classes, for instance, were killed by a penny-pinching government. The best education at high school and university remained private, yet in those sectors a bias toward classical studies and a neglect of science prevailed. From 1910 to 1929, 39 per cent of middle class boys went to secondary school, and 8.5 per cent to university. The figures for working class boys are 10 per cent and 1.5 per cent respectively. Those for girls in both classes were, needless to say, even lower. Leaving aside the fact that this made social mobility (and gender equality) extremely difficult to achieve, the figures also demonstrate that the country wasted huge resources of talent. According to one estimate, in the period before the Second World War, 73 per cent of able children never made it to secondary school, while nearly half of those who did make it did not, on the basis of their intelligence alone, belong there.[43]

The war revealed many problems worthy of attention, but their solutions were often incompatible with the traditional ethos. Social improvement was seen as a luxury which only a prosperous society could afford, and throughout the interwar period Britain did not feel prosperous. The cul de sac of working class existence became a little less drab, and a bit more secure, but it remained difficult to escape. It was not that the privileged classes were intent upon keeping the working class down, but rather that they wished to preserve their own way of life. Unfortunately the consequence of doing so was to keep the working class down. And the workers, better off than they had been before the war, did not complain. Rudimentary social

43 Wilson, pp. 817–18.

welfare, cheap entertainment, better working conditions and improved health were effective opiates for the people.

FREEDOM AND EMANCIPATION V. HOMES, HUSBANDS AND BABIES

War imposed masculine values upon society, thus reinvigorating notions of separate spheres. Because men fight wars and women stay at home, women are forced back into feminine roles of mother, nurturer and carer which are themselves symbolic of the values men imagine themselves to be defending. It is no wonder that many women allowed the helpless victim mentality to engulf them. While they sat knitting socks by the fire,[44] fantasies involving chivalric heroes took the place of sexual gratification. Traditional, patriotic and patriarchal ideals 'proved hard to eradicate once rooted in the blood of young men who had apparently died in their belief'.[45]

Granted, during the war many women broke the constricting chains of femininity, but the culture quickly adapted to the escapees. Female munitions workers were often depicted in war propaganda in stylised drawings which disguised the dirt, darkness and drudgery of a real factory. The reality of what they were doing – creating weapons of destruction – was also obscured. Two wartime heroines, Mairi Chisholm and Elsie Knocker, drove motorcycles and ambulances close to the British line. They did this because they were attracted to the idea of being men – doing what women were not supposed to do. Yet to the public they became the Angels of Pervyse – the masculinity of motorcycle riding subsumed by the femininity of angels of mercy. A hero was made of Chisholm, who retained some feminine qualities, but not of Flora Sandes, who actually fought for the Serbian Army and in so doing squandered all femininity.

The number of women in paid employment increased from 4.93 million to 6.19 million during the war. This seems a significant increase, but the vast majority who took up new jobs were working class women who had worked previously or, being teenagers, expected to enter employment shortly. Wartime work was different in that it was generally better paid, more stable and was crucially important to the nation's survival, thus giving women a sense of pride. But these differences and the experiences they engendered were

44 See S. Sassoon, 'Glory of Women', in J. Silkin, ed., *The Penguin Book of First World War Poetry*, p. 132.

45 C. Tylee, *The Great War and Women's Consciousness*, p. 74.

fleeting. Working class women were changed by the war, but few could enjoy those changes after it.

Excessive attention has been given to the war experiences of young middle class women. The Voluntary Aid Detachments (VADs), popularised by Vera Brittain, did make a significant contribution. But very few of the largely upper and middle class women who joined (one-third, incidentally, were men) saw it as anything other than a brief and adventurous hiatus in an otherwise conventional life. The experience essentially replicated in a war context the voluntary and charitable activities in which women of similar social status had long engaged.[46] Yet, quite unwittingly, middle class women unaccustomed to employment of any type did undergo a metamorphosis. By their actions they contradicted Victorian notions of female frailty, which had never really applied to working class women.[47] Many of them found fulfilment by escaping the stifling predictability of middle class existence. Few of these women were feminists, some had even opposed the extension of suffrage, but by their actions they contributed to the feminist cause. They advanced along the road to emancipation, largely because they had the means to realise their newfound sense of freedom after the war. They could, after all, pay working class women to look after their homes and children.

The Great War has customarily been seen as a step forward for women because it broke down gender-based barriers to achievement. But even while women were striding forward toward emancipation, a conservative counter-reaction was under way. Pay scales symbolically confirmed women's inferior status. Separation allowances, as we have seen, underlined women's status as dependants of their husbands and, in the sense that allowances could be withdrawn on evidence of moral delinquency, they reiterated the husband's ownership of his wife's body, with the state as trustee.[48] The counter-reaction intensified after the armistice. Women were under intense pressure to leave wartime jobs. 'The idea that because the State called for women to help the nation, the State must continue to employ them is too absurd for sensible women to entertain', argued the *Daily Graphic*. 'As for women formerly in domestic service, they at least should have no difficulty in finding vacancies.'[49] Most women willingly sur-

46 See A. Summers, *Angels and Citizens: British Women as Military Nurses*, p. 178.

47 H. Jones, *Health and Society in Twentieth-Century Britain*, p. 39.

48 A point discussed by S. Pedersen in 'Gender, Welfare, and Citizenship in Britain during the Great War', *American Historical Review* 95 (1990), p. 1000.

49 D. Mitchell, *Women on the Warpath*, p. 266.

rendered their jobs to returning soldiers. 'Far from being the selfish creatures the Press described, they were only too meek and yielding', commented Ray Strachey.[50] As for those who refused to leave jobs, the government was quick to use legislation, in particular the 1919 Restoration of Pre-War Practices Act, to force them to do so. Various official studies proposed bans upon married women working, limits upon the hours women could work, and prohibitions on women in trades deemed 'unsuitable'.[51] While not all these ideas were practicable, one is struck by the revulsion against the changes war had wrought. 'The attitude of the public towards women', commented the *Daily News* in March 1921, 'is more full of contempt and bitterness than has been the case since the suffragette outbreaks.'[52] According to Strachey, 'public opinion assumed that all women could still be supported by men, and that if they went on working it was from some sort of deliberate wickedness'.[53] Before the war a woman doing a man's job was considered an interesting anomaly. After the war she was a threat. Women had proved that they could do men's work, and were henceforth more dangerous.

Thus, 'reconstruction' meant a return to traditional family life, which militated against female emancipation. Yet many of those most enthusiastic for a return to normality were women. 'Why', complained Winifred Holtby after the war, 'are women themselves often the first to repudiate the movements of the past hundred and fifty years, which have gained for them at least the foundations of political, economic, educational and moral equality?'[54] Holtby (like so many radical feminists ever since) simply could not understand that women might actually enjoy the prosaic pleasures of motherhood and the home. Employment outside the home has become a symbol of emancipation, but at the time it was a necessary evil caused by the low pay or unstable employment of a husband – or the lack of one entirely. If the work was unfulfilling or badly paid, and if the woman had no access to childcare or no assistance around the home, it merely added to her considerable burdens. In this sense, social improvement meant being able to stay home and look after a family. After the war, the largest women's union, the National Federation of Women Workers, expressed the opinion that married women

50 R. Strachey, *The Cause*, p. 371.
51 M. Pugh, *Women and the Women's Movement in Britain, 1914–1959*, pp. 29–30.
52 K. Kent, 'The Politics of Sexual Difference: World War I and the Demise of British Feminism', *Journal of British Studies* 27 (1988), p. 238.
53 Strachey, p. 371.
54 Kent, 'The Politics of Sexual Difference', p. 236.

should ideally not have to work.[55] Behind the 'land fit for heroes' rhetoric lurked a rigidly patriarchal implication: men would get jobs and women would retreat to their separate sphere. But the incomplete achievement of this ideal meant that many women were forced, out of necessity, back into ill-paid, low status jobs.

'Throughout history', Holtby commented, 'whenever society has tried to curtail the opportunities, interests and powers of women, it has done so in the sacred names of marriage and maternity.'[56] Serious attempts were made to create a social system more conducive to motherhood and family life. 'Let us glorify, dignify and purify motherhood by every means in our power', proclaimed John Burns, President of the Board of Trade.[57] Due to fiscal orthodoxy and an abhorrence of the interventionist state, real improvements fell short of rhetoric. Nevertheless, the provision of health visitors was dramatically improved and the benefits of breastfeeding were widely publicised. The maternalist ethic was not merely a male conspiracy to keep women shackled by the burdens of motherhood. Some of the most enthusiastic supporters of these campaigns were feminists like Mrs Fawcett, Eleanor Rathbone, Selina Cooper and even Sylvia Pankhurst. But, by raising motherhood to a function of citizenship equivalent to soldiering, these women inadvertently played into the hands of those keen on restoring Victorian notions of separate spheres.[58]

While maternalists promoted motherhood, sexologists promoted intercourse. The postwar sex reformer Magnus Hirschfield argued that the war had provided 'an opportunity for throwing off, for a while, all the irksome repressions which culture imposes and for satisfying temporarily all the repressed desires'.[59] Walter Gallichan, in *The Poison of Prudery*, warned that 'Many daughters of cold mothers die spinsters' – a rather insensitive remark at a time when war had limited the supply of available husbands. In a direct attack upon feminists and spinsters, Janet Chance advocated the banning of 'non-orgasmic' women from politics, fearing that they would spread their repressive ways throughout society.[60] Yet advice to wives

---

55 G. Braybon and P. Summerfield, *Out of the Cage: Women's Experiences in Two World Wars*, p. 130.

56 Kent, 'The Politics of Sexual Difference', p. 244.

57 Pugh, p. 16.

58 See S. Kent, 'Gender Reconstruction after the First World War', in H. Smith, ed., *British Feminism in the Twentieth Century*, pp. 80–1.

59 Ibid., p. 68.

60 Ibid., p. 74.

to set free their libidos was in truth pressure upon them to do their duty by their husbands in the bedroom. This was sexuality of the most conventional kind, with men dominant and women conquered, lying back, thinking of England. Contrary to the fantasies of Arthur Marwick, women did not win 'sexual liberty' during the war, nor did 'official opinion [come] very near to condoning any consolation which might be offered to war heroes briefly returned from the trenches'.[61] If the newspapers are to be believed, those war heroes, when they returned for good, could be very violent in the pursuit of sexual needs.[62] And society still scorned women whose sexual impulses tempted them beyond propriety. The *Manchester Guardian* reported on the widely accepted 'unwritten law' that a man was 'held to be justified in killing his wife on obtaining proof, as to the sufficiency of which he is himself the judge, of her infidelity'.[63] In mid-1915, the Newcastle Assizes heard the trial of William Simpson, a soldier, who cut the throat of his young son. His defence was provocation – his wife had 'not behaved properly during his absence at the front'. The jury found him guilty but recommended mercy.[64]

After fulfilling her duties as mother and sexual plaything, it is a wonder how women had any time for housework (which perhaps explains the increased demand for domestic servants). Yet, after the war, housekeeping (an extension of maternalism) was, within some circles, elevated to the status of a science or profession, albeit one which did not carry a salary. Magazines like *Good Housekeeping* encouraged greater cleanliness, professionalism and creativity in the housewife, in so doing curbing her pursuit of interests outside the home and setting standards often impossible to meet. One (obviously male) 'expert' blamed industrial unrest on bad digestion and indirectly on bad cooking. 'Girls [leave] school knowing all about William the Conqueror in 1066, but very little about the method of preparing a first-class steak and kidney pudding.'[65] Conspiracy theorists might see all this as part of the concerted campaign to confine women to traditional roles.

61 A. Marwick, *The Explosion of British Society 1914–62*, p. 26.
62 Kent, 'Gender Reconstruction', p. 70.
63 Wilson, p. 723.
64 *The Times*, 1 July 1915.
65 Ibid., 2 December 1918.

POSTSCRIPT

Vera Brittain's *Testament of Youth* has been admired by feminists and pacifists alike because it supposedly evokes both the futility of the war and the opportunities for women's emancipation which occurred during it. Yet a close reading of that book reveals a very different Brittain who subordinated her identity to that of the men around her, mainly her brother and Roland Leighton.[66] As for recognising the futility of war, Brittain was closer to Brooke than to Sassoon, as her poem 'To My Brother' reveals:

> (In Memory of July 1st, 1916)
> Your battle-wounds are scars upon my heart,
>   Received when in that grand and tragic 'show'
> You played your part
>   Two years ago,
>
> And silver in the summer morning sun
>   I see the symbol of your courage glow –
> That Cross you won
>   Two years ago.
>
> Though now again you watch the shrapnel fly,
>   And hear the guns that daily louder grow,
> As in July
>   Two years ago,
>
> May you endure to lead the Last Advance
>   And with your men pursue the flying foe
> As once in France
>   Two years ago.[67]

Brittain's diaries reveal that she was an enthusiastic supporter of the war who, in contrast to her father (treated rather unfairly in the book), felt that, for duty's sake, her brother must enlist.[68] The extent to which she was herself intoxicated by chivalric notions of war is evident in her horror when her beloved Leighton showed her his 'vicious-looking short steel dagger', a thoroughly 'uncivilised' weapon.[69]

66 Tylee, p. 65.
67 Captain E. H. Brittain, M.C. written four days before his death in action in the Austrian offensive on the Italian front, June 15th, 1918. V. Brittain, 'To My Brother', in C. Reilly, ed., *Scars Upon My Heart*, p. 15.
68 Pugh, p. 11.
69 See Chapter 4, page 71.

Nor is Brittain's sense of sisterhood very striking. Hers was an individual quest; her book reveals little cognisance of the plight of women (especially working class women) of her generation. She was one of the foremost marketers of the Lost Generation myth, yet apparently failed to understand its implications for women. The myth reinforces women's inferiority and helplessness by attributing catastrophic consequences to the loss of a small group of men.[70] In 'This Generation of Men' (1934), Brittain actually warned that society was becoming increasingly matriarchal because men who survived the war were poor physical specimens with weak wills who lacked vitality and dynamism.[71] The elevation of Brittain into an icon of modern woman has meant that we have willingly swallowed her misguided conception of the world in which she lived, where naive idealism, chivalric war, the end of innocence and forever departed masculine heroes figure prominently.

Monica Cosens, author of *Lloyd George's Munitions Girls*, ended her book by unconsciously demonstrating that the war had done little to change attitudes to class and gender:

> And last of all the Nation – what will it think of Miss Tommy Atkins when the War is over, and it has the time to stand still, to look back and think how these light-hearted, gay, simple-minded children – for that is what they are – have borne the heat of battle, how they fought smiling all the time, no matter if the day was hard and long?
>
> Then it will be the turn of the country to shake them by the hand and echo the words spoken by Mr. Tommy Atkins:
>
> 'It's great what you have done!'[72]

In fact, feelings of gratitude quickly diminished, though condescending attitudes did not. Anecdotal as the Cosens quotation might be, it is nevertheless a great deal more accurate than Brittain's retrospective impressions of a world changed beyond recognition. Subsequent generations have revered Brittain because she provides a bridge across the deluge. Both a victim and a survivor of the war, she seems a link between the age of innocence and the modern age who confirms the status of the Great War as the watershed of the twentieth century. Yet both the age of innocence and the idea of modernism are arbitrary constructs, relevant to high culture but meaningless to real life. Brittain's turbulent world existed only in her mind and in the minds of those unrepresentative elites to whom far too much attention has

70 Tylee, p. 218.
71 Pugh, p. 79.
72 M. Cosens, *Lloyd George's Munitions Girls*, pp. 159–60.

subsequently been given. The real world was much more prosaic and boringly stable. War was tragic, in some cases catastrophic. But for most people it was an extraordinary event of limited duration which, as much as it brought change, also inspired a desire to reconstruct according to cherished patterns. If war is the locomotive of history, the rolling stock in this case was typically British: slow, outmoded and prone to delay and cancellation.

16 POLITICS AND THE PEOPLE: THE TRIUMPH OF THE HARD-FACED MEN

After the election of December 1918, Stanley Baldwin described the new House of Commons as 'a lot of hard-faced men who look as if they had done very well out of the war'.[1] It was an accurate description of the new political order, particularly of the Conservative Party Baldwin would eventually lead. Yet that new order was 'new' only in the sense that it contained a great number of men who entered the Commons for the first time in 1918. The political instincts of the hard-faced men were decidedly traditional. They were determined to limit the changes war had brought into being and were remarkably successful at so doing. But, by their success, they rendered Britain ill-equipped to thrive in a decidedly different postwar world.

THE 1918 REPRESENTATION OF THE PEOPLE ACT

It is a measure of the strength of conservatism in British politics that the political complexion hardly changed after the electorate expanded from eight million to 21 million as a result of the 1918 Representation of the People Act. That Act will forever be synonymous with votes for women. Yet female enfranchisement was but a clause in an act which dealt primarily with male suffrage. Existing residency requirements (at least one year in the same dwelling) disfranchised many soldiers and industrial workers. This injustice could not be allowed to continue. The residency requirement was therefore reduced to six months, with the prospective voter no longer required to stay in one dwelling, rather only in the same general area. The Act also enfranchised a group deemed to have made a special contribution to the war, namely men aged nineteen or twenty on active service. Otherwise, the voting age for men remained 21. Displaying conspicuous pique, Parliament disfranchised all conscientious objectors for five years, unless they could prove they had performed work

1 T. Wilson, *The Myriad Faces of War*, p. 820.

312

of national importance. Men in receipt of poor relief were no longer disfranchised. Plural voting, by which an elector could vote in the constituencies of his residence, his university and his places of business, was henceforward reduced to two constituencies only.

The Act was heartily supported by the Tories, for two reasons. Firstly, they realised that some reform was inevitable, therefore it made sense to be associated with it. They did not want enfranchisement to become an electoral issue, exploited by a demagogue like Lloyd George. Secondly, the party no longer had reason to fear mass democracy. The big change had come in 1884, the last time suffrage was determined strictly along class lines. Relaxing registration requirements would first enfranchise a layer of middle class natural Liberal supporters; relaxing them further would bring in a large contingent of workers, many of whom, evidence suggested, would be inclined to vote Conservative.[2]

By a majority of 387 to 57 the Commons extended the franchise to women aged over 30 who were themselves ratepayers or who were married to a ratepayer. On first glance this seems an enthusiastic recognition of the contribution women made to the war. But enthusiasm for women's emancipation remained in short supply. The war had little to do with hastening women's suffrage. Instead, as the previous chapter demonstrated, it revived notions of separate spheres as much as it encouraged ideas of equality. The argument for female enfranchisement had essentially been won before 1914; all that was required were specific terms acceptable to the Commons. Of the 194 MPs who voted in both the 1911 and 1917 divisions on the issue, eighteen had moved in favour and four against, a net shift of a mere fourteen.[3] Success came not as a consequence of war-inspired good feelings toward women, but because the terms of the reform were more acceptable than those of 1911. The 1918 reform was tolerable because it was limited. The age and marriage restriction addressed fears that women would constitute a majority of the electorate, fears made more acute because so many male voters had died in the war. (A total of 8,479,156 women were enfranchised, as against 12,913,166 men; or almost exactly four women for every six men.[4]) The vast majority of those women who had made a significant contribution to the war effort by working in factories were barred by the age requirement. Those given the vote were acceptable essentially

---

2 M. Pugh, *Electoral Reform in War and Peace*, p. 182.
3 Idem, *Women and the Women's Movement in Britain, 1914–59*, pp. 40–1.
4 Ibid., p. 34.

because they seemed stable and unaffected by war's disruption. In other words, the typical female voter would be a mature wife and mother primarily concerned with the preservation of her home life. She would not, it was presumed, be interested in a career, nor in radical feminist causes. Tories drew additional solace from the fact that women tended to be more conservative than their male counterparts, since they were less likely to be influenced by trade unionism.[5]

Most suffrage campaigners pragmatically accepted the measure as the most they could expect. Realising that postwar competition for jobs would inspire fresh antagonism between the sexes, Mrs Fawcett wisely decided that it would be foolish to hold out for more. She in fact saw logic in the householder stipulation attached to female suffrage:

> There was some outcry against this on the part of ardent suffragists as being derogatory to the independence of women. While understanding this objection, I did not share it; I felt, on the contrary, that it marked an important advance in that it recognized in a practical political form a universally accepted and most valuable social fact – namely the partnership of the wife and mother in the home.[6]

Thus the hour of woman's emancipation was an anticlimax. Had women been granted the vote before August 1914, militant campaigners could have claimed a monumental victory. Direct action would have been vindicated. Instead, the franchise was extended during the war, in a limited fashion and as a minor part of a bill concerned primarily with male enfranchisement. The change had occurred despite the quiescence of feminists and, sandwiched between events on the war fronts, hardly created a stir. A cynic would argue that women had been rewarded for behaving.

POLITICS AND THE 1918 ELECTION

The expanded electorate first exercised its muscle at the General Election on 14 December 1918 – a schizophrenic contest. On the one hand politicians espoused reconstruction and magnanimous victory. 'We must not allow any sense of revenge, any spirit of greed, any grasping desire, to over-ride the fundamental principles of righteousness', argued Lloyd George on 12 November.[7] The ideal

---

5 Pugh, *Electoral Reform*, p. 180.

6 M. Fawcett, *The Women's Victory – And After: Personal Reminiscences, 1911–1918*, p. 141. See also M. Fawcett, *What I Remember*, pp. 243–53.

7 C. Haste, *Keep the Home Fires Burning*, p. 181.

of 'a fit land for heroes to live in' harmonised with these noble aims. Unfortunately, the nation had until recently been whipped into a state of blind anger. Only a few months had passed since the worst anti-German riots of the war. The press and many politicians preferred malice to magnanimity. The *Daily Mail* made strident demands for the Kaiser to be hung, while it exhorted readers to 'Refuse to vote for any Member of Parliament who will not give a definite pledge that he will stand for the total eradication of German influence from our country.'[8] The government eventually realised that it was easier to go along with this mood than to tame it. Auckland Geddes signalled the new direction when he promised that the government would 'squeeze the German lemon till the pips squeak'. Xenophobic fury conveniently distracted the electorate's attention from noble (and expensive) ideals of peace and social reconstruction. Churchill wrote in retrospect that the election 'woefully cheapened' Britain[9] – rich comment from the man who built his campaign in Dundee around hysterical references to the Bolshevik menace.

Though it was extremely difficult, in the atmosphere of proud patriotism, for a candidate not supporting the Coalition to succeed, the election must be seen as a victory for Conservatism. Liberals outside the Coalition managed just 28 seats, Labour 63, while the Conservatives won 348. The war had turned the country rightward. Wartime bellicosity harmonised best with the Conservative temper. Thus, though Lloyd George remained Prime Minister of a supposedly national Coalition, his government was in fact an electoral abomination which would not survive the first energetic attempt by Conservatives to assert their authority.

Beyond being a reflection of the previous four years, the election was a harbinger of the future. The three-party pattern of British politics, with Conservatives dominant, Labour ambitious but weak, and Liberals hopelessly distant but not quite dead, had been established. It would take a few elections before contemporaries (especially Liberals) accepted this pattern as inevitable, but, aside from a few anomalies, it would continue until the present day. Labour never achieved a sufficiently broad appeal to kill off the Liberals completely. The beneficiary of this untidy transference of power was the Conservative Party, which profited immensely from a split opposition.[10]

8 Ibid., pp. 188–9.
9 Ibid., p. 178.
10 See D. Tanner, *Political Change and the Labour Party, 1900–1918*, especially pp. 426–42.

Britain became the closest thing to a one-party state; Labour would achieve a majority government only under extraordinary circumstances.

A popular and comfortable assumption holds that the Great War destroyed liberalism. The ideals of individual liberty were supposedly smashed by the exigencies of war, in particular by the ever-expanding state. But, though individual freedom declined, liberalism did not die. Radical liberalism, espoused by John Maynard Keynes and William Beveridge, is one of the success stories of twentieth-century British history. The Liberal Party, not liberalism, was crippled by war. How this happened is a subject too complicated and contentious to cover adequately here. Some Liberals found wartime belligerence (especially that of their one-time hero Lloyd George) too abhorrent. For others, alienation predated the war – they were troubled by the conundrum that further extension of liberty required state intervention (in the form of welfare provision) which by definition restricted individual liberty. Still other Liberals felt too strongly about pacifism, free trade, conscription, or any of their other favourite causes to compromise principles. The war provided too many opportunities for inflexible Liberals to draw a line in the sand. Doctrinal differences were exacerbated by personal rivalries which endured long after the armistice. Thus the party never capitalised on the return to normality after 1918; old antagonisms never healed.

Watching Liberals fight with themselves may have been entertaining, but it did not encourage the confidence of the electorate. Voters deserted the party in droves. One-time Whigs moved toward the Tories, while social democrats opted for Labour. A rump of hardcore ideologues, with free trade as their shibboleth, remained loyal. Thus, the one party genuinely interested in the individual and ideologically committed to social mobility was rendered impotent. Though many of the cudgels of the Liberal Party would be taken up by Labour, individualism was not one of them. Labour's *raison d'être* was the advancement of the working class.

This meant that class conflict was henceforward enshrined in the party system. Post-1918 politics would be dominated by the labour–capital rivalry. But conflict was neither violent nor particularly destructive. The British political system accommodated the working class in a way unknown before the war. The precarious manpower situation during the war had forced the government to deal with trade union representatives on a more equal footing, a change symbolically demonstrated by the inclusion of Labour members in the War Cabinet. Labour's status did not completely evaporate after the war, even though mass unemployment emasculated workers. Capital and labour cooperated in constructing mechanisms for the accommodation of their competing interests, at the expense of the nation as a whole. The historian Elie Halevy, who attended the National Industrial Conference in February 1919, inadvertently recognised this development:

> The National Industrial Conference, far from denying the idea of class struggle, is organized to permit the struggle to go on, in forms as legal and, so to speak, as 'peaceable' as they can be. . . . We shall see the class struggle, acclimatized on English soil, adapting itself to the traditional party system.[11]

The NIC was intended to establish consensus between capital and labour, a very different thing from the accommodation which eventually transpired. Though it failed, Halevy's prediction was essentially accurate: class conflict was institutionalised. During the war, Whitley Councils were a harbinger of this development. The councils grew out of the government's desire to establish joint committees of employers and workers which would meet regularly to discuss wages and conditions, and eventually establish a national bargaining system. In a similar fashion, the 1919 Restoration of Pre-War Practices Act was an enticement to the main body of workers to unify and join the political mainstream. Meanwhile, radical firebrands were marginalised by evidence of a government willing to bargain.[12] This trend of accommodation and consolidation continued during the interwar period with national pay awards, collective bargaining and the creation of corporatist behemoths like the Trades Union Congress and the Federation (later Confederation) of British Industries.[13]

The Labour Party was henceforward accepted, by both labour and capital, as a legitimate mechanism for working class expression. As John Hill of the Boilermakers told the TUC in 1917, 'the prejudice of Trade Unionists against politics has hitherto held us back . . . but the events of the last three years have taken the scales from our eyes'. The best way forward was a 'strong and intelligent Trade Unionism linked with our political arm, the Labour Party'.[14] The change is illustrated by the inclusion of Clause Four – calling for the

11 R. Lowe, 'The Failure of Consensus in Britain: the National Industrial Conference, 1919–1921', *Historical Journal* 21 (1978), p. 650.

12 G. Rubin, 'Law as a Bargaining Weapon: British Labour and the Restoration of Pre-War Practices Act 1919', *Historical Journal* 32 (1989), pp. 926, 940.

13 B. Waites, *A Class Society at War*, p. 30.

14 R. McKibbin, *The Evolution of the Labour Party 1910–1924*, p. 105.

common ownership of the means of production, distribution and exchange – in the 1918 Labour Party constitution. On the surface this seems the first salvo in the new class war. But seen in the light of the party's 1918 manifesto, *Labour and the New Social Order*, which advocated only modest nationalisation, the essentially symbolic nature of Clause Four is revealed. The manifesto was 'a Fabian blueprint for a more advanced, more regulated form of capitalism'.[15] Clause Four thus expressed the newfound solidarity of the working class, but the workers' potentially volatile power was restrained by the limiting context of a party committed to constitutional reform. The 'studiously vague' Clause Four, writes James Hinton, 'was intended as much to contain as to express the ambitions of the Labour Party's rank and file'.[16] The moderate nature of the party is revealed by the marginalisation of the mainly middle class socialists:

> in Britain alone the left wing of the working-class movement did not emerge from the war in some way stronger than it entered it. . . . Were socialists suspect because they were socialist or because they were supposedly not working class? – it is often hard to tell. But in a way the result was the same, and if the war did not necessarily mean the defeat of socialism in Britain, it did mean the defeat of socialists.[17]

Liberalism through the Liberal Party was replaced not by socialism, but by Labourism through the Labour Party. Labourism had much in common with Liberalism, most importantly the desire for improved social welfare, but the importance of the individual had given way to that of the workers as a class.

After 1918, Labour would never be as formidable an opponent for the Tories as the Liberals had been before the war. The Great War helped Labour establish itself as a party, but in terms of its popularity, progress was less impressive. Its electoral support had increased by nearly two million since 1906, but many more constituencies were contested. And, when it is considered that the electorate had more than doubled and trade union membership had increased during the war from four million to six and a half million, Labour's attractiveness to working class voters hardly seems striking. During the interwar period 60 per cent of working class voters consistently refused to support Labour.[18]

Many of the men disfranchised by residency requirements prior

---

15 R. Miliband, *Parliamentary Socialism*, p. 62.
16 J. Hinton, *Labour and Socialism*, p. 103.
17 McKibbin, pp. 105–6.
18 M. Pugh, *The Making of Modern British Politics*, pp. 255–6.

to 1918 did not turn out to be natural Labour supporters. The existing franchise had discriminated against young single men who did not stay long in one dwelling – salesmen, junior managers and the socially mobile. In contrast, the typical Labour supporter tended to be tied to an industry or locale from a very young age.[19] Labour after 1918 drew its support from the same source it had begun to tap before 1914, namely older skilled workers from the industrial areas of the North, Wales and Scotland, most of whom were already organised into trade unions. With the decline of the Liberal Party and the rise in popularity of trade unions, the voters in these areas were more inclined to vote Labour. 'Labour was presented with a half open door and it took the opportunity to obtain a hearing in areas in which hitherto it had had the door slammed in its face', argues Duncan Tanner. 'It became a larger, more significant force than it need have done because of the Liberals' failure and its own ability to duplicate aspects of the Liberal appeal.'[20] But Labour was conspicuously unsuccessful in attracting those one-time Liberal voters in the south-east or in the suburbs who were disinclined to interpret politics in class terms.[21] Thus, at the hour of its emergence, Labour in its cloth cap already looked old-fashioned.

The chief beneficiary of mass democracy was the party most inclined to elitism. The new voters, both young males and women, leaned toward the Conservatives and would continue to do so. It is perhaps understandable that newly enfranchised middle class voters should behave in this way, but one might expect something different from those of working class stock. But as was demonstrated in the previous chapter, increased working class awareness was not automatically translated into support for Labour. Competing loyalties pulled workers in different directions. Thus, the political reper-cussions of the war contradict images of the war as a deluge: the war facilitated the rise to dominance of the party most committed to holding back the flood of social progress. Devotees of the military

19 See D. Tanner, 'The Parliamentary Electoral System, the "Fourth" Reform Act, and the Rise of Labour in England and Wales', *Bulletin of the Institute of Historical Research* 56 (1983), passim.

20 Idem, *Political Change and the Labour Party*, p. 430.

21 See T. Adams, 'Labour and the First World War: Economy, Politics and the Erosion of Local Peculiarity?', *Journal of Regional and Local Studies* 10 (1990), pp. 27ff.; J. Turner, 'The Labour Vote and the Franchise after 1918: An Investigation of the English Evidence', in P. Denley and D. Hopkin, eds, *History and Computing II*, pp. 136–43; M. Hart, 'The Liberals, the War and the Franchise', *English Historical Review* 97 (1982), pp. 820–32.

participation ratio should take note: the Conservatives were the party most responsible for increasing participation during the war and also the group most determined to limit its political and social consequences.[22]

The war diversified political participation. Opportunities were provided for those who had previously found the traditional party system too confining. Milner, Beaverbrook, Amery, Carson, Maclay and the Geddes brothers are the most prominent examples. Yet after the war their sort declined in prominence as politics became dominated by selfishly possessive party machines. An opportunity to give those of independent temperament greater influence was lost when Parliament rejected proportional representation in 1917. Lloyd George's lieutenants (and Lloyd George) were lukewarm toward PR, because it implied a strengthening of legislative power at the expense of the executive. But, given that they were already a minority politically, they would have been among the chief beneficiaries.[23] The rejection of PR sealed the fate of the Liberals and continued Parliament's emasculation at the hands of an increasingly powerful executive. As the *Manchester Guardian* complained: 'In rejecting P.R. a House willing to be weak has refused the remedy that might make it strong.'[24]

WOMEN AND POLITICS

The 1918 Act was followed by the demise of British feminism. This is not surprising, given that the only thing holding feminists together before the war had been the quest for the vote. Once it was granted, activist women splintered into myriad special interest groups. But the majority turned apathetic toward politics, not unlike their male counterparts. At the risk of over-simplification, those women who remained active came in two types. The first, concerned about sexual equality, campaigned for legal reform, equal access, equal pay, the removal of the marriage bar to employment, liberalisation of divorce laws, further electoral reform (the removal of the age bar) and the like. The second type consisted of women for whom war had confirmed the legitimacy of separate spheres. They campaigned for reforms to make the home more comfortable, safe and secure, and to enhance motherhood.

22 See Pugh, *Electoral Reform*, p. 183.
23 Ibid., pp. 183–4.
24 *Manchester Guardian*, 21 June 1917.

This dichotomy was reflected in the split within the National Union of Societies for Equal Citizenship, the successor to the NUWSS. NUSEC was originally established to press for 'all other reforms, economic, legislative and social as are necessary to secure a real equality of liberties, status and opportunities between men and women'.[25] But its leader, Eleanor Rathbone, felt that the 1918 Act had rendered women 'virtually free'. Therefore,

> we can stop looking at all our problems through men's eyes and discussing them in men's phraseology. We can demand what we want for women, not because it is what men have got, but because it is what women need to fulfil the potentialities of their own natures and to adjust themselves to the circumstances of their own lives.

Rathbone specifically sought to enhance 'the occupation of motherhood – in which most women are at some time or another engaged and which no man . . . is capable of performing'. 'Women working are only birds of passage in their trades', she argued. 'Marriage and the bearing and rearing of children are their permanent occupations.'[26] To old feminists this was far too close to the notion of separate spheres, and to the antifeminist argument which gained strength after the war. Yet it is probably safe to say that this was the first time a woman calling herself a feminist articulated a position which the rest of society generally supported.

The showdown within NUSEC came in March 1927. Old feminists, fearing that gender-based protective legislation would give employers an excuse not to hire women, proposed a motion arguing that 'legislation for the protection of workers should be based not upon sex, but upon the nature of the occupation'. Protective legislation, Winifred Holtby argued,

> perpetuates the notion that [women] are not quite persons; that they are not able to look after themselves; to secure their own interests, to judge whether they are fit or unfit to continue employment after marriage, to enter certain trades, or to assume equal responsibility with men in the state. It fosters the popular fallacy that women are the weaker sex, physically and mentally.[27]

Rathbone disagreed. She proposed an amendment which completely destroyed the spirit of the old feminist motion. When it was carried by the narrowest of margins, 81 to 80, NUSEC essentially gave its blessing

---

25 Pugh, *Women and the Women's Movement*, p. 50.

26 S. K. Kent, 'The Politics of Sexual Difference: World War I and the Demise of British Feminism', *Journal of British Studies* 27 (1988), pp. 240–1.

27 Ibid., pp. 243–4.

to any measures designed to discriminate against women in employment. Shortly afterwards, eleven members of the executive resigned, arguing that the decision was 'a betrayal of the women's movement'.[28] Old feminists, by standing still while the rest of Britain moved backwards, found themselves uncomfortably ahead of their time.

Granting votes to women did not highlight women's issues in politics. Women voted not unlike men; gender had little influence upon political allegiance. The absence of a women's party (an attempt by Christabel Pankhurst to form one failed miserably) demonstrates that agreement among women on 'women's issues' was impossible. During the interwar period women interested in politics but not in non-party feminism joined the women's sections of established parties, such as the Women's Labour League and the Primrose League. But this did not lead to their empowerment within the parties, a much slower process. Women were accommodated sufficiently to avoid their complete alienation from politics but were not given significant influence. Female enfranchisement thus reinforced the party machines after 1918, without fundamentally altering the nature of politics and the issues considered important.

RECONSTRUCTION

It fell to the government elected in December 1918 to carry out the reconstruction of British society. According to Peter Cline, early discussions of reconstruction, based on very different circumstances than those which prevailed at the armistice, focused not on social improvement but on national security.[29] Cline cites a number of different postwar scenarios which the government discussed, beginning as early as December 1915. All of these assumed that, given the inconclusive fighting on the Western Front, a complete military defeat of Germany would be impossible. Since an armistice would leave Germany economically strong and able to undersell British and Entente producers in key areas, the Allies would have to carry on the war by other means. Cooperation in protecting import and export markets, and supplies of essential raw materials, might have to continue, even to the extent of continuing the blockade against Germany. The Paris Economic Resolutions, agreed between the Allies in March

---

28 Ibid., p. 243.

29 P. Cline, 'Winding Down the War Economy: British Plans for Peacetime Recovery', in K. Burk, ed., *War and the State*, pp. 157–81.

1916, established just such a programme.[30] But during the last year of the war an even more dismal scenario worried politicians: 'the overriding concern about access to supplies was no longer how to *deny German access . . .* rather, it was how to *ensure British access*'.[31] Britain, it was further assumed, would suffer profound turmoil arising from the problems of reintegrating a huge demobilised army and redundant munitions workers into a peacetime economy ill-equipped to accommodate them. Scarcity of essential commodities, combined with severe economic depression and labour unrest, would create an explosive, potentially revolutionary, situation.[32]

These scenarios and the planned responses to them arose from profound fears of a resurgent Germany. Both the Asquith and Lloyd George governments saw reconstruction primarily in terms of stealing a march on Germany while the great industrial giant lay wounded. This thinking echoed the 'Business as Usual' strategy with which Britain began the war; in other words, since competition with Germany on even terms was difficult, Britain needed to exploit fortuitous opportunities which might arise while Germany was vulnerable. It was further anticipated that, in order to take advantage of these opportunities, the government would have to assume an active role in directing the economy. Reconstruction would not, therefore, permit an immediate return to liberal economics. Tariffs, cartels and the like would protect British markets and access to raw materials. The more dire the scenario, the more comprehensive government intervention would have to be. Under the worst case outlined above, the government anticipated not only trade restrictions, but also constraints upon labour and upon the distribution of goods and services. Wartime rationing and controls would be continued and possibly extended. Shortly after he left the government, Carson warned that 'restrictions hardly less drastic' than those already in force would be essential during peacetime, for 'In no other way can the country hope to escape from the perils of hunger, unemployment, social disorganization, industrial paralysis, and financial chaos.'[33]

The necessity of comprehensive government intervention seemed all the more urgent because of the heavy involvement of the state in the German economy. In other words, state intervention was not accepted as good *per se*, but, since the Germans were doing it, so

30 Ibid., p. 163.
31 Ibid., p. 177.
32 Ibid., p. 160.
33 Ibid., p. 173.

too must the British. Since Lloyd George was more sanguine than Asquith about positive state intervention, he was also more confident about reconstruction. Businessmen and industrialists tagged along because they did not want to be left defenceless against a rampaging German industrial oligarchy. But, for them, government controls remained a necessary evil.

All of these discussions were rendered moot by the manner of Germany's defeat. Her army was beaten, her economy collapsed and her government ruined. The postwar world, with Germany crippled, seemed Britain's oyster. Reconstruction along the lines planned therefore appeared unnecessary. Instead, the focus shifted to creating a better world. This task was first discussed formally by Asquith's Reconstruction Committee. It was continued under Lloyd George, most prominently by Montagu and Addison, the latter heading the Ministry of Reconstruction. The amount of energy expended on the subject from mid-1916 is indeed impressive, but one must be wary of ulterior motives. Promises that reconstruction would be 'not so much a question of rebuilding society as it was before the war, but of moulding a better world out of the social and economic conditions which have come into being during the war'[34] were cleverly calculated to inspire soldiers and workers at a time when the fighting front provided few grounds for hope. While radical Liberals like Montagu, Fisher and Addison occupied themselves in earnest discussion, the government moved steadily to the right – away from the ideals Liberal reconstruction implied.

The great problem with reconstruction was that it meant different things to different people. To the soldiers, it meant compensation for the sacrifices of the war – a fit land for heroes to live in. To the workers reconstruction meant capitalising upon the gains made on the shop floor. They hoped that their enhanced status could be used to make jobs safer, more secure, with pay and conditions improved. In addition, some workers hoped that wartime amalgamation of industries like coal would proceed logically toward nationalisation. But workers were not exclusively progressive: many wanted to turn the clock back to a time when skill implied status.

To radical Coalition Liberals, and indeed to Lloyd George, reconstruction meant sustaining the mood of cooperation which had supposedly existed during the war. Conflict would disappear and with it the rigidity of the class system. The government saw itself as not just a political but also a social coalition. Within Addison's Ministry

34 A. Marwick, *The Deluge*, pp. 279–80.

of Reconstruction, social reform came to mean not only an amelioration of poverty, but the dynamic development of mechanisms designed to ease conflict. The King's Speech which opened the first postwar Parliament set forth this agenda:

> since the outbreak of the war every party and every class have worked and fought together for a great ideal . . . we must continue to manifest the same spirit. We must stop at no sacrifice of interest or prejudice to stamp out unmerited poverty, to diminish unemployment and mitigate its sufferings, to provide decent homes, to improve the nation's health and to raise the standard of well-being throughout the country.[35]

'Lloyd George', according to Kenneth Morgan, 'believed that the war had been a solvent of traditional social barriers: conflict between classes was now as outmoded as conflict between political parties.'[36]

But to the economist Arthur Shadwell, this thinking was hopelessly naive:

> The war was generally expected to lead to a sort of Utopia, in which the lion would lay down with the lamb. . . . There was no substance in this sanguine vision; it was simply a nebulous hope, born of war excitement and fed by politicians' phrases . . . such as the nebulous word 'reconstruction'. I can remember no such prolific begetter of nonsense as this idea of 'reconstruction'.[37]

As was indicated in the previous chapter, Ernest Bevin, like Shadwell, also saw through the misty sentimentality. He denied that any profound change in the relationship between labour and management had occurred and predicted that, with the return to a more competitive peacetime economy, workers' rights would be won only after long and bitter struggle. Bevin and his ilk therefore wanted reconstruction to be about concrete reforms rather than esoteric ideals.

Those of conservative temperament saw reconstruction as a return to a pre-1914 normality. Their vision was clouded by overly romanticised images of the past: a world where workers were content and obedient, where business was conducted free of government interference and where profits were not prey to voracious tax collectors. They argued, with considerable logic, that the war had been about international issues, not domestic ones; Britain had fought to preserve and protect, not to change. While they were clever enough not to attack ideals of a land fit for heroes, they did cast doubt upon the capacity of Britain to afford social improvement. Progressive

35 *Hansard*, 11 February 1919.
36 K. O. Morgan, *Consensus and Disunity*, p. 280.
37 Waites, p. 73.

reforms, they advised, should await the stabilisation of Britain's economy and the re-establishment of trade. Groups like the Anti-Waste League warned that a rapacious and uncontrollable 'spendocrat' bureaucracy would destroy fragile prosperity. Dire scenarios of big government running rampant struck a popular chord even among those who supported humanitarian ideals of reconstruction. The war years had left both capital and labour deeply suspicious of government power. A Ministry of Labour official complained as early as 1918 that 'Everybody – employers and workers alike – are saying they don't want the State to act, they want the State to keep out and let them handle their own problems.'[38] 'The major actors', writes John Turner, 'were convinced . . . that it would be better to be left alone, to fight the class war, or negotiate its end.'[39]

Fears of big government and high taxes eventually overwhelmed reconstruction sentiment. In a seminal article published in 1943, R. H. Tawney explained that reconstruction faltered because the instinct to de-control overwhelmed amorphous and disparate desires to create a better world. Governmental controls were easily abolished because intervention had always been ad hoc and temporary. During the war,

> a collectivism was established which was entirely doctrineless. The most extensive and intricate scheme of state intervention in economic life which the country had seen was brought into existence, without the merits or demerits of state intervention being even discussed.[40]

But Cline disagrees:

> The defeat of the 'British revolution' of social and economic reconstruction was only secondarily the result of the reassertion of orthodox economic thinking in 1919: the primary cause was the unexpected collapse of Germany [which] . . . removed the politically strongest, least vulnerable, justification for . . . state-initiated economic development.[41]

Cline's insistence upon primary and secondary causes is unnecessarily pedantic. There is room for both arguments. State intervention did contradict Britain's instincts, as Tawney contended. Only under the most extraordinary circumstances (war or imminent peacetime economic collapse) would she consider going against her instincts. And

---

38 R. Lowe, 'The Erosion of State Intervention in Britain, 1917–24', *Economic History Review* 31 (1978), p. 286.

39 J. Turner, *British Politics and the Great War*, p. 389.

40 R. H. Tawney, 'The Abolition of Economic Controls, 1918–1921', *Economic History Review* 13 (1943), p. 7.

41 Cline, 'Winding Down the War Economy', p. 159.

Once the war was over, what had been a source of strength became a weakness. War collectivism had not been accompanied by any intellectual conversion on the subject of the proper relations between the state and economic life, while it did not last long enough to change social habits. With the passing, therefore, of the crisis that occasioned it, it was exposed to the attack of the same interests and ideas as, but for the war, would have prevented its establishment.[42]

The acts which established the big wartime interventionist ministries like those of food and munitions all had specific deadlines for disbandment, usually one year after the cessation of hostilities. Rolling back the state was therefore a passive act which consisted of letting deadlines run.

The government had two choices: it could manage the postwar recovery by continuing and perhaps extending controls, or it could let an inflationary boom set the pace and determine the character of the transition to a peacetime economy. Since powerful capitalists demanded their freedom and workers (particularly those marooned in a now redundant army) were impatient to return to old jobs and old patterns of spending, the second option had a certain inevitability and the first option was not really an option at all. It was left to the advocates of state control to demonstrate its continued necessity. Given that the war had not established an ideological shift on the subject of intervention, there were few so inclined. Since the government had committed itself to a restoration of pre-war labour practices, fairness (and instinct) suggested that restrictions upon the management of capital should also be relaxed.

Here Cline's argument is especially germane. It was easy to assume that the more profound Germany's defeat, the more promising Britain's postwar economic fortunes would be. The immediate aftermath of war seemed to bear out these optimistic predictions. Consumer demand, held in check for over four years, burst forth, producing an impressive demand for British goods and, consequently, healthy industrial employment. But in its overwhelming and irrational desire to get the economy moving again, the government threw caution to the wind. It held all too much faith in the idea that wartime domestic harmony would inspire capital and labour to cooperate in the construction of a better world. In fact, left alone, labour and capital acted like two snakes trying to swallow each other: the workers demanded rewards which the system was not strong enough to provide and industrialists feverishly pursued specu-

---

42 Tawney, 'The Abolition of Economic Controls', p. 7.

lative profits which seriously jeopardised economic stability. The government, through its rhetoric, encouraged both of these attitudes and refused to employ the fiscal mechanisms at its disposal to promote restraint and to force economic adversaries to work together.[43]

Nor did the government provide a very good example of fiscal prudence. 'I think you have to consider this year [1919] as really almost a war condition year', Lloyd George told his Chancellor, Austen Chamberlain.[44] Sir Eric Geddes, Minister of Transport in the new government, lent his weight to efforts to ease the fears of the cautious Chancellor:

> You must be prepared to spend money on after-the-war problems as you did during the during-the-war problems. That must be found, and added to our war-debt if necessary. It is the period of reconstruction, and money has to be spent generously, and on those [social welfare] schemes. If we get over that period I think the trade of the country will revive.[45]

The result was inevitable inflation, to which the government reacted first with prevarication, then with panic. Boom quickly turned into bust. Unemployment, which stood at just 3.1 per cent in late 1920, rocketed to 13.5 per cent in the following year. For the next twenty years, the number of unemployed did not drop below one million.

The sudden recession seemed to justify the fears of those who had urged restraint. Reconstruction suddenly seemed unaffordable – at the very time when it was most needed. Hysterical rantings about squandermania in the Northcliffe and Rothermere press, pressure from the Anti-Waste League, by-election defeats in the Coalition heartland and demands from within his own government for tax cuts convinced Lloyd George to set up a committee under Eric Geddes to execute sweeping budgetary cuts. Against this onslaught, embattled radicals were unable or unwilling to provide a coherent defence of social welfare programmes. Geddes proposed economies of £87 million which drove a bulldozer through the already shaky reconstruction edifice. Social spending, it was suggested, should fall by £24 million, which included £18 million off the education budget.[46] But, argues Andrew McDonald,

---

43 J. Dowie, '1919–20 is in Need of Attention', *Economic History Review* 28 (1975), p. 447.

44 P. Cline, 'Reopening the Case of the Lloyd George Coalition and the post-War Economic Transition, 1918–19', *Journal of British Studies* 10 (1970), p. 167.

45 Ibid., p. 169.

46 Morgan, pp. 289–90, 293. In the end, education cuts totalled £6.5 million.

the most important element in the committee's reports was not the schedule of cuts . . . but rather it was the manner in which they went beyond those cuts to raise questions about the future activities and role of the state. Implicit in their repeated comparisons with the position of the state in 1914 was an assumption that in most respects the scope and character of the pre-war state were adequate to the nation's needs and that nothing had happened since then to diminish that adequacy.[47]

The government responded to recession by taking refuge in orthodox economics, never mindful that the accepted orthodoxy pertained to a pre-war context of relative abundance. In contrast, after 1920 the world suffered from severe *scarcity* of goods, raw materials and services. The government was nevertheless confident that producers would be able on their own to lead the country back to abundance, through the miracle of the free market. Government control had become, in the words of one minister, 'a thoroughly abominable thing'.[48] Normal practices, it was confidently assumed, would restore normality.

Intervention would not have enabled the government to avoid the slump, which was a worldwide phenomenon. But, whether one trusts in state intervention or not, it is impossible to deny that immediate de-control was foolhardy. The war had resulted in comprehensive changes in the British economy. In November 1918 factories were operating at full capacity in controlled markets producing goods which often had no peacetime utility. It required extraordinary temerity to believe that producers could automatically shift to domestic production and adjust smoothly to the return of unbridled competition without government help. British producers were blithely set loose on a world economy ravaged by war. In no time at all many were mown down by the machine-guns of reckless competition or left to drown in shellholes of stagnation. Or, to borrow Tawney's metaphor:

The patient required to be nursed through a long period of convalescence, and could not be expected, even at the end of this, to lead the same life as before the operation. [The government] thought it sufficient, having removed his bandages, to exhort him to take up his bed and walk.[49]

47 A. McDonald, 'The Geddes Committee and the Formulation of Public Expenditure Policy, 1921–1922', *Historical Journal* 32 (1989), p. 664.
48 Tawney, 'The Abolition of Economic Controls', p. 17.
49 Ibid, p. 27.

To thrive in the conditions which prevailed after 1918 necessitated sustained economic management. The increasing complexity of world markets required a government prepared to act as overseer. As Cline points out, even by 1920 the government still exercised control over important commodities and still supervised industries like the mines, shipping, railways and banking. It would thus have been possible to provide significant direction to the economy. 'Parliament never lost the power to control production, allocation and prices; what it did lose was the will to use that power.'[50] To leave the economic direction to thousands of independent producers all tugging in different directions was to invite chaos, waste, inefficiency and eventual suffering.

Reconstruction presented the last opportunity for establishing consensus in Britain and avoiding the cul-de-sac of class conflict. It might have weaned both workers and industrialists from their purely sectional interests and encouraged them to think in terms of national progress. But the drive for economy after 1920, with its potent symbol of the Geddes axe, destroyed that opportunity. By its policies and its budgetary priorities, a government supposedly committed to social unity made class divisions deeper and antagonism more profound. Morgan argues that reconstruction 'ran aground for reasons that really would have defeated any government'. Up to 1921, he contends, real progress was made.

> For two years [the government] made unemployment and structural poverty more bearable, strong and interventionist government more acceptable, [while] it tried to create an image of social concern and communal involvement.[51]

Granted, the coalition has received a great deal more criticism than it perhaps deserves.[52] But the real problem with reconstruction lay in its ideals. It aimed to create social harmony instead of an efficient society. As we saw in the previous chapter, housing and education reforms were not designed to destroy class barriers but rather to make them more tolerable. Judged according to this standard, reconstruction was an impressive success. Despite the ravages of the Geddes axe, enough survived of social welfare programmes to cushion the workers from the worst ravages of the slump. Thus, it could be argued, Britain avoided the turmoil which occurred on the continent. But, as has been the case throughout the twentieth century,

50 Cline, 'Reopening the Case', pp. 172–3.

51 Morgan, pp. 107–8.

52 As, for instance, in the Tawney article and in P. Abrams, 'The Failure of Social Reform: 1918–1920', *Past and Present* 24 (1963), pp. 43–64.

social legislation during the reconstruction period was ameliorative rather than preventative. Social programmes provided relief for society's dispossessed, but did not attempt to solve the core problems of long term decline. Morgan argues that reconstruction was the casualty of Britain's 'external financial predicament'.[53] That may be true, but one struggles to find politicians with the courage, imagination and foresight to address that predicament. In 1917 Lloyd George told a delegation of labour leaders that 'the whole state of society is more or less molten and you can stamp upon that molten mass almost anything so long as you do it with firmness and determination'.[54] For various reasons, he failed to act upon his own rhetoric.

Argument rages regarding the war's long term effect upon the British economy. Some historians believe that it merely magnified already inevitable trends, others that definite shifts in economic direction are discernible. Those who favour the second view disagree whether the balance sheet of good changes versus bad leaves profit or loss. There were undoubtedly some positive effects. Necessity forced Britain to develop more efficient industrial techniques which had productive peacetime applications. For instance, dyestuff production (in which Germany had enjoyed a near monopoly) received massive stimulation, rendering Britain much more competitive after the war. Likewise the aircraft, motor, chemical and food preservation industries, to name but a few, made significant progress.

On the debit side, the coal industry suffered badly from the loss of skilled labour and the exhaustion of valuable seams but, more importantly, from the collapse of the world market for British coal after the war. The same could be said for shipbuilding and cotton. Seemingly secure markets in Asia and South America were absorbed by Britain's competitors while she was preoccupied with war. These were never completely recovered. One suspects, however, that this decline was inevitable and was merely hastened by war. Even more profound was the change in Britain's financial position. She entered the war a creditor nation and exited a debtor. Her supreme position at the top of the world financial markets was surrendered permanently to the United States. In order to pay for the necessities of war and to supply these to her allies, Britain had to sell 25 per cent of her overseas foreign investments.[55] She also borrowed at a prodigious rate. Loans of more than £1,350 million accumulated, over £1,000

---

53 Morgan, p. 108.
54 Lowe, 'The Erosion of State Intervention in Britain', p. 270.
55 G. Hardach, *The First World War 1914–18*, p. 290.

million from the United States. A greater amount (£1,750 million) was loaned to allies, but afterwards Britain was more faithful in her repayments than her debtors were in theirs. Money loaned to Russia was, for instance, unrecoverable.[56]

From a position of pre-eminence before 1914, Britain in the subsequent three-quarters of a century has been surpassed by countries once considered minnows in the world economy. None of this was inevitable, but rather resulted from consistently poor (or absent) economic management. It would require an obsessive belief in the sanctity of the free market to maintain that the interwar slump saw too much intervention rather than not enough. Nor can British decline be blamed on the unfortunate effects of war, since countries more ravaged by war subsequently performed better. In fact, Britain's decline began well before the Great War, which seems to underline the folly of attempting a return to pre-war practices. Before 1914, Britain's export trade was still concentrated on patterns and products developed in the eighteenth and nineteenth centuries. 'She had sidestepped increasing competition on the Continent by having recourse to overseas markets; instead of looking for new products for her old markets, she had sought new markets for her old products.'[57] Britain's once great lead over her economic rivals had encouraged complacency and conservatism. After the war, the long-delayed readjustment of the economy suddenly became urgent.

But, as has been seen, readjustment was not embraced with the energy and commitment clearly required. After 1918 the British were remarkably successful at re-creating pre-war society. Social and political change was absorbed or contained. The quality of life improved, but class stratification was not measurably eroded. If it is in the power of governments to assist social mobility, the British government failed. Ambitious housing, health and education programmes, cautious politicians argued, jeopardised economic recovery. Yet in conditions of economic decline, Britain could hardly afford *not* to address the problem of social stasis. The pre-1914 working class, in its deference, lack of imagination, fatalism and lack of ambition was ideally suited to the type of war Britain had been called upon to fight. But recovery in the harsh conditions which prevailed after 1918 required a wholly different society in which a dynamic, educated and ambitious work force was free to pursue its full potential. During discussion of Geddes's proposals for education cuts, Lloyd George

56 Wilson, p. 792.
57 Hardach, p. 288.

332

had the audacity to argue that 'brighter children would learn as readily and as quickly in a class of seventy as they would in a much smaller class'.[58] That sort of complacency was costly; Britain could no longer afford to allow skills to go untapped because of the obstruction of class barriers or the fear of spending money on genuine social improvement. Stability and social harmony were expensive luxuries bought at the cost of growth and prosperity.

It would be easy to blame the Conservative Party for the stagnation which has prevailed since 1918. After all, the period of sustained decline has also been one of extraordinary domination by the Tories. Yet governments are not alien beings which appear from nowhere and inflict their will upon a defenceless people. Britain is a democracy. If her people have at times failed to act democratically, that is their fault. There is remarkable similarity between the way the country supported the war from 1914 to 1918 and the way it has supported the Conservatives since. Similar emotions seem at play. Nationalism, traditionalism and an enduring sense of cultural superiority saw the British through the war and have since encouraged an acquiescence in their own decline.

---

[58] Morgan, p. 292.

BIBLIOGRAPHY

BOOKS

(Place of publication is London unless otherwise stated. Dates of publication are for the edition used in the preparation of this work.)

Adams, R. J. Q., *Arms and the Wizard*, 1978
Adams, R. J. Q. and Poirer, P., *The Conscription Controversy*, 1987
Aldington, Richard, *Death of a Hero*, 1984
Andreski, Stefan, *Military Organization and Society*, 1968
Angell, Norman (Ralf Lane), *The Great Illusion*, 1909
Balfour, F., *Elsie Inglis*, 1918
Barker, Pat, *The Eye in the Door*, Harmondsworth, 1994
Barnett, L. M., *British Food Policy During the First World War*, 1985
Barr, Niall, 'Service not Self: The British Legion 1921–1939', unpublished Ph.D. thesis, St Andrews, 1994
Beckett, Ian and Simpson, Keith, eds, *A Nation in Arms*, Manchester, 1985
Bennett, Arnold, *Journal 1896–1926*, Oxford, 1954
Beveridge, William, *British Food Control*, Oxford, 1928
Bond, Brian, *The Victorian Army and the Staff College*, 1972
Boston, Sarah, *Women Workers and the Trade Unions*, 1980
Bourne, J. M., *Britain and the Great War, 1914–1918*, 1989
Bourne, Kenneth, *The Foreign Policy of Victorian England*, Oxford, 1970
Bowley, M., *Housing and the State 1919–1941*, 1945
Bradley, M. J. and Simon, B., eds, *The Victorian Public School*, 1975
Braybon, Gail, *Women Workers in the First World War*, 1981
Braybon, Gail and Summerfield, Penny, *Out of the Cage: Women's Experiences in Two World Wars*, 1987
Brittain, Vera, *Chronicle of Youth: War Diary 1913–1917*, 1981
Brittain, Vera, *Testament of Experience*, 1980
Brittain, Vera, *Testament of Youth*, 1944
Buitenhuis, Peter, *The Great War of Words*, 1989
Burk, Kathleen, ed., *War and the State*, 1982
Burnett, J., *A Social History of Housing 1815–1970*, 1978
Carrington, C. E., *Soldier from the Wars Returning*, 1945
Carsten, F. L., *War Against War*, 1982
Chapman, Guy, *A Passionate Prodigality*, 1933

Chapman, Guy, ed., *Vain Glory*, 1937
Churchill, Randolph, *Lord Derby: King of Lancashire*, 1959
Clegg, H., *The System of Industrial Relations in Britain*, Oxford, 1956
Clegg, H., Fox, A. and Thompson, A. F., *A History of British Trade Unions Since 1889*, Oxford, 1985
Cole, G. D. H., *Labour in War Time*, 1915
Cole, G. D. H., *Trade Unionism and Munitions*, 1923
Cole, G. D. H., *Workshop Organization*, 1923
Constantine, Stephen, ed., *The First World War in British History*, 1995
Cook, Chris and Stevenson, John, *The Longman Handbook of Modern British History 1714–1980*, 1983
Coppard, George, *With a Machine Gun to Cambrai*, 1969
Cosens, Monica, *Lloyd George's Munitions Girls*, 1916
Cross, Tim, ed., *The Lost Voices of World War I*, 1988
Dakers, Caroline, *The Countryside at War*, 1987
Dallas, Gloden and Gill, Douglas, *The Unknown Army*, 1985
DeGroot, Gerard, *Douglas Haig, 1861–1928*, 1988.
DeGroot, Gerard, *Liberal Crusader: The Life of Sir Archibald Sinclair*, 1993
Denley, P. and Hopkin, D, eds, *History and Computing II*, Manchester, 1989
Dilks, David, *Neville Chamberlain*, Cambridge, 1984
Drake, Barbara, *Women in the Engineering Trade*, 1915
Dutton, David, *Austen Chamberlain, Gentleman in Politics*, Bolton, 1985
Eksteins, Modris, *Rites of Spring*, New York, 1989
Ellis, John, *Eye-Deep in Hell*, 1976
Fawcett, Millicent, *What I Remember*, 1925
Fawcett, Millicent, *The Women's Victory – And After: Personal Reminiscences, 1911–1918*, 1920
Ford, F. M., *Parade's End*, New York, 1950
French, David, *British Economic and Strategic Planning, 1905–1915*, 1982
French, David, *British Strategy and War Aims, 1914–1916*, 1986
Fussell, Paul, *The Great War and Modern Memory*, New York, 1977
Garvin, J. L., *The Life of Joseph Chamberlain*, 1932
Gauldie, Enid, *Cruel Habitations*, 1974
Gibbs, Phillip, *Now It Can Be Told*, New York, 1920
Gleason, Arthur, *What the Workers Want*, 1920
Graham, John, *Conscription and Conscience*, New York, 1969
Graves, Robert, *Goodbye to All That*, New York, 1929
Gregory, Adrian, *The Silence of Memory*, Oxford, 1994
Grey, Sir Edward, *Twenty-Five Years, 1893–1916*, 1925
Grieves, Keith, *The Politics of Manpower, 1914–1918*, Manchester, 1988
Guinn, Paul, *British Strategy and Politics 1914 to 1918*, Oxford, 1965
Haldane, R. B., *Autobiography*, 1929
Haldane, R. B., *Before the War*, 1927
Halsey, A. H., *Trends in British Society Since 1900*, 1972
Hamilton, Mary Agnes, *Dead Yesterday*, 1916

Hamilton, Mary Agnes, *Our Freedom*, 1922
Hankey, Maurice, *The Supreme Command, 1914–1918*, 1961
Hardach, Gerd, *The First World War 1914–1918*, Harmondsworth, 1987
Harries-Jenkins, Gwyn, *The Army in Victorian Society*, 1977
Harrison, Jane, *Alpha and Omega*, 1915
Haste, Cate, *Keep the Home Fires Burning*, 1977
Henty, G. A., *With Kitchener in the Soudan*, 1903
Hinton, James, *The First Shop Stewards' Movement*, 1973
Hinton, James, *Labour and Socialism*, Brighton, 1983
Hinton, James, *Protests and Visions*, 1989
History of the Ministry of Munitions, HMSO 8 vols (1921–22).
Holmes, Richard, *Firing Line*, Harmondsworth, 1987
Horn, Pamela, *Rural Life in England in the First World War*, Dublin, 1984
Howard, Michael, *The Continental Commitment*, 1972
Howard, Michael, ed., *Soldiers and Governments*, 1957
Howard, Michael, *Studies in War and Peace*, 1970
Hunt, Barry and Preston, Adrian, ed., *War Aims and Strategic Policy in the Great War 1914–1918*, 1977
Hyman, A., *The Rise and Fall of Horatio Bottomley*, 1972
Hynes, S., *A War Imagined*, New York, 1990
James, Robert Rhodes, *Rosebery*, 1963
Jameson, M. Storm, *No Time Like the Present*, 1933
Janowitz, Maurice, *The Professional Soldier*, New York, 1960
Jenkins, Roy, *Asquith*, 1964
Johnston, Paul Barton, *Land Fit for Heroes*, Chicago, 1968
Jones, Helen, *Health and Society in Twentieth-Century Britain*, 1994
Keegan, John, *The Face of Battle*, Harmondsworth, 1976
Kendall, W., *The Revolutionary Movement in Great Britain*, 1969
Kennedy, Paul, *The Realities Behind Diplomacy*, 1981
Kennedy, Paul, ed., *The War Plans of the Great Powers*, 1979
Koss, Stephen, *The Rise and Fall of the Political Press*, 1984
Laslett, Peter, *The World We Have Lost*, 1971
Lasswell, Harold, *Propaganda Technique in the World War*, 1938
Lauder, Harry, *Roamin' in the Gloamin'*, 1928
Lewis, Jane, *The Politics of Motherhood*, 1980
Liddle, Peter, ed., *Home Fires and Foreign Fields*, 1985
Lloyd, E. M. H., *Experiments in State Control*, Oxford, 1924
Lloyd George, David, *War Memoirs*, 1938
McFeely, Mary Drake, *Lady Inspectors*, Oxford, 1988
McKibbin, Ross, *The Evolution of the Labour Party 1910–1924*, Oxford, 1973
McLean, Iain, *The Legend of Red Clydeside*, Edinburgh, 1983
Magnus, Phillip, *Kitchener: Portrait of an Imperialist*, Harmondsworth, 1958

Mangan, J. A., *Athleticism in the Victorian and Edwardian Public School*, 1981

Mangan, J. A. and Walvin, James, eds, *Manliness and Morality*, Manchester, 1987

Marwick, Arthur, *The Deluge* (2nd edn), 1991

Marwick, Arthur, *The Explosion of British Society 1914–62*, 1963

Marwick, Arthur, *Women at War*, 1977

Masterman, C. F. G., *England After the War*, 1922

Masterman, Lucy, *C. F. G. Masterman*, 1939

Messinger, G. S., *Propaganda and the State in the First World War*, Manchester, 1992

Middlemas, R. K., *The Clydesiders*, 1965

Middlemas, R. K., *Politics in Industrial Society*, 1979

Miliband, Ralph, *Parliamentary Socialism*, 1972

Milward, A. S., *The Economic Effects of the Two World Wars Upon Britain*, 1970

Mitchell, David, *Women on the Warpath*, 1966

Montague, C. E., *Disenchantment*, 1968

Morgan, K. O., *Consensus and Disunity*, Oxford, 1979

Morgan, K. O., *Lloyd George*, 1974

Mosley, Nicholas, *Rules of the Game*, 1983

Mosse, G., *Fallen Soldiers*, Oxford, 1990

Mowat, C. L., *Britain Between the Wars*, 1968

Newbolt, Henry, *Naval Operations (Official History of the Great War)*, 1931

Newbolt, Henry, *Poems New and Old*, 1912

Newsome, David, *Godliness and Good Learning*, 1961

Oxford and Asquith, Lord, *Memories and Reflections*, 1928

Oxford Dictionary of Quotations, The, 3rd edn, Oxford, 1979

Pakenham, Thomas, *The Boer War*, 1982

Panayi, Panikos, *The Enemy in Our Midst*, Oxford, 1991

Panichas, G. A., ed., *Promise of Greatness*, 1968

Pankhurst, Sylvia, *The Home Front*, 1987

Parker, P., *The Old Lie: The Great War and the Public School Ethos*, 1987

Pearce, R., *Britain: Industrial Relations and the Economy 1900–39*, 1993

Peel, C. S., *How We Lived Then*, 1929

Phelps Brown, Henry, *The Origins of Trade Union Power*, Oxford, 1986

Playne, Caroline, *The Pre-War Mind in Britain*, 1928

Ponsonby, Arthur, *Falsehood in War-Time*, 1928

Porter, Bernard, *The Lion's Share*, 1975

Pugh, Martin, *Electoral Reform in War and Peace*, 1978

Pugh, Martin, *The Making of Modern British Politics*, Oxford, 1982

Pugh, Martin, *Women and the Women's Movement in Britain, 1914–1959*, 1992

Rae, John, *Conscience and Politics*, Oxford, 1970

Reader, W. J., *At Duty's Call*, Manchester, 1988

Reilly, Catherine, ed., *Scars Upon My Heart: Women's Poetry and Verse of the First World War*, 1981.

Reiss, R., *The Home I Want*, 1918

Repington, C. a'Court, *The First World War 1914–1918*, 1920

Robertson, William, *From Private to Field Marshal*, 1921

Royle, Trevor., *The Kitchener Enigma*, 1985

Rubin, G. R., *War, Law and Labour*, Oxford, 1987

Sanders, Michael and Taylor, Phillip, *British Propaganda during the First World War*, 1982

Sassoon, Siegfried, *Collected Poems*, 1947

Sassoon, Siegfried, *Memoirs of an Infantry Officer*, 1930

Sassoon, Siegfried, *Sherston's Progress*, 1936

Silkin, Jon, ed., *The Penguin Book of First World War Poetry*, Harmondsworth, 1979

Silkin, Jon, ed., *The Penguin Book of First World War Prose*, Harmondsworth, 1990

Sillars, S., *Art and Survival in First World War Britain*, New York, 1987

Simkins, Peter, *Kitchener's Army*, Manchester, 1988

Sitwell, Osbert, *Laughter in the Next Room*, 1949

Smith, Harold, ed., *British Feminism in the Twentieth Century*, 1990

Spiers, Edward, *Haldane, An Army Reformer*, Edinburgh, 1980

Stapledon, O., *Last Men in London*, 1963

Steiner, Zara, *Britain and the Origins of the First World War*, 1986

Stevenson, John, *British Society 1914–45*, Harmondsworth, 1984

Strachey, Ray, *The Cause*, 1928

Summers, Anne, *Angels and Citizens: British Women as Military Nurses*, 1988

Swartz, M., *The Union of Democratic Control in British Politics During the First World War*, Oxford, 1971

Swenarton, M., *Homes Fit for Heroes*, 1981

Tanner, Duncan, *Political Change and the Labour Party, 1900–1918*, Cambridge, 1990

Taylor, A. J. P., *English History 1914–1945*, Harmondsworth, 1965

Taylor, A. J. P., ed., *Lloyd George: A Diary by Frances Stevenson*, 1971

Terraine, John, *The Smoke and the Fire*, 1980

Thorpe, Andrew, *The Longman Companion to Britain in the Era of the Two World Wars*, 1994

Travers, T. H. E., *The Killing Ground*, 1987

Turner, John, *British Politics and the Great War*, New Haven, Connecticut, 1992

Turner, John, ed., *Britain and the First World War*, 1988

Tylee, C., *The Great War and Women's Consciousness*, Basingstoke, 1990

Vachell, H. A., *The Hill*, 1905

Vansittart, Peter, *Voices from the Great War*, 1981
Vaughan, E. C., *Some Desperate Glory*, 1981
Waites, Bernard, *A Class Society at War*, Leamington Spa, 1987
Wallace, Stuart, *War and the Image of Germany*, Edinburgh, 1988
Wall, R. and Winter, J. M., eds, *The Upheaval of War*, Cambridge, 1988
Walvin, James, *Leisure and Society 1830–1950*, 1978
Waugh, Alec, *The Loom of Youth*, 1929
Wavell, Archibald, *Soldiers and Soldiering*, 1953
Webb, Sydney, *The Restoration of Trade Union Conditions*, 1918
Weeks, Jeremy, *Sex, Politics and Society*, 1989
Weintraub, S., *A Stillness Heard Round the World*, New York, 1985
Wilkinson, Alan, *The Church of England and the First World War*, 1978
Wilkinson, Rupert, *The Prefects*, Oxford, 1964
Wilson, Keith, ed. *Empire and Continent*, 1987
Wilson, Keith, *The Policy of the Entente*, Cambridge, 1985
Wilson, Trevor, *The Myriad Faces of War*, Cambridge, 1988
Wilson, Trevor, ed., *The Political Diaries of C. P. Scott*, 1970
Wiltsher, Anne, *Most Dangerous Women*, 1985
Winter, Denis, *Death's Men*, Harmondsworth, 1979
Winter, J. M., *The Great War and the British People*, 1985
Winter, J. M., ed., *War and Economic Development*, Cambridge, 1975
Wolfe, Humbert, *Labour Supply and Regulation*, Oxford, 1923
Woodward, David, *Lloyd George and the Generals*, 1983
Woodward, E. L., *Great Britain and the War of 1914–1918*, 1967
Wrigley, C., *David Lloyd George and the British Labour Movement*, Hassocks, Sussex, 1976
Wrigley, C., *Lloyd George and the Challenge of Labour*, Hemel Hempstead, 1990
Wrigley, C., ed., *Warfare, Diplomacy and Politics: Essays in Honour of A. J. P. Taylor*, 1986
Younghusband, George John, *A Soldier's Memories*, 1917

ARTICLES

Abrams, Phillip, 'The Failure of Social Reform: 1918–1920', *Past and Present* 24 (1963)
Adams, R. J. Q., 'Asquith's Choice: the May Coalition and the Coming of Conscription, 1915–1916', *Journal of British Studies* 25 (1986)
Adams, Tony, 'Labour and the First World War: Economy, Politics and the Erosion of Local Peculiarity?', *Journal of Regional and Local Studies* 10 (1990)
Bond, Brian, 'The Late Victorian Army', *History Today* 11 (1961)
Boswell, J. and Johns, B., 'Patriots or Profiteers? British Businessmen and the First World War', *Journal of European Economic History* 11 (1982)
Brodick, George, 'A Nation of Amateurs', *The Nineteenth Century* 48 (1900)

Bryder, L., 'The First World War: Healthy or Hungry?', *History Workshop Journal* 24 (1987)

Cline, Peter, 'Reopening the Case of the Lloyd George Coalition and the post-War Economic Transition, 1918–19', *Journal of British Studies* 10 (1970)

Davidson, Roger, 'The Myth of the "Servile State"', *Bulletin of the Society for the Study of Labour History* 29 (1974)

DeGroot, Gerard, 'Educated Soldier or Cavalry Officer?: Contradictions in the pre-1914 Career of Douglas Haig', *War and Society* 4 (1986)

Demm, E., 'Propaganda and Caricature in the First World War', *Journal of Contemporary History* 28 (1993)

Dewey, P. E., 'Agricultural Labour Supply in England and Wales during the First World War', *Economic History Review* 28 (1975)

Dewey, P. E., 'British Farming Profits and Government Policy During the First World War', *Economic History Review* 37 (1984)

Dewey, P. E., 'Food Production and Policy in the United Kingdom, 1914–1918', *Transactions of the Royal Historical Society*, Fifth Series, 30 (1980)

Dewey, P. E., 'Military Recruiting and the British Labour Force During the First World War', *Historical Journal* 27 (1984)

Douglas, Roy, 'The National Democratic Party and the British Workers' League', *Historical Journal* 15 (1972)

Douglas, Roy, 'Voluntary Enlistment in the First World War and the Work of the Parliamentary Recruiting Committee', *Journal of Modern History* 42 (1970)

Dowie, J., '1919–20 is in Need of Attention', *Economic History Review* 28 (1975)

Doyle, Barry, 'Who Paid the Price of Patriotism? The Funding of Charles Stanton during the Merthyr Boroughs By-Election of 1915', *English Historical Review* 109 (1994)

Englander, D. and Osborne, J., 'Jack, Tommy and Henry Dubb: The Armed Forces and the Working Class', *Historical Journal* 21 (1978)

Fraser, P., 'British War Policy and the Crisis of Liberalism in May 1915', *Journal of Modern History* 54 (1982)

French, David, 'The Meaning of Attrition', *English Historical Review* 103 (1988)

French, David, 'Spy Fever in Britain, 1900–1915', *Historical Journal* 21 (1978)

Fry, M., 'Political Change in Britain, August 1914 to December 1916: Lloyd George Replaces Asquith: The Issues Underlying the Drama', *Historical Journal* 31 (1988)

Gilbert, Bentley B., 'Pacifist to Interventionist: David Lloyd George in 1911 and 1914. Was Belgium an Issue?', *Historical Journal* 28 (1985)

Gill, Douglas and Dallas, Gloden, 'Mutiny at Etaples Base in 1917', *Past and Present* 69 (1975)

Gordon, M., 'Domestic Conflict and the Origins of the First World War: The British and the German Cases', *Journal of Modern History* 46 (1974).

Graubard, S. R., 'Military Demobilization in Great Britain Following the First World War', *Journal of Modern History* 19 (1947)

Harris, Bernard, 'The Demographic Impact of the First World War: An Anthropometric Perspective', *Journal of the Society for the Social History of Medicine* 6 (1993)

Hart, Michael, 'The Liberals, the War and the Franchise', *English Historical Review* 97 (1982)

Hazlehurst, Cameron, 'Asquith as Prime Minister, 1908–1916', *English Historical Review* 85 (1970)

Hiley, N., 'The Failure of British Counter-Espionage Against Germany, 1907–1914', *Historical Journal* 28 (1985)

Hiley, N., ' "Lord Kitchener Resigns": The Suppression of the *Globe* in 1915', *Journal of Newspaper and Periodical History* 8 (1992)

Horne, John and Kramer, Alan, 'German "Atrocities" and Franco-German Opinion, 1914: The Evidence of German Soldiers' Diaries', *Journal of Modern History* 66 (1994)

Kent, Susan Kingsley, 'The Politics of Sexual Difference: World War I and the Demise of British Feminism', *Journal of British Studies* 27 (1988)

Koven, Seth, 'Remembering and Dismemberment: Crippled Children, Wounded Soldiers, and the Great War in Britain', *American Historical Review* 99 (1994)

Koven, Seth and Michel, Sonya, 'Womanly Duties: Maternalist Politics and the Origins of Welfare States in France, Germany, Great Britain and the United States, 1880–1920', *American Historical Review* 95 (1990)

Levine, Philippa, ' "Walking the Streets in a Way No Decent Woman Should": Women Police in World War I', *Journal of Modern History* 66 (1994)

Loudon, I., 'Deaths in Childbed from the Eighteenth Century to 1935', *Medical History* 30 (1986)

Low, S., 'The Future of the Great Armies', *The Nineteenth Century* 47 (1899)

Lowe, Rodney, 'The Erosion of State Intervention in Britain, 1917–24', *Economic History Review* 31 (1978)

Lowe, Rodney, 'The Failure of Consensus in Britain: the National Industrial Conference, 1919–1921', *Historical Journal* 21 (1978)

McDermott, J., ' "A Needless Sacrifice": British Businessmen and Business as Usual in the First World War', *Albion* 21 (1989)

McDonald, A., 'The Geddes Committee and the Formulation of Public Expenditure Policy, 1921–1922', *Historical Journal* 32 (1989)

McEwan, J. M., 'The Press and the Fall of Asquith', *Historical Journal* 21 (1978)

Marquis, A. G., 'Words as Weapons: Propaganda in Britain and Germany During the First World War', *Journal of Contemporary History* 13 (1978)

Maxwell, Sir Herbert, 'Are We Really a Nation of Amateurs?', *The Nineteenth Century* 48 (December 1900)

Melling, Joseph, ' "Non-Commissioned Officers": British Employers and their Supervisory Workers, 1880–1920', *Social History* 5 (1980)

Money, Leo Chiozza, 'British Trade and the War', *Contemporary Review* 106 (October 1914)

Pedersen, Susan, 'The Failure of Feminism in the Making of the British Welfare State', *Radical History Review* 43 (1989)

Pedersen, Susan, 'Gender, Welfare, and Citizenship in Britain during the Great War', *American Historical Review* 95 (1990)

Petter, Martin, ' "Temporary Gentlemen" in the Aftermath of the Great War: Rank, Status and the Ex-Officer Problem', *Historical Journal* 37 (1994)

Rawlings, G., 'Swindler of the Century', *History Today* 43 (July 1993)

Razzell, P. E., 'Social Origins of Officers in the Indian and British Home Army: 1758–1962', *British Journal of Sociology* 14 (1963)

Reeves, N., 'Film Propaganda and Its Audience: The Example of Britain's Official Films During the First World War', *Journal of Contemporary History* 18 (1983)

Rubin, G., 'Law as a Bargaining Weapon: British Labour and the Restoration of Pre-War Practices Act 1919', *Historical Journal* 32 (1989)

Rubinstein, W. D., 'Henry Page Croft and the National Party 1917–22', *Journal of Contemporary History* 9 (1974)

Samuel, Raphael, 'The Deference Voter', *New Left Review* (January 1960)

Sheffield, G. D., 'The Effect of the Great War on Class Relations in Great Britain: The Career of Major Christopher Stone DSO MC', *War and Society* 7 (1989)

Smith, Harold, 'The Issue of "Equal Pay for Equal Work" in Britain, 1914–19', *Societas* 8 (1978)

Stubbs, J. O., 'Lord Milner and Patriotic Labour', *English Historical Review* 87 (1972)

Summers, Anne, 'Militarism in Britain Before the Great War', *History Workshop Journal* 2 (1976)

Tanner, Duncan, 'The Parliamentary Electoral System, the "Fourth" Reform Act, and the Rise of Labour in England and Wales', *Bulletin of the Institute of Historical Research* 56 (1983)

Tawney, R. H., 'The Abolition of Economic Controls, 1918–1921', *Economic History Review*, 13 (1943)

Travers, T. H. E., 'The Hidden Army: Structural Problems in the British Officer Corps, 1900–1918', *Journal of Contemporary History* 17 (1982)

Travers, T. H. E., 'The Offensive and the Problem of Innovation in British Military Thought 1870–1915', *Journal of Contemporary History* 13 (1978)

Travers, T. H. E., 'Technology, Tactics and Morale: Jean de Bloch, the Boer War, and British Military Theory, 1900–1914', *Journal of Modern History* 51 (1979)

Veitch, Colin, ' "Play up! Play up! and Win the War!" Football, the Nation and the First World War 1914–15', *Journal of Contemporary History* 20 (1985)

Ward, S. R., 'Intelligence Surveillance of British Ex-Servicemen, 1918–20', *Historical Journal* 16 (1973)

Weinroth, H., 'Norman Angell and *The Great Illusion*: An Episode in Pre-1914 Pacifism', *Historical Journal* 18 (1974)

Whiteside, Noelle, 'Industrial Welfare and Labour Regulation in Britain at the Time of the First World War', *International Review of Social History* 25 (1980)

Whiting, R. C., 'Taxation and the Working Class, 1915–24', *Historical Journal* 33 (1990)

Wilkinson, G., ' "Soldiers by Instinct, Slayers by Training": The *Daily Mail* and the Image of the Warrior, 1899–1914', *Journal of Newspaper and Periodical History* 8 (1992)

Wilson, Trevor, 'Britain's "Moral Commitment" to France in August 1914', *History* 64 (1979)

Wilson, Trevor, 'Lord Bryce's Investigation into Alleged German Atrocities in Belgium, 1914–15', *Journal of Contemporary History* 14 (1979)

Winter, J. M., 'Aspects of the Impact of the First World War on Infant Mortality in Britain', *Journal of European Economic History* 11 (1982)

Winter, J. M., 'The Impact of the First World War on Civilian Health in Britain', *Economic History Review* 30 (1977)

Winter, J. M., 'Public Health and the Political Economy of War: A Reply to Linda Bryder', *History Workshop Journal* 26 (1988)

Winter, J. M., 'Some Aspects of the Demographic Consequences of the First World War on Civilian Health in Britain', *Population Studies* 30 (1976)

Woodward, David, 'Did Lloyd George Starve the British Army of Men Prior to the German Offensive of March 1918?', *Historical Journal* 27 (1984)

Woollacott, Angela, 'Khaki Fever and Its Control: Gender, Class, Age and Sexual Morality on the British Homefront in the First World War', *Journal of Contemporary History* 29 (1994)

Woollacott, Angela, 'Maternalism, Professionalism and Industrial Welfare Supervisors in World War I Britain', *Women's History Review* 3 (1994)

343

INDEX